A HISTORY OF
BABYLONIA AND ASSYRIA

BY

ROBERT WILLIAM ROGERS

PH.D. (LEIPZIG), D.D., LL.D., F.R.G.S., PROFESSOR IN DREW
THEOLOGICAL SEMINARY, MADISON, NEW JERSEY

THIRD EDITION

IN TWO VOLUMES
VOLUME I

Published 2003
Lost Arts Media
Long Beach, CA

Printed on Acid-Free Paper

The History of Babylonia and Assyria: Volume One
by Robert William Rogers
ISBN 1-59016-316-8

To order VOLUME TWO in this series use ISBN 1-59016-317-6

©2003
LOST ARTS MEDIA
All Rights Reserved

LOST ARTS MEDIA

Published by
LOST ARTS MEDIA
P.O. Box 15026
Long Beach, CA
VISIT WWW.LOSTARTSMEDIA.COM OR CALL
1 (800) 952-LOST FOR OUR FREE CATALOG

LOST ARTS MEDIA publishes, markets and distributes a variety of products and services. Our mission it to provide fascinating and educational books, videos and mutlimedia products to help inform, enlighten and inspire humanity at large. We specialize in bringing rare and classic books back into print. We are also involved in document research, video production, e-books, DVD authoring, broadcasting, screenwriting, conference promotion, online services, amongst many other creative endeavors. We carry Books, Booklets, Audio, CD, Video, DVD, Music, Multimedia and other products on Acting and Cinematography, Alchemy, Alternative Medicine, American History, Ancient America, Ancient Astronauts, Ancient Civilizations, Ancient History, Ancient Mysteries, Ancient Religion and Worship, Angels, Anthropology, Anti-Gravity, Archaeology, Apocrypha, Area 51, Astrology, Astronomy, Astro-Physics, Atlantis, Biblical Studies, Biology, Books on Books, Townsend Brown, Buddhism, Children's Books, Cold Fusion, Colloidal Silver, Comparative Religions, Cooking and Household, Coursework and Study Guides, Craftwork and Hobbies, Crop Circles, Dictionaries and Reference, Early History, Education and Schooling, Electromagnetics, Electro-Gravity, Egyptian History, Electromagnetic Smog, Entertainment, European History, Famous People, Michael Faraday, FBI Files Revealed, The Federal Reserve, Fluoride, Folklore and Mythology, the Freedom of Information Act, Free Energy, Freemasonry, Furniture and Decorating, Games, General History, Geology and Minerals, Ghosts, Global Manipulation, Gnosticism, Gravity and Gravity Waves, Greek History, Gyroscopic Anti-Gravity, Healing Electromagnetics, Health and Nutrition, Health Issues, Hermetic Studies, the Hidden History of Holidays, History of the Americas, HIV, Human Origins, Humor, John Keely, Knights Templar, Lost Cities, Lost Continents, Medieval History, Mercury Poisoning, Mesopotamian History, Mesopotamian Religion, Metaphysics, Mithraic Studies, Money and Business, Music Studies, Natural History, Novelty Books, Occultism, Oriental Philosophy, Painting and Drawing, Paganism, Paleontology and Prehistoric World, Paradigm Politics, the Paranormal, Pesticide Pollution, Personal Growth, Phallicism, The Philadelphia Experiment, Philosophy, Physics, Powerlines, Prophecy, Psychic Phenomena, Pyramids, Questions and Answers, Quotations, Rare Books, Religion, Remote Viewing, Roman History, Roswell, Walter Russell, Sasquatch, Scalar Waves, Science and Technology, SDI, John Searle, Secret Societies, Sex Worship, Short Stories, Sitchin Studies, Smart Cards, Solar Power, Song Books, Sovereignty, Space Travel, Spiritualism, Spirituality, Sports and Athletics, Stage Magic and Tricks, Stonehenge, Story of Language, Sumeria, Sun Myths, Symbolism, Tachyon Fields, Nikola Tesla, Theater and Drama, Theology, Time Travel, Translations from the Past, Travel and Adventure, The Treasury, UFOs, Underground Bases, Vedic Philosophy, World Control, The World Grid, World History, Writing and Authorship, Yoga, Zero Point Energy and so much more. Call 1 (800) 952-LOST or 1 (562) 596-ARTS or write for our free catalog.

INTRODUCTION

Babylonia and Assyria were two of the greatest nations the history of mankind has brought forth. These two great Mesopotamian civilizations were best known for their massive armies and instruments of war. This is not surprising, since they were rarely at peace with one another. They were, however, heavily influenced by each other, as well as their predecessors, the Sumerians. Much of what we taken for granted today, the arts and science of industry and invention, were bequeathed to us from these ancient cultures. This two-volume series is remarkable in that it offers an exceedingly comprehensive and detailed looked at ancient Babylonia and Assyria. The way in which these reference works were compiled and written will bring noteworthy enjoyment for the curious reader.

These two volumes are based mostly on the archaeological discoveries of the late 19th Century, and are well-referenced and cited with footnotes from that period. As a result, much of what they have to say is timeless, in a sense, because of nature of how the information is presented. For example, randomly thumbing through this 900 page tome and stopping to read a passage will normally result in the reader being completely preoccupied in whatever annal of history is being revealed. As a professor of ancient Oriental literature at Princeton University at the turn of the twentieth century, professor Robert William Rogers provides a competent perspective concerning the past history of Babylonia and Assyria. This book was skillfully written from the author's vast scholarship and understanding on these subjects.

Volume one begins with a discussion of the earliest European explorations of the Middle East. It began in 1320, when a wandering friar made contact, and continued into the 15th and 16th centuries, when a number of explorers took a closer look at some of the ancient ruins that dot the Arabian landscape, but did not pay particular attention to them. It wasn't until the early 1800s that scientifically minded men began to detail a history on the great archaeological discoveries found throughout the Middle East. As a result, there were a number of cursory explorations conducted from 1820-1834, but it wasn't until 1842, when the French established a consulate at Mosul, that excavations began. Also included in this volume is story concerning the decipherment of the Vannic, Sumerian and Assyrian scripts. This volume also includes the additional explorations conducted in the Middle East from 1872 to 1900. Beginning in 1872, a new round of excavations began after nearly 20 years of dormancy. In times past, excavations were conducted slowly, or even halted, because the work of translation and decipherment many times failed to keep up with new discoveries. In these cases, artifacts that had become unearthed were but meaningless curiosities. It wasn't until the late 1800s that learned people were able to make sense of what was found. Several chapters within this volume detail the various sources which scholars used to establish the chronology of the Kings list, as well as the characteristics of the land and of the peoples who inhabited the Mesopotamian valley. Also included is a history of Babylonia to the fall of Larsa, the Kassite tenure, and the dynasty of Isin.

Tédd St. Rain

PREFACE.

DURING the past ten years, when not absorbed in the duties of a busy professorship, I have given my time to the preparation of this work. In its interest I have made repeated journeys to Europe, and also to the East, and the greater part of the text has been written in the University Library at Leipzig, the British Museum in London, and the Bodleian Library in Oxford. In the last named I have had especial opportunity to investigate the early history of cuneiform research in the almost unrivaled collections of early travelers and decipherers. Large parts of the book have been rewritten twice or thrice as changes in opinion and the discovery of fresh monumental material have modified the views previously entertained. Whatever may be the judgment of my fellow-investigators in this difficult field, it will not truthfully be said that I have not taken pains.

Every part of the two volumes rests upon original sources, yet I have tried to consider all that modern Assyriologists have brought forward in elucidation of them, and have sought to give due credit for every explanation which I have accepted, and to treat with courtesy and respect any that I have ventured to reject. The progress of

Assyriology in the past twenty years has been so rapid that every book on the history of Babylonia and Assyria published prior to 1880 is hopelessly antiquated, and many issued much later would need extensive revision. The work of investigation has fallen necessarily into the hands of specialists, and so vast has the field grown that there are now specialists in even small parts of the subject. The results of all this detailed research are scattered in scientific journals and monographs in almost all the languages of Europe. To sift, weigh, and decide upon their merits is no easy task, and I am sadly conscious that it might have been better done; yet am I persuaded that scholars who know the field intimately will recognize the difficulties and be most ready to pardon the shortcomings which each may discover in his own province.

I have sought to tell the whole story as scholars now generally understand it, rather being disposed to yield to the *consensus* of opinion, when any exists, than eager to set forth novel personal opinions. Yet in parts of the field at least I may claim to be an independent investigator, and to have made contributions to the knowledge of the subject.

In travel and in research in the libraries and museums of Paris, Berlin, Cairo, Constantinople, and elsewhere I have received many courtesies which I should gladly acknowledge here did it not seem disproportionate to carve great names on so small a structure. The obligations to my friend Professor Sayce are, however, so unusual that they must be expressed. He has read the entire book in manuscript, and made many suggestions, some of which led me to change my view, while others showed me wherein I had written obscurely or had failed to defend my position adequately. I am grateful to him for this new illustration of his unfailing kindness and generosity to younger men.

I take leave of the book with mingled pleasure and regret, hoping only that it may prove sufficiently useful to demand and deserve a revision at no distant day.

ROBERT W. ROGERS.

MADISON, NEW JERSEY,
September 18, 1900.

CONTENTS.

BOOK I: PROLEGOMENA.

CHAPTER I.

EARLY TRAVELERS AND EARLY DECIPHERERS.

ix

CHAPTER III.

EARLY EXPLORERS IN BABYLONIA.

CHAPTER IV.

EXPLORATIONS IN ASSYRIA AND BABYLONIA, 1734–1820.

CHAPTER V.

EXCAVATIONS IN ASSYRIA AND BABYLONIA, 1843–1854.

2

CHAPTER VI.

THE DECIPHERMENT OF ASSYRIAN.

CHAPTER VII.

THE DECIPHERMENT OF SUMERIAN AND OF VANNIC.

CHAPTER VIII.

EXPLORATIONS IN ASSYRIA AND BABYLONIA, 1872–1900.

CHAPTER IX.

THE SOURCES.

CHAPTER X.

THE LANDS OF BABYLONIA AND ASSYRIA.

CHAPTER XI.

THE PEOPLES OF BABYLONIA AND ASSYRIA.

CHAPTER XII.

THE CHRONOLOGY.

BOOK II: THE HISTORY OF BABYLONIA.

CHAPTER I.

The History of Babylonia to the Fall of Larsa.

CHAPTER II.

THE FIRST AND SECOND DYNASTIES OF BABYLON.

CHAPTER III.

THE KASSITE DYNASTY.

CHAPTER IV

The Dynasty of Isin.

LIST OF PLATES AND DIAGRAMS.

A HISTORY

OF

BABYLONIA AND ASSYRIA.

BOOK I:
PROLEGOMENA.

CHAPTER I.

EARLY TRAVELERS AND EARLY DECIPHERERS.

PRIOR to 1820 the only knowledge possessed by the world of the two cities Babylon and Nineveh, and of the empires which they founded and led, was derived from peoples other than their inhabitants. No single word had come from the deep stillness of the ruins of Babylon, no voice was heard beneath the mounds of Nineveh. It would then have seemed a dream of impossible things to hope that some future day would discover buried libraries in these mounds, filled with books in which these peoples had written not only their history and chronology, but their science, their operations of building, their manners and customs, their very thoughts and emotions. That the long-lost languages in which these books

were written should be recovered, that men should
read them as readily and as surely as the tongues
of which traditional use had never ceased among
men—all this would then have seemed impossible
indeed. But this and much more has happened.
From these long-lost, even forgotten materials the
history of Babylonia and Assyria has become
known. These are now the chief sources of our
knowledge, and before we begin our survey of the
long line of the centuries it is well that we should
look at the steps by which our sources were
secured.

The story of the rediscovery of Babylonia and
Assyria is really twofold. Two lines of research,
pursued separately for a long time, at last formed
a union, and from that union has resulted present
knowledge. By the one line the ancient sources
were rediscovered, by the other men learned how
to read them.

The first clue which led to the rediscovery of the
ancient language of Babylonia and of Assyria was
not found in either of these two lands. It was
not found by a scholar who set out to search for
it. It was not a brilliant discovery made in a day,
to become the wonder of ages. It was rather
the natural result of a long, tedious, and somewhat involved process. It began and long continued to be in the hands of travelers, each learning a little from his predecessors, and then adding
a mite as the result of his own observation. It
was found in the most unlikely place in Persia,

far from Babylonia and Assyria. The story of its finding is worth the telling, not only because it is necessary to any just appreciation of our present knowledge of Assyria and Babylonia, but because it has its own interest, and is instructive as a history of the progress of knowledge.

In Persia, forty miles northeast of Shiraz, once the capital of the kingdom, there is a range of everlasting hills, composed of a marble of dark grey limestone, which bears the name of Mount Rachmet. In front of this ridge, and in a semicircular hollow, there rises above the plain a vast terracelike platform. Nature built this terrace in part, but man at some time erected a wall in front of it, leveled off the top, and there built great palaces and temples. In the Middle Ages this land of Persia became full of interest for various reasons. It had an important commerce with Europe, and that naturally drew men of trade from Europe into its extensive plateaus, that were reeking with heat in summer, and equally uncomfortable in the bleak cold of winter. The commercial contact of Persia led, also, most naturally to diplomatic intercourse of various kinds with European states, and this intercourse gradually made the land known in some measure to the West.

The earliest European, at present known to us, who visited the great terrace at the foot of Mount Rachmet was a wandering friar, Odoricus, or Odoric, by name. He was going overland to Cathay, and on the way passed between Yezd and Huz, about

1320 A. D.   He had no time to look at ruins,
and appears hardly to have seen them at all.
Yet his record is the first word heard in Europe
concerning the ruins at Persepolis:

"I came unto a certaine citie called Comum, which
was an huge and mightie city in olde time, con-
teyning well nigh fiftie miles in circuite, and hath
done in times past great damage unto the Romanes.
In it there are stately palaces altogether destitute
of inhabitants, notwithstanding it aboundeth with
great store of victuals."[1]

The passage is disappointing.   Odoric was a
"man of little refinement"[2] and, though possessed
of a desire to wander and see strange sights, cared
little for the intellectual or spiritual meaning of
great places.   It is an oft-recurring statement with

---

[1] *The Second Volume of the Principal Navigations, Voyages, Traffiques,
and Discoveries of the English Nation,* etc. By Richard Hakluyt, Preacher,
and sometime Student of Christ Church, Oxford. Imprinted at London,
anno 1599, p. 54. [Here beginneth the iournall of Frier *Odoricus,* one of
the order of the Minorites, concerning strange things which hee sawe
among the Tartars of the East.] The following is the original Latin text:
" Ab hac, transiens per civitates et terras, veni ad quamdam civitatem
nomine Coprum, quae antiquitatus civitas magna fuit: haec maximum
damnum quondam intulit Romae; eius autem muri bene quadraginta milia-
rum sunt capaces. Et in ea sunt palacia adhuc integra, et multis victuali-
bus haec abundat." (See *Sopra la Vita e i Viaggi del Beato Odorico da
Pordenone, Stuni del Chierico Francescano Fr. Teofilo Domenichelli.* In
Prato, 1881, pp. 156, 157.) The name of the place called Comum, above,
is variously written by different authorities: Comerum, YULE; Conium,
VENNI; Comum, UTIN.; Coman, MUS.; Comerum, FARS. The manuscript
readings are very diverse, but I believe with Yule (*Cathay and the Way
Thither,* by Col. Henry Yule, C. B., London, Hakluyt Society, 1866, p. 52,
note) that the reading to be preferred is Comerum, which is the Camara of
Barbaro, the Kinara of Rich, and the Kenaré of Mme. Dieulafoy.

[2] This is the judgment of Colonel Yule [*ib.* i, p. 8], and everything seems
to me to bear it out.

him that he found good "victuals," and with that
his simple soul was content. He evidently did
not know what place the ancient ruins marked,
and that he cared at all does not appear. So
simple is his word that men have even doubted
whether he ever saw the ruins with his own eyes;
but there is no real reason to doubt that he did.
But even though he saw little and said less, his
narrative was almost a classic before the invention
of printing, and was copied frequently, as the numerous manuscripts still in existence show.[1] Not
very long after the invention of printing his story
found expression in type. Then it became a call
to others to go and see also. It is only a first
voice in the dark—this word of Odoric—and long
would it be ere another wayfarer should see the
same relics of the past.

In the year 1472 the glorious republic of Venice dispatched an envoy to the Court of Uzun

---

[1] Cordier enumerates seventy-nine as still existing in London, Oxford,
Cambridge, Paris, etc.

See for biographical and critical material: *Les Voyages en Asie au XIV*
Siècle du Bienheureux Frère Odoric de Pordenone Religieux de Saint-François,
publiés avec une introduction et des notes par Henri Cordier. Paris, 1891.

The narrative of Odoricus was first published in 1513 under the title,
"*Odorichus de rebus incognitis*, Pesaro [per Girolamo Soncino], 1513, in 4."
Only one copy of this extraordinarily rare book is known to exist, and that
is in the Reale Biblioteca Palatina de Parme, and I have not seen it. It
is described with facsimiles in Cordier, pp. cxvii–cxxiii.

A second edition appeared in 1528, at Paris, and the third reprinting was in
Ramusio, *Navigationi et Viaggi*, ii, Venetia, 1583, pp. 245–253. This beautiful edition I have seen. The title of the section is "Viaggio del Beato
Odorico da Vdine, dell' ordine de' frati Minori, Delle usanze, costumi, &
nature, di diverse nationi & genti del Mondo, & del maritirio di quattro
frati dell'ordine predetto, qual patirono tra gl'Infedeli."

Hassan. His name was Josophat Barbaro, and he passed the same way as Odoric, but saw a little more, which he thus describes:

"Near the town of Camara is seen a circular mountain, which on one side appears to have been cut and made into a terrace six paces high. On the summit of this terrace is a flat space, and around are forty columns, which are called Cilminar, which means in our tongue Forty Columns, each of which is twenty cubits long, as thick as the embrace of three men; some of them are ruined; but, to judge from that which can still be seen, this was formerly a beautiful building. The terrace is all of one piece of rock, and upon it stand sculptured figures of animals as large as giants, and above them is a figure like those by which, in our country, we represent God the Father inclosed in a circle, and holding a ring in his hand; underneath are other smaller figures. In front is the figure of a man leaning on his bow, which is said to be a figure of Solomon. Below are many others which seem to support those above them, and among these is one who seems to wear on his head a papal miter, and holds up his open hand, apparently with the intention of giving his benediction to those below, who look up to him, and seem to stand in a certain expectation of the said benediction. Beyond this there is a tall figure on horseback, apparently that of a strong man; this they say is Samson, near whom are many other figures, dressed in the French fashion and wearing long cloaks; all these figures are in half relief. Two days' journey from this place there is a village called Thimar, and two days further off another village, where there is a tomb in which they say the mother of Solomon was buried. Over this is built an edifice in the form of a chapel, and there are Arabic letters upon it, which say, as we understand from the inhabitants of the place, Messer Suleimen, which means in our tongue Temple of Solomon, and its gate looks toward the east."[1]

Barbaro had not made much advance upon Odoric, but his account was not altogether fruitless, though soon to be superseded.

When Shah Abbas the Great, king of Persia, began his long and remarkable reign (1586) Persia was a dark land to European eyes. It was he who opened it freely to ambassadors from Europe, all of whom he treated with a magnificent courtesy. The first of these ambassadors to arrive in his kingdom came from the kingdom of Portugal, sent out by Philip III, king of Spain and Portugal. This man was an Augustinian friar, Antonio de Gouvea, who came with messages both of peace and of war. It was his aim to endeavor to carry Christianity among the Persians—a message of peace—but also to induce Abbas to make war on the Osmanli Turks. He was somewhat more successful in the second than in the first object,

---

[1] *Viaggi Fatti da Vinetia, alla Tana, in Persia, in India et in Constantinopli*, con la descrittione particolare di Citta, Luoghi, Sitti, Costumi, et della Porta del gran Turco & di tutte le intrate, spese, & modo di governo suo, & della ultima Impressa contra Portoghesi. In Venezia, M.D.XLIII, p. 51.

though he did establish an Augustinian society at
the Persian court.   After many and sore adventures at the hands of sea pirates he again saw his
native land, and published an account of his adventures.   In this story he tells of a visit to Persepolis, and in these terms:

"We continued our journey as far as a village
called Chelminira, which in their language means
Forty Minarets, because that was the number in
the tomb of an ancient king which stood there. . . .
We went to see the tomb of which I have spoken,
and it is my firm belief that the mausoleum which
Artemisia erected to her husband was not more
notable, though it is held as one of the wonders of
the world; but the mausoleum has been destroyed
by time, which seems to have no power against
this monument, which has also resisted the efforts
of human malice. . . . The place is between two
high ridges, and the tomb of which I have made
mention is at the foot of the northern ridge.   Those
who say that Cyrus rebuilt the city of Shiraz,
affirm also that he built for himself this famous
tomb.   There are indications that Ahasuerus, or
Artaxerxes, erected it for himself, besides another
near it which he made for Queen Vashti; and this
opinion is made more probable by the consideration of the short distance from this site to the city
of Suzis, or Shushan, in which he generally re-
sided. . . . At the foot of the ridge began two
staircases facing one another, with many steps
made of stones of so great a size that it will be

beyond belief when I affirm that some of them,
when they were first hewn, were more than
twenty-five palms in circumference, ten or twelve
broad, and six or eight high ; and of these, there
were very many throughout the whole structure,
for the building was chiefly composed of them ;
and it was no small wonder to consider how they
could have been placed one upon the other, particularly in the columns, where the stones were
larger than in any other part. That which astonished us most was to see that certain small chapels
were made of a single stone—doorway, pavement,
walls, and roof. . . . The staircases, of which I
have spoken, met on a broad landing, from which
the whole plain was visible. The walls of the
staircases were entirely covered with figures in relief, of workmanship so excellent that I doubt
whether it could be surpassed ; and by ascending
the staircases access was gained to an extensive
terrace, on which stood the forty columns which
gave their name to the place, each formed, in spite
of their great size, of no more than three stones. . . .
The bases might be thirty palms round, and on
the columns were beautifully carved figures. The
porches through which the terrace was entered
were very high and the walls very thick ; at each
end stood out figures of lions and other fierce animals, carved in relief in the same stone ; so well executed that they seemed to be endeavoring to terrify
the spectators. The likeness of the king was drawn
life-size upon the porches and in many other parts.

3

"From this place was an ascent to another much higher, where was a chamber excavated in the hillside, which must have been intended to contain the king's body, although the natives, imagining that it contained a different treasure, have broken into it, having little respect for the ancient memory of him who constructed it. . . .

"The inscriptions—which relate to the foundation of the edifice, and, no doubt, also, declare the author of it—although they remain in many parts very distinct, yet there is none that can read them, for they are not in Persian, nor Arabic, nor Armenian, nor Hebrew, which are the languages current in those parts; and thus all helps to blot out the memory of that which the ambitious king hoped to make eternal. And because the hardness of the material of which it is built still resists the wear of time, the inhabitants of the place, ill treated or irritated by the numbers of visitors who came to see this wonder, set to work to do it as much injury as they could, taking as much trouble perhaps to deface it as the builders had done to erect it. The hard stone has resisted the effect of fire and steel, but not without showing signs of injury." [1]

---

[1] Relaçam, AM | em que se tra- | tam as gueras e gran | des victorias que alcan- | çou grâde Rey da Persia Xá Abbas do grão Tur | co Mahometto, & seu filho Amethe: as quais | resultarão das Embaixadas, q̃ por mandado | da Catholica & Real Magesta de del Rey | D. Felippe segundo de Portugal fize- | rão algũs Religiosos da ordem dos Eremitas de S. Augusti- | nho a Persia. |

Composto pella Padre F. Antonio de Gouvea | Religioso da mesma ordem.

From this narrative it is plain that the militant friar had learned more of the ruins than had Odoric or Barbaro. He no longer believes that Solomon had aught to do with them, but connects them with fair degree of exactness with the Persian kings. He also is more accurate and explicit concerning the inscriptions which he saw. They had already begun to exercise over his mind some little spell—a spell which was soon to hold a large part of Europe beneath its sway.

The next ambassador whom Philip III sent out to Shah Abbas was Don Garcia de Sylva y Figueroa, who likewise visited the great ruins. On his return to Isfahan he wrote a letter, in 1619, to the Marquess de Bedmar. It was written originally in Spanish, but immediately was done into Latin and published at Antwerp in 1620. This letter of a brilliant man completely superseded Gouvea's account, and evidently made a profound impression in Europe. Within five years it was

---

Reitor do Col | legio de sancto Augustinho de Goa, & | professor da sagrada Theologia.

Impresso em Lisboa per Pedro Crasbeeck.—Anno M.DCXI, fol. 30, recto et seq.

Relation | des Grandes | Guerres et | victoires obtenues par | le Roy de Perse | Cha Abbas | contre les Empereurs de Turquie | Mahomet et Achmet son fils. | En suite du voyage de quelques | Religieux de l'Ordre des Hermites de S. Augustin envoyez | en Perse par le Roy Catholique Dom Philippe Second | Roy de Portugal.

Par le P. Fr. Anthoine de Gouvea, Religieux du mesme | Ordre, Recteur du College de S. Augustin de Goa, | Professeur en Theologie.

Traduit de l'Original Portugais, imprimé à Lisbonne avec Licence | de l'Inquisition, de l'oridinaire & du Palais.

A Rouen, | chez Nicolas Loyselet, près S. Lo, | derriere le Palais, à l'Oyselet.—1646, pp. 78, ff.

translated into English, so receiving still greater publicity.   His description of the ruins of Persepolis runs after this fashion :

"There are yet remayning most of those huge wilde buildings of the Castle and Palace of Persepolis, so much celebrated in the monuments of ancient writers.   These frames do the Arabians and Persians in their owne language call Chilminara : which is as much as if you should say in Spanish *Quarenta Columnas*, or *Alcoranas* : for so they call those high narrow round steeples which the Arabians have in their Mesquites.   This rare, yea and onely monument of the world (which farre exceedeth all the rest of the World's miracles that we have seen or heard of), sheweth it selfe to them that come to this Citie from the Towne of Xiria, and standeth about a league from the River Bandamir, in times past called Araxis (not that which parteth Media from the greater Armenia), whereof often mention is made by Q. Curtius, Diodorus, and Plutarch : which Authors doe point us oute the situation of Persepolis, and doe almost lead us unto it by the hand.   The largenesse, fairnesse, and long-lasting matter of these Pillars appeareth by the twentie which are yet left of alike fashion ; which with other remaynders of those stately Piles do move admiration in the minde of beholders, and cannot but with much labour and at leisure be layed open.   But since it is your Lordships hap to live now at Venice, where you may see some resemblance of the things which I am about to

write of, I will briefly tell you that most of the
pictures of men, that, ingraven in marble, doe seele
the front, the sides, and statelier parts of this building, are decked with a very comely cloathing, and
clad in the same fashion which the Venetian Mag-
nificoes goe in : that is Gownes downe to the heeles,
with wide sleeves, with round flat caps, their hair
spred to the shoulders, and notably long beards.
Yee may see in these tables some men sitting with
great maiestie in certayne loftier chayres, such as
use to bee with us in the Quires and Chapter—
Houses of Cathedrall Churches, appointed for the
seates of the chiefe Prelates; the seate being supported with a little foote-stoole neatly made, about
a hand high.   And, which is very worthy of wonder
in so divers dresses of so many men as are ingraven
in these tables, none cometh neere the fashion
which is at this day, or hath beene these many
Ages past, in use through all Asia.   For though
out of all Antiquitie we can gather no such arguments of the cloathing of Assyrians, Medes, and
Persians, as we finde many of the Greekes and
Romanes; yet it appeareth sufficiently that they
used garments of a middle size for length, like the
Punike vest used by the Turks and Persians at
this day, which they call Aljuba, and these Cavaia :
and shashes round about their heads, distinguished
yet both by fashion and colour from the Cidaris,
which is the Royall Diademe.   Yet verily in all
this sculpture (which, though it be ancient, yet
shineth as neatly as if it were but new-done) you

can see no picture that is like or in the workmanship resembleth any other, which the memorie of
man could yet attaine to the knowledge of from
any part of the World : so that this worke may
seeme to excede all Antiquities. Now nothing
more confirmeth this than one notable Inscription
cut in a Jasper table, with characters still so fresh
and faire that one would wonder how it could
scape so many Ages without touch of the least
blemish. The Letters themselves are neither
Chaldean, nor Hebrew, nor Greeke, nor Arabike,
nor of any other Nation which was ever found of
old, or at this day to be extant. They are all
three cornered, but somewhat long, of the forme
of a Pyramide, or such a little Obeliske as I have
set in the margin (Δ) ; so that in nothing do they
differ from one another but in their placing and
situation, yet so conformed that they are wondrous
plaine, distinct and perspicuous. What kind of
building the whole was (whether Corinthian,
Ionick or mixt) cannot be gathered from the re-
maynder of these ruines : which is otherwise in the
old broken walls at Rome, by which that may
easily be discerned. Notwithstanding the wondrous
and artificiall exactness of the worke, the beautie
and elegancy of it shining out of the proportion
and symmetrie, doth dazzle the eyes of the beholders. But nothing amazed me more than the
hardnesse and durablenesse of these Marbles and
Jaspers; for in many places there are Tables so
solide, and so curiously wrought and polished that

ye may see your face in them as in a glasse. Besides the Authors by me alreadie commended, Arrianus and Justine make special mention of this Palace; and they report that Alexander the Great (at the instigation of Thaïs) did burne it downe. But most delicately of all doth Diodorus deliver this storie.

"The whole Castle was encompassed with a threefold circle of walls, the greater part whereof hath yielded to the time and weather. There stand also the sepulchres of their kings, placed on the side of that hill, at the foote whereof the Castle itself is built; and the monuments stand just so farre from one another as Diodorus reporteth. In a worde, all doth so agree with his discourse of it that he that hath seene this and read that cannot possibly be deceived." [1]

Sylva y Figueroa had evidently more interest in the peoples of the ancient Orient than in their languages. He had not given much attention to the inscriptions which he saw, and the idea of attempting to copy any of these strange characters never seems to have entered his mind. It was a pity that this did not occur to him, for the wide dissemination of his letter would have earlier intro-

---

[1] Garciae Silva Figueroa | Philippi III | Hispaniarum Indiarumq. Regis | Ad Persiae Regem Legati | De | Rebus Persarum | Epistola. | v Kal. an. M.DC.XIX.

Spahani exarata | Ad Marchionem Bedmari | nuper ad Venetos, nunc ad Sereniss. | Austrriae Archiduces, Belgarum Principes | Regium Legatum | Antverpiae | ex officina Plantiniana.—M.DC.XX, p. 6, ff.

English translation in *Purchas His Pilgrimes*. London, 1625. Part ii, 1533–1534.

duced Europe to the idea that here was another
great field for study. These mysterious signs would
even then have attracted attention. But Europe
was now soon to learn something of the appearance of these strange signs.

In the years 1614–1626 Pietro della Valle traversed a large part of Turkey, Persia, and India.
On this journey he wrote "familiar" letters, which
were in reality almost treatises upon geography,
history, and ethnology, to a friend and physician,
Mario Schipano, at Naples. In passing through
Persia he visited the ruins of Persepolis, once the
capital of ancient Persia. Here he marked that the
city was surrounded upon three sides by mountains
which broke off abruptly, leaving smooth precipice
surfaces around it. Upon this smooth rock in
a number of places he found strange marks, evidently made by the hand of man, and intended to
mean something. What language this might be or
what letters he had no idea. In a letter written
October 21, 1621, he described the appearance of
these strange signs, and even went so far as to copy
down into his letter a few of them:[1]

and that without very great exactness. Comment-
ing upon these signs, he remarks that in the sec-

[1] *Viaggi di Pietro della Valle, il Pellegrino. . . . Descritti da lui medeimo
in 54. Lettere familiari . . . All' erudito, e fra' più cari, di molti anni suo
Amico Mario Schipano.* In Roma MDCL. Vol. iii, p. 206. Printed 1658.

ond one of them, consisting of three strokes downward and one pointing toward the right, there
seemed to be indications that it was made from
left to right, and not from right to left. He had
thus already begun to speculate upon the question
as to whether this unknown language was read
from right to left, as were most of the oriental
tongues of which he had knowledge, or whether it
was to be read, like the European languages, from
left to right. On the ground already alleged, and
upon other grounds which he then proceeds to
state, he decided that this tongue was really to be
read from left to right. The appearance of these
few signs in his published letters were the first
sight which Europe gained of the appearance of
the written language of ancient Persia. His letters were repeatedly reprinted and must have had
an extensive circulation. So came the learned of
Europe to know that the ancient Persians had
carved some sort of language on the rocks at
Persepolis, but what these signs might mean none
knew, and there was apparently no clue to their
meaning. But to Pietro della Valle belongs the
honor of beginning the long line of men who contributed little by little toward the reading of Assyrian and Babylonian books.[1]

---

[1] Pietro della Valle was a man of learning in his age, writing and speaking Turkish, Persian, and Arabic, and possessing some knowledge of Coptic. He was a close and careful observer, and accurate, for the greater
part, in the reproduction of his observations. A brief sketch of his life is
printed in the introduction to *The Travels of Pietro della Valle in India*,
from the old English translation of 1664, by G. Havers. In 2 vols.
Edited by Edward Grey. London. Printed for the Hakluyt Society, 1892.

Pietro della Valle was, however, not long left in possession of the honors of primacy in his examination of Persepolis. In 1627 Sir Dodmore Cotton, accredited to the Persian court as ambassador, sailed away from England. In his suite was a boy of nineteen years of age, by name Thomas Herbert. The party landed at Gombrun, Persian Gulf, on January 10, 1627–8, and thence proceeded to Ashraff for an audience with the king. They later visited Mount Taurus and Casbin, where Cotton and Sir Robert Shirley, who was also in the suite, died, and Herbert was left free to continue his travels. Herbert saw much of Persia and of Babylonia before reaching England at the end of 1629. In 1634 he published an account of these travels and devoted a few pages to Persepolis and Chilmanor.¹ In his description he is very entertainingly discursive concerning the " Images of Lions, Tygres, Griffins, and Buls of rare sculpture and proportion "² which he saw there, but he says not a word about inscriptions. In 1638 he issued a second edition, considerably enlarged, in which Persepolis receives more attention, and is introduced in quaint and enthusiastic phrase, thus :

"Let us now (what pace you please) to Persepolis, not much out of the road: but were it a thousand times further, it merits our paines to

---

¹ A | Relation | of some yeares | travaile, begunne | Anno 1626 | Into Afrique and the greater Asia, especially | the Territories of the Persian Monarchie : and | some parts of the Orientall Indies, | and isles Adjacent. . . . by T. H. Esquier. London, 1634, pp. 56–60.

² *Ibid.,* p. 59.

view it; being indeed the only brave Antique-
Monument (not in Persia alone) but through all
the Orient." [1]

In this edition he comes up to the question of
inscriptions, and so alludes to them:

"In part of this great roome (not farre from the
portall) in a mirrour of polisht marble, wee noted
above a dozen lynes of strange-characters, very faire
and apparent to the eye, but so mysticall, so odly
framed, as no Hierogliphick, no other deep conceit
can be more difficultly fancied, more adverse to
the intellect. These consisting of Figures, obelisk,
triangular, and pyramidall, yet in such Simmetry
and order as cannot well be called barbarous. Some
resemblance, I thought some words had, of the An-
tick Greek, shadowing out Ahasuerus Theos. And,
though it have small concordance with the Hebrew,
Greek, or Latine letter, yet questionlesse to the In-
venter it was well knowne; and peradventure may
conceale some excellent matter, though to this day
wrapt up in the dim leafes of envious obscuritie." [2]

Even here Herbert did not cease the work of
elaborating his description of Persepolis. He did,
however, rest a few years, and in that time another
traveler had seen the ruins. This was J. Albert
de Mandelslo, a member of an "Embassy sent by
the Duke of Holstein to the great Duke of Mus-
covy and the King of Persia," who traveled in the
East 1638–1640. The account of his wanderings

---

[1] *Ibid.*, second edition, p. 143.

[2] Some yeares | Travels | into | Divers Parts of | Asia and Afrique | . . .
Revised and enlarged by the Author. London, 1638, pp. 145, 146.

was written down by Olearius, secretary to the embassy, and an English translation appeared in 1662. Mandelslo also described the columns as usual and then added this statement:

"Near these chambers may be seen, engraven upon a square pillar, certain unknown characters, which have nothing common with either the *Greek*, *Hebrew*, or *Arabian*, nor indeed with any other language. There are twelve lines of these characters, which, as to their figure, are triangular, Piramidal, or like obelisques, but so well graven and so proportionate, that those whot did them cannot be thought Barbarians: Some believe, they are Telesmes, and that they contain some secrets which Time will discover." [1]

In 1677 Herbert issued the fourth impression of the account of his travels. In this he devotes still more space to Persepolis and its inscriptions, and it is altogether probable that he was moved to this by Mendelslo's book, and being desirous that he should not lose the credit of being first to publish a copy of the inscriptions, he includes a specimen plate. In its revised form the account deserves quotation here:

"Adjoyning these toward the West is a Jasper

---

[1] The first edition which I have been able to find of Mendelslo's travels appeared at Utrecht in 1651, *in Neer duyts overgeset door D. V. Wageninge.* The first German edition which I have seen was published at "Schleszwig In Jahr MDCLVI." The first English edition bears title-page thus: *The Voyages & Travels of the Ambassadors sent by Frederick, Duke of Holstein* . . . written originally by Adam Olearius, Secretary to the Embassy. Faithfully rendered into English, by John Davies of Kidwelly. London, M.DC.LXII. P. 5.

or Marble Table about twenty foot from the pavement, wherein are inscribed about twenty lines of
Characters, every line being a yard and a half broad
or thereabouts; all of them are very perfect to the
eye, and the stone so well polished that it reserves
its lustre. The Characters are of a strange and unusual shape; neither like Letters nor Hieroglyph-
icks; yea so far from our deciphering them that
we could not so much as make any positive judgment whether they were words or Characters;
albeit I rather incline to the first, and that they
comprehended words or syllables, as in *Brachy-
ography* or Short-writing we familiarly practise :
Nor indeed could we judge whether the writing
were from the right hand to the left, according
to the *Chaldee*, and usual manner of these Orien
tal Countreys; or from the left hand to the right,
as the Greeks, Romans and other Nations imita-
ting their Alphabets have accustomed. Nevertheless, by the posture and tendency of some of the
Characters (which consist of several magnitudes)
it may be supposed that this writing was rather
from the left hand to the right, as the *Armenian*
and *Indian* do at this day. And concerning the
Characters, albeit I have since compared them
with the twelve several Alphabets in *Postellus*, and
after that with those eight and fifty different Alphabets I find in *Purchas*, most of which are borrowed
from that learned Scholar Gromay, which indeed
comprehend all or most of the various forms of
letters that either now or at any time have been

in use through the greatest part of the Universe,
I could not perceive that these had the least resemblance or coherence with any of them: which
is very strange, and certainly renders it the greater
curiosity; and therefore well worthy the scrutiny
of some ingenious Persons that delight themselves
in this dark and difficult Art or Exercise of deciphering. For, how obscure soever these seemed
to us, without doubt they were at some time understood, and peradventure by *Daniel*, who probably might be the surveyour and instruct the Arch-
itector of this Palace, as he was of those memorable Buildings at *Shushan* and *Ecbatan;* for it
is very likely that this structure was raised by
Astyages or his Grandson *Cyrus;* and is acknowledged that this great Prophet (who likewise was
a Civil Officer in highest trust and repute during those great revolutions of State under the
mighty Monarchs *Nebuchodonosor*, *Belshazzar*,
Astyages, *Darius*, and *Cyrus*) had his mysterious
Characters: So as how incommunicable soever
these Characters be to us (for they bear the resemblance of pyramids inverted or with bases up-
wards, Triangles or Delta's, or (if I may so compare them) with the Lamed in the *Samaritan*
Alphabet, which is writ the contrary way to the
same letter in the *Chaldee* and *Hebrew*), yet doubtless in the Age these were engraven they were
both legible and intelligible; and not to be imagined that they were there placed either to
amuse or to delude the spectators; for it cannot

be denied but that the *Persians* in those primitive times had letters peculiar to themselves,
which differed from all those of other Nations,
according to the testimony of a learned Author,
*Persae proprios habebant Characteres, qui hodie in
vestigiis antiquorum Monumentorum vix inveni-
unter.* However, I have thought fit to insert a
few of these for better demonstration:

which nevertheless whiles they cannot be read,
will in all probability like the *Mene Tekel* without the help of a Daniel hardly be interpreted." [1]

These quotations from the successive editions
of Herbert show a book in the very process of
growth, but they unfortunately do not show much
development of the author's knowledge. Herbert
had, however, in the fourth impression consulted
his notes to greater advantage, and brought forth
from them some copies of cuneiform signs. These
were the first that had been published in England,
but unhappily they did not form a complete inscription. The first two lines come from one inscription, and the third from another, and the
copying was not very well done. It was a pity

---

[1] Some Years | Travels | into | Divers Parts | of | Africa and Asia the
Great | . . . | In this fourth Impression are added (by the Author now
living) as well many Addi | tions throughout the whole work, as also sev-
eral Sculptures, never before Printed. | London, 1677, pp. 141, 142.

that Herbert had not taken the time and pains
necessary to make a complete as well as a correct
copy of one inscription however small. That
would have been a genuine contribution to learning. As it happened Herbert's book contributed
nothing of scientific importance to the pursuit of
knowledge concerning the East. It is, however,
certainly true that this entertainingly written narrative may have influenced later work by arousing
fresh interest in the ruined palaces, and the mystic
inscriptions at Persepolis.

The copies of a few signs by Pietro della Valle
and by Herbert, however, aroused no special interest, and there was in reality hardly enough of these
signs even to awaken curiosity.

In the same manner the few signs which an
English traveler, Mr. S. Flower, copied and published in England failed of arousing any interest
in the rocks and their inscriptions at Persepolis.[1]

The first real impulse to an attempt at unraveling the secrets of Persepolis was given by Sir John
Chardin. Born at Paris in 1643, and early a wan-
derer, this man, after long voyages, saw the rocks
at Persepolis.[2] Many things he had learned in
his journeyings, and among them had found how
important it was to make copies of inscriptions,
whether one could read them or not. He was the
first to copy one of these little Persian inscriptions

---

[1] These copies of Mr. Flower had a most singular history, an outline of
which is given in the Excursus below, see p. 74.

[2] *Voyages de Monsieur le Chevalier Chardin, en Perse et autres lieux de
l'Orient,* 3 tom. Amsterdam, 1711.

entire. When this was published[1] it was at last
possible for students to see some of the peculiarities of this method of writing. It was now plainly
seen that the characters were made up of little
wedges and arrowheads—of which the latter were
formed by the combination of two of the former.
By combinations of these wedges and arrowheads
the most complex-looking signs were produced.
In all of them this one abiding rule seemed to be
followed, that the wedges always pointed to the
right or downward, and that the arrowheaded
forms were always open toward the right. The
prevalence of this rule seemed to confirm the guess
already hazarded more than once that the language
was really to be read from left to right. But,
though Chardin's published inscription awakened,
for the first time, some genuine interest in the
matter, there was found no man so bold as to essay
a decipherment of the enigmatic signs.

After Chardin the next man to see the ruins of
Persepolis was Jean Baptiste Tavernier, who was,
however, too much interested in himself and in his
reception by the king to pay much attention to
the past and its great monuments. But in a short
time there came another traveler who was interested in the past more than the present. On June
13, 1693, Giovanni Francesco Gemelli-Carreri
started away from Naples to make the circuit of
the globe, and to the same city he returned December 3, 1699, having accomplished the task. In 1694

4　　　　　　　[1] *Ibid.*, tom. iii, plate at p. 118.

he was in Persia and naturally visited the ruins of Persepolis. He is very explicit in his statements as to how he traveled to the ruins and is careful in reporting the dimensions of everything which he saw. After some preliminary description he makes some statements about the inscriptions in this form :

" On the South Side outwards there is an Inscription cut on an empty space 15 spans long, and 7 broad, in such a character that there is now no understanding Person in the World that can make anything of it. It is neither Caldee, nor Hebrew, nor Arabick, nor Greek, nor of any of those Languages the Learned have Knowledge, but only Triangles of several Sorts, severally plac'd, the various placing whereof perhaps formed divers words, and express'd some Thoughts. The most receiv'd Opinion is, that they are Characters of the ancient Goris, who were Sovereigns of Persia; but this is not easily to be made out, the Goris themselves being at present very ignorant as to their Antiquities, and unfit to give any Judgment of such things. . . . Not far off on a Pilaster of the same black marble, is an Inscription in the same Character, and another on such another Stone; which I observing, and remembering those I had seen before, began to consider with myself, how easily human Judgment is mistaken, and how different things happen to what Man proposes to himself; for whereas the Author thought by means of those inscriptions to have

Reduced from the Plate in Chardin's Voyages.

Vol. III, Page 118.

The inscription at the top of the page is Persian, the one on the left hand is Susian, the one on the right is Babylonian.

THE FIRST PERSEPOLIS INSCRIPTIONS COPIED ENTIRE.

eterniz'd his Memory with Posterity, which the
beauty of the work well deserv'd, yet quite the
contrary we see is fallen out. . . .

"Such precious Remains of Antiquity well deserve to be cut in Copper for the satisfaction of the
Ingenious, before they are quite lost through the
fault of the natives; but it is a difficult matter to
draw above two thousand Basse Relieves, and a
vast charge to print them. The Reader therefore
will think it enough that I have drawn the Plan
of the Palace, with some of the principal Figures;
that there may be some knowledge of the several
Habits of the antient *Persians;* and two lines
of twelve there are in the inscription on the Pilaster of the first Floor; perhaps hereafter some more
fortunate searcher into the oriental languages may
employ his wit on it.

"Having very well spent all the Day in seeing
and distinctly observing the best part of those
Antiquities, I returned, and was scarce come to
the place where I had left my Armenian Servant
before I hear'd him as'k me whether I had found
the Treasure; he believing the Inscriptions were
in Portugese, and that I had Read them and taken
the Treasure, as the *Carvansedar* had told him;
which made me laugh heartily all the Way."

By the side of this narrative Carreri presents a
copperplate illustration of the platform at Persepolis, showing the columns of the palace still
standing in front of the mountain. Above this
picture are two lines of inscription as follows:

[Reproduced in the same size as the copy given in Churchill's republica-
tion of Carreri's narrative.[1]]

It is evidently the purpose of Carreri to leave
upon the reader's mind the impression that he had
copied these characters himself. This, however,
is certainly not true. A slight examination and
comparison reveal the fact that these two lines
are made up out of the three lines of Herbert,
with but slight changes. Here, then, is a clear
case of deception proved at once upon the Nea-
politan. He has borrowed, and that rather stu-
pidly, from his English predecessor. In this
matter, at least, he has made no contribution to
the search for facts about records at Persepolis.
To make the matter rather worse, the picture of
the platform at Persepolis, which he gives beneath
his plate of inscriptions, is also borrowed without
acknowledgment. It had already appeared in
Daulier-Deslandes.[2]

His punishment has been severe. It has even

---

[1] *A Collection of Voyages and Travels* [Churchills]. Vol. iv. London,
MDCCIV. Containing pp. 1–606. *A Voyage round the World.* By Dr. John
Francis Gemelli-Carreri. . . . Translated from the Italian, pp. 172, 174.
Plate p. 175. The plate is better reproduced in *Voyage du Tour du Monde
Traduit de l'Italien de Gemelli Careri*, par M. L. N. Paris, MDCCXXVII.
P. 246. Should be p. 402. The pagination is incorrect.

[2] *Les Beautez de la Perse* . . . par le Sieur A. D. D. V. (*Andraé
Daulier Des Lands Vardomois.*) Paris, M.DC.LXXIII.

been this, that men have been moved to say that
Carreri copied much more than the plate of inscriptions and the Plan of Persepolis; that he
copied, indeed, everything in his book, and had
never been absent from Naples at all, nor had
seen anything which he describes. This is, however, an excess of skepticism. He doubtless borrowed much from his predecessors, a common
habit then, and not altogether unknown among
travelers even now, but there is really no reason
to believe that the whole of Carreri's narrative
was fictitious.

But that question aside, the book of Carreri is
of importance in the history of decipherment; not
indeed that his copy or his description was of
any practical use, but because his book was widely
read in Europe, and had its share in keeping alive
the interest in Persepolis and in stimulating more.
And that was no mean service.

The slow assaults upon these inscriptions at Persepolis were now becoming international. The
Spanish, Italians, English, and French had all
made their observations. It was now in order
that a German, Engelrecht Kaempfer, should make
his contribution to the unraveling of the mystery.
Kaempfer was a physician, born and trained in
Germany, but largely become a Hollander by residence and service. He had already made important
contributions to science through long residence in
Japan, where he had studied the botany and then
the manners, customs, and the history of that then

unknown land. From the mystery of Japan he
turned to the mystery of Persia, and not knowing
exactly what he did, copied again the little three-
line inscription which Chardin had already prepared for publication. That would have been no
new contribution to the work had he gone no
further, but he made a gain by publishing for the
first time a long inscription, which was not in old
Persian at all, but in Assyro-Babylonian.[1] The
difference between the two inscriptions he does
not appear to have noticed, and he certainly did
not know in what language or languages these texts
might be written. The longer inscription appears
to have interested him most, and upon this he made
some observations which sprang naturally out of his
former studies in Chinese and Japanese. His question was in simplest form this : Have we in these
strange-looking inscriptions a language written in
alphabetic, in syllabic, or in ideographic characters?
Or, in another form ; do these little wedge-shaped
signs represent in each case a letter, a syllable, or
a word ? His decision was that the signs were
ideographic, each of them representing an idea or
a word. If he had reference in this judgment only
to his longer inscription, and not to the smaller
one at all, his decision was correct, and may very

---

[1] Kaempfer's important investigations are published in his great book,
*Amoenitatum exoticarum politico-physico-medicarum, fasciculi v, quibus
continenter variae relationes, observationes & descriptiones rerum Persica-
rum & ulterioris Asiae, multa attentione, in peregrinationibus per univer-
sum Orientem, collectae ab auctore Engelberto Kaempfero.* D. Lemgoviae,
1712. Quart.

possibly have influenced those who came after him to a proper decision at the beginning of their researches.

Kaempfer spent the later days of his life in the Netherlands. His work might almost entirely be claimed as Holland's contribution to this international enterprise if there were any need so to do. But Holland was now to make its own direct contribution through one of its own sons, Cornelis de Bruin, who visited the ruins in 1704, and also copied inscriptions there. Ten years later an account of his travels over Moscovia, Persia, and India was published in sumptuous style in Amsterdam. In this new work there were reproduced two inscriptions in a threefold form. In reality the threefold form was later discovered to be three languages, but Bruin believed that he had really published six inscriptions, and not merely two inscriptions repeated in three languages. Bruin reproduced two other inscriptions each in a single language. Bruin's book was first published in Dutch,[1] but afterward appeared in French.[2] Its influence upon the progress of these studies was surprisingly small. The very costliness of its magnificent original publication might have made it accessible to few, and in this

---

[1] *Cornelis de Bruins Reizen over Moskovie, door Persie en Indie.* t'Amsteldam, 1714. Folio. Between pages 216 and 217 are magnificent copperplate views of the ruins at Persepolis, and between 217 and 218 are the copies of the inscriptions, numbered 131, 134.

[2] *Voyages de Corneille le Brun par la Moscovie, en Perse, et aux Indes Orientales,* 2 tom. à Amsterdam, 1718. The plates in this edition are inserted in vol. ii, between pages 270 and 271, and between 272 and 273.

there is possibly some explanation of its slight influence. But the French edition, in a language more extensively used, and in a form more simple, must have had a considerable circulation. Yet even from this there came no impulse. Europe looked idly over the plates in which these strange characters appeared and apparently made no attempt to get at their secret. They were still matters of curiosity, but their publication at all was an achievement which could not be permanently fruitless. The restless spirit of man would be in pursuit of them shortly, and then each line published by one traveler after another would be eagerly scanned, and every single suggestion or hint weighed and considered. Other travelers planning to visit these same lands in the age before guidebooks, would read the accounts of their predecessors, and, inspired by them, would go to see the same ruins and to bring back more complete copies of these little inscriptions. In this was the chief hope for the future. All the copies which were yet made were too brief to offer a good chance for translation, or even decipherment. They were furthermore inaccurate in very important matters. There could be no hope of a successful decipherment until the quiet scholar in his library had copies in which every line, every wedge, every little corner, was accurately reproduced. The improvement in this respect had thus far not been great. The gain had been chiefly in the number of texts offered. If the proposition made by the Royal Society of London, when Mr. Flower's copies were first presented, in 1693, had been followed, and a complete copy made of all these inscriptions by a competent hand, the attempts to decipher would have undoubtedly begun much earlier than they did.

In this story of a slow-moving effort at decipherment the small must find its mention along with the great; and there is need to turn for a moment from Persepolis to mention the publication made in 1762 of a beautiful vase.[1] Upon this were inscribed at the upper part one long line of cuneiform characters, followed by a shorter line of the same. By the side of this shorter line were some hieroglyphic characters. Like the publications which preceded it, this also failed of any influence upon the progress of research at this time. The hieroglyphic signs were not yet deciphered, for the Rosetta stone had not yet been found by Napoleon's soldiers as they threw up their breastworks. If the Egyptian could have then been read, men would certainly have seized upon this little vase as containing a clue to the decipherment of the cuneiform characters. It would then have appeared as a bilingual text, in which the Egyptian formed one part and the cuneiform the other. By this means Egyptian would have become the mother study for Assyrian. Later this vase played a part both in Egyptian and in Assyrian studies, and then it became known that, like the monuments at Per-

---

[1] *Recuil d'Antiquités.* . . . tom. cinquieme, planche xxx.   Paris, 1762.

sepolis, the two lines of cuneiform texts were in reality written in *three* separate languages. The publication of the inscriptions on the vase was made by the French. So were the European nations, one by one, giving their share of time and labor to the international work. The greater ones among them had now done something, the smaller had yet hardly begun. One of these, the people of Denmark, was now to begin making contributions of great importance which should carry the investigations far beyond anything that had yet been attained. In the month of March, 1765, the ruins of Persepolis were visited by Carsten Niebuhr. He, like some of his predecessors, had had long experience of travel, and, unlike the others, was a man of exact and methodical habits of work. He had, furthermore, prepared for just this work by a perusal of Bruin and Chardin, and apparently, also, even by the reading of Pietro della Valle. The references which he gives to the two former show the continuity of study and indicate afresh how much these early voyagers had really accomplished, even when their work appeared to count for little at the time. Niebuhr's description of the ruins of Persepolis makes careful note of the changes which had come to the ruins by the ravages of time and the hand of man since Bruin had seen them, and then hurries on the real matter which most concerned him. His distinguished son has thus set forth the enthusiasm and the methods of Niebuhr in these researches:

"These ruins, inscriptions, and bas-reliefs had been sufficiently well represented by three former travelers to arouse the attention of Niebuhr as the most important monument of the East. The number of inscriptions and sculptures made him hope that an interpreter might be found who, by comparing them, would be able to understand them, if once correct copies of them were placed before him; and Niebuhr's keen eye told him how insufficient the drawings hitherto published were. Nothing out of all that he saw in Asia attracted him so powerfully in anticipation; he could not rest until he had reached Persepolis, and the last night saw him sleepless. The remembrance of these ruins remained ineffaceable all his life long; they were for him the gem of all that he had viewed.

"Three weeks and a half he remained beneath them, in the midst of a wilderness; and during this time he worked without interruption at the measurement and drawing of the ruins. The inscriptions are placed high up on the walls, and were clearly to be distinguished only when the sun shone upon them; as in this atmosphere the hard, originally polished marble is not weather-worn, his eyes, already affected by the uninterrupted work, were dangerously inflamed; and this, as well as the death of his Armenian servant, obliged him, much against his will, to leave the old Persian sanctuary before he had completed his drawings."

It would seem from this that it was the design of Niebuhr to copy every inscription which he could find at Persepolis. That would have been a great task indeed. Even without this completeness he achieved a result attained by no one who had preceded him. He republished several of the texts which Bruin and Kaempfer had published before him, but in a form far excelling them for accuracy. To these he added four texts which had not before appeared in any work. But Niebuhr made other contributions besides merely reporting the state of the ruins and giving copies of the inscriptions. His long journeyings ended in Denmark on November 20, 1767. A certain amount of leisure was now secured, and while writing the narrative of his travels[1] for the press he went over these little inscriptions and made some discoveries concerning them. It was in the first place clear to him that the conjectures of earlier students, that this writing was to be read from left to right, were correct. That was a good point of approach, and with that in mind he compared all his copies and soon determined that in them there were really three separate systems of writing. These three systems were always kept distinct in the inscriptions. In one of them the little wedges were not so complex in their combinations, in the second the complexity had some-

---

[1] Carsten Niebuhr, *Reisebeschreibung nach Arabien und andern umliegenden Ländern.* Kopenhagen, 1774–1837, 3 vols. The description of Persepolis is in vol. ii.

what increased, while in the third it had become much greater. He did not, however, come to what now seems a natural conclusion, that three languages were here represented. He held rather to the view that the proud builders of Persepolis had carved their inscriptions in a threefold form, the same words being written in more complicated characters. Having come thus far, he made still another step in advance. He divided these little inscriptions into three distinct classes, according to the manner of their writing, calling them Class I, II, and III. He then arranged all those, which he had copied, that belonged to Class I, and by careful comparison decided that in them there were employed altogether but forty-two (42) signs. These he copied out and set in order in one of his plates.[1] This list of signs was so nearly complete and accurate that later study has made but slight changes in it. When Niebuhr had made his list of signs he naturally enough decided that this language, whatever it might be, was written in alphabetic characters. This much was finally determined, and future investigation would not overthrow it. Far beyond all his predecessors had Niebuhr gone. It is a pity that he was not able to go still further and essay the decipherment of one of these little inscriptions of the first class. For this, however, he did not possess the requisite linguistic genius, nor had he at command the various historical data necessary for its solution. He had given the

---

[1] *Ibid.*, vol. ii, plate xxiii, between pp. 132 and 133.

world the material in a new and substantially correct form, and he had pointed out the proper place
to begin; the rest must be left for another.

For just this which Niebuhr had furnished the
learned world had been waiting. The words of
Bruin and Chardin had awakened no scholar to
attempts to decipher the texts which they had
copied, simply because so little had been offered
by them. Soon after the richer store of Niebuhr
had been published, two scholars were at work
seriously attempting to decipher these texts. The
first was Olav Gerhard Tychsen, professor of oriental languages in the University of Rostock, in
Germany; the other was Friedrich Münter, the
Danish academician of Copenhagen. Tychsen
made a very important discovery in the beginning
of his researches, that remained to guide future
workers. He observed that there occurred at
irregular intervals in the inscriptions of the first
class a wedge that pointed neither directly to the
right nor downward, but inclined diagonally. This
wedge Tychsen suggested was the dividing sign
used to separate words.[1] This very simple discovery later became of very great importance in the
hands of Münter. Of more general importance
was his statement that " all the inscriptions of
Niebuhr, with a single exception, are trilingual."[2]
In that sentence spoke a linguist; the previous

---

[1] *De cuneatis inscriptionibus Persepolitanis lucubratio.*   Rostochii, 1798,
p. 24.

[2] *Ibid.*, p. 5.

workers had been travelers, men of science, men of skill. The matter was now in the hands of men accustomed to deal with languages, and the promise of ultimate success was yearly growing brighter. The rest of Tychsen's work was not of enduring character. He argued wrongly as to the age of the buildings at Persepolis, and reached the erroneous conclusion that these inscriptions had been written during the Parthian dynasty (246 B. C.—227 A. D.). This error in history vitiated his promising attempt at the decipherment of one small inscription which had been found above the figure of a king. He rendered it thus:

"This is the king, this is Arsaces the great, this is Arsaces, this is Arsaces, the perfect and the king, this is Arsaces the divine, the pious, the admirable hero." [1]

But a later investigator was to show that this was not an inscription of Arsaces at all, and that scarcely a word of it had been correctly rendered. This statement makes the work of Tychsen appear almost abortive, but such a judgment would not be just. He had indeed failed in the greater effort, but in making that he had, nevertheless, gained several smaller steps, and at the place thus attained another might begin and travel farther.

Münter was more fortunate than Tychsen in his historic researches, and that made him also more successful in his linguistic attempts. He rightly identified the builders of Persepolis with the Achæ-

---

[1] *Ibid.*, p. 29.

menides, and so located in time the authors of the inscriptions. This was great gain, the full force of which he was not able to appreciate nor to utilize. He also agreed with the judgment of the former workers that the texts were to be read from left to right, and was beyond them in his full recognition of three languages, of which the last two were translations of the first. Independently of Tychsen, he recognized the oblique wedge as the divider between words, and was able to go far beyond this, even to the recognizing of the vowel " a " and the consonant " b." This was the first sure step in the decipherment. From our present point of view it may sound small, but it is to be remembered that it was made without the assistance of any bilingual text, taken bodily out of the darkness and gloom which had settled over this language centuries before. It was an achievement far exceeding that of the decipherment of the Egyptian hieroglyphics, which was secured by the aid of a bilingual text containing Greek. The name of Münter may well be held in honor among all who covet knowledge of the past of the Orient.

With the material which Münter had it would have been difficult to go farther, but events were now to make accessible to another man of genius, adapted to such work, new material which would greatly simplify the labor of decipherment. This new material did not directly concern the inscriptions of Persepolis, but it did cast welcome light upon them. It is connected with three great names

in the annals of oriental studies, and romantic in
its personal, as in its scientific connections.

In the year 1731 there was born at Paris a boy
whose parents gave him the name of Abraham
Hyacinthe Anquetil-Duperron, and destined him
to the priesthood. In the seminary studies, carried
on for this purpose, the young man learned Hebrew, and that introduced him to the fascination
of the oriental world, as it has many another since
his day. His soul forgot its dedication to the priesthood and became absorbed in oriental study at the
Royal Library of Paris. Here he attracted the notice of Abbé Sallier, who secured for him a small
stipend as a student of Arabic and Persian. In
that treasure-house of human knowledge there fell
into his hands a few leaves of an oriental manuscript, in which were written words sacred in the
religion of Zoroaster. The language best known
as Avestan, but long erroneously called Zend, he
could not read, and his soul burned with longing
to learn what these strange characters should be,
and what the language which they expressed. He
determined, even in his hopeless poverty, to get
out to India, there to learn from the priests of
Zoroastrianism the language of their sacred books.
The times were troubled; war was likely at any
time to begin between France and England in India, and even now French troops were about to be
dispatched thither. With these lay his only hope
of reaching the land of his dreams. He enlisted
as a common soldier, but before he had sailed from

5

L'Orient his friends had appealed to the minister, who gave him a discharge, provided free passage, with a seat at the captain's table, and ordered a salary paid him on arrival at his destination. He landed, on the 10th of August, 1755, at Pondicherry, and waited a short time to study modern Persian, and later at Chandernagore to study Sanskrit. When the war broke out between France and England he suffered terrible privations. At last his reward came at Surat, where he ingratiated himself with the priests and acquired enough knowledge of the language to translate the dictionary Vedidad-Sade and other works. In May, 1762, he arrived at Paris poor and exhausted, but laden with oriental manuscripts to the number of one hundred and eighty. Out of this store he published in 1771 the Zend-Avesta, which brought to Europe its first sight of the sacred books of the followers of Zoroaster. This publication was of immense value to the study of religion and of history, but it was now destined to exert another potent influence. The linguistic collections of Anquetil-Duperron were organized and systematized by Eugène Burnouf, and it was this fact that was to have an important bearing upon the study of the inscriptions of Persepolis.

After Anquetil-Duperron and Eugène Burnouf there is to be added the name of Silvestre de Sacy, the greatest Arabic scholar of his age, as one who, without intending so to do, cast a valuable side light upon Persepolitan research.

In Persia travelers had long been noticing inscriptions written during the Sassanian period in the Pehlevi character (227–641 A. D.). In the years 1787–1791 Sylvestre de Sacy, who was later to lay the foundations of Arabic philology on which its present structure is still standing, began the decipherment of these inscriptions, and soon conquered their mystery sufficiently to gain at least their general sense. He found that they had a stereotyped form from which there was scarcely ever a departure, and that they run about in this style:

"N., the great king, the king of kings, the king of Iran and Aniran, son of N., the great king, etc."

That discovery had its own importance in its own field, but, like the work of Duperron and Burnouf, it was now to be applied to other uses by a man whose aim was to decipher much older inscriptions.

If now we look back over this long story, reaching from the earlier part of the fourteenth century down to the very beginning of the nineteenth, and gather up the loose threads of our story, we shall be the better able to understand the method and the results which were now to be revealed.

Out of Persepolis, by the combined efforts of a long line of travelers, Italian, Spanish, Dutch, German, English, Danish, and Portuguese, there had been brought to Europe copies of some little inscriptions written in cuneiform characters. It had already been learned concerning them that they

belonged to the age of the Achæmenides, that they
were written in three languages, of which the first
was ancient Persian, that this ancient Persian was
almost, if not quite wholly, an alphabetic language,
with possibly some syllabic signs, and that of these
alphabetic signs two, namely, "a" and "b," were
almost certainly made out, while of some others
possible or even probable meanings were suggested.
To this were now to be added two valuable side
lights. The decipherment of the Avestan language had supplied the grammatical structure and
much of the vocabulary of a language spoken
over the very same territory as that in which Persian had formerly held dominion. It was exceedingly probable that it had taken up many words,
with some changes, from the more ancient tongue
which scholars were now trying to decipher. It
was likely, also, to represent in its grammatical
structure, in its declensions or conjugations, some
reminiscence of old Persian. In grammar, syntax,
or lexicon of Avestan there was a good hope of
finding something that might be made useful to
the decipherer. Some of this material was accessible to Tychsen and to Münter, but they had not
known how to use it with best effect. There is a gift
for deciphering, as there is a gift of tongues. But
not only from this work of Duperron and Burnouf
was there new material; valuable hints might be
had from the discoveries of De Sacy concerning
the inscriptions of Sassanian kings. The style in
which the Sassanian kings wrote their inscriptions

was very probably copied from the style in which the older Achæmenides had written. That was not certain, but as a hypothesis upon which to work it might prove useful.

In this we have shown what the material was, what the problem, and what the essays made for its solution, and now there was a call for a man able to practice a method by which all that existed of fact or of hypothesis could be brought to bear, and the successful result be achieved. But even while this preliminary work was going on the genius who should achieve the result was preparing.

CHAPTER II.

GROTEFEND AND RAWLINSON.

IT were difficult, if not impossible, to define the qualities of mind which must inhere in the decipherer of a forgotten language. He is not necessarily a great scholar, though great scholars have been successful decipherers. He may know but little of the languages that are cognate with the one whose secrets he is trying to unravel. He may indeed know nothing of them, as has several times been the case. But the patience, the persistence, the power of combination, the divine gift of insight, the historical sense, the feeling for archæological indications, these must be present, and all these were present in the extraordinary man who now attacked the problem that had baffled so many.

On June 9, 1775, Georg Friedrich Grotefend was born at Münden, in Hanover, Germany. He was destined to become a classical philologist, and for this purpose studied first at Ilfeld and later at the University of Göttingen. Here he attracted much attention, not only as a classical scholar of promise, but also as an ingenious man with a passion for the unraveling of difficult and recondite questions. He formed the friendship in Göttingen of Heyne, Tychsen, and Heeren. On the recommendation of the first named, he was appointed in

1797 to an assistant mastership in the Göttingen Gymnasium. Two years later appeared his first work, which brought him reputation and a superior post in the Gymnasium at Frankfort-on-the-Main. Up to this time he had given no attention to the study of oriental languages. But in 1802 his friend, the librarian Fiorillo, drew the attention of Grotefend to the inscriptions from Persepolis, and placed in his hands all the literature which had hitherto appeared.

Grotefend was at once enlisted, and, though he had no oriental learning, set himself to the work, probably little dreaming of how many years of his life would be spent upon these little inscriptions or upon the work which grew out of them. His method was exceedingly simple,[1] and may be made perfectly clear without the possession of any linguistic knowledge. His fundamental principles and his simplest facts were taken over bodily from his predecessors. He began with the assumption that there were three languages, and that of these the first was ancient Persian, the language of the Achæmenides, who had erected these palaces and caused these inscriptions to be written. For his first attempts at decipherment he chose two of

---

[1] Grotefend's first paper was written in Latin (*De cuneatis, quas vocant inscriptionibus persepolitanis legendis et esplicandis relatio*) and presented by a friend to the Göttingen Academy September 4, 1802. It was followed by others on October 2, November 13, 1802, and May 20, 1803. None of these were published by the society. The original papers were found by Professor Wilhelm Meyer, of Göttingen, in the society's archives and published in the *Nachrichten von der Königlichen Gesellschaft der wissenschaften zu Göttingen*, 1893, No. 14.

these old Persian inscriptions and laid them side by side. The ones which were chosen were neither too long nor too short; the frequent recurrence of the same signs in them seemed to indicate that their contents were similar, and finally they were clearly and apparently accurately copied by Niebuhr. The inscriptions thus selected were those numbered "B" and "G" by Niebuhr (see plate), which, for the purpose of this exposition, may be designated simply as first and second (I and II). Following Tychsen and Münter, he held that these inscriptions, which accompanied figures of kings, were the titles of these monarchs, and were presumably similar to the inscriptions of Sassanian kings which De Sacy had just deciphered. Grotefend placed these two inscriptions side by side and carefully examined them. In the work of Münter a word had been pointed out which appeared frequently in these inscriptions, sometimes in a short form and sometimes longer, as though in the latter case some grammatical termination had been added to it. In these two inscriptions this word appeared both in the shorter and in the longer form. Grotefend was persuaded that this word meant king, as Münter had discovered, and that when it appeared twice in each of these texts in exactly the same place, first the shorter and then the longer form, the expression meant "king of kings." A glance at the plate will show that in these two inscriptions, in the second line, after the first word divider, appear the two sets of signs exactly alike, thus:

(a) 《》𒁹 . 𒌋 . 𒌅 . 𒅗 . 𒅗𒁹 . 𒐊 . 𒅗 .

this is followed by the same word, but much increased in length, thus:

(b) 《》𒁹 . 𒌋𒌋 . 𒌅 . 𒅗 . 𒁹𒌋𒁹 . 𒐊 . 𒅗 . 𒐊 .
𒂊 . 𒐊 . 𒐊 .

The supposition was that (a) meant *king* while (b)
was the plural and meant *kings*, the whole expression signifying *king of kings*. But further
this same word, supposed to be king, occurred
again in both inscriptions, namely, in the first line,
and in both instances it was followed by the
same word, namely:

(c) 𒁹 𒐊 𒐊 𒐊

Here, then, was another expression containing the
word king. What could it mean? Grotefend looked
over De Sacy's translations of Sassanian inscriptions and found that the expression "great king"
occurred in them, and then made the conjecture
that this was the same expression, and that (c)
meant "great," hence "king great," that is, *great
king*. All this looked plausible enough, but it
was, after all, only conjecture. It must all be supported by definite facts, and these words must
each be separated into its alphabetic constituents
and these understood, and supported by clear evidence, before anyone would or could believe in

the decipherment. To this Grotefend now bent every energy. His method was as simple as before. He had made out to his own satisfaction the titles "great king, king of kings." Now, in the Sassanian inscriptions the first word was always the king's name, followed immediately by "great king, king of kings;" it was probably true in this case. But, if true, then these two inscriptions were set up by different kings, for the name in the first was:

(d) 𒁹 . 𒈨 . 𒂖 . 𒅗 . 𒉺 . 𒌋 . 𒌋𒌋 .

while in the other it was :

(e) 𒌋𒌋 . 𒌋𒌋 . 𒉺 . 𒈨 . 𒂖 . 𒌋𒌋 . 𒈨 .

But to simplify, or to complicate the matter, as one will, this name with which I begins appears in II in the third line, but changed somewhat in its ending, so that it stands thus:

(f) 𒁹 . 𒈨 . 𒂖 . 𒅗 . 𒉺 . 𒂗 . 𒌋 . 𒌋𒌋 .

From its situation in the two places Grotefend concluded that (d) was the name in the nominative and (f) was the same name in the genitive. Thus I begins " *N great king, king of kings,*" and this same king appears in II thus: " *of N.*" In number II this name was followed by the word for king, and after this another word which might mean "son," so that the whole phrase in II would be " *of N king son,*" that is, " *son of N king,*" the order

of words being presumably different from that to
which we are accustomed. But this same word,
which is supposed to mean *son*, appears also in I,
line five, thus:

$$(g) \quad \text{𒅆 𒆠 𒅆}$$

where it follows a name which does not possess
the title king. From all these facts Grotefend
surmised that in these two inscriptions he had the
names of three rulers: (1) the grandfather, who
had founded a dynasty, but did not possess the
title of king; (2) the son, who succeeded him and
bore the title of king; and (3) the grandson, who
also had the same title. The next thing to do
was to search through all the known names of the
Achamenides to find three names which should
suit. The first names thought of were Cambyses,
Cyrus, and Cambyses. These will, however, not
do, because the name of the grandfather and grandson are exactly alike, whereas on the two inscriptions they are different. The next three to be
considered are Hystaspes, Darius, Xerxes. If
these be correct, then the seven signs with which
I begins must be the name Darius (see d above).
The next thing in order was to find the form of
the name Darius in ancient Persian. Of course
Grotefend did not expect to find it written in that
way exactly, for the modern European spelling
has come to us from the Greek, and the Greeks
were not careful to reproduce exactly the names
of other peoples who were, in their view, only

barbarians. He ascertained from the Hebrew
lexicon that the Hebrews pronounced the word
Daryavesh, while Strabo in one passage, in trying
to represent as accurately as possible the Persian
form, gave it as Dareiaves. Neither of these would
work very well into the seven characters, and on
a venture Grotefend gave the word the form of
Darheush, and so the first word was thus to be set
down

That seemed to fit well enough, and as later investigations have shown, it was almost wholly
correct, there being only errors in H and E, which
did not vitiate the process, nor interfere with carrying it out further.   The next task was to make
out the name at the beginning of II.   This was
comparatively easy, for nearly all these same
letters were here again used, and only the first was
wanting.   It was easy to supply this from the
Hebrew form of the name and also from the
Avestan language so recently deciphered.   This
name was therefore read thus:

The error in this also was exceedingly slight,
when one considers the extreme difficulty of the
task and the comparative bluntness of this tool of
conjecture or surmise or, to put it boldly, guess.

This name was supposed to be the Persian form
for Xerxes.

The next thing in order was to find the letters
for the third name, and that was a much more
difficult problem. This was the name which appears in I, line four, last word, thus:

(*h*) 𒀭 . 𒀭 . 𒀭 . 𒀭 . 𒀭 . 𒀭 . 𒀭 . 𒀭 .
𒀭 . 𒀭 .

Here were ten signs. Grotefend believed that
this word was in the genitive case, and some signs
at the end must be cut off as the genitive ending.
But how many? That was the question. Perhaps the Avestan language (then called Zend)
would help him. To the study of this he now
had recourse, and after much doubt decided to
cut off the last three as ending, and take what
remained as the king's real name. The name
which he was seeking, as we have already seen,
was Hystaspes, the late Persian form of which
Grotefend followed, and thus made out the name:

(*h'*) 𒀭 . 𒀭 . 𒀭 . 𒀭 . 𒀭 . 𒀭 . 𒀭 .
   G   O   SH   T   A   S   P

In this word, as in the other two, later discovery
showed that he had made a mistake, but this
time only in the first two characters. To Grotefend's own mind the whole case seemed clear and
indisputable, for the same characters occurred in

all three names, and thus each supported the other. At this time the Persian alphabet was supposed to contain forty-two alphabetic characters, of which Grotefend believed that he had found thirteen. To this he soon added more, by a simple process of combination, using the word for the name of god in these texts, namely, Aurmazda. He now felt himself able to translate these inscriptions in part, thus:

I. Darius, the mighty king, king of kings . . . son of Hystaspes.

II. Xerxes, the mighty king, king of kings . . . son of Darius, the king.

This was an epoch-making result, and even Grotefend with all his enthusiasm and with all the confidence of genius, did not fully realize it. This much he was anxious to get before the learned world for acceptance, or perhaps for criticism. That should have been easy indeed, but, in fact, it was not easy. The Göttingen Academy of Sciences refused absolutely to believe in his methods or his results, and would not take the risk of disgracing itself by publishing Grotefend's paper, describing his work, in its transactions.[1] He was not an orientalist at all by training or experience, and the learned men of Göttingen who were oriental-

---

[1] This refusal is the more noticeable as the Academy had, in the very beginning, announced that Grotefend "had been led by certain historical presuppositions, and also by the analogy of the Sassanian inscriptions, to discover in the shorter cuneiform inscriptions of Persepolis, written in the first and simplest of the three forms of character, which he had examined with this purpose in view, the names and titles of Darius and Xerxes."— *Göttingische Gelehrte Anzeigen*, September 18, 1802 (No. 149).

ists asked whether "any good thing could come
out of Nazareth," that is, whether a man who was
not an orientalist could possibly offer a contribution of value to oriental learning. The case was
a sad one for the patient, plodding decipherer, for
it was not easy to see how he could gain any publicity for his work. At this juncture a personal
friend, A. H. L. Heeren, who was about to publish a book on the ancient world,[1] offered to give
space in the appendix to Grotefend for the purpose of setting forth his theories and discoveries.
Grotefend eagerly seized the opportunity, and
there appeared his work. It met, on the whole,
with a cold reception. Volney denounced it as
resting on forms of names which were at least
doubtful and might be incorrect, and with him
joined many German voices. On the other hand
Anquetil-Duperron, now an aged man, waiting
"with calmness the dissolution of his mortal
frame," and the immortal De Sacy received it with
enthusiasm and hailed it as the beginning of the
sure reading of these inscriptions.

Those who doubted the whole scheme were
later to receive a severe setback, and that from

[1] *Ideen über die Politik, den Verkehr und den Handel der vornehmsten
Völker der alten Welt*, von A. H. L. Heeren. 3 vols. Göttingen, 1815.
The paper by Grotefend is printed in vol. i, pp. 563, ff., under the title
Ueber die Erklärung der Keilschriften, und besonders der Inschriften von
Persepolis.

Heeren's book was translated into English with the title, *Historical
Researches into the Politics, Intercourse, and Trade of the Principal Nations
of Antiquity*, by A. H. L. Heeren. Oxford, 1833. In this edition Grotefend's essay appears in vol. ii, pp. 313, ff., accompanied by plates better
executed than those of the German edition.

an unexpected source. It will be remembered that while the Persepolis inscriptions were still in the copying stage a beautiful vase had come to Paris which contained some Egyptian hieroglyphics, and also some signs like those found at Persepolis. After the publication of Grotefend's work in Heeren's book the Abbé Saint-Martin, in Paris, devoted much thought and time to its criticism and study. At this same time Champollion was engaged in the decipherment of the Egyptian hieroglyphics. He suggested to the abbé that they should try to decipher together the marks upon the vase. When this was attempted the abbé found that the name on the vase in cuneiform characters should be transliterated thus:

CH. SH. A. R. SH. A [1]

and this was remarkably confirmed by the finding of the same name, according to Champollion, in the Egyptian signs. This was a small matter in some ways, but it increased the faith of many in the method and results of Grotefend.

Meanwhile Grotefend himself was continuing his efforts to get beyond these few words and decipher a whole inscription. At this stage, however, entirely different traits of mind were needed, and a completely changed mental furnishing. In the preliminary work the type of mind which Grotefend possessed was admirably adapted to

---

[1] *Nouvelles observations sur les inscriptions de Persepolis*, par M. Saint-Martin. (*Memoires de l'Academie Royale des Inscrip. et Belles-Lettres.* Tome xii, part 2, 1839, pp. 113, ff.) This paper was read before the Academy, December 20, 1822.

the work to be done. The mental training derived from long study of the classics of Greek
and Latin was likewise of constant service. He
had, however, now reached the point where extensive and definite knowledge of the oriental languages was imperatively necessary. In order to
secure words of ancient Persian he must know
words in the related oriental languages or in those
other languages which, though not related, had
been used in or about the same territory, and so
might have borrowed words from old Persian. He
must also know the oriental spirit, have a feeling
for oriental life, be able to understand in advance
just about what an oriental was likely to say.
None of these possessions were his. His later
work was therefore largely abortive. He tried to
translate entire inscriptions, and failed almost completely, though he devoted much time for all the
rest of his life to this matter, without, however,
abandoning his real field of classical literature.

However unsuccessful the later efforts of Grotefend may have been, nothing can ever dim the
luster of his fame as a decipherer. It was he who
first learned how to read an ancient Persian word.
From this, in due course, came the power to read
the words of Babylonian and Assyrian. In other
words, through the discoveries of Grotefend the
world of ancient Persia was reopened, and men
learned to read its ancient inscriptions. By them
also the much greater worlds of Assyria and Babylonia were likewise rediscovered. Much of what

we know of ancient Persia came from them; almost
all that we know of Assyria and Babylonia was
derived from them. To very few men, in all
time, has it happened to make discoveries of such
moment.

While he still lived and worked others with
better equipment in a knowledge of the oriental
languages took up his work. The first of these
was a Norwegian by birth, R. Rask. It was his
good fortune to discover the plural ending in
ancient Persian, which had baffled Grotefend. In
the work of decipherment Grotefend never got so
far as to determine all the characters in the phrase,
king of kings, and this was now achieved by Rask,[1]
who correctly apportioned the characters. The
same ending appears also in another word after
the word "king." Rask also for this suggested
a very plausible rendering. In the Sassanian inscriptions the phrase is "king of lands;" why
might not this be the same? That question would
find its answer at a later day.

And now appeared a man to grapple with the
problem of the inscriptions of Persepolis, who was
in learning far better equipped than any who had
preceded him. This was the French savant,
Eugène Burnouf.[2] He had already gained fame

---

[1] R. Rask, *Ueber das Alter und die Echtheit der Zend Sprache und des
Zend-Avesta und Herstellung des Zend-Alphabets nebst einer Uebersicht der
gesammten Sprachstammes; uebersetzt von* Fried. Heinrich von der Hagen.
Berlin, 1826, p. 28.

[2] *Mémoire sur deux inscriptions cunéiformes trouvées près d'Hamadan,*
par M. Eugène Burnouf. Paris, 1836.

as the man who had given the grammar of Avestan
a scientific basis. He knew that language in all
its intricacies. To this he added a knowledge of
Persian life and religion in the period following
that to which these inscriptions belonged. All
this learning could be brought to bear upon these
inscriptions, and Burnouf used it all as a master.
He found in one of the little inscriptions which
Niebuhr had copied at Naksh-i-Rustam a list of
names of countries. To this he gave close study,
and by means of it accomplished almost at a
stroke several distinct achievements. In the first
place he found the equivalent for almost every
character in the Persian alphabet. In the next he
determined finally that old Persian was not the
same language as Avestan, but that it was closely
related to it, and that therefore there was good
hope that Avestan as well as certain Indo-European
languages would contribute important light to the
study of old Persian.

Before his own discoveries were made in full,
and before their publication, Burnouf had called
the attention of Lassen to this list of names. Induced by the remarks of Burnouf, Lassen made
this same list of names the subject of investigation,
and at about the same time as Burnouf published
the results of his study, which were almost identical.[1] He had, however, made, in one respect at

---

[1] Some believe that Lassen borrowed these results from Burnouf's com-
munications to him, and therefore count him dishonest in making no acknowledgment.

least, very definite progress over Burnouf. He
discovered that, if the system of Grotefend were
rigidly followed, and to every letter was given the
exact equivalent which Grotefend had assigned, a
good many words could not be read at all, while
others would be left wholly or almost wholly
without vowels. As instances of such words he
mentioned ÇPRD, THTGUS, KTPTUK, FRA-
ISJM. This situation led Lassen to a very important discovery, toward which his knowledge of
the Sanskrit alphabet did much to bring him. He
came, in one word, to the conclusion that the
ancient Persian signs were not entirely alphabetic,
but were, partially at least, syllabic, that is, that
certain signs were used to represent not merely an
alphabetic character like "b," but also a syllable
such as "ba," "bi," "bu." He believed that he
had successfully demonstrated that the sign for
"a" (see second sign in "f," below) was only used
at the beginning of a word, or before a conso·
nant, or before another vowel, and that in every
other case it was included in the consonant sign.
For example, in inscription I the first word of the
second line ought to be read thus :

while in inscription II the middle word in line
three should be so read :

This discovery was of tremendous importance, and may be said to have completely revolutionized the study of these long puzzling texts. To it two other scholars made important contributions, the one being Beer, and the other Jacquet, a Parisian savant.

This long line of successful decipherment had been carried on with only a small portion of the inscriptions of ancient Persia, that were still in existence. Other and better copies of the inscriptions were even at this time in Europe, but had not been published. In 1811 an English traveler, Claudius James Rich, had visited Persepolis and copied all the texts that were to be found, including those which Niebuhr and his predecessors had copied. These were discovered in the papers of Rich, and in 1839 were published, coming naturally at once into the hands of Lassen, who found in them much new material for the testing of his method and for the extension of the process of decipherment.

Still greater and more valuable material was placed in Lassen's hands through the travels of Westergaard, a Dane, who, in this, imitated worthily his fellow-countryman Niebuhr. Westergaard had again gone over the old ground at Persepolis and had there recopied and carefully collated all the well-known inscriptions.[1] In this he had not

---

[1] Lassen, *Die Alpersischen Keilinschriften nach Herrn N. L. Westergaard's Mittheilungen. Zeitschrift für die Kunde des Morgenlandes.* Band vi. Bonn, 1845. See especially pages 1-3.

done a useless task, for only by oft-repeated copying
and comparing could the finally definite and perfect text be attained, without which the decipherment would always be subject to revision.   But
Westergaard went further than this; he visited
at Naksh-i-Rustam the tombs of the Persian kings,
and there copied all the tomb inscriptions which
were hitherto unknown.   On his return this new
material was also made accessible to Lassen, who
was now fairly the leader in this work of decipherment.   Lassen found that the new copies of the
old texts were so important that he went over
some of the ground afresh and found it useful to
reedit some of his work which had before seemed
final.   The same material called a new worker into
the field in the person of Holtzman,[1] of Karlsruhe,
in Germany, whose work, however, made no very
deep impression on the general movement.

In the work of decipherment thus far the chief
positions had been held by Grotefend and Burnouf, but for the maintaining of its international
character the time was calling for workers from
other lands.   As it happened, at this very time
an Englishman was at work on the same task,
from a different point of view, and with different
materials.   It was well that this was so, for the
conclusions thus far reached would probably have
failed of general acceptance but for the support
obtained by the publication of similar results

---

[1] *Beiträge zur Erklärung der Persischen Keilinschriften*, von Adolf Holz-
mann.   Erstes Heft.   Carlsruhe, 1845.

achieved by a man of different nationality and
diverse training. The history of all forms of
decipherment of unknown languages shows that
skepticism concerning them is far more prevalent
than either its opposite, credulousness, or the happy
mean of a not too ready faith.

The man who was thus to rebuke the gainsayer
and put the capstone upon the work of the decipherment of the Persian inscriptions was Major,
(afterward Sir) Henry Rawlinson, who was born at
Chadlington, Oxford, England, on April 11, 1810.
While still a boy Rawlinson went out to India in
the service of the East India Company. There he
learned Persian and several of the Indian vernacu-
lars. This training hardly seemed likely to produce a man for the work of deciphering an unknown language. It was just such training as had
produced men like the earlier travelers who had
made the first copies of the inscriptions at Persepolis. It was, however, not the kind of education
which Grotefend, Burnouf, and Lassen had received. In 1833 the young Rawlinson went to
Persia, there to work with other British officers in
the reorganization of the Persian army. To Persia
his services were of extraordinary value, and met
with hearty recognition. It was in Persia, while
engaged in the laborious task of whipping semi-
barbarous masses of men into the severe discipline
of the soldier's life, that the attention of Rawlinson was attracted by some inscriptions. The first
that roused an interest in him were those at Hama-

dan, which he copied with great care. This was in the year 1835, at a time when a number of European scholars were earnestly trying to decipher the inscriptions from Persepolis. Of all this eager work Rawlinson knew comparatively little. It is impossible now to determine exactly when he first secured knowledge of Grotefend's work, for Norris, the secretary of the Royal Asiatic Society, has left us no record of when he first sent copies of Grotefend's essays to the far-distant decipherer. Whatever was sent in the beginning, it is quite clear that Rawlinson worked largely independently for a considerable time. He had certainly begun his work and adopted his method before he learned of what was going on in Europe.[1]

Rawlinson's method was strikingly like that adopted in the first instance by Grotefend. He had copied two trilingual inscriptions. That he had before him three languages, and not merely three styles of writing, he appears to have understood at once. To this ready appreciation of the presence of three languages Rawlinson's experience of the polyglot character of the East had probably contributed. In 1839 he thus wrote concerning his method of decipherment:

" When I proceeded . . . to compare and interline the two inscriptions (or, rather, the Persian columns of the two inscriptions, for as the com-

---

[1] On Rawlinson's life, and also on his work as a decipherer, see now *A Memoir of Major-General Sir Henry Creswicke Rawlinson*, by George Rawlinson. London, 1898. The notice of Rawlinson's work here given was written before the appearance of this memoir.

partments exhibiting the inscription in the Persian language occupied the principal place in the tablets, and were engraved in the least complicated of the three classes of cuneiform writing, they were naturally first submitted to examination) I found that the characters coincided throughout, except in certain particular groups, and it was only reasonable to suppose that the groups which were thus brought out and individualized must represent proper names. I further remarked that there were but three of these distinct groups in the two inscriptions; for the group which occupied the second place in one inscription, and which, from its position, suggested the idea of its representing the name of the father of the king who was there commemorated, corresponded with the group which occupied the first place in the other inscription, and thus not only served determinately to connect the two inscriptions together, but, assuming the groups to represent proper names, appeared also to indicate a genealogical succession. The natural inference was that in these three groups of characters I had obtained the proper names belonging to three consecutive generations of the Persian monarchy; and it so happened that the first three names of Hystaspes, Darius, and Xerxes, which I applied at hazard to the three groups, according to the succession, proved to answer in all respects satisfactorily and were, in fact, the true identifications."[1]

In the autumn of 1836, while at Teheran, Raw-

---

[1] *Journal of the Royal Asiatic Society*, x, pp. 5, 6.

linson first secured an acquaintance with the works of St. Martin and Klaproth, but found in them nothing beyond what he had already attained by his own unaided efforts, and in certain points he felt that he had gone further than they, and with greater probability.

Rawlinson's next work was the copying of the great inscription of Darius on the rocks at Behistun. This was a task of immense difficulty, carried on at the actual risk of his life, from its position high up on the rocks and beneath a blazing sun.[1] In 1835, when he first discovered it, Rawlinson was able to study it only by means of a field glass. At this time he could not copy the whole text, but gained more of it in 1837, when he had become more skilled in the strange character. In that year he forwarded to the Royal Asiatic Society of London his translation of the first two paragraphs of this Persian inscription, containing the name, titles, and genealogy of Darius. It must be remembered that Rawlinson had accomplished this without a knowledge of the related languages, except for what he could extract from the researches of Anquetil-Duperron. In the autumn of 1838, however, he came into possession of the works of Burnouf on the Avestan language, which proved of immense value in his work. He also secured at the same time the copies of the Persepolis inscriptions made by Niebuhr, Le Brun, and Porter, and the names of countries in them

---

[1] See *Athenæum*, November 8, 1884, No. 2976, p. 593.

were of great assistance to him, as they already had been to Burnouf and Lassen. With the advantage of almost all that European scholars had done, Rawlinson was now able to make rapid progress, and in the winter of 1838–1839 his alphabet of ancient Persian was almost complete. He was, however, unwilling to publish his results until he had ransacked every possible source of information which might have any bearing on the matter. In 1839 he was settled in Baghdad, his work in reality finished and written out for publication, but still hesitating and waiting for more light. Here he obtained books from England for the study of Sanskrit, and a letter from Professor Lassen, which greatly pleased him, though from it he was able to obtain only one character which he had not previously known. Here also he received the copies which Mr. Rich had made at Persepolis, and a transcript of an inscription of Xerxes at Van which had been made by M. Eugène Boré. In this year (1839) he wrote his preliminary memoir, and expected to publish it in the spring of 1840.

Just at this juncture he was suddenly removed from Baghdad and sent to Afghanistan as political agent at Kandahar. In this land, then in a state of war, he spent troublous years until 1843. He was so absorbed in war, in which he won distinction, and in administration as well, that his oriental studies had to be given up entirely.

In December, 1843, he was returned to Baghdad, the troubles in Afghanistan being for the time ended, and at once resumed his investiga- tions. Here he obtained the fresh copies and cor- rections of the Persepolitan inscriptions which Wes- tergaard had made, and later made a journey to Behistun to perfect his copies of those texts which had formed the basis of his first study. At last, after many delays and discouragements, he pub- lished, in 1846, in the *Journal of the Royal Asiatic Society*, his memoir, or series of memoirs, on the an- cient Persian inscriptions, in which for the first time he gave a nearly complete translation of the whole Persian text of Behistun. In this Rawlinson attained an imperishable fame in oriental research. His work had been carried on under difficulties, of which the European scholars had never even dreamed, but he had surpassed them all in the making of an in- telligible and connected translation of a long in- scription. Remarkable as this was, perhaps the most noteworthy matter in connection with his work was this, that much of it had been done with small assistance from Europe.' He had, indeed,

---

¹ George Rawlinson has attached himself to the view that Sir Henry Raw- linson had almost completed the work of decipherment of the Old Persian alphabet before he learned anything of the work of Grotefend. He says : "Up to this time [end of 1836] he had no knowledge at all of the antece- dent or contemporary labors of continental scholars, but had worked out his conclusions entirely from his own observation and reasoning " (*Memoir*, p. 309). This view rests upon the decipherer's own recollections of his work. It is, however, almost certain that Sir Henry Rawlinson forgot just when he first learned of Grotefend's work, and thought that he was independent, when in reality he was assisted by Grotefend, Burnouf, and Lassen. In 1884 he carried on a spirited controversy with Professor F. Max Müller concerning the right of priority of discovery. In one of his letters he

received from Norris, Grotefend's results, though
not at the very beginning, and he was later supplied with all that other scholars had been able to
accomplish. Furthermore, as early as 1837 he was
in correspondence with Burnouf and Lassen, from
both of whom he gained assistance. When all allowance is made for these influences, his fame is not
diminished nor the extent of his services in the decipherment curtailed. His method was settled
early and before he knew of Lassen's work. That
two men of such different training and of such
opposing types of mind should have lighted upon
the same method, and by it have attained the
same results, confirmed, in the eyes of many, the
decipherment.

The whole history of the decipherment of these
ancient Persian inscriptions is full of surprises,
and another now followed immediately. In January, 1847, the *Dublin University Magazine* contained an unsigned article with the taking title,
"Some Passages of the Life of King Darius," the
opening sentences of which were as follows:

speaks thus of the matter: "Now, for my own part, I take leave to say
that, though I worked independently, and with some success, in my early
attempts to decipher the Persian cuneiform inscriptions (from 1835 to
1839), still I never pretended to claim priority of discovery over Grotefend,
Burnouf, and Lassen. . . . As I was in pretty active correspondence with
Burnouf and Lassen from 1837 to 1839 on the values of the cuneiform
characters, it is impossible to say by whom each individual letter became
identified" (*Athenæum*, November 8, 1884, p. 593). This letter makes it
sufficiently plain that Rawlinson himself when he carefully considered the
matter did not make so great a claim for himself as does his brother in
the admirable memoir. His fame is secure, and needs not to be established by any attempt to prove that he was wholly independent of European scholars in all his earlier work.

"In adding this new name to the catalogue of royal authors, we assure our readers that we are perfectly serious. The volume which contains this monarch's own account of his accession, and of the various rebellions that followed it, is now before us; and unpretending as it is in its appearance, we do not hesitate to say that a more interesting—and on many accounts a more important—addition to our library of ancient history has never been made." [1]

After this introduction the writer proceeds to narrate how Major Rawlinson had copied at Behistun the inscription of Darius and how he had successfully deciphered it. As the paper proceeds, the anonymous writer goes beyond the work of Rawlinson to tell of what had been done in Europe by Grotefend and others, displaying in every sentence the most exhaustive acquaintance with the whole history of the various attempts at decipherment. Then he falls into courteous and gentle but incisive criticism of some of Major Rawlinson's readings or translations, and herein displays a mastery of the whole subject which could only be the result of years of study. There was but one man in Ireland who could have written such a paper as that, and he was a quiet country rector at Killyleagh, County Down, the Rev. Edward Hincks.[2]

---

[1] *Dublin University Magazine*, Dublin, 1847, p. 14.

[2] Apart from the internal evidence there is now no doubt that this paper was written by Hincks, though published anonymously. See Adler, *Proceedings of the American Oriental Society*, October, 1888, p. civ; and compare Stanley Lane Poole, *Dictionary of National Biography*, xxvi, p. 439

He was born at Cork, in 1792, and was therefore
the senior of Rawlinson by about eighteen years.
After an education at Trinity College, Dublin,
that wonderful nursery of distinguished Irishmen,
where he took a gold medal in 1811, he was settled in 1825 at Killyleagh, to spend the remainder of his life. His first contributions to human
learning appear to have been in mathematics, but
he early began to devote himself to oriental languages, publishing in 1832 a Hebrew grammar.
He was one of the pioneers of Egyptian decipherment, and his contributions to that great work
are acknowledged now to be of the highest rank.
Unhappily his life has never been worthily written, and it is impossible to determine just when he
first began to study the inscriptions of Persepolis.
It is, however, clear that, independently of Rawlinson, he arrived at the meaning of a large number
of signs, and had among his papers, before Rawlinson's work appeared, translations of some of the
Persepolitan texts. His first published memoir
was read before the Royal Irish Academy on June
6, 1846, having been written in the month of
May in that year. In this paper Hincks shows
an acquaintance with the efforts at decipherment
which had been made by Westergaard and Lassen, but he seems not to have seen the works
of the other continental decipherers. He had
much surpassed these two without the advantage which they enjoyed of more complete literature.

In the work of Hincks the Persepolitan inscriptions had been now for the third time independently deciphered and in part translated. With this Dr. Hincks did not cease his work, but went on to larger conquests, of which we shall hear later in this story.

The work of decipherment was now over as far as the ancient Persian inscriptions were concerned. There was, of course, much more to be learned concerning the language and concerning the historical material which the inscriptions had provided. On these and other points investigation would go on even to this hour. But the pure work of the decipherer was ended, the texts were read. A language long dead lived again. Men long silent had spoken again. It seemed a dream; it was a genuine reality, the result of long and painful study through a series of years by scores of men, each contributing his share.

Though the work upon Persian was in this advanced stage, very little had yet been done with the other two languages upon these same inscriptions. What might be the result of a similar study of them nobody now knew. It was believed that the columns written in two other languages contained the same facts as those which had been so laboriously extracted from old Persian, and there was, therefore, little incitement to their study. Before the end of this period, however, there were beginning to be hints that these other two languages were important, and that one of them was the representative of a great people who possessed an extensive literature. The proofs that this was indeed true were now slowly beginning to accumulate, and, when enough of them were gathered to make an impression, the men who were gifted with the decipherer's skill would turn from the Persian to unravel the secrets of the unknown and unnamed languages which the kings of Persia had commanded to be set up by the side of their own Persian words. Great results had already flowed from the Persian studies. New light had been cast upon many an enigmatical passage in Herodotus; a whole kingdom had been permitted to speak, not through its enemies, as before, but for itself. But all this was as nothing compared with the untold, unimagined results which were soon to follow from a study of the third language which existed in all the groups at Persepolis. To this study men were now to be wrought up by the brilliant work of explorers.

We have traced one story—the story of decipherment. We turn now to a second story, the story of exploration.

7

EXCURSUS.

THE ROMANTIC HISTORY OF FLOWER'S COPIES OF INSCRIPTIONS.

The first characters from Persepolis which were published in England appeared in the *Philosophical Transactions* for June, 1693, and their history was so peculiar and of such considerable importance that they are here reproduced and the story of their misuse in various forms is set forth.

The beginning of the story is found in a letter sent by Francis Aston to the publisher, which, with all its solecisms, runs thus :

" Sir, I here send you some Fragments of Papers put into my hands by a very good Friend, relatlating to antique and obscure Inscriptions, w^h were retrieved after the Death of Mr. *Flower*, Agent in *Persia* for our East India Company ; who while he was a Merchant at *Aleppo* had taken up a resolution to procure some Draught or Representation of the admired Ruines at *Chilmenar*, pursuant to the third Enquiry for *Persia*, mentioned in the Philosophical Tranactions, pag. 420, viz., whether there being already good Descriptions in words of the Excellent Pictures and Basse Relieves that are about Persepolis at Chilmenar yet none very particular, some may not be found sufficiently skilled in those parts, that might be engaged to make a Draught of the Place, & the Stories their [*sic*] pictured & carved. This Desire of the Royal Society, as I believe, it hinted at a Summary Delineation,

w[h] might be perform'd by a Man qualify'd in
a few days, taking his own opportunity for the
avoiding much Expence, (w[h] you know they
are never able to bear :) So I cannot but think
Mr. *Flower* conceived it to be a business much
easier to perform then [*sic*] he found it upon
the place, where he spent a good deal of Time
and Money, & dying suddainly after, left his
Draughts & Papers dispersed in several hands,
one part whereof you have here, the rest its hoped
may in some wise be recovered, if Sir John Chardin's exact & accurate Publication of the entire
Word do not put a period to all further Curiosity,
w[h] I heartily wish."

Accompanying this letter was a lithographed
plate of inscriptions from Nocturestand, that is
Naksh-i-Rustam, and from Chahelminar, that is,
Persepolis. They had been copied by Flower in
November, 1667. The first, second, and fourth of
these inscriptions are Sassanian and Greek, while
the third and sixth are Arabic. The fifth consists of two lines of cuneiform characters as follows:

To these cuneiform characters Mr. Flower had
added this explanatory note:

" This character, whether it be the ancient
writing of the *Gawres* and *Gabres*, or a kind of

Telesmes is found only at *Persepolis*, being a part
of what is there engraven in white Marble, &
is by no man in Persia legible or understood at
this Day. A Learned Jesuit Father, who deceased three years since, affirmed this character to
be known & used in *Egypt*."

The editor appended to this a note which
showed that he was a man of some penetration :
"it seems written from the Left Hand to the
Right, and to consist of Pyramids, diversely pos-
ited, but not joined together. As to the Quantity
of the Inscriptions, *Herbert* reckon'd in one large
Table Twenty Lines of a prodigious Breadth. Of
this sort here are distinct Papers, each of several
Lines."

Aston appears to have been much interested
in these papers of his deceased friend, for he re-
curs to the matter again to say that in February,
1672, Flower had compared these cuneiform signs
with twenty-two characters, "Collected out of the
Ancient Sculptures, to be found this day extant in
the admired Hills of Canary."

It is unfortunate that Flower died without publishing his own copies of inscriptions. If he had
lived to give them forth, a curious catalogue of
mistakes might have been avoided.

Mr. Aston doubtless supposed that the characters formed an inscription either complete or at
least connected. These characters, as a matter of
fact, were selected by Flower from the three languages at Persepolis, and do not form an inscrip-

tion at all. As published by Aston they are
taken at random from Persian, Susian, and Assyrian, as the following list will show. The first
line begins with three Persian characters (a, ra, sa),
the next is Assyrian (u), and after it the Persian
word-divider. After these come one Persian (th)
and three Assyrian (bu, ša, si) syllabic signs;
then one Susian (sa), one Assyrian (rad), one
Persian (h), and finally one Assyrian (i) character.
The second line is equally mixed. It begins with
a Persian sign (probably *bumi*) followed by three
Assyrian (a, ú, nu), one Susian (ak) and then another Assyrian (kha) sign. These are followed by
one Susian (ti), one Persian (kh), one Assyrian
(ya), and finally one Susian (ta). The signs were
exceedingly well copied, and it is a pity that a
man who could copy so well had not been able to
issue all his work. It might have hastened the
day of the final decipherment.

Instead of really contributing to a forward
movement in the study of the Persepolis inscriptions, Flower's copies resulted in actual hindrance
to the new study.

The history of this retrograde movement is a
curious chapter in the history of the science of
language. It deserves to be followed step by step
if for naught else than for its lessons in the weak-
nesses of human nature.

The cuneiform characters of Flower now began
an extraordinary and unexpected career. The
first man who appears to have noticed them was

Thomas Hyde. Hyde was professor of Hebrew in the University of Oxford, but, like other Hebrew professors in later days, devoted much energy to other oriental study. His great book was on the religion of the Persians,[1] in which he discussed many things, without always displaying much willing receptiveness for things that were new. He reproduced in a plate the cuneiform characters of Flower, along with some Sassanian and Palmyrene inscriptions. Over the Sassanian and Palmyrene texts Hyde waxes eloquent of denunciation. He bewails the sad fact that these "wretched scribblings, made perhaps by ignorant soldiers," had been left to vex a later day. Then he comes to a discussion of the cuneiform characters, and gives them that very name (*dactuli pyramidales seu cuneiformes.*)[2] Next he quotes Aston's statement that Herbert had mentioned twenty lines of cuneiform writing at Persepolis. Hyde waves this statement majestically aside, and gives a long argument to show that these signs were not letters, nor intended for letters, but are purely ornamental.[3] He attached great importance to the interpunction in Flower's copy, and adds that Herbert and Thevenot had given three

---

[1] Thomas Hyde, *Historia Religionis veterum Persarum, eorumque Magorum.* Oxonii, 1700. The second edition appeared at Oxford, in 1760, under the title *Veterum Persarum et Parthorum et Mediorum Religionis Historia.*

[2] *Ibid.,* first edition, p. 526 ; second edition, p. 556.

[3] "Me autem judice non sunt Literae, nec pro Literis intendebantur; sed fuerunt solius Ornatûs causâ. . . ."—*Ibid.,* first edition, p. 527 ; second edition, p. 557.

lines of the same kind of ornamentation, but as they did not give any interpunction, he pronounces their copies worthless. Just here he made a series of mistakes. In the first place, of course, the interpunction was the invention of Flower, and was, as we now see, merely his way of indicating that he had copied only separate and selected signs. In the next place, Thevenot gives no copies of inscriptions at all. Hyde had evidently seen some copies in some place and was quoting from memory. One wonders whether he had not seen the copies of Mandeslo, and had in memory confused him with Thevenot.

The next man who was moved to make use of the characters of Flower was a Dutchman, Witsen, who was gifted with a keen eagerness for the marvelous. He calmly reproduces Flower's characters, which he had most probably copied from Hyde, and introduces them to his readers in a remarkable narrative. "In the lands beyond Tarku, Boeriah, and Osmin," he says, "is a country where a German medical man, who had traversed it when flying from the anger of Stenko Rasin, has told me he had seen on arches, walls, and mountains sculptured letters of the same form as those found on the ruins of Persepolis, which he had also seen. This writing belonged, it is said, to the language of the ancient Persians, Gaures, Gabres, or worshipers of fire. Two specimens of them are given here, though these characters are now unintelligible. Throughout the whole country, said this medical man, above all at a little distance from Derbent, in the mountains beside which the road passes, one sees sculptured on the rock figures of men dressed in strange fashion like that of the ancient Greeks, or perhaps Romans, and not only solitary figures, but entire scenes and representations of men engaged in the same business, besides broken columns, aqueducts, and arcades for walking over pits and valleys. Among other monuments there is there a chapel built of stone, and reverenced by some Armenian Christians who live in its neighborhood, and on the walls of which were engraved many of the characters of which I have spoken. This chapel had formerly belonged to the pagan Persians who adored a divinity in fire." [1]

This whole account bears every mark of having been manufactured to fit the inscriptions. No such ruins have been seen by any person in the country described, and no inscriptions have been found there. The cuneiform characters had to be accounted for in some way, and this was Witsen's method.

But more and worse things were still to be invented to account for these same little characters of Flower.

In 1723 Derbent and Tarku were visited by

---

[1] Nicolaus Witsen, *Noord en Oost Tartarye*, II Part, p. 563. Amsterdam, 1705. Quoted by Burnouf, *Mémoire sur deux inscriptions*. Paris, 1836, pp. 177, 178.

Dimitri Cantémir, Prince of Moldavia, who had the patronage of the czar, Peter the Great, in his search for antiquities and inscriptions. He died at Derbent, and the inscriptions he saw are all catalogued by Frähm, and there is no cuneiform inscription among them. The prince's papers passed into the hands of Th. S. Bayer, who utilized them in a book, *De Muro Caucaseo*, in which he tried to prove that this wall was built in the time of the Medo-Persian empire. Now, Bayer was acquainted with Witsen's book, and made references to it, but he evidently did not believe in the marvelous story which Witsen told concerning the cuneiform inscriptions, for he makes no reference to it at all, whereas that would have given the most conclusive proof of the main thesis of his book which could possibly be suggested. Here were inscriptions of the Medo-Persian people, found at the very wall which he desired to prove was Medo-Persian in origin. But the end was not yet concerning the papers of the unfortunate Prince of Moldavia. Professor Guldenstädt planned a trip through the Caucasus in 1766–69, and friends put in his hands certain papers to be used on the journey. Among them was a copy of Flower's cuneiform characters. It seems probable that he was informed that this copy belonged to Cantémir's papers, for when Guldenstädt's papers came into the hands of Klaproth he attached to the Flower characters this note: " Inscriptions de Tarkou, d'après un Dessin du prince Dimitri Cantémir, qui se trouvait avec les Instruc-

tions de Guldenstädt.   St. P. 4 Aug., 1807."[1]   Now
here, by a chapter of accidents, mistakes, and de-
ceits, were Flower's signs localized at Tarku, and
of course considered a veritable inscription.

In 1826 F. E. Schulz was sent by the French
government to the East to search for inscriptions,
and he took with him the Flower signs, with Klaproth's note attached.   It was probably his intention
to go to Tarku and collate the copy with the original inscription, for of course he had no doubt that
it really existed.   Schulz, however, was murdered
at Julameih in 1829, and when many of his papers
were recovered, here was found among them the
same old copy of Flower.   Schulz's copies were
published, and the "inscription of Tarku" appears
with the rest.

The next man to allude to it was Saint Martin,
who gravely informs his readers that this inscription was carved above the gate of Tarku,[2] thus
adding a little definiteness to the tradition.

Naturally enough the Flower copy made its way
to Grotefend, who was, however, not deceived by
it.[3]   He recognized at once that it really consisted
of a number of characters selected from all three
languages which were found at Persepolis, though
he did not know that Flower was the copyist.
This was in 1820, and one might have expected

[1] Burnouf, *ibid.*, p. 178.

[2] *Nouvelles Observations sur les inscriptions de Persepolis*, par M. Saint
Martin, Mem. de l'Acad. des Inscriptions et Belles-Lettres, IIe Série, tom.
xii, p. 114.

[3] *Hall. allgem. Lit.-Zeitung*, April, 1820, p. 845.

that this would end the wanderings and the ficti- tious history of Flower's copies. But not just yet; there was still vigor in the story and the race was not yet over.

In 1836 Burnouf got a copy of the same lines and set to work earnestly to decipher them. He found that they contained the name of Arsakes, re- peated three times.[1]

In 1838 Beer discussed the lines, and attached himself to Grotefend's view, recognizing the fact that they did not form an inscription at all.

Burnouf's translation did not suit the next in- vestigator very well, and he began afresh to de- cipher and translate. This was A. Holtzmann, who argued learnedly that the lines formed a gen- uine Persepolitan text of great interest. The in- scription was indeed a memorial of Arses, who was murdered in B. C. 336 by Bagoas. Holtzmann thus translated the text:

"Arses (son) of Artaxerxes, King of Provinces, the Achamenian, made (this)."

Here was indeed a fitting conclusion of the whole matter. Flower had copied a few signs out of three different languages, and out of them had been woven this elaborate history. It is a melancholy story from one point of view. But it is instructive also as showing that progress in knowledge is not uniform, but has its undertow as well as its ad- vancing wave. Happily there is a dash of humor in it as well.

---

[1] Burnouf, *Mémoire sur deux inscriptions.* Paris, 1836, pp. 176, ff.

CHAPTER III.

EARLY EXPLORERS IN BABYLONIA.

WHEN the city of Nineveh fell, and when Babylon was finally given over to the destroyer, a deep darkness of ignorance settled over their ruins. The very site of Nineveh was forgotten, and, though a tradition lived on which located the spot where Babylon had stood, there was almost as little known of that great capital as of its northern neighbor. In the Middle Age the world forgot many things, and then with wonderful vigor began to learn them all over again. In the general spell of forgetfulness it cast away all remembrance of these two great cities. Even the monk in his cell, to whose industry as a copyist the world owes a debt that can never be paid, recked little of barbarous cities, whose sins had destroyed them. He knew of Jerusalem and of Bethlehem, for these had imperishable fragrance in his nostrils. They were sacred cities in a sacred land, and he sighed as he thought that they were now in the hands of infidels. But Nineveh and Babylon, they were mentioned, it is true, in the prophets; but then Nahum had cursed the one and Isaiah predicted the destruction of the other, and they had received their deserts. Where they might be he knew not, nor cared. But after a time came the period when Europe began to relearn, and that with wonderful avidity. The Crusades roused all Europe to a passionate interest in the Orient. Palestine, Syria, and Egypt were traversed by one after another of travelers who visited sacred scenes and came home to tell wonderful stories in Europe. Of these almost all were Christians, who knew in greater or less degree the New Testament, but were for the more part hopelessly ignorant of the Old Testament. They would fain see the land of the Lord, but cared little for associations with Old Testament prophets, heroes, or kings.

But at last there appeared a man who had wider interests than even those that concerned the land of Palestine. He was a Jewish rabbi of Tudela, in the kingdom of Navarre. The Rabbi Benjamin, son of Jonah, set out from home about 1160 A. D., and journeyed overland across Spain and France, and thence into Italy. As he went he made the most careful notes of all that he saw, and gave much attention to the learned and pious men of his own faith whom he met. From Italy he passed over to Greece, and then on to Constantinople, with which he was profoundly impressed. After he had visited the sacred spots in Palestine he went over the desert by way of Tadmor, and crossed the Euphrates, and then journeyed on eastward to the Tigris, where he visited the Jews of Mosul. Of Mosul and its surroundings he has this to relate:

"This city, situated on the confines of Persia, is of great extent and very ancient; it stands on the banks of the Tigris, and is joined by a bridge to Nineveh. Although the latter lies in ruins, there are numerous inhabited villages and small towns on its site. Nineveh is on the Tigris distant one parasang from the town of Arbil."[1]

From Nineveh Benjamin of Tudela passed on down the river and visited Baghdad, then a great center of culture both Mohammedan and Jewish, and this was more to him than even its wealth, and it is as to a climax that his last sentence concerning this city comes:

"The city of Baghdad is three miles in circumference, the country in which it is situated is rich in palm trees, gardens, and orchards, so that nothing equals it in Mesopotamia. Merchants of all countries resort thither for purposes of trade, and it contains many wise philosophers, well skilled in sciences, and magicians proficient in all sorts of enchantment."[2]

From Baghdad Benjamin went on to Gihiagin or Ras-al-Ain, which he mistakenly identified with Resen (Gen. x, 12), and then continues his narrative thus:

"From hence it is one day to Babylon. This is the ancient Babel, and now lies in ruins; but the streets still extend thirty miles. The ruins of the

---

[1] *Itinerarium Beniamin Tudelensis. Ex Hebraico Latinum factum Bened. Aria Montano interprete.* Antverpiæ, M.D.LXXV, p. 58.

[2] *Ibid.*, pp. 69, 70.

palace of Nebuchadnezzar are still to be seen, but people are afraid to venture among them on account of the serpents and scorpions with which they are infested. Twenty thousand Jews live about twenty miles from this place, and perform their worship in the synagogue of Daniel, who rests in peace. This synagogue is of remote antiquity, having been built by Daniel himself; it is constructed of solid stones and bricks. Here the traveler may also behold the palace of Nebuchadnezzar, with the burning fiery furnace into which were thrown Hananiah, Mishael, and Azariah; it is a valley well known to everyone. Hillah, which is at a distance of five miles, contains about ten thousand Jews and four synagogues. . . . Four miles from hence is the tower built by the dispersed Generation. It is constructed of bricks called al-ajurr; the base measures two miles, the breadth two hundred and forty yards, and the height about one hundred canna. A spiral passage, built into the tower (in stages of ten yards each), leads up to the summit, from which we have a prospect of twenty miles, the country being one wide plain and quite level. The heavenly fire, which struck the tower, split it to its very foundation." [1]

That Benjamin of Tudela actually did visit

---

[1] *Ibid.*, pp. 70, 71. Compare also Martinet, *Reisetagbuch des Rabbi Benjamin von Tudela.* Bamberg, 1858, pp. 16, 18. For English translations see Thomas Wright, *Early Travels in Palestine*, London (Bohn), 1848, pp. 94, 100, and especially A. Asher, *The Itinerary of Rabbi Benjamin of Tudela.* London and Berlin, 1840, i, pp. 91, 92, 105–107.

Mosul, and that he there saw across the river the great mounds which marked the ruins of Nineveh there is no reason to doubt, but it is not so clear that he also saw the ruins of Babylon. He did make the visit to Baghdad, for that city is described in the terms of an eyewitness. It is, however, not certain that he had really seen the ruins of Babylon, for his description lacks the little touches which accompanied the former narrative. He is here probably reproducing simply what he had heard from others concerning these ruins.

Benjamin of Tudela wrote his narrative in Hebrew. It was known to the learned during the thirteenth, fourteenth, and fifteenth centuries, but was not printed until 1543, when it appeared at Constantinople in the rabbinic character. In 1633 it appeared, with a Latin translation, at Leyden. It later appeared in English and French, and thus became known over a large part of Europe. Though thus well known, the book of Benjamin appears to have attracted no attention to the buried cities of Nineveh and Babylon.

Like the first scant notices of Persepolis given by the earlier travelers, these notes of Benjamin of Tudela would bear fruit in a later day, for they would incite other travelers to visit the same mysterious ruins.

The next word of information concerning the ancient sites was brought to Europe by another Jew, the Rabbi Pethachiah of Ratisbon, whose recollections were set down by one of his disciples, after the scanty notes which he had made by the way.

The time was now hastening on toward the period when men of Europe began to travel extensively in the Orient, and of these many visited both Mosul and Baghdad. Most of them, however, did not pay any attention to the ruins which lay near these cities. Many, like Sir John Mandeville (1322–56), made no journey to these sites, but were contented to report what they had heard concerning them. Marco Polo appears to have cared nothing for the ruins, and, though he visited both Mosul and Baghdad, never refers to them. Others confounded Baghdad with Babylon, and really believed that the Mohammedan capital was the same city as that which Nebuchadrezzar had made powerful.

In 1583 the Orient was visited by John Eldred, an English traveler and merchant, whose quaint notice of Babylon and of Nineveh was among the very first hints which came directly to England concerning these great cities. His account is as follows:

"We landed at Felugia the 8th and 20th of June, where we made our abode seven dayes, for lack of camels to carie our goods to Babylon. The heat at that time of the yeare is such in those parts that men are loath to let out their camels to travell. This Felugia is a village of some hundred houses, and a place appointed for discharge-ing of such goods as come downe the river: the inhabitants are Arabians. Not finding camels here, we were constrained to unlade our goods, and hired an hundred asses to carie our English merchandizes onely to New Babylon over a short desert; in crossing whereof we spent eighteen houres, travelling by night and part of the morning, to avoid the great heat.

"In this place which we crossed over stood the olde mightie citie of Babylon, many olde ruines whereof are easilie to be seene by daylight, which I John Eldred have often behelde at my goode leisure, having made three voyages between the New citie of Babylon and Aleppo over this desert. Here also are yet standing the ruines of the olde tower of Babell, which being upon a plaine ground seemeth a farre off very great, but the nearer you come to it, the lesser and lesser it appeareth: sundry times I have gone thither to see it, and found the remnants yet standing about a quarter of a mile in compasse, and almost as high as the stone worke of Paules steeple in London, but it sheweth much bigger.' The brickes remaining in

---

¹ " For about seven or eight miles from Bagdad, as men passe from Felugia, a towne on Euphrates, whereon Old Babylon stood, to this newe citie on Tigris (a worke of eighteene houres, and about forty miles space) there is seen a ruinous shape, of a shapelesse heape and building, in circuit less than a mile, about the height of the stoneworke of Paule's steeple in London, the bricks being six inches thicke, eight broad, and a foot long (as Master Allen measured) with mats of canes laid betwixt them, yet remaining as sound as if they had beene laid within a yeere's space. Thus Master Eldred and Master Fitch, Master Cartwright, also, and my friend Master Allen, by testimony of their own eyes, have reported. But I can scarce think it to be that tower or temple, because authors place it in the midst of old Babylon, and neere Euphrates; whereas this is neerer

this most ancient monument be half a yard thicke and three quarters of a yard long, being dried in the Sunne only, and betweene every course of brickes there lieth a course of mattes made of canes, which remaine sounde and not perished, as though they had beene layed within one yeere. The citie of New Babylon joyneth upon the aforesaid desert where the Olde citie was, and the river of Tygris runneth close under the wall, and they may if they will open a sluce, and let the water of the same runne round about the towne. It is about two English miles in compasse, and the inhabitants generally speake three languages, to wit, the Persian, Arabian, and Turkish tongues : the people are of the Spanyards complexion : and the women generalie weare in one of the gristles of their noses a ring like a wedding ring, but somewhat greater, with a pearle and a Turkish stone set therein, and this they doe be they never so poore." [1]

The old confusion between Baghdad and Babylon plainly exists in the mind of Eldred, but apart from that error his words have a magical ring in them, and might well induce others to set out to see such sights.   He appears not to have seen the

Tigris."—*Purchas his Pilgrimage*, 1626, p. 50 (folio edition), quoted in *Narrative of a Journey to the Site of Babylon*, etc., by the late Claudius James Rich, edited by his widow. London, 1839, p. 321.

[1] *The Principall Navigations, Voiages and Discoveries of the English Nation.* By Richard Hakluyt, Master of Artes, and Student sometime of Christ-Church in Oxford. Imprinted at London by George Bishop and Ralph Newberie, Deputies to Christopher Baker, Printer to the Queen's most excellent Majestie. 1589, p. 232.

ruins of Nineveh at all, but another Englishman,
who sailed from Venice in 1599, was more fortunate
and also more romantic.

There is more of eloquence in Anthony Shirley
(or Sherley), who thus wrote of both cities:

" I will speake…of Babylon; not to the intent
to tell stories, either of the huge ruines of the first
Towne or the splendour of the second, but —
because nothing doth impose anything in man's
nature more than example—to shew the truth of
God's word, whose vengeances, threatened by His
Prophets, are truely succeeded in all those
parts. . . .'

" All the ground on which Babylon was spred
is left now desolate; nothing standing in that
Peninsula between the Euphrates and the Tigris,
but only part, and that a small part, of the greate
Tower, which God hath suffered to stand (if man
may speake so confidently of His greate impenetrable counsels) for an eternal testimony of His
work in the confusion of Man's pride, and that
Arke of Nebuchadnezzar for as perpetual a memory of his greate idolatry and condigne punishment.'

" Nineve, that which God Himself calleth That
greate Citie, hath not one stone standing which
may give memory of the being of a towne. One
English mile from it is a place called Mosul, a

---

[1] Sir Anthony Sherley, *His Relation of His Travels into Persia.* London,
1613, p. 21.

[2] *Ibid.*

small thing, rather to be a witnesse of the other's mightinesse and God's judgment than of any fashion of magnificence in it selfe." [1]

In these words is sounded for the first time the note which would bring eager explorers to these mounds. The former travelers had looked curiously upon these mounds and then passed on; this man saw in them facts which illustrated the Hebrew prophets. In a later day expeditions would go out from England for the very purpose of seeking in them books which might confirm or illustrate the history and the prophecy of the Hebrew people. The real force behind the large contributions of money for these explorations was this desire to know anything that had any possible bearing on the scriptures of the Old Testament. Anthony Shirley did not see that day, but he belonged to it in spirit.

In all these notices of passing travelers ignorance was mingled with credulity, and definite knowledge was wanting. The most that had been accomplished was the perpetuation and the stimulation of interest in these cities. The very small amount of progress that had been made is indicated by the publication in 1596, at Antwerp, of the great Geographical Treasury of Ortelius,[2] an

---

[1] Ibid.

[2] Abrahami Ortellii Antverpiani Thesaurus Geographicus Recognitus et Auctus. Antwerp, Plantin, 1596. The copy which the writer used in the Bodleian Library had belonged to Joseph Scaliger, and contained manuscript notes of his. On Nineveh he had nothing to add, and on Babylon merely wrote in the margins some Arabic words which had been transliterated in the text of Ortelius.

alphabetic list of places, with such descriptive geographical facts added as were then known. Ortelius states that certain writers identified Nineveh with Mosul, but as he had no definite information, he had to let the matter rest at that. Of Babylon even less was known. All the authorities quoted by Ortelius, except Benjamin of Tudela, identify Babylon with Baghdad, and that position he accepts. It is clear from this that there was need for more travelers who should see, and understand as well what they saw.

A beginning is made by an English traveler, John Cartwright, whose tone is very similar to that of Sherley, though he makes more of a contribution to the knowledge of the subject:

"Having passed over this river [the Choaspes] we set forward toward Mosul, a very antient towne in this countrey, six dayes journey from Valdac, and so pitched on the bankes of the river Tigris. Here in these plaines of Assiria, and on the bankes of the Tigris, and in the region of Eden, was Ninevie built by Nimrod, but finished by Ninus. It is agreed by all prophane writers, and confirmed by the Scriptures that this citty exceeded all other citties in circuit, and answerable magnificence. For it seemes by the ruinous foundation (which I thoroughly viewed) that it was built with four sides, but not equall or square; for the two longer sides had each of them (as we gesse) an hundredth and fifty furlongs, the two shorter sides, ninty furlongs, which amounteth to foure hundred and eighty furlongs of ground, which makes three score miles, accounting eight furlongs to an Italian mile. The walls whereof were an hundredth foote upright, and had such a breadth, as three Chariots might passe on the rampire in front: these walls were garnished with a thousand and five hundreth towers, which gave exceeding beauty to the rest, and a strength no lesse admirable for the nature of those times." [1]

After these descriptions of the past and present of Nineveh, Cartwright supplied some extracts from its history and then concluded thus:

" Finally, that this city was farre greater than Babilon, being the Lady of the East, the Queene of Nations, and the riches of the world, hauing more people within her wals, than are now in some one kingdome: but now it is destroyed (as God foretold it should be by the Chaldæans) being nothing else, then (sic) a sepulture of her self, a litle towne of small trade, where the *Patriarch* of the *Nestorians* keeps his seate, at the deuotion of the Turkes. Sundry times had we conference with this *Patriarch:* and among many other speeches which past from him, he wished us that before we departed, to see the Iland of Eden, but twelue miles up the riuer, *which he affirmed was undoubtedly a part of Paradise.*"

Keen as Cartwright was after historical and legendary material, he continued the error of confusion

---

[1] *The Preacher's Travels*, penned by I. C. (preface signed Iohn Cartwright). London, 1611, pp. 89, 90.

of Baghdad and Babylon.   His descriptions, however, contained some new matter:

"Two places of great antiquity did we thoroughly
view in the country: the one was the ruines of the
old tower of *Babel*, (as the inhabitants hold unto
this day) built by Nymrod, the nephew of Cham,
Noahs sonne. . . .

"And now at this day that which remayneth,
is called, the remnant of the tower of Babel: there
standing as much, as is a quarter of mile in compasse, and as high as the stone-worke of Paules
steeple in London.   It was built of burnt bricke
cimented and joyned with bituminous mortar, to
the end, that it should not receiue any cleft in the
same.   The brickes are three quarters of a yard in
length, and a quarter in thicknesse, and between
euery course of brickes, there lyeth a course of
mats made of Canes and Palme-tree leaves, so
fresh, as if they had beene layd within one yeere.

"The other place remarkable is, the ruines of
old Babilon, because it was the first citie, which
was built after the Floud. . . . This city was built
upon the riuer *Euphrates*, as we found by experience, spending two dayes journey and better, on
the ruines thereof.

"Amongst the other stately buildings was the
temple of Bel, erected by Semiramis in the middle
of this citie. . . . Some do thinke, that the ruines
of Nimrods tower, is but the foundation of this
temple of Bel, & that therefore many trauellers
haue bin deceiued, who suppose they haue seene

a part of that tower which Nimrod builded. But who can tell whether it be the one or the other? It may be that confused Chaos which we saw was the ruines of both, the Temple of *Bel* being founded on that of Nimrod." [1]

There are not wanting indications in this narrative that Cartwright knew the description of Sherley, whom he almost seems to quote in the comparison with St. Paul's Cathedral.

The visiting of Babylon and Nineveh was now becoming as much of an international matter as was the observing of the ruins of Persepolis at a slightly later time. Gasparo Balbi,[2] a Venetian, Alexander Hamilton, an Englishman, and Don Garcia de Silva y Figueroa, a Spaniard, followed soon after Cartwright, but made no advance in their investigations beyond that which had been seen by their predecessors. Following these came the great traveler, Pietro della Valle, who has received so much attention already in a former narrative concerning Persepolis.[3] He made the same mistake of confusing Baghdad with ancient Babylon, but he visited Hillah, which probably few of his predecessors had done. He also visited the great mound near Hillah, called Babil by the natives. This, Pietro della Valle believed, was the ruin of the Tower of Babel. This mound he had sketched by an artist, and from it he collected some bricks, which he

---

[1] *Ibid.,* pp. 99, 100.

[2] *Viaggio nelle Indie Orientali,* Venise, 1590. See also *Recueil des Voyages aux Indes Orientales,* par les fréres de Bry. Francfort, 1660.

[3] See p. 16.

afterward took back to Rome. One of these was presented to Athanasius Kircher, the Jesuit, who wrote a learned treatise on the Tower of Babel. Kircher believed that this brick had formed part of the original Tower of Babel, wrecked by the hand of God, a silent monitor from the great age of the dispersion of tongues. He placed it in his museum, and it is still preserved. This is probably the very first Babylonian antiquity which came into Europe, and must always have a great interest on that account. Though it was not what Pietro della Valle and Kircher supposed, it was, nevertheless, a brick from the glorious period of Babylonian history, and to the world of letters had a meaning of tremendous import. It was the harbinger of great stores of tablets and of building bricks which were soon to flow from that land. Far beyond the dreams of the mediæval student of the Tower of Babel were this first brick and those which were to follow, to carry the thoughts of men.

After these men of the world, others bent on errands of religion passed up and down the valley —Augustinians, Jesuits, Carmelites, and Franciscans—some of whom visited the sites covered with ruins, while others were content to report what they had heard. They were generally impressed with the thought that they were in lands where God had signally manifested his displeasure with the sons of men, but none of them appear to have felt any quickening of imagination at the thought of the great deeds of human history which had there been enacted. They naturally knew no more of the meaning of the mounds than did those who had preceded them.

So the end of the seventeenth century had come, and no man knew more of the history of Babylon or of Nineveh than could be gathered out of the pages of the Greeks or the Latins, or from the stirring words of the Old Testament. The day of the traveler who went and saw, and no more, was now nearly over, and the day of the scientific explorer was rapidly hastening on. Before men should be led to dig up these great mounds they must be roused to interest in them, and that the traveler had done in some measure. The age of the explorer and of the decipherer had come, and the intellectual quickening of the times manifested itself in a thorough study of the mounds of Nineveh and Babylon.

CHAPTER IV.

EXPLORATIONS IN ASSYRIA AND BABYLONIA, 1734–1820.

THE man who began the new age of exploration was not himself an explorer, nor were several of his immediate successors. He was, however, a man of scientific spirit, and in that differed from the men who had gone before him. He was not seeking marvels, nor anxiously inquiring for evidences of strange dealings in dark days. He was a student of geography and history, and went into the Orient specially charged to study them. Jean Otter, member of the French Academy of Inscriptions and Belles-Lettres, and afterward professor of Arabic at the College de France, spent ten years in western Asia, being sent thither for the purpose of study by the Comte de Maurepas. His notice of the city of Nineveh is very different indeed from all that preceded it. Its tone of criticism, of sifting out the false from the true, is the tone of the new age that had now begun:

"Abulfeda [the Arabian Geographer] says that Nineveh was on the eastern bank of the Tigris, opposite the modern Mosul; either he must have been mistaken, or the inhabitants of the district are greatly in error, for the latter place Nineveh on the western bank of the Tigris, on the spot which they call Eski-Mosul. If we attempt to

conciliate the two opinions by supposing that
Nineveh was built on both sides of the river,
nothing is gained, for Eski-Mosul is seven or eight
leagues higher up the stream. One point seems to
favor the belief of Abulfeda, and that is, that
opposite Mosul there is a place called Tell-i-Tou-
bah—that is to say, the Hill of Repentance—
where, they say, the Ninevites put on sackcloth
and ashes to turn away the wrath of God." [1]

Otter also visited the mounds at Hillah, and,
with a better knowledge of the Arabian geographers than any of his predecessors, located the
ancient city of Babylon near Hillah. The true
location of the city even he did not make out, but
the site was almost determined. A scientifically
trained scholar, as Otter was, had not found it,
but the thoughts of men were at least pointed
away from the identification with Baghdad.

After Otter the land of Babylonia was visited by
a Carmelite missionary, Father Emmanuel de Saint
Albert. He saw the ruins at Hillah and made a
very important report upon them to the Duke of
Orleans. His account was not published, but in
manuscript form came into the hands of D'Anville,
who presented to the Academy of Inscriptions at
Paris a paper on the site of Babylon. This paper
was based, in its conclusive portions, upon the description of southern Babylonia given by Pietro
della Valle, and especially that now offered by the

---

[1] *Voyage en Turquie et en Perse*, par M. Otter, de l'Académie Royale des
Inscriptions et Belles-Lettres, Paris. 1748, pp. 133, 134.

Carmelite missionary. The words of the latter
differ in important respects from the descriptions
of any travelers who had preceded him. He
says :

" Before reaching Hillah a hill is visible which
has been formed by the ruins of some great building. It may be between two and three miles in
circumference. I brought away from it some
square bricks, on which were writing in certain unknown characters. Opposite this hill, and distant
two leagues, another similar hill is visible, between
two reaches of the river at an equal distance. . . .
We went to the opposite hill, which I have already
mentioned ; this one is in Arabia, about an hour's
distance from the Euphrates, and the other is in
Mesopotamia, at the same distance from the Euphrates, and both exactly opposite to each other.
I found it very like the other, and I brought
away some square bricks, which had the same impressions as the first-mentioned ones. I remarked
upon this hill a fragment of thick wall, still standing on the summit, which, from a distance, looked
like a large tower. A similar mass was lying
overturned beside it ; and the cement was so solid
that it was quite impossible to detach one brick
whole. Both masses seemed as if they had been
vitrified, which made me conclude that these ruins
were of the highest antiquity. Many people in-
sist that this latter hill is the remains of the real
Babylon ; but I know not what they will make
of the other, which is opposite and exactly like

this one. The people of the country related to
me a thousand foolish stories about these two
mounds; and the Jews call the latter the prison
of Nebuchadnezzar."[1]

Unlike the travelers who had preceded him,
this missionary cared nothing for the marvelous,
and would have none of the stories of the natives.
He had, however, so completely and accurately
described these ruins that the work of D'Anville
was comparatively easy. He decided that this
was really Babylon, and that Baghdad was not
its modern representative. The final word of
D'Anville is interesting, and opens up the new era
of study of this part of the Orient:

"The written characters which, as Father
Emmanuel says in his report, are impressed upon
the bricks which remain of buildings so ancient
that they may have formed part of the original
Babylon would be for scholars who wish to pene-
trate into the most remote antiquity an entirely
new matter of meditation and study."[2]

These words were written in 1755, in the very
middle of the eighteenth century. They show
how the study of the city of Babylon lagged behind the investigation of the cities of Persia. At
this very time, as we have already seen, Europe
was stirring with interest in the great Achæmenian dynasty, and not only was the site of Per-

[1] *Mémoire sur la Position de Babylone*, par M. d'Anville. Mémoires des
Inscriptions et des Belles-Lettres, t. xxviii, p. 256, année 1755 [published
1761].

[2] Comp. trans. in Evetts, *ibid.*, p. 44.

sepolis well known, its inscriptions had been several times copied, and men were eagerly trying to decipher them. It was not yet time to turn from the study of Persepolis to the study of Babylon, but the hour was rapidly hastening on. Father Emmanuel and his skillful interpreter before the Academy had done much to bring the hour nearer.

In December, 1765, Carsten Niebuhr, whose name has already filled a large place in this story in connection with the ruins of Persepolis, visited Hillah. He was absolutely certain in his own mind that these ruins belonged to the city of Babylon.[1] He was deeply impressed by their vast size, but still more by the evidences of a high state of civilization which they indicated. He found lying upon the ground and about the great mounds numerous bricks covered with inscriptions. Niebuhr could not read a line upon them, and no man living could have done so; but that they existed, and that the writing was the writing of the ancient Babylonians, was now well known in Europe. Europe had, however, entirely failed to grasp the meaning of these important facts. Europe believed that a people who could only write upon clay must have been a people in a low state of civilization indeed, and must have possessed but a small literature. Niebuhr quotes from Bryant

---

[1] "Dass Babylon in der Gegend von Helle [Hillah] gelegen habe, daran ist gar kein Zweifel."—*Reisebeschreibung nach Arabien und andern umliegenden Landern.* Kopenhagen, 1778, ii, p. 287.

these words, and they were fairly representative
of the general opinion entertained in Europe : " I
cannot help forming a judgment of the learning
of a people from the materials with which it is
expedited and carried on, and I should think that
literature must have been very scanty, or none at
all, where the means above mentioned were applied." To Niebuhr such reasoning appeared to
be folly. To his mind the presence of these inscribed bricks was evidence of a very high state
of civilization.[1] He lamented that he could not
remain longer at the site, the more thoroughly to
study its ruins, and calls earnestly for others to
continue the work which he had to leave un-
finished.

Niebuhr also visited the mounds near the Tigris
and opposite the city of Mosul. Here also he was
as clear and cogent in his reasoning as he had been
at Hillah. The site of Nineveh he identified without difficulty,[2] but it appears to have impressed
him much less than the more ancient, and the
greater, mother city of Babylon.

The hope and wish of Niebuhr that others
would soon follow him to carry on researches at
Babylon were soon gratified. In 1781, on July 6,
M. de Beauchamp sailed away from Marseilles to
carry on astronomical observations at Baghdad
and to make historical and geographical studies

---

[1] "Man kann daraus vielmehr den Schluss machen, dass die Babylonier
es in der Schreibkunst und den Wissenschaften schon sehr weit gebracht
haben müssen.—*Ibid.*, pp. 290, 291.

[2] *Ibid.*, p. 353.

in the neighborhood. He visited Hillah, and contributed further to its exact localization. His knowledge of the languages and the archæology both of the past and the present of the Orient was not equal to that of Niebuhr, and he therefore made curious mistakes concerning the names which the Arabs had given to certain portions of the mounds, but withal he marks a fresh step of progress. The mound which had now long been known to travelers as the mound of Babel he now designates under the name of Makloube. For the first time he directs attention to a second mound close by the first, which he considers the site of Babylon; it is the mound called El-Kasr by the Arabs.

Of the mound at Hillah he says: "Here are found those large and thick bricks, imprinted with unknown characters, specimens of which I have presented to Abbé Bartholomy.[1] . . . I was informed by the master mason employed to dig for bricks that the places from which he procured them were large, thick walls, and sometimes chambers. He has frequently found earthen vessels, engraved marbles, and, about eight years ago, a statue as large as life, which he threw amongst the rubbish. On one wall of a chamber he found the figures of a cow and of the sun and moon formed of varnished bricks. Some idols of clay are found representing human figures. I

---

[1] Afterward published in beautiful copies by Millin, *Monuments Antiques inédits*. Paris, 1802, vol. ii, pp. 263, ff.

found one brick on which was a lion, and on others a half moon in relief. The bricks are cemented with bitumen, except in one place, which is well preserved, where they are united by a very thin stratum of white cement, which appears to be made of lime and sand."

"Most of the bricks found at Makloube have writing on them; but it does not appear that it was meant to be read, for it is as common on bricks buried in the walls as on those on the outside. . . .

" The master mason led me along a valley which he dug out a long while ago to get at the bricks of a wall, that, from the marks he showed me, I guess to have been sixty feet thick. It ran perpendicularly to the bed of the river, and was probably the wall of the city. I found in it a subterranean canal, which, instead of being arched over, is covered with pieces of sandstone six or seven feet long by three feet wide. These ruins extend several leagues to the north of Hella, and incontestably mark the situation of ancient Babylon. . . .

" Besides the bricks with inscriptions, which I have mentioned, there are solid cylinders, three inches in diameter, of a white substance, covered with very small writing, resembling the inscriptions of Persepolis mentioned by Chardin. Four years ago I saw one; but I was not eager to procure it, as I was assured that they were very common. I mentioned them to the master mason, who told me that he sometimes found such, but left them among the rubbish as useless. Black stones which have inscriptions engraved on them are also met with."[1]

In these descriptions and narratives of the learned and inquiring abbé are found the first notices of excavations and the first accounts of the finding of inscriptions beyond the mere building bricks stamped with names and titles of kings. These had been seen often before and several had been taken to Europe. The period of description of mounds has now come to an end and the period of excavation has fully come. These little inscriptions which at first awakened so slight an interest in Abbé Beauchamp would soon be eagerly sought with pick and shovel. Then would come the effort to read them, and later the full knowledge of the past history of the great valley. One observation of the abbé is of great importance in this story. The cylinders, he says, were "covered with very small writing, resembling the inscriptions of Persepolis mentioned by Chardin." That showed, as by prophetic instinct, the very line which would be pursued for the decipherment of the literature of Babylon.

As definite knowledge of the site of Nineveh, as

---

[1] Abbé Beauchamp made at least two visits to Hillah. The description of the first is found in *Journal des Savants*, Mai, 1785, pp. 852, ff. The second is published in *Journal des Savants*, December, 1790, pp. 2403, ff. The extracts given above are from the latter, pp. 2418, ff. This second paper is translated into English in the *European Magazine*, May, 1792, pp. 338, ff; for extracts see pp. 340, ff.

Abbé Beauchamp had achieved of the site of Babylon, was now soon secured by a French physician, Guillaume A. Olivier, who was sent into the East for the purpose chiefly of scientific study. He had no such knowledge of the ancient world as the abbé, and therefore failed to make any independent contribution to the progress of knowledge respecting Nineveh. His references to the city are scanty enough, and he does not appear to have seen any inscriptions.[1] At this time the knowledge of ancient Babylon very far exceeded the knowledge of Nineveh. It is, however, proper to say that both sites had been found, and excavations on a very small scale had been begun at Babylon. These excavations, it is true, were primarily made to obtain building material which was to be used in the construction of dwellings for the people about the neighboring country. Incidentally, however, inscriptions were found, and these were recognized as being pieces of writing from the ancient people of Babylon. The words of Beauchamp produced an uncommon impression in Europe, and were the subject of much discussion. In England especially were men aroused by them to a sense of eager thirst for a sight of these inscriptions—the books of the Babylonians—and for an effort to read them. So soon as this desire should crystallize it was certain to result in an attempt to secure some of them for an English museum. The first move in this direction

---

[1] *Voyage dans l'Empire Ottoman, l'Egypte et la Perse,* par **G. A.** Olivier. Paris, an. 12, iv, pp. 283, 284 [published 1801-7].

was made by the East India Company of London, which forwarded, on October 18, 1797, a letter to the governor of Bombay instructing him to give orders to the company's resident at Bussorah to have search made for some of these inscribed bricks. He was then to have them carefully packed and sent as soon as possible to London. Early in 1801 the first case arrived at the East India House in London. These inscriptions were the first that had reached London. It was true, indeed, that no man could read them. They stood, however, as silent monuments of the past, and their very position in London called upon men to attempt their decipherment. Their resemblance to the inscriptions of Persepolis had also been pointed out, and of that there was now no doubt. At this time the work was in progress which resulted in the reading of ancient Persian. Here were now inscriptions in ancient Babylonian, and they must also be read.

There were at last enthusiasm and real interest in Babylon. This general interest was focused by a remarkable book by Joseph Hager,[1] which was the direct result of his inspection of the Babylonian inscriptions that were now in the East India House. Hager's small book was epoch-making both in its suggestions and in its conclusions. In a few pages he reviewed the history of the obser-

---

[1] *A Dissertation on the Newly Discovered Babylonian Inscriptions*, by Joseph Hager, D.D. London, 1801. At the end this beautifully printed little volume contains five plates reproducing the Babylonian inscriptions which had been found on the East India House antiquities. The reproductions have probably never been surpassed for beauty or accuracy.

vations made at Babylon, and then connected the inscribed stones there found with the Persepolitan inscriptions. His statements on these points well deserve repetition:

"It is well known that for more than a century past, about which time the *Persepolitan* inscriptions were first discovered by European travellers, the opinions have been much divided respecting these characters. Some have believed them to be *talismans*, and others the characters of the *Guebres*, or antient inhabitants of *Persia*; others held them for mere *hieroglyphics*, and others for *alphabetic* characters, like ours. KAEMPFER supposed them to express whole ideas, like the *Chinese* characters, but that they had been appropriated solely for the palace of *Istakhar*. . . .

"By the Babylonian bricks here exhibited, the whole difficulty in regard to their origin is removed; as it is evident that *Babylon*, in point of cultivation, was much earlier than *Persepolis*, and that the *Chaldeans* were a celebrated people, when the name of the Persians was scarcely known."[1]

It must be remembered that this little book of Hager was written before the Persepolis inscriptions had been deciphered at all, and this makes all the more remarkable the generalizations of this gifted man, who seemed to foresee the very conclusions to which men would come when both the inscriptions of Persepolis and these new texts were finally deciphered. Even beyond these deductions

---

[1] *Ibid.*, pp. xvii, xviii.

was Hager led to go, when he summed up his conclusions at the end of his volume,[1] for there he claimed that even the Assyrians must have used the same method of writing—and this before he had even so much as seen an Assyrian inscription of any kind.

Hager's little book had an influence out of all proportion to its size. The great tomes of many travelers had utterly failed to excite more than a passing interest. His book was soon translated into German and made a distinct impression upon Grotefend, then deeply absorbed in his efforts to decipher the records of the Achæmenian kings. In its English form it became known in France, there to inspire the archæologist, A. L. Millin, to publish in facsimile[2] a small inscribed stone brought several years before from the neighborhood of Baghdad to Paris by the botanist Michaux. The article of Millin called this little inscription a "Persepolitan monument," though his own statements show that it came not from Persepolis, but from Babylonia. His copy of this beautiful little inscription was another added to the increasing list of objects which awakened in men the belief that beneath the mounds at and about Hillah must

---

[1] That these characters were the *Chaldaic* characters with which, according to ATHENÆUS, the epitaphium of SARDANAPALUS at Nineveh was engraved; the *Assyriac* characters mentioned by HERODOTUS, DIODORUS, POLYÆNUS, and other ancient authors.—*Ibid.*, p. 61.

[2] *Monuments Antiques inédits ou nouvellement expliqués*, par A. L. Millin. Paris, 1802, tome i, pp. 58, sqq. *Déscription d'un monument persépolitain, qui appartient au Muséum de la Bibliothèque Nationale*, with two beautiful plates.

lie buried great stores of monuments of the past of
Babylonia.

 While these publications were appearing, and
while men were still curiously examining the
East India House inscriptions, a man was preparing for a work which would demonstrate the truth
of these hopes and astonish the world with un-
suspected discoveries.

 Claudius James Rich, who had been born at
Dijon, France, in 1787, but spent his childhood at
Bristol, England, and there secured his earliest
education, went early in life to Bombay in the
service of the East India Company. Gifted extraordinarily with a love for languages and with
a readiness in their acquiring, he there made himself acquainted with Latin and Greek, and especially with Hebrew, Aramæan, Persian, Arabic,
and even somewhat with Chinese. Later, by fortunate accidents, he had found opportunity to continue his oriental studies at Constantinople and
at Smyrna, and then in Egypt; while a sojourn in
Italy put the language of that people at his service.
Before he was twenty-four years of age he had
been appointed the resident of the East India
Company at Baghdad. Though he had not probably been consciously preparing for this particular
post, all that he had learned and much that he
had experienced now became of the greatest
service to him. In the beginning of his residence
at Baghdad he appears to have been most interested by the city itself and its immediately sur-

rounding country, and began the collection of materials for a history of its Pashalic. In 1811, however, he was in some way led to visit the ruins of ancient Babylon, and at once there was awakened in him a new passion. On December 10, 1811, he saw for the first time the great mounds, to which he was now to devote so much energy and enthusiasm. His first impressions were distinctly disappointing. When he could secure the first opportunity to write them down he said:

"From the accounts of modern travelers I had expected to have found on the site of Babylon more, and less, than I actually did. Less, because I could have formed no conception of the prodigious extent of the whole ruins, or of the size, solidity, and perfect state of some of the particular parts of them; and more, because I thought that I should have distinguished some traces, however imperfect, of many of the principal structures of Babylon. I imagined, I should have said: 'Here were the walls, and such must have been the extent of the area. There stood the palace, and this most assuredly was the tower of Belus.' I was completely deceived; instead of a few insulated mounds, I found the whole face of the country covered with the vestiges of building; in some places consisting of brick walls surprisingly fresh, in others merely of a vast succession of mounds of rubbish of such indeterminate figures, variety, and extent as to involve the person who should have formed any theory in inextricable confusion and contradiction." [1]

This first visit of Rich to Babylon was brief, for he was back again in Baghdad on December 21. In that short time, however, he had planned all the mounds, and had correctly located them by astronomical observations. He also tested the mounds by digging into them in several places, of which the following words may serve as a sufficient description :

" I went with ten men with pickaxes and shovels to make experiments on the Mujelibè; they dug into the heaps on the top, and found layers of burnt bricks, with inscriptions laid in mortar. A kind of parapet of unburnt bricks appears to have surrounded the whole. On the western face the mud bricks were not only laid on reeds, but mixed up with them. In the northern face, where a part is also still standing, the bricks are not mixed up with reeds, but only laid on layers of them; here I found some beams of the date tree, specimens of which I brought away. The part of the mud wall standing on the west front is not thick; that on the northern side is more so, but none of them are of any considerable thickness. On the north front the height of the whole pile to the top of the parapet is 132 feet. The southeast angle is higher." [2]

[1] *Fundgraben des Orients, bearbeitet durch eine Gesellschaft von Liebhabern.* Wien, 1813, p. 129. The narrative of Rich extends pp. 129–162, and also pp. 197–200. The pages 129–162 are reprinted in the volume edited by his widow, *Narrative of a Journey to the Site of Babylon in 1861, now first published*, etc. London, 1839.   [2] *Ibid.*, p. 20.

From these walls he took specimens of the in-scribed building bricks, and likewise, when pos-sible, purchased from the inhabitants various smaller inscriptions, which were later to form a part of the treasures of the British Museum. Rich's work at that time seemed small in amount, but it was the first serious survey of all the mounds, and has formed from that day to this the basis for every subsequent examination of them. So care-fully had his work been done that he required, upon later acquaintance, to change his conclusions but slightly. His first account was, strangely enough, published in Vienna, but it was eagerly read and discussed in London. Free as it had been from theorizing, it, nevertheless, called forth a review and criticism from Major Rennell, who argued that Rich had not properly considered the allusions of classical historians and geographers, and had therefore improperly identified some ruins. Rennell's paper determined Rich to visit the ruins again, to verify or to correct his first statements. In his second visit he did find some things to correct, but in the main confirmed and established his former conclusions. The results of this visit were written out at Baghdad in the month of July, 1817, and, like the first publication of Rich, carried forward very distinctly the in-vestigation of the ancient city.

Rich had already achieved enough to gain fame, but he was to do still more for oriental study, not, indeed, at Babylon, but at the other chief center,

the city of Nineveh. In April, 1820, he set out
from Baghdad to escape its heat by a journey in
Kurdistan, and this was productive of valuable
results in the geography of a land then but little
visited by Europeans. In this journey Mr. Rich
reached Mosul on October 31, 1820, and there
spent four months. The experience which had
been gained in his work at Babylon was now
splendidly used. He visited and sketched with
plans every one of the great mounds which
might be considered as forming a part of the
ancient city of Nineveh. The first of these
mounds to be explored was that known among
the natives as Neby Yunus, because it was
supposed to contain the tomb of the prophet
Jonah. Here he learned that even a cursory examination by means of the spade would uncover
inscriptions, and some that had been found by the
natives were shown to him. They were written
in cuneiform characters, which Rich of course
could not read, but some were secured for the
British Museum, where their influence would soon
be felt. From Neby Yunus Rich transferred his
investigations to Kuyunjik, where he surveyed
the mound, drafted a plan of it, and conversed
with the natives, learning from them little more
than that most of the inscriptions were found at
Neby Yunus.

After the investigations at these two mounds
Rich went down the river and studied the
mound of Nimroud, where, as the natives said,

Nimrod is buried. In every Arab village which he visited Rich found inscriptions in the cuneiform character. Some which were small enough to be easily transported he purchased for his collection. Many were, however, monumental in character, being cut into stones, which the Arabs had used in the erection of their miserable hovels. Rich appears to have found no opposition among the natives to his study of the mounds, but he did find various suspicions of himself and of his motives among the more ignorant of them. In one of his tours about Mosul the remark was overheard that he was probably seeking a suitable place to plant guns and take the city. The cupidity and fear which rendered miserable the lives of later explorers did not trouble him, partly because he knew by long association the temper of the natives, and so did not unnecessarily wound their sensibilities, and partly because he did not dig up the ground, as was necessary in the work of his successors.

The inscriptions which Rich had secured soon came to London, and there formed the nucleus of the great Assyrian and Babylonian collections of the British Museum. They showed at the very first glance that the daring guess of Hager was correct. They were indeed written in the same kind of characters as those which had been sent home to London from the ruins of Babylon. That fact alone was of so great moment as to make distinguished all the work of Rich at Nineveh. He had laid the basis for all future work in that city, as he had previously done in Babylon. His plans and drawings must be used by whoever should next take up the work.

To all this work at Babylon and at Nineveh Rich was to add useful labor at Persepolis, which he visited in August, 1821. His approach to the city was graphically described in these words:

"It was dark when we left the bridge of the Araxes. My expectation was greatly excited. Chardin, when I was a mere child, had inspired me with a great desire to see these ruins, and the desires excited in us in childhood are too vivid ever to be effaced. Their gratification has a relish which motives suggested by reason and judgment are unable afterward to equal. My late antiquarian researches had, however, also added their interest to my other inducements; and as I rode over the plain by the beautiful starlight, reflections innumerable on the great events that had happened there crowded on my memory. I was in the moment of enjoying what I had long waited for; and what a delightful moment that is! At last the pointed summit began to detach itself from the line of the mountains to which we were advancing. Mr. Tod pointed it out: 'Under that lie the ruins.' At that moment the moon rose with uncommon beauty behind it. Ages seemed at once to present themselves to my fancy." [1]

---

[1] *Narrative of a Residence in Koordistan and on the Site of Ancient Nineveh*, with Journal of a voyage down the Tigris to Baghdad, and an

Here at Persepolis he made more exact copies of the inscriptions to which already so much discussion had been given in Europe, and his copies proved to be of great value to those who were to engage in the criticism and the perfecting of the work of Grotefend. On the way back to Baghdad from this visit to Persepolis Rich died of cholera, at Shiraz, while bravely serving others who were suffering from the disease. The man who had wrought so wonderfully for the study of the ancient world now died a hero in the humblest service for the poorest of humanity.

The impulse which Claudius James Rich gave to Babylonian and Assyrian study has never yet lost its effect. Others had done much, indeed, in awakening interest, and Rich's own testimony, quoted above, shows that Chardin had done this for him; still others had made observations of lasting value, while a very few had accurately determined ancient sites, and so had made possible his work. All these things, and more, Rich had accomplished. None who preceded him had excelled him in inspirational power, for even his Journal, intended only as the basis of future careful writing, possessed it, and none had equaled him in the collecting of definite information concerning the ruins both of Nineveh and of Babylon.

---

account of a visit to Shiraz and Persepolis, by the late Claudius James Rich, Esq. Edited by his widow. Two volumes. London, 1836, vol. ii, p. 218.

His quickening and informing influence worked
wonders in his immediate successors.

While Rich was still living in Baghdad, surrounded by a great retinue of servants and soldiers, in the almost regal state which was then
deemed necessary in order to overawe the impress-
ible natives, he received a visit from a fellow-
countrymen, Sir Robert Ker Porter. This was
October 14, 1818, and Rich had, as we have seen,
made his investigations at Babylon, and published
them in Europe. It was natural that he should
discuss them with this newcomer. Porter had
already visited Persepolis, and by the copying of
inscriptions had added his name to the long
and worthy line of those who had made the
work of Grotefend possible. Of all those who
had yet been in Babylonia none were endowed
in the same manner as this new visitor. Others
had possessed greater experience in travel,
though even in this his experience was not
small. Others had had better scientific equipment in knowledge of surveying and in acquaintance with oriental languages. In these matters
Porter was far behind Rich and the former wan-
derers. But Porter was an artist, an artist who
had made his name famous in England by many a
canvas depicting the glory of England in war, and
the history of her people in Church and State. To
this he added the unique distinction of having
been court painter at St. Petersburg. A man of
talent, if not even a man of genius, a man of
10

great social following in Great Britain and in Russia, where he had entered the highest circles and even married a Russian princess—such was Sir Robert Ker Porter. His skill as a painter qualified him admirably to sketch the ruins of Babylon, and his trained eye was ready to observe the lay of land and the external conditions of the modern surroundings of ancient sites. He had had experience in the copying of texts at Persepolis, and could now copy at Babylon with additional sureness. He had a gift for striking description in words, and his brush added vividness to his pen. Rich gave him willing assistance, and Rich's admirably trained secretary, Bellino, accompanied him to the ruins at Hillah. Though Porter was lacking in many things, his observations were useful and served well in directing later workers bent on definite work. Upon his return the account of his travels was published in sumptuous style,[1] beautifully illustrated by his own brush. The big book was received with acclaim in England, and apparently also on the continent. A man with greater scientific equipment but with less social following might have written a work more valuable scientifically, which would, nevertheless, have completely failed in influence on the age. Porter's work, however, offered the needed supplement to the

---

[1] *Travels in Georgia, Persia, Armenia, Ancient Babylonia, etc., etc., during the years* 1817, 8, 9, *and* 20, by Sir Robert Ker Porter. In two volumes. London, 1821, 1822.

work of Rich. Rich had written very little indeed, and that was concerned with details, and at
times was very dry indeed. It was, besides this,
not published in a complete form until after the
author's death. Porter saw his own book published,
and heard the popular plaudits. Here was at last a
description of Babylon as it now was, duly inter-
mingled with quotations from previous observers,
and fortified by the word of Mr. Rich and Mr.
Bellino. Here were pictures of mounds and ruined
walls and inscribed bricks, and here was the expressed opinion that they had not yet been fully
explored. What better thing could have been
done for the recovery of Babylon at this time
than the publication of just such a book as this
of Sir Robert Ker Porter! It was impossible
that its publication should not be followed by a
rekindling of zeal in the pursuit of oriental learning; or that its glowing and pictured pages
should fail to excite the wonder of even the ordinary reader, who may to-morrow become an explorer himself or a patron of such pursuits in
others. Just as the book of Chardin had roused
the boyish enthusiasm of Rich and sent him in his
early manhood to the scenes which it described,
so would this new book exert a similar influence
upon others. Though its scientific contributions
are not to be named with those of Rich, its popular influence was great, and it is to be ranked
with the greatest of all the influences which contributed to the recovery of Nineveh and Babylon.

With the work of Sir Robert Ker Porter another period of exploration in Babylonia and in Assyria closes. The progress had been indeed very slow. The whole story is a narrative of description, rising at times to measurement and survey, and very rarely to the summit of actually recovering inscribed monuments. But all this was absolutely indispensable work. It was foundation work, preparatory and perhaps little more. But it represented a clear step forward beyond that of the days of the credulous seeker for marvels. It was, further, an era of popularization, and before governments or peoples, in monarchies or democracies, would join heartily in costly excavations, the people must get some promise of interesting result, some zeal for the learning of the past history of humanity, and some taste for the color of the Orient. In the greatest of the democracies, also, it was well that the people should come to believe that a study of the mounds of Babylon and Nineveh might give results of value to the study of their Bible, for the English people were then willing to give much if there were promise of any such result. Of that issue assurance was given in many a word from Shirley to Rich, and that the people had heard it was soon clearly shown. In France there was probably less diffusion of popular biblical knowledge; yet from France was to come the first real step which should prove that England's hesitation had been unwise. In France that which failed in the popular interest and enthusiasm was supplied by the love of learning in the few and by the great liberality of the government, in a land where governments have always done marvels for the pursuit of learning.   But the story of this great work belongs to the new era, that now follows the period closed by two Englishmen whose names belong high up on the record—Claudius James Rich and Sir Robert Ker Porter.

CHAPTER V.

EXCAVATIONS IN ASSYRIA AND BABYLONIA,
1843–1854.

THE period of exploration in Babylonia was succeeded by the era of excavation, but the succession was not so rapid as might have been expected. The whole history of the progress was slow, and there was now a pause before the really culminating work was begun. But this pause was full of preparation.

In 1823 Julius Mohl came from Tübingen, where he had taken in the previous year the doctor's degree, to Paris, to become the pupil of the greatest Arabist of the day, Silvestre de Sacy, whose name has already appeared in the story of decipherment. In 1840 Mohl became one of the secretaries of the Société Asiatique, and thus became permanently attached to the French capital. Though his masters had taught him the Arabic classics rather than the learning of the older Orient, he was, nevertheless, full of a desire to know of its history, language, and literature. At about the time of the pause in the progress of Babylonian exploration Mohl visited London, and there saw the inscribed Babylonian bricks which the East India Company had brought together. He was filled with an overmastering belief that these little bricks were the promise of an immense literature which lay buried, awaiting the excavator's spade. He returned to Paris to read of mounds in Babylonia and Assyria, and to reflect upon the untold treasures which must come to light if properly sought. There was no opportunity found for Mohl himself to go to Assyria or Babylonia to seek these long-lost monuments, but there soon came a time when he could arouse another to this call.

In 1842 the French government created at Mosul a vice consulate. French commerce with the district did not warrant or demand this, and the new departure was really made in the interest of archæological study—to establish at this happily chosen place a French archæological mission. The man selected to fill the new post was admirably suited to it. Paul Emil Botta was now but thirty-seven years of age, with the full ardor of youth and the steadying influence of experience of the world. He had had service as the French consul at Alexandria, and must there have learned of the methods of archæological study in which the French had already met with distinguished success. Before Botta departed from Paris for his new post Mohl had impressed strongly upon his mind that a great opportunity was now his to *dig*, and not merely to describe, explore, and plot the mounds opposite Mosul. The preliminary work of plotting and examining these mounds had been well done, and no more of it was needed. Rich had made it entirely unnecessary for any follower of his to repeat more of that work. It was now Botta's duty to dig beneath the surface of the oft-de-scribed mounds, and determine finally whether they covered any remains of the ancient city of Nineveh. Botta was persuaded, and went out to Mosul to occupy his consulate on May 25, 1842. That was an historic day in the annals of Assyrian study.

The French diplomat and archæologist, whose face bore the fine lines of the scholar rather than the marks of a man of the world, found himself in a place little suited to one who had lived in Paris, or even in the comparative comfort of Alexandria. Mosul was a mean little city, built more of mud than of stone, lying upon the right or western bank of the Tigris. It had once possessed an ex-tensive commerce with the East, of which it still retained the remnants. Botta seems to have cared little for the town or its fanatical inhabitants, and were it not for the comments of Layard, we should know little of what it was at this time. Botta's own letters give it scarcely more than a passing reference. When he stood by the banks of the river Tigris he could see the river Choser dis-charging its sluggish and muddy waters into the great river. The eye could follow the little river back over a plain which melted away into the mountains of Kurdistan upon the east and north-east. Upon this plain there were a few squalid villages, the homes of a peasantry more fearful of

the taxgatherer than of death. Over these the
pasha of Mosul exercised a sway, patriarchal only
in its severe authority. The land had once supported a vast population; of that the history left
by Greeks, Romans, and Hebrews made no doubt
possible. Besides these wretched villages the
most noticeable objects were several vast mounds.
They had been often described before, and Botta
knew just what they were supposed to be. As
he swept his eyes over them, the first that was
noticeable was south of the Choser, on his right
hand as he looked across the river. It might
seem to the untrained eye at first glance merely a
hill, a bit of nature's own handiwork, but the top
was too flat, the sides unnaturally regular and
steep. Upon its top rose a mosque, and grouped
round this were several poor houses forming a
little village. The mound was called Neby Yunus
—that is, Prophet Jonah—and to his honor and
memory the mosque was dedicated. Beneath, in
the mound, lay the prophet's bones, according to
the tradition of the natives. As he looked farther
north on the opposite side of the Choser lay a
larger mound called Kuyunjik, where also there
were some human habitations. This mound was
larger than the other, and beyond them was a
raised line which seemed to unite these two
mounds, and might mark the remains of an ancient
line of wall which inclosed them both. Farther
back from the Tigris, upon the rising ground
along the upper Choser and distant about fourteen

miles north-northeast from Mosul, was another
mound with a village called Khorsabad.   Other
lesser mounds were either in sight or were known
from the descriptions of travelers or from native
residents.   Botta looked the field over and doubted
where to begin.   His first discouraging experience
resulted from a careful survey of the town of
Mosul itself.   He had been led to believe that as
the towns about the ruins of Babylon had been
built of brick dug from the remains of the ancient
city, so he would find in Mosul huts erected of
bricks taken from the ancient city.   His plan,
therefore, was to go over Mosul and seek for signs
of ancient-looking bricks, and especially for any
that were inscribed with cuneiform characters.
He would then ascertain from what mound these
had come.   To his great surprise and discomfiture
he found no such memorials of the past, and was
therefore left without this hint as to the proper
place to begin excavations.   The mounds were so
large as to discourage aimless seeking, and he began
a process of questioning the natives concerning
any finds that might be known.   Gradually some
pieces of inscribed stone were brought forth from
hiding places, and these he bought from their own-
ers.   This surprising news that a man had come
to Mosul who would buy old stones became noised
about the whole country, and he had numerous
offers of bits of stone and clay.   But even with
all this advertising of his wishes the number of
antiquities offered was much less than that which

the passing traveler reported at Baghdad or at Hillah. Furthermore, it was difficult to ascertain where the natives had secured what was offered him, for they naturally desired to work these mines for their own gain and not permit the Frank to learn of their exact whereabouts. Botta's own mind swerved gradually round to the notion that the most promising mound was Neby Yunus, and he carefully considered the possibility of digging there. From this purpose he was finally dissuaded by the awkward fact that a village occupied the better part of the top of the mound, which would make digging almost impossible without the utter collapse and ruin of the miserable hovels. Besides this there were Mohammedan graves in the mound, and, above all, was not Jonah himself buried beneath its surface? To disturb a spot thus sacred would mean a revolution among the natives which might set the whole region ablaze with fanaticism. This plan was therefore abandoned and the mound by Kuyunjik was selected for the first efforts. At the western edge of this mound near the southern extremity a few large bricks could be seen which were joined with bitumen. These seemed to offer a hope that they belonged to some ancient building. Here, therefore, Botta began to dig in December, 1842. His funds were very limited and he could employ but a few workmen, whose slow movements promised little results. The workmen, however, discovered some fragments of bas-reliefs and broken bits of clay inscriptions. For three months the work went on and nothing large or valuable or beautiful came out of the little ditches or wells. What was found was interesting indeed, for it offered proof positive that this mound really did cover some ancient building or buildings. It was, however, discouraging to find only broken pieces, and not complete monuments.

While this work was in progress the inhabitants gathered round the ditches and watched curiously the slow and careful work. They did not know what it all meant, but it was perfectly clear that this man was seeking inscriptions, whatever they might be. Every little fragment found which contained any of these strange little wedge-shaped marks was carefully numbered and laid aside. One of the bystanders whose home was at Khorsabad observed this proceeding, and within the first month of the excavations brought down from Khorsabad two large bricks with inscriptions, which he offered to sell to Botta. This gave him the hint that perhaps Khorsabad might be a more profitable mound for excavations. He was, however, still hopeful of success at Kuyunjik, and continued to work on. At last, on March 20, 1843, his faith in this mound gave out, and he determined to send a few men to Khorsabad to try the mound there. It was a fortunate resolve. In three days word was brought to him at Mosul that antiquities and inscriptions had already been found. He was, however, skeptical, fearing lest the records

might be some late Arabic graffiti, and was therefore unwilling to go himself lest those which had
been found should prove valuless. He sent a servant with instructions to copy a few of the inscriptions and then report. The reply showed beyond
a doubt that the antiquities were really Assyrian.
Thereupon Botta went to the scene, to behold a
sight that thrilled him.

His workmen had lighted upon a very well-preserved ancient wall, not of a city, but of a building.
This they had followed round and so uncovered
a large room, in which were lying fragments of
sculptures, calcined by fire, together with a number of well-preserved inscriptions. The full meaning of this new room was not ascertained until long
after, but some appreciation of it was Botta's own,
as he looked down into the rude excavation. He
believed at once that this was but one room, perhaps of a great palace, and proved the supposition
at once by causing wells to be driven near by in
several places, out of which came other bas-reliefs,
almost perfectly preserved. In these his eyes
looked upon a sight which no man had seen since
the great royal city fell before its enemies more
than two thousand four hundred years before.
Only one day could Botta remain at Khorsabad,
and then had to return to Mosul for other duties.
Thence he wrote on April 5, 1843,[1] a quiet, digni-

---

[1] *Lettres de M. Botta sur les Decouvertes à Khorsabad*, publiées par M.
J .Mohl. Paris, 1845. M. Botta's *Letters on the Discoveries at Nineveh*,
translated from the French by C. T. London, 1850.

fied letter to the author of his first enthusiasm, M. Mohl. There is scarcely a word of enthusiasm in the letter, but it roused Mohl to contribute of his own small purse and also sent him to the Academy of Inscriptions with Botta's letter and the accompanying diagrams. Meanwhile the excavations went slowly on, though with some opposition on the part of the pasha. A month later a second and more important letter moved the French government to its old line of generous assistance to archæological research, and three thousand francs were placed at Botta's disposal for further researches.

Thus supported by France, and cheered on by the ever-active Mohl, Botta's course seemed clear and his success certain. He was, however, sorely pressed by great difficulties. The climate was dangerous, and he almost fell a victim. The natives were suspicious beyond measure, and hampered his work at every turn. Some supposed that he was digging for buried treasure, and that these inscriptions which he copied were talismanic guardians from which he would learn its exact location. Yet others supposed that he was searching for old title deeds by which to prove that all this land had belonged to Europeans, who thus might claim its restoration. These and similar stories came to the ears of Mohammed Pasha, then governing the pashalic of Mosul, and he entered gradually upon a policy of oppression. He first set guards over Botta's workmen, whose business it

was to seize any piece of metal that might be
found and dispatch it to him, that it might be
carefully examined to determine whether it was
gold. This caused so little inconvenience to Botta
that it was scarcely worth the trouble, and he soon
felt compelled to resort to more strenuous measures. He had given permission to Botta to erect
for himself a small hut where he might find a resting
place when he came up on visits from Mosul. The
wily pasha now pretended that this was in reality
a fortress and that the trenches were its defenses.
It was evidently Botta's intention to overawe the
country by force of arms and detach it from the
sultan's dominions. Upon these representations
the Sublime Porte ordered that all the excavations should at once cease. Botta was equal to
the painful emergency. On October 15, 1843, he
dispatched a courier to the French ambassador at
Constantinople, begging him to make such representation to the Porte as might secure permission
for the continuance of the excavations.

While these petitions were pending amid the
usual delays at Constantinople the wily pasha was
pretending to Botta that all his difficulties were
due to the people of Khorsabad, and not to his
own machinations. "I told him one day," says
Botta, "that the first rains of the season had
caused a portion of the house erected at Khorsabad
to fall down. 'Can you imagine,' said he, laugh-
ing in the most natural manner, and turning to the
numerous officers by whom he was surrounded,

'anything like the impudence of the inhabitants of Khorsabad? They pretend that the French consul has constructed a redoubtable fortress, and a little rain is sufficient to destroy it. I can assure you, sir, that, were I not afraid of hurting your feelings, I would have them all bastinadoed till they were dead; they would richly deserve it, for having dared to accuse you.' It was in this manner that he spoke, while he himself was the author of the lie, and his menaces alone were the obstacles which prevented the inhabitants from exposing it."[1]

At Constantinople difficulties innumerable and delays uncounted were found, and not until May 4, 1844, did the firmans allowing the work to proceed reach Botta at Mosul. They were brought from Constantinople by M. E. Flandin, who had been sent from Paris to copy and sketch all the antiquities which were too bulky or heavy to be removed. It was already decided in Paris that everything else should be carried thither.

When Botta attempted to begin excavations again he found that it would be necessary to raze the little village and thus be free to dig over the whole mound. This was accomplished by paying the inhabitants to remove to the level ground at the foot of the mound and then entering into an agreement to restore the mound's surface as it was for their rebuilding. The work now went on apace. Botta copied the inscriptions, while Flandin planned all the rooms and buildings that were

---

[1] Quoted in Bonomi, *Nineveh and Its Palaces*. London, 1852, p. 15.

found, and three hundred native laborers worked
lustily with pick and shovel to lay bare this portion of the ruined city. Scores of inscriptions,
chiefly upon stone and monumental in character,
were now found. Great winged bulls that once
had guarded palace doors came to light. Bas-reliefs of much beauty portraying scenes of peace
and war arose out of dust and dirt. The success
of the work passed all the hopes of Botta and all
the enthusiastic predictions of Mohl, and almost
exceeded the belief of the learned world in Paris.
In October, 1844, Botta stopped the work and
soon began to arrange for the transportation of
the antiquities to Paris. The difficulties were
great and the delays annoying, but at last, in December, 1846, the entire mass of material was successfully landed at Havre, thence to be transported
to Paris and deposited in the Louvre.

To crown the work the French government
published all the drawings of Flandin, all the
copies of inscriptions, and all the descriptive
matter of Botta in five magnificent folio volumes,[1]
in a style worthy of French traditions and of
French liberality to archæological research.

So ended in a worthy publicity the first great
expedition to Assyria which had succeeded in
bringing to Europe the first Assyrian monuments

---

[1] *Monument de Ninive découvert et décrit*, par M. P. E. Botta, mesuré et
dessiné par M. E. Flandin. Ouvrage publié par ordre du gouvernement
sous les auspices de M. le Ministre de l'Interieur, et sous la direction d'une
Commission de l'Institut. Tomes i-v. Paris, Imprimerie Nationale,
1849—.

which the Occident had ever seen.   It was a noble work of Botta, of Flandin, of Mohl, and of France.

Botta would probably have gone back to Khorsabad or to some other mound in the district of Nineveh after the publication of his discoveries had he not been sent into government service elsewhere.   His work might well call him to re-turn, but another would soon continue it.

On March 5, 1817, there was born in Paris an English boy of Huguenot descent, whose early training, gathered here and there in England, France, and Italy,[1] awakened in him a love for the fine arts, an interest in archæology, and a passion for travel.   In the boyish days of Austen Henry Layard his eager reading of the *Arabian Nights* was mixed with study of Fellowe's travels in Asia Minor and with the perusal of Rich's accounts of discovery at Babylon and Nineveh.   Rich's jour-nal filled him with desire to see these great mounds beneath which lay ancient memorials of untold interest.   Herein again, as often before, is seen the continuity of research in these lands, the influence of enthusiasm carried over from man to man.

Fortunately for science Layard's education had been too uneven to fit him for the pursuit of a profession, and the law, for which he was destined, did not awake in him an enthusiasm sufficient to

---

[1] The early life of Layard is sketched very briefly by Lord Aberdare in the introduction of the second edition of Layard, *Early Adventures in Persia, Susiana, and Babylonia.*   London, 1894.

overcome the early defects. The restless fever was in his blood, and the quiet ways of England were too tame for the almost Gallic spirit within him. He determined, therefore, to seek a career in Ceylon, and in 1839, when a mere boy in appearance and but twenty-two years of age, he set out to make the journey overland in company with Edward Ledwich Mitford, who was bent upon the same business. Mitford was nearly ten years older than Layard and had had experience in Morocco, where he had learned the Arabic dialect there in use. Before setting out upon this journey Layard had learned a little Arabic and Persian, and had tried to make other hasty preparations for the dangerous voyage over lands almost unknown, amid savage animals and even more savage men. Upon reaching Hamadan, Persia, Layard abandoned the plan of seeking his fortune in Ceylon, and therein archæology triumphed over commerce. Mitford pursued his way on to Ceylon, and Layard returned into western Asia.[1]

It was upon May 10, 1840, that Layard and Mitford first saw Mosul and examined somewhat curiously the mounds on the opposite bank, which Layard had learned from Rich to consider the re-

---

[1] The story of Layard's early wanderings is told in *A Land March from England to Ceylon, forty years ago*, by Edward Ledwich Mitford, F. R. G. S., two volumes, London, 1884, which describes the European travels and the oriental as far as Hamadan. The story is continued in *Early Adventures in Persia, Susiana, and Babylonia*, by Sir Henry Layard, G. C. B., two volumes, London, 1887. Mitford's book very curiously refrains from mentioning Layard's name.

mains of Nineveh. The mounds of Kuyunjik and Neby Yunus did not make so great an impression upon Layard as did the great mound of Nimroud, farther south. But all aroused in him a deep longing to learn their secrets. Even then he could say, " These huge mounds of Assyria made a deeper impression upon me, gave rise to more serious thought and more earnest reflection, than the temples of Baalbec or the theaters of Ionia." This spell deepened as he saw more of Nimroud by rafting down the Tigris toward Baghdad. His words are a promise of the work that was to follow :

" It was evening as we approached the spot. The spring rains had clothed the mounds with the richest verdure, and the fertile meadows, which stretched around it, were covered with flowers of every hue. Amidst this luxuriant vegetation were partly concealed a few fragments of bricks, pottery, and alabaster, upon which might be traced the well-defined wedges of the cuneiform character. Did not these remains mark the nature of the ruin, it might have been confounded with a natural eminence. A long line of consecutive narrow mounds, still retaining the appearance of walls or ramparts, stretched from its base, and formed a vast quadrangle. The river flowed at some distance from them, its waters, swollen by the melting of the snows on the Armenian hills, were broken into a thousand foaming whirlpools by an artificial barrier built across the stream. On the eastern bank the soil had been washed away by the current, but a solid mass of masonry still withstood its impetuosity. The Arab who guided my small raft gave himself up to religious ejaculations as we approached this formidable cataract, over which we were carried with some violence. Once safely through the danger, my companion explained to me that this unusual change in the quiet face of the river was caused by a great dam which had been built by Nimrod, and that in the autumn, before the winter rains, the huge stones of which it was constructed, squared, and united by clamps of iron, were frequently visible above the surface of the stream. It was, in fact, one of those monuments of a great people to be found in all the rivers of Mesopotamia, which were undertaken to insure a constant supply of water to the innumerable canals, spreading like network over the surrounding country, and which, even in the days of Alexander, were looked upon as the works of an ancient nation. No wonder that the traditions of the present inhabitants of the land should assign them to one of the founders of the human race! The Arab was telling me of the connection between the dam and the city built by Athur, the lieutenant of Nimrod, the vast ruins of which were now before us—of its purpose as a causeway for the mighty hunter to cross to the opposite palace, now represented by the mound of Hammum Ali— and of the histories and fate of kings of a primitive race still the favorite theme of the inhabitants of the plain of Shinar, when the last glow of twilight faded away, and I fell alseep as we glided onward to Baghdad.

"My curiosity had been greatly excited, and from that time I formed the design of thoroughly examining, whenever it might be in my power, these singular ruins." [1]

The resolve expressed in this last sentence is very striking when one remembers that it was taken in April, 1840. This was more than two years before Botta had even seen the mounds. At least in the thought of excavation Layard anticipated Botta, though the good fortune of the latter gave him the precedence in the field.

In May, 1842, Layard passed through Mosul on his way to Constantinople, and found Botta established as consular agent and already engaged in carrying on excavations at Kuyunjik. Layard was too much a man of dignity, even in his youth, to feel any envy of the fortunate Frenchman, who was now doing what he had been dreaming. In the two years which had passed Layard had attempted to secure aid to enable him to undertake just such work as this, but in vain. His own government was not as easily induced to aid archæologists as the government of France, whether monarchical or republican, has always

---

[1] *Nineveh and Its Remains;* with an account of a visit to the Chaldean Christians of Kurdistan, and the Yezidis, or Devil-worshippers; and an enquiry into the Manners and Arts of the Ancient Assyrians, by Austen Henry Layard, Esq., D.C.L. Two volumes. London, 1849, i, pp. 7, 8.

been. Layard then formed terms of friendship with Botta, and entered upon a correspondence. When Botta was discouraged at his small success it was Layard who wrote urging him to persevere.

At the time of this second visit to Mosul, Layard was on his way home to England. At Constantinople, however, he was detained and sent thence to Salonica upon service for the British embassy. The British ambassador at Constantinople was now Sir Stratford Canning, afterward Lord Stratford de Redcliffe, who had secured for the British Museum the marbles of Halicarnassus. The skill, patience, and ardor with which he had pursued the efforts required to obtain these had increased his own interest in the monuments of the past. To him Layard told the story of the mounds, and described his eagerness to try excavations in them. At last he had found the right man, and Sir Stratford gave him £60, to which Layard was to add an equal amount collected among friends. With this small sum Layard left Constantinople October, 1845, and traveled with all haste to Mosul. Mohammed Pasha was now governor of the province, and from him Layard could expect no help, but every possible interference. He therefore concealed the object of his mission, but after a few days gave out that he was going to hunt wild boars, and then left Mosul by a raft to float down to Nimroud, where he had determined to begin excavations. Here an Arab tent sheltered him, and hearts more tender than the pasha's watched over him. His record of the night before the first spade was struck into the ground reveals the enthusiasm of the man, and gives some clue to his great success :

" I had slept little during the night. The hovel in which we had taken shelter, and its inmates, did not invite slumber; but such scenes and companions were not new to me; they could have been forgotten had my brain been less excited. Hopes long cherished were now to be realized or were to end in disappointment. Visions of palaces underground, of gigantic monsters, of sculptured figures, and endless inscriptions floated before me. After forming plan after plan for removing the earth and extricating these treasures, I fancied myself wandering in a maze of chambers from which I could find no outlet. Then, again, all was reburied and I was standing on the grass-covered mound. Exhausted, I was at length sinking into sleep when, hearing the voice of Awad [his Arab host], I rose from my carpet and joined him outside the hovel. The day had already dawned ; he had returned with six Arabs, who agreed for a small sum to work under my direction." [1]

The excavations thus begun were carried on until December amid constant difficulties set on foot by the pasha. The plans pursued were exactly the same as were followed against Botta. When the excavations were resumed, after a visit

---

[1] *Nineveh and Its Remains,* i, p. 25.

to Baghdad, they were again interrupted by the
fanatacism of the Arabs, operating upon the new
governor of the province, Ismail Pasha. When
they were again resumed, in February, 1846, Layard
left the mound to visit a neighboring sheikh, and
was returning to the mound when he observed
two Arabs hastening to meet him with excited
faces. The narrative of what followed is best
told by Layard himself:

"On approaching me they stopped. 'Hasten,
O Bey,' exclaimed one of them—'hasten to the
diggers, for they have found Nimrod himself.
Wallah, it is wonderful, but it is true! we have
seen him with our eyes. There is no God but
God;' and both joining in this pious exclamation,
they galloped off, without further words, in the
direction of their tents.

"On reaching the ruins I descended into the
new trench, and found the workmen, who had
already seen me as I approached, standing near a
heap of baskets and cloaks. Whilst Awad advanced and asked for a present to celebrate the
occasion, the Arabs withdrew the screen they had
hastily constructed and disclosed an enormous
human head sculptured in full out of the alabaster
of the country. They had uncovered the upper
part of a figure, the remainder of which was still
buried in the earth. I saw at once that the head
must belong to a winged lion or bull, similar to
those of Khorsabad and Persepolis. It was in
admirable preservation. The expression was calm,

yet majestic, and the outline of the features showed a freedom and knowledge of art scarcely to be looked for in the works of so remote a period. The cap had three horns, and, unlike that of the human-headed bulls hitherto found in Assyria, was rounded and without ornament at the top.

"I was not surprised that the Arabs had been amazed and terrified at this apparition. It required no stretch of imagination to conjure up the most strange fancies. This gigantic head, blanched with age, thus rising from the bowels of the earth, might well have belonged to one of those fearful beings which are pictured in the traditions of the country as appearing to mortals, slowly ascending from the regions below. One of the workmen, on catching the first glimpse of the monster, had thrown down his basket and run off toward Mosul as fast as his legs could carry him. I learned this with regret, as I anticipated the consequences.

"While I was superintending the removal of the earth, which still clung to the sculpture, and giving directions for the continuation of the work, a noise of horsemen was heard, and presently Abd-ur-rahmar, followed by half his tribe, appeared on the edge of the trench. As soon as the two Arabs had reached the tents and published the wonders they had seen everyone mounted his mare and rode to the mound, to satisfy himself of the truth of these inconceivable reports. When

they beheld the head they all cried together,
'There is no God but God, and Mohammed is his
prophet!' It was some time before the sheikh
could be prevailed upon to descend into the pit
and convince himself that the image he saw was
of stone. 'This is not the work of men's hands,'
exclaimed he, 'but of those infidel giants of whom
the prophet, peace be with him! has said that
they were higher than the tallest date tree; this
is one of the idols which Noah, peace be with
him! cursed before the flood.' In this opinion,
the result of a careful examination, all the bystanders concurred.

"I now ordered a trench to be dug due south
from the head, in the expectation of finding a corresponding figure, and before nightfall reached the
object of my search, about twelve feet distant.
Engaging two or three men to sleep near the
sculptures, I returned to the village and celebrated
the day's discovery by a slaughter of sheep, of
which all the Arabs near partook. As some wandering musicians chanced to be at Selamiyah, I
sent for them, and dances were kept up during
the greater part of the night. On the following
morning Arabs from the other side of the Tigris
and the inhabitants of the surrounding villages con-
gregated on the mound. Even the women could
not repress their curiosity, and came in crowds,
with their children, from afar. My cawass was
stationed during the day in the trench, into which
I would not allow the multitude to descend.

"As I had expected, the report of the discovery of the gigantic head, carried by the terrified Arab to Mosul, had thrown the town into commotion. He had scarcely checked his speed before reaching the bridge. Entering breathless into the bazaars, he announced to everyone he met that Nimrod had appeared. The news soon got to the ears of the cadi, who, anxious for a fresh opportunity to annoy me, called the mufti and the ulema together to consult upon this unexpected occurrence. Their deliberations ended in a procession to the governor, and a formal protest on the part of the Mussulmans of the town against proceedings so directly contrary to the laws of the Koran. The cadi had no distinct idea whether the bones of the mighty hunter had been uncovered or only his image; nor did Ismail Pasha very clearly remember whether Nimrod was a true believing prophet or an infidel. I consequently received a somewhat unintelligible message from his excellency to the effect that the remains should be treated with respect, and be by no means further disturbed, and that he wished the excavations to be stopped at once, and desired to confer with me on the subject.

"I called upon him accordingly, and had some difficulty in making him understand the nature of my discovery. As he requested me to discontinue my operations until the sensation in the town had somewhat subsided, I returned to Nimroud and dismissed the workmen, retaining only two men

to dig leisurely along the walls without giving
cause for further interference. I ascertained by
the end of March the existence of a second pair
of winged human-headed lions, differing from those
previously discovered in form, the human shape
being continued to the waist and finished with
arms. In one hand each figure carried a goat or
stag, and in the other, which hung down by the
side, a branch with three flowers. They formed
a northern entrance into the chamber of which
the lions previously described were the southern
portal. I completely uncovered the latter, and
found them to be entire. They were about
twelve feet in height, and the same number in
length. The body and limbs were admirably portrayed; the muscles and bones, though strongly
developed to display the strength of the animal,
showed at the same time a correct knowledge of
its anatomy and form. Expanded wings sprung
from the shoulder and spread over the back; a
knotted girdle, ending in tassels, encircled the
loins. These sculptures, forming an entrance, were
partly in full and partly in relief. The head and
fore part, facing the chamber, were in full; but
only one side of the rest of the slab was sculptured, the back being placed against the wall of
sun-dried bricks. That the spectator might have
both a perfect front and side view of the figures
they were furnished with five legs; two were
carved on the end of the slab to face the chamber,
and three on the side. The relief of the body

and three limbs was high and bold, and the slab was covered in all parts not occupied by the image with inscriptions in the cuneiform character. These magnificent specimens of Assyrian art were in perfect preservation; the most minute lines in the details of the wings and in the ornaments had been retained with their original freshness. Not a character was wanting in the inscriptions.

"I used to contemplate for hours these mysterious emblems, and muse over their intent and history. What more noble forms could have ushered the people into the temple of their gods? What more sublime images could have been borrowed from nature by men who sought, unaided by the light of revealed religion, to embody their conception of the wisdom, power, and ubiquity of a Supreme Being? They could find no better type of intellect and knowledge than the head of the man; of strength, than the body of the lion; of rapidity of motion, than the wings of the bird. These winged human-headed lions were not idle creations, the offspring of mere fancy; their meaning was written upon them. They had awed and instructed races which flourished three thousand years ago. Through the portals which they guarded kings, priests, and warriors had borne sacrifices to their altars long before the wisdom of the East had penetrated to Greece, and had furnished its mythology with symbols long recognized by the Assyrian votaries. They may have been buried, and

their existence may have been unknown, before
the foundation of the Eternal City. For twenty-
five centuries they had been hidden from the eye
of man, and they now stood forth once more in
their ancient majesty. But how changed was the
scene around them! The luxury and civilization
of a mighty nation had given place to the wretched-
ness and ignorance of a few half-barbarous tribes.
The wealth of temples and the riches of great
cities had been succeeded by ruins and shapeless
heaps of earth. Above the spacious hall in which
they stood the plow had passed and the corn now
waved. Egypt has monuments no less ancient
and no less wonderful, but they have stood forth
for ages to testify her early power and renown,
while those before me had but now appeared to
bear witness, in the words of the prophet, that
once 'the Assyrian was a cedar in Lebanon with
fair branches, and with a shadowing shroud of an
high stature; and his top was among the thick
boughs . . . his height was exalted above all the
trees of the field, and his boughs were multiplied,
and his branches became long, because of the
multitude of waters when he shot forth. All the
fowls of heaven made their nests in his boughs,
and under his branches did all the beasts of the
field bring forth their young, and under his shadow
dwelt all great nations;' for now is 'Nineveh a
desolation and dry like a wilderness, and flocks lie
down in the midst of her: all the beasts of the
nations, both the cormorant and bittern, lodge in

the upper lintels of it; their voice sings in the
windows; and desolation is in the thresholds.'"[1]

In one respect this narrative of Layard's far
excels all that had been written by the men who
before his day had seen or measured or worked in
these mounds. None before had ever told the
story of their experiences or of their discoveries
in words so full of color, life, and movement; none
had ever displayed so much of enthusiasm and so
great a power of description. In another respect
Layard becomes a successor of one of the earliest
of English travelers and explorers. Like Shirley, he
knew how to make all that he saw bear upon the
words of the Bible. He could quote the very
words out of the Scriptures and make the dust-
covered monument reflect a bright light upon
them. These two powers—the power of description in color and the power of biblical comparison
—ranged all England at his back. They who
cared nothing for the Bible were moved by the
fire and the beauty of his description; they who
loved the Bible saw in him a man who was making discoveries which promised to illustrate or
confirm records to them most dear. In due time,
also, these influences became so potent that the
British government was moved to lend a hand to
this work, and so that which had been begun upon slender private means became a great national
enterprise.

The colossal figures which so deeply moved

---

[1] Layard, *Nineveh and Its Remains*, i, 65, ff.

Layard were indeed a noble sight, but they were not so important as the smaller inscriptions which were later to be dug out of their resting places. Layard had supposed that the winged lions had guarded the entrance of some great temple, the spade was later to show that they had stood at the portals of the palace of Shalmaneser II.

The work which revealed these monuments had been carried on under many difficulties and with a constant dread of interruption from the suspicious natives or their rulers. It was therefore a great relief to Layard's anxieties when he received from Constantinople a " vizirial letter, procured by Sir Stratford Canning, authorizing the continuation of the excavations and the removal of such objects as might be discovered." This put another face upon Layard's work, and enabled him to do openly work which had hitherto been carried on with as much concealment as possible. He now made some small attempts upon the mound of Kuyunjik, but his funds were extremely limited and the results were not encouraging. He therefore resumed with fresh vigor the work at Nimroud, from which he was shortly able to send a large consignment of monuments on a raft to Baghdad and thence to Bassorah, for transportation to England. Soon after which his health, already undermined by the enervating climate, compelled him to cease work and make a mountain journey for recuperation.

Upon his return to Mosul he found letters from
12

England advising him that Sir Stratford Canning had presented to the British Museum the antiquities which had been found, and that furthermore the Museum had received from the government a grant of funds for continuing the work. This was good news indeed, though Layard had to lament that it was so much smaller than Botta had enjoyed, and that therefore he must stint and economize and strive to utilize every penny.

With such resources as he had the work was resumed in October, 1846, and a winter campaign was carefully planned. Huts were erected for shelter from the storms; wandering Arabs were induced to pitch their tents near by, and instead of living by plunder draw wages for labor in the trenches. Many a new plan of dealing with troublesome natives was tried and the better adopted. In all this Layard had the valuable assistance of Mr. Hormuzd Rassam, whose brother, Charles Rassam, was British vice consul at Mosul. Hormuzd Rassam was native born and understood the people as no European could hope to do. He conducted most of the dealings with them, and kept the peace without use of force.

The excavations carried on under these auspices, and with the powers which Layard then possessed, were successful beyond his wildest dreams. As the trenches followed round the walls of room after room they uncovered great slabs of alabaster, with which the chamber walls were wainscoted, and these were found to be richly carved in relief

with scenes of hunting, of war, and of solemn
ceremony. The very life of palace, camp, and
field in Assyrian days came back again before the
astonished eyes of the explorer, while these received an addition to their verisimilitude by the
discovery in some of the ruins of pieces of iron
which had once formed parts of the same kind of
armor as that portrayed on the reliefs, together
with iron and bronze helmets, while in others
were found vases and ornamentally carved pieces
of ivory. Here were the pictures and there were
the objects which they represented. As the
trenches were dug deeper or longer monuments
carved or inscribed were found daily. One trench
ten feet beneath the surface uncovered the edge of
a piece of black marble. It was the corner of "an
obelisk about seven feet high, lying on its side."
It was covered on three sides with inscriptions and
with twenty small bas-reliefs. The inscriptions
recorded and the bas-reliefs illustrated various
forms of gift and tribute which had been received
by Shalmaneser II, though when found these facts
were of course unknown. No inscription equal in
beauty and in the promise of valuable historical
material had yet been found in Assyria. Layard
was therefore particularly anxious to get it away
from the place lest some mishap should befall it.
He therefore set Arabs to sleep and watch by it
overnight and had it speedily packed for ship-
ment. Day after day the work went on with the
regular and constant discovery of stone slabs

similar to those which had been found before, and with the finding of inscribed bricks which, though not so beautiful as the stone, contained much more historical material.

When the trenches began to yield less material Layard determined to try elsewhere. Had his funds not been so severely limited, he would have continued still further the excavations at Nimroud, even though they did not appear to be immediately productive. This would have been the best method of procedure, but the means would not permit it, and Layard had to seek fresh soil.

For his next adventure he chose the mound of Kalah Shergat, where he had before desired to make excavations. Out of these ruins were taken an interesting sitting figure and many small bricks with inscriptions, some of which belong to the earliest of the great Assyrian conquerors, Tiglath-pileser I. But what ancient city this might be Layard was unable to ascertain. That it was none other than the city of Asshur,' first capital of the kingdom, was a discovery made afterward.

A few days were also given to excavation in the mound of Kuyunjik with similar good fortune, and then the work had to cease because of the consumption of the means for its carrying on. On June 24, 1847, Layard left Mosul for the land journey to Constantinople, after having sent the last of his discoveries down the Tigris.

After a few months' rest in England, devoted

' See *infra*, p. 297.

in considerable measure to the preparation of the
narrative of his expedition and of the copies of
the monuments which he had found, Layard was
ordered to Constantinople to service with the
British embassy. He had not been able to finish
for the press the work which he had written, and
went out to his duty not knowing whether his
story would awaken any interest or not. He does
not appear even to have dreamed that any special
call would come to him to resume the excavations again. But the books[1] were published after
his departure, and at once all England rang with
his praise and with an eager expression that this
work must go on further. The British Museum
secured more funds for the work and he was directed to set out for Assyria again. From England Hormuzd Rassam, Mr. F. Cooper, an artist,
and Dr. Sandwith, a physician, were induced to
accompany him. They set sail from the Bos-
phorus on August 28, 1849, for Trebizond, and
landed there on the thirty-first day and began the
journey to Mosul.

In this expedition he laid the chief emphasis
upon the mound of Kuyunjik and Neby Yunus.
In the former he discovered the great palace of
Sennacherib, and so keen was he now become in
the examination of inscriptions and tables of genealogy that he recognized the fact that this edifice

---

[1] These books were *Nineveh and Its Remains* (see references above) and
The Monuments of Nineveh, by Austen Henry Layard, Esq., D.C.L.,
London, 1849. The latter contained one hundred plates, many well exe-
cuted, but far below the standard of beauty set by Botta's superb volumes.

belonged to the king whose son was the builder of
the palace at Nimroud and whose father built the
palace discovered by Botta at Khorsabad. It is
to be remembered that he made this conjecture
without being able to read Assyrian at all. Later
study has determined that he had correctly ascertained the facts. Sargon built the palace at
Khorsabad; his son Sennacherib built the palace
at Kuyunjik, while his son Esar-haddon erected
the palace at Nimroud. Even greater than in the
first expedition were his discoveries at Kuyunjik both for the history, the literature, and the
art of ancient Assyria. But he also conducted
excavations at Kalah Shergat, Nimroud, and
Khorsabad. From Mosul he made excursions to
various sites in northern and southern Babylonia.
Upon these excursions he visited and for the first
time described the great mound of Niffer, where a
later expedition was to achieve unparalleled successes. At Hillah he made some excavations, but
met with little success.

After another season he returned in April,
1852, to England. His first work was the writing
of his narrative and the preparing of his inscriptions for publication.[1] He found that his pre-

---

[1] *Discoveries in the Ruins of Nineveh and Babylon*, with travels in
Armenia, Kurdistan, and the Desert: being the result of a second expedition undertaken for the trustees of the British Museum, by Austen H. Layard, M.P. London, 1853.

A Second Series of the Monuments of Nineveh, including bas-reliefs from
the palace of Sennacherib and bronzes from the ruins of Nimroud, from
drawings made on the spot during a second expedition to Assyria, by
Austen Henry Layard, M.P. Seventy-one plates. London, 1853.

vious books had made him famous, while the new discoveries would be certain to add much to his reputation. This secured for him honored diplomatic posts, notably at Constantinople, where he was able to serve Assyrian study by dealing with the Turkish government in the interest of explorers, as he had once served it by his own labors.

Layard's two expeditions to Assyria had been fruitful indeed beyond those of Botta, and their influence lived far beyond even Layard's own life. His books had, as we have already seen, touched the popular heart in many points, and, though he laid the work down to take up diplomatic service, in which he appears not to have been so happy, others were found to continue it.

Even while Layard was still at work in Nineveh the French government sent Victor Place, an architect of great skill, to hold the post of consular agent at Mosul and continue Botta's work. He had not accomplished much when Layard's work ended, but remained and made important discoveries in the department of Assyrian art, cooperating afterward with a French expedition, to which attention must later be paid.

Meanwhile in England interest in the whole of Babylonia and Assyria grew apace, manifesting itself in many ways. The government had been moved to assist Layard's investigations, and it now joined in the work in still another way. For a long time the frontier between Turkey and Persia had been a bone of contention, each land gaining or losing as the fortune of war might be, while predatory bands belonging neither to the one nor the other made reprisals upon both. In 1839 and 1840 war almost ensued between the two nations, whereupon England and Russia intervened, and a commission was appointed to sit at Erzerum to conduct negotiations for a peaceful settlement of difficulties. This commission, after a session lasting four years, agreed upon a treaty, the basis of which lay in a survey of the doubtful territory between the two states, and a proper delimitation of the border. This work was carried on by representatives of England, Russia, Turkey, and Persia. The most prominent of these was Colonel W. F. Williams. In January, 1849, Mr. William Kennett Loftus was sent out from England to serve as geologist upon his staff. Loftus found time amid other duties to visit large numbers of mounds in Babylonia, and the very sight of them filled him with enthusiasm. Of one, the mound of Hammam, he says:

" I know of nothing more exciting or impressive than the first sight of one of these great Chaldean piles looming in solitary grandeur from the surrounding plains and marshes. A thousand thoughts and surmises concerning its past eventful history and origin—its gradual rise and rapid fall—naturally present themselves to the mind of the spectator. The hazy atmosphere of early morning is peculiarly favorable to considerations and impressions of this character, and the gray mist intervening between the gazer and the object of his reflections imparts to it a dreamy existence. This fairylike effect is further heightened by mirage, which strangely and fantastically magnifies its form, elevating it from the ground, and causing it to dance and quiver in the rarefied air. No wonder, therefore, that the beholder is lost in pleasing doubt as to the actual reality of the apparition before him." [1]

In the spring of 1850 Loftus carried on small excavations at Warka, the ancient city of Erech, but, though many interesting antiquities were found, they were not to be compared with the results of Layard's work. This was due in chief measure to the exceedingly meager means at the disposal of Loftus, and further to the great difficulties of excavating in Babylonia. Upon this first expedition Loftus rendered distinguished services by his long, and often dangerous, travels over southern Babylonia. Upon these trips he visited Niffer, Mukayyar (Mugheir), and a number of lesser sites, most of which had never before been visited by Europeans. These he carefully described, and minutely located, rendering thereby access easy for others. Even to this present some of Loftus's work remains useful. He had also a keen eye for the peculiarities of mounds, and expressed a longing to dig in some spots which have since proved exceedingly productive. An oppor-

---

[1] *Travels and Researches in Chaldæa and Susiana*, by William Kennett Loftus, F.G.S. London, 1857.

tunity to do some of the work he had planned was soon to come to him through private enterprise in England.

While travelers and explorers were busy among almost savage peoples English interest in the mounds continued, and finally eventuated in the organization of an Assyrian Excavation Fund, which undertook to gather popular subscriptions and to direct excavations in Assyria and Babylonia with the means thus acquired.   At this time Sir Henry C. Rawlinson was British resident and consul general at Baghdad, and to him was intrusted the general oversight of such excavations as might be planned and carried on.   This direction could hardly have been placed in better hands.   His extensive travels, and long residence in the East and his remarkable attainments in the decipherment of ancient Persian had fitted him in the fullest degree to take charge of efforts intended to make the buried records of the great valley accessible to the world.

Loftus was sent by the fund to conduct excavations and carry on explorations in the southern part of the country.   His work was successful in bringing to London considerable numbers of inscribed tablets, with many vases, and a considerable mass of mortuary remains.   It attracted, however, little popular attention, not that it was unimportant, though less in amount than Layard's, but chiefly because Loftus did not possess Layard's popular gifts, and was unable to set forth his discoveries in such attractive fashion. Had it not been for the notes which Rawlinson sent home, he would have remained almost unknown.

Rawlinson's next move was to send J. E. Taylor, British vice consul at Bassorah, to Mugheir, probably the ancient Babylonian city of Ur.[1] Taylor dug straight into the center of the mound, finding almost nothing as a reward for his pains. It was rather at the southwestern corner that his great discovery was to be made. Of it he has this story to tell:

"I began excavating the southwest corner, clearing away large masses of rubbish formed of the remains of burnt, mingled with sun-dried, bricks. I worked along at a depth of 10 feet and a breadth of 6 without finding anything. I then returned, and worked a few feet north along the brick casing of the western wall; here, 6 feet below the surface, I found a perfect inscribed cylinder. This relic was in the solid masonry; it had been placed in a niche formed by the omission of one of the bricks in the layer, and was found standing on one end. I excavated some little distance further without any success, and then relinquished this corner for the northwest one. Here, also, I found a second cylinder similar to the one above mentioned, but at 12 feet from the surface. At this corner I sank a shaft 21 feet deep by 12 broad. The sun-dried bricks, composing this solid mass within were here of an amazing thickness; their

---

[1] See *infra*, p. 290.

size was 16 inches square and 7 inches thick. Just below the cylinder were two rough logs of wood, apparently teak, which ran across the whole breadth of the shaft. . . .

"Having thus found two cylinders in the solid masonry in two corners, I naturally concluded the same objects would be found in the two corners still remaining. I sank a shaft in each, and found two other cylinders precisely in the same position, and in the same kind of structure, one at 6 and the other at 2 feet from the surface. This is easily accounted for when looking at the irregular surface of the ruin, which, at the southeast corner and south side generally, has been subject to greater ravages from rain than the other sides, owing to the greater depression of the surface toward these points."[1]

Taylor also conducted excavations at Abu Sharein and Tel-el-Lahm, but without important results.[2]

At this time expeditions were so numerous and the work of different men in various places so constantly in progress that it is impossible to follow them in detail and almost impossible to arrange them in chronological order.

While yet Loftus was still at work and Taylor had not even begun his labors the French government was taking steps to resume excavations upon

---

[1] "Notes on the Ruins of Muqeyer," by J. E. Taylor, Esq., *Journal of the Royal Asiatic Society*, xv, p. 263, 264.

[2] *Ibid.*, pp. 404, ff.

a large scale. It was the indefatigable Mohl who kept government and people in France ever incited to good works in this matter. At last he moved M. Leon Fancher, the minister of the interior, to ask the assembly for a credit of 70,000 francs, and on October 9, 1851, an expedition set out from Marseilles for Hillah, which was reached July 7, 1852. The members of this expedition were MM. Fulgence Fresnel, formerly consul at Jeddah, Jules Oppert, professor of German at the Lycée, Reims, and F. Thomas, an architect.

Oppert had already done important work upon old Persian and was a trained orientalist. He made important researches at Babylon and visited a large number of mounds, some of which Loftus had already seen. This expedition excavated at Birs Nimroud and found rich treasures of art and of inscriptions. At the same time Place was continuing excavations at Khorsabad. The materials found both by Place and by the expedition at Birs Nimroud were loaded on rafts to be floated down the river to Bassorah. Unhappily, and as it is stated by "sheer carelessness and mismanagement," the rafts were overturned and the whole collection was lost in the river.[1] Though this sore mishap had occurred, Oppert brought back to Europe much fresh knowledge, and the published results of the expedition were notable.[2]

---

[1] *Journal of Sacred Literature*, iii, p. 471 (July, 1856).

[2] *Expédition Scientifique en Mésopotamie*, par Jules Oppert. 2 vols. Paris, 1863–1867.

In the same year that the French expedition, which ended so unhappily, was being planned the trustees of the British Museum secured a grant from Parliament to begin anew the work at Nineveh. Layard was now absorbed in the diplomatic service, and would not go out to take up the work again. His former assistant was, however, now studying at Oxford, and to him the authorities appealed. To his lasting honor Mr. Hormuzd Rassam accepted the post, and set out at the end of 1852 to begin excavations at Kuyunjik, under the general direction of Sir Henry Rawlinson. Rassam was fitted for the work of excavator as few who had ever dug in these mounds. He knew land and people from his birth up; he had served a long and useful apprenticeship to Layard; he was devoted to the business he had in hand, and eager to give every energy to its successful accomplishment. In one respect he was unfortunately not so well equipped as the brilliant Oppert, who was now busy among the mounds of Babylon. Oppert knew all that was then known of the cuneiform writing, while Rassam knew nothing of the language in which the ancient records of his country were written.

When he reached Mosul he found that Sir Henry Rawlinson had drawn a line across the mound at Kuyunjik, assigning the northern half of the mound to the French and retaining the remainder for the "English sphere of influence." Place had, however, not yet dug at all in this mound, but was busy with the continuing of excavations at Khorsabad. Rassam was endowed beyond Place in a feeling for archæological investigations, and believed that the northern part of the mound was by far the most promising. From the very beginning he desired most to try excavations there, but felt himself prevented by the arrangement which Sir Henry Rawlinson had made. He concealed from Place his feelings and went sturdily to work upon other parts of the mound. For nearly a year and a half his work continued, and from his trenches and wells there were constantly brought out inscribed records of the past, now fragments of tablets, now obelisks, now clay cylinders, and now beautifully preserved tablets, with the fine, neat writing of the ancient Assyrians. During all this time M. Place made no move toward even the beginnings of excavation at Kuyunjik, and Rassam finally concluded that, after all, Sir Henry Rawlinson had exceeded his authority in setting off a part of the mound to the French, and therefore determined, " come what might," to move over to the top of the mound and see what might be found. His first essays were to be made at night so as to prevent any possible interference by Place if it should be attempted. The story is romantic, and Rassam's own laconic sentences best describe it :

" After having waited a few days for a bright moonlight night,[1] I selected a number of my old

---

[1] December 20, 1853.

and faithful Arab workmen who could be de-
pended on for secrecy, with a trustworthy over-
seer, and gave them orders to assemble at a certain spot on the mound about two hours after
sunset. When everything was ready I went and
marked them three different spots on which to
dig. There had been already a number of trenches
dug there on a former occasion, but at this time I
directed the workmen to dig across them and go
deeper down; and having superintended the work
myself till midnight, I left them at work (after
telling them to stop work at dawn) and went to
bed.

"The next morning I examined the trenches,
and on seeing some good signs of Assyrian remains I doubled the number of workmen the second night and made them work hard all night.
As usual, I superintended the work till midnight, and then went to bed, but had not been
asleep two hours before my faithful Albanian over-
seer came running to give me the good tidings of
the discovery of some broken sculptures. I hur-
ried immediately to the spot, and on descending
one of the trenches I could just see in the moonlight the lower part of two bas-reliefs, the upper
portion having been destroyed by the Sassanians
or other barbarous nations who occupied the
mound after the destruction of the Assyrian empire. I could only find out this from experience,
by examining the foundation and the brick wall
which supported the bas-reliefs; so I directed the

workmen to clear the lower part of the sculptures,
which clearly showed that the slabs belonged to
a new palace; but on digging around them we
came upon bones, ashes, and other rubbish, and no
trace whatever was left of any other sculptures.
On the third day the fact of my digging at night
oozed out in the town of Mosul, which did not
surprise me, seeing that all the families of the
workmen who were employed in the nocturnal
work knew that they were digging clandestinely
somewhere; and, moreover, the workmen who were
not employed at night must have seen their fellow-
laborers leaving their tents and not coming to
work the next day.   Not only did I fear the
French consul hearing and coming to prevent me
from digging in what he would call his own
ground, but, worse than all, that it should be
thought I was digging for treasure by the Turkish
authorities and the people of Mosul, who had
always imagined that we were enriching ourselves
by the discovery of fabulous treasures; consequently, on the third night, I increased the workmen, and resolved to remain in the trenches till
the morning, superintending the work.   It can be
well imagined how I longed for the close of the
day, as there was no doubt in my mind that some
Assyrian structure was in existence near those
broken slabs which had been found the night before.   I was not disappointed in my surmises, for
the men had not been at work three hours on the
third night before a bank under which they were

13

digging fell and exposed a most perfect and beautiful bas-relief, on which was represented an Assyrian king (which proved afterward to be Assurbanipal or Sardanapalus) in his chariot hunting lions. The delight of the workmen was past all bounds; they all collected and began to dance and sing from their inmost heart, and no entreaty or threat of mine had any effect upon them. Indeed, I did not know which was most pleasing, the discovery of this new palace or to witness the joy of my faithful and grateful workmen. We kept on working till morning, and seeing that by this time three perfect sculptures had been uncovered, I had no doubt in my mind that this was quite a new palace. The night workmen were changed, and new hands put to work in the daytime, as I had now no more fear of being thwarted by my rivals, because, according to all rules, I had secured this palace for the British nation. During the day we cleared out all the lion-hunt room of Assurbanipal, which is now in the basement room of the British Museum. In the center of this long room or passage there were heaps of inscribed terra cottas, among which I believe was discovered the famous Deluge Tablet. Undoubtedly this was the record chamber of Assurbanipal." [1]

The discovery thus made was the greatest which had yet been made either in Assyria or Babylonia.

[1] *Excavations and Discoveries in Assyria*, by Hormuzd Rassam, *Transactions of the Society of Biblical Archæology*, vii, pp. 39–41. Rassam has told the story again in *Asshur and the Land of Nimrod* (New York, 1897), pp. 24, ff.

Rassam, by the exercise of a skilled judgment and the fortunate combination of circumstances, had actually uncovered the long-buried library of the royal city of Nineveh—the library which Assurbanipal had gathered or caused to be copied for the learning of his sages. Here was a royal storehouse of literature, science, history, and religion brought to light, ready to be studied in the West, when the method of its reading was fully made out. Well might Rawlinson join with Layard in applause over this happy and fortunate discovery, which had linked Rassam's name forever with the history of Assyrian research.

In March, 1854, Rassam returned to England, and Loftus, who had finished his researches in the south, was sent to Kuyunjik to complete Rassam's work. This task he fulfilled with complete success, recovering many more tablets, to be sent, as Rassam's were, to the British Museum.

While these works were in progress the East India Company again took part, in a most valuable manner, in the work of Assyrian study. On the request of the trustees of the British Museum the company dispatched Commander Felix Jones, assisted by Dr. J. M. Hyslop, from Baghdad to Mosul to survey the whole Nineveh district. This was accomplished in a masterly fashion during the month of March, 1862, and three great maps were published, which remain the standard records until to-day.[1]

---

[1] "Topography of Nineveh," illustrative of the maps of the chief cities of

And now the long and brilliant series of excavations was drawing near to another period of rest. But at the very end Sir Henry Rawlinson was the author of a remarkable discovery. During the months of August and September, 1854, he had placed "an intelligent young man, M. Joseph Tonetti by name," in charge of excavations at Birs Nimroud, where the ill-fated French expedition had carried on its work. For two months the work was not very successful, and then Sir Henry Rawlinson visited the works in person, and after some examination determined to break into the walls at the corners, in the hope of finding commemorative cylinders, such as Taylor had found at Mugheir. He first directed the removal of bricks down to the tenth layer above the plinth at the base, and while this was being done busied himself elsewhere. When this had been finished he was summoned back, and thus describes the happy fortune which ensued:

"On reaching the spot I was first occupied for a few minutes in adjusting a prismatic compass on the lowest brick now remaining of the original angle, which fortunately projected a little, so as to afford a good point for obtaining the exact magnetic bearing of the two sides, and I then ordered the work to be resumed. No sooner had the next layer of bricks been removed than the workmen called out there was a *Khazeneh,* or 'treasure

Assyria; and the general geography of the country intermediate between the Tigris and the upper Tab, by Felix Jones, Commander Indian Navy, and Surveyor in Mesopotamia. [With three large folded maps.] *Journal of the Royal Asiatic Society,* xv, pp. 297, ff.

hole'—that is, in the corner at the distance of two bricks from the exterior surface there was a vacant space filled up with loose reddish sand. 'Clear away the sand,' I said, 'and bring out the cylinder;' and as I spoke the words the Arab, groping with his hand among the débris in the hole, seized and held up in triumph a fine cylinder of baked clay, in as perfect a condition as when it was deposited in the artificial cavity above twenty-four centuries ago. The workmen were perfectly bewildered. They could be heard whispering to each other that it was *sihr*, or 'magic,' while the graybeard of the party significantly observed to his companion that the *compass*, which, as I have mentioned, I had just before been using, and had accidentally placed immediately above the cylinder, was certainly 'a wonderful instrument.' " [1]

The cylinder thus recovered was one of four originally set in four corners of the building, and a little later a second was found. The remaining two were not recovered, as the corners in which they had presumably been placed had long before been broken down. Nebuchadrezzar had taken great pains to preserve the records of his great works of building and restoration.

And now the long series of excavations was ended. Men of learning in the history of the

[1] "On the Birs Nimroud; or, The Great Temple of Borsippa," by Sir Henry Rawlinson, K.C.B., *Journal of the Royal Asiatic Society*, xviii (1860), pp. 2, ff. [This paper was read January 13, 1855.]

ancient Orient had been overwhelmed by the mass
no less than by the startling character of the
great discoveries. The spade and the pick might
now be suffered to lie idle and rust for several
years. There was great work to do in the reading
of these long-lost books. Europe waited for the
results before beginning new excavations.

CHAPTER VI.

THE DECIPHERMENT OF ASSYRIAN.

WHEN the masters of decipherment, Grotefend, Rawlinson, and Hincks, had brought to happy conclusion the reading of the ancient Persian inscriptions which had been copied at Persepolis, Behistun, and other less important sites, they were still confronted by a great series of problems.

Many of these inscriptions were threefold in form, and, as has already been shown, it was now generally believed that they represented three separate languages. The first was now read, and it was ancient Persian. The second called for attempts at its decipherment. None knew what people these were whose language appeared side by side with ancient Persian, and opinion now called them Scythians, and now Medes. But whatever their language might be named, some one must essay its decipherment. In reality a number of men in different places were at work simultaneously upon the fascinating problem. It was to be expected that Grotefend would attempt the task, and this he did, but, unfortunately, without complete success. He was, indeed, hardly fitted by his training for work of this kind. The great achievement of really beginning this decipherment was reserved for Niels Louis Westergaard, whose very first paper[1] laid the foundations for the successful reading of the second class of Persepolitan writing. His method was very similar to that used by Grotefend in the decipherment of Persian. He selected the names for Darius, for Hystaspes, for the Persians, and for other nationalities, and compared them with their equivalents in the Persian texts. By this means he learned a number of the signs and sought by their use in other words to spell out syllables or words, whose meanings were then ascertained by conjecture and by comparison. He estimated the number of separate characters at eighty-two or eighty-seven, and judged the writing to be partly alphabetical and partly syllabic. The language he called Median, and classified it in the " Scythian," rather than the " Japhetic," family. But Westergaard's results were tentative at the best, and needed the severe criticism of another mind. These they obtained in two papers by Dr. Hincks, read before the Royal Irish Academy.[2] Hincks clearly advanced upon Westergaard, and again, as before, showed himself a master of all the processes of cuneiform decipherment.

After Westergaard and Hincks the work was

---

[1] " Zur Entzifferung der Achämenidischen Keilschrift zweiter Gattung," von N. L. Westergaard, *Zeitschrift für die Kunde des Morgenlandes*, vi, pp. 337, ff.

[2] On the first and second kinds of Persepolitan writing, by the Rev. Edward Hincks, D.D., *Transactions of the Royal Irish Academy*, xxi, 114, ff. On the three kinds of Persepolitan writing, and on the Babylonian lapidary characters, *ibid.*, pp. 233–248.

taken up by a French scholar, F. de Saulcy, who
was able to see farther than either. De Saulcy
looked back upon the decipherment of ancient
Persian and compared the signs of the Median
language, for so he also named this second language. He observed that they were similar, then
he looked ahead and saw that they appeared
almost identical with the characters in the third
language, to which he gave the name *Assyrian*.
De Saulcy was not the first to give this title to
the third form of writing found at Persepolis—
that designation was now becoming common—but
he was the first to point out the remarkable resemblance between the signs or characters in the
second and third groups of the texts. It was now
clearer than ever that if the second language,
whatever it was, whether Median or Scythian,
could be deciphered, the way would be open to
the reading of Assyrian. To this great end de
Saulcy contributed by his increased success in the
study of Median.

All three, Westergaard, Hincks, and de Saulcy,
had done their work with very defective materials.
It was very improbable that the study of the
Median or Scythian would get beyond de Saulcy's
attempts without the publication of fresh material.
This was soon forthcoming, through the generosity
of Sir Henry Rawlinson. At great personal cost
of money, time, and dangerous labor he had completed the copy of the inscription at Behistun.
The first column was in ancient Persian, and in

the decipherment of this he had won imperishable fame. The second column he had not time to publish at once himself, and therefore gave it over to Mr. Edwin Norris, with full permission to use it as he wished. Norris, leaning in the beginning strongly upon Westergaard, succeeded in decipher-ing almost all of it. His paper, read before the Royal Asiatic Society of London on July 3, 1852,[1] was almost epoch-making in the history of the study, and it was long before it was superseded. The work of Norris drew Westergaard[2] once more into the arena with criticism, with fresh con-jectures, and with several marked improvements. Mordtmann[3] followed him in a paper too little leaning upon the work of predecessors, and there-fore containing useless combinations and repetitions, but, nevertheless, making a few gains upon the problems. He named the language Susian—and the name was happily chosen. A. H. Sayce[4]

---

[1] "Memoir on the Scythic Version of the Behistun Inscription," by Mr. E. Norris, *Journal of the Royal Asiatic Society*, xv, pp. 1–213; addenda, pp. 431–433.

[2] Westergaard, Om den anden eller den sakiske Art af Akhaemenidernes Kileskrift, in "*Det kongelike Danske Vedenskabernes Selskabs Skrifter.*" Femte Raekke; Historisk og philosophisk Afdeling; Andet Binds, forste Hefte, pp. 39–178. Kjöbenhavn, 1856.

[3] "Erklärung der Keilinschriften zweiter Gattung," von A. D. Mordt-mann, *Zeitschrift der Deutschen Morgenländischen Gesellschaft*, xv, pp. 1–126. "Ueber die Keilinschriften zweiter Gattung," *ibid.*, xxiv, pp. 1–84.

[4] "The Languages of the Cuneiform Inscriptions of Elam and Media," by A. H. Sayce, *Transactions of the Society of Biblical Archæology*, iii, pp. 465–485. "The Inscriptions of Mal-Amir and the Language of the Second Column of the Akhæmenian Inscriptions," by A. H. Sayce, *Actes du VIième Congrès International des Orientalistes, tenu en 1883 à Leide*, 2ième partie., section 1: Semitique, pp. 637–756.

attacked the problem next in two brilliant papers, the first of which even went so far as to present a transcription and partial translation of two small inscriptions. The translation was necessarily fragmentary, but none of the former workers had equaled it. He argued learnedly for the name Amardian for the language, and returned again to this matter in a second paper, which likewise registered progress in the decipherment. Oppert,[1] who gave most of his great skill to other questions, also studied these texts shortly after Sayce, and made contributions of importance to the problem. The problem of the second form of writing at Persepolis and at Behistun was solved, and in 1890 Weissbach[2] was able to gather up all the loose threads and present clear and convincing translations of the long-puzzling inscriptions.

If now we pause for a moment and look back, we cannot fail to be moved by the patience, skill, and learning that had been employed in the unraveling of these tangled threads of ancient writing. It was a long and a hard hill, and many a weary traveler had toiled up its slope. Persian and Susian at last were read. The progress, slow at first, had at last become very rapid. As yet, however, the historical results had been comparatively meager. The inscriptions were not numerous, and their words were few. But how

---

[1] See especially Jules Oppert, *Le Peuple et la Langue des Mèdes.* Paris, 1879.

[2] F. H. Weissbach, *Die Achämemdeninschriften Zweiter Art.* Leipzig, 1890.

different this would be if only the third language could be deciphered. That third language at Persepolis and at Behistun was undoubtedly Assyrian or Babylonian. Here in Susian and in Persian were the clews for its deciphering. If it could be read, men would have before them all the literatures of Assyria and Babylonia. What that meant was even now daily becoming more clear. While Norris was working quietly in England Botta and Layard were unearthing inscriptions by the score in Assyria, and the first fruits of Babylonian discovery were likewise finding their way to Europe. With such a treasure-trove it was not surprising that men almost jostled each other in their passionate eagerness to learn the meanings of the strange complicated signs which stood third at Persepolis and at Behistun.

Grotefend had picked out among the Assyrian transcripts of the Persepolis inscriptions the names of the kings, just as he had in the old Persian texts, but was able to go but little further. More material was imperatively necessary before much progress could possibly be made. As soon as the letters from Botta to Mohl were published announcing the discoveries at Khorsabad a man was found who plunged boldly into the attempt at deciphering Assyrian. Isidore de Loewenstein made his chief point of departure in a comparison of the Assyrian and Egyptian inscriptions on the Caylus vase.[1] It was hardly a good place to be-

---

[1] *Essai de déchiffrement de l'Écriture Assyrienne pour servir a l'explica-*

gin, and it is therefore surprising that his success was so great as it really was. Loewenstein made the exceedingly happy stroke of suggesting that the Assyrian language belonged to the Semitic family of speech, and was therefore sister to Hebrew, Arabic, and Aramæan.[1] This suggestion would alone dignify his work, for it became exceedingly fruitful in the hands of later workers. He was, however, not very successful in determining the values of the signs, and in that there was the greatest need for success. In the second memoir[2] Loewenstein was much more successful, for his point of departure was more happily chosen. He now chose for comparison the proper names of Persians,[3] which were transliterated in the Assyrian texts. With such comparisons a beginning might well be made, and this beginning Loewenstein made in happy fashion. To him, however, it was not given to read an Assyrian text; that proved to be a task much more difficult than anyone had imagined.

But workers were increasing in numbers, and all had hope that at last the way out to the light must be found.

Of all these none was gifted with such marvelous skill in decipherment as Edward Hincks. He

---

tion du Monument de Khorsabad, par Isidore Löwenstein. Paris and Leipzig, 1845.

[1] Ibid., pp. 12, 13.

[2] Exposé des élements constitutifs du systéme de la troisième écriture cuneiforme de Persépolis, par Isidore Löwenstein. Paris and Leipzig, 1847.

[3] Ibid., p. 10, footnote 1, where a complete list of the names used is given.

had already had a goodly share in the decipherment of the first form of the Persepolis inscriptions, and, as we have just seen, his work upon
the second was exceedingly important. Both these
services he was now to surpass, and apparently
with ease. Upon November 30, and again upon
December 14, 1846, he read before the Royal
Irish Academy two papers, afterward printed
as one,[1] in which he plunged boldly into the decipherment of the Babylonian. In a third paper,
read on January 11, 1847,[2] he modified somewhat
the views expressed in the two former papers, and
advanced a step farther. In the preparation of
these papers it seems quite clear that Hincks had
received no help from any other worker. Loewenstein's first paper he had not seen, and the second
paper was not yet published. The work of
Hincks was independent in every way. What he
accomplished in those three papers it would be
difficult to exaggerate. A number of Babylonian
signs were definitely determined in meaning, and
the meanings then assigned remain the standard
to this day. He even succeeded at this time in
determining correctly a large part of the numerals.
He was on the clear high road to a reading of the
texts, but he was too careful to venture to translate. His method, even under the pressure of the

---

[1] On the three kinds of Persepolitan writing, and on the Babylonian lapidary characters. *Transactions of the Royal Irish Academy,* xxi, " Polite
Literature," pp. 233, ff.

[2] On the third Persepolitan writing, and on the mode of expressing numerals
in cuneatic characters, *ibid.,* pp. 249, ff.

enthusiasm that must have tingled in his veins, remained rigidly scientific.

And now the inscriptions which Botta had unearthed at Khorsabad began to come to Paris.
From the heavy wooden cases came slabs of stone,
covered with dust, but bearing strange wedge-
shaped characters. Henri Adrien de Longperier
was now to arrange them in the same order in the
Museum of the Louvre. He could not do this
work without a longing to read these unknown
characters, and so, like others elsewhere, he began
to ponder over the hard problem. He was familiar with Loewenstein's work, and so began his own
efforts standing upon Loewenstein's shoulders. It
is true that Loewenstein could not give him much
help with individual signs, but he had at least
selected a group of signs, after comparison with old
Persian, which he believed represented the word
"great," and was probably to be pronounced *rabou.*
Loewenstein had learned this from the Persepolis
inscriptions. Longperier found the same group in
the inscriptions from Khorsabad. He assumed its
correctness and pushed on a bit further. In these
texts of Botta a little inscription was often repeated, and after long comparison A. de Longperier
translated the whole inscription in this way:

"Glorious is Sargon, the great king, the [. . .]
king, king of kings, king of the land of Assyria."[1]

---

[1] *Journal Asiatique,* x, pp. 532, ff. Comp. also *Revue Archéologique,*
1847, pp. 501, ff., "Lettre à M. Isidore Löwenstern sur les inscriptions
cunéiformes de l'Assyrie" (20 Septembre, 1847).

But the strange thing about this translation was this, that he could not name or pronounce a single word in it all except the one word, *rabou* "great." Yet the researches that were to follow showed that the translation was almost a full and correct representation of the original. If de Longperier had had before him the list of signs and meanings which Hincks had already proposed, he might have gone further. As it was, he made out the name of Sargon, and there paused. When one looks back upon all this work in France, England, and Ireland, and sees the little gain here and another there, he cannot but think that the slow progress was chiefly due to lack of communication. If, by some means, each worker might have known at once the move of his friendly rival, the progress must inevitably have been more rapid. It is in. deed true that the men who worked in France managed through published paper or letter or society meeting to keep fairly well in touch. But the much more brilliant Irishman beyond two stormy channels found no way of learning promptly what they were thinking, and, still worse, was not readily able to make known his work to them. So much was this latter fact painfully true that the keen Frenchmen worked steadily on without his invaluable aid. This lack of ready communication of hypotheses and of results still continues in a measure, in spite of all improvements in printing and in dissemination of documents, and appears to be increased rather than diminished by the vast number of societies and of journals devoted to the pursuit of science.

Botta was now back again in Paris and was publishing in parts a memoir [1] upon the language of the inscriptions which he had brought back to the world. He made but little effort to decipher or to translate, but he collated all the inscriptions which he had found, and made elaborate lists of the signs which he found upon them. He differentiated no less than 642 separate signs—enough to make the stoutest heart of the decipherers quail. For every one of these signs a value, or a meaning, or both, must be found. This at once and forever settled all dispute about an alphabet. If there were 642 characters, some of them certainly must represent syllables. But how could there possibly be so many syllables? Botta looked over the Persepolis inscriptions, comparing inscription No. 1, that is Persian, with inscription No. 3, that is Babylonian. In No. 1 he sometimes found the name of a country represented by *several signs*, whereas in No. 3, in the proper place, he found the same country represented by only *one* sign. It now became clear that this Babylonian language was partly at least written in ideograms. Here was another added difficulty, for even if

---

[1] This memoir of Botta began in the *Journal Asiatique*, Mai, 1847, and continued until Mars, 1848. It was published entire under the title *Mémoire sur l'écriture cunéiforme Assyrienne*, par M. Botta, Consul de France à Mossul. Paris, 1848. For a rather more detailed account of Botta's method in this investigation see Hommel, *Geschichte*, pp. 94, 95, and Kaulen, *Assyrien und Babylonien*, 5te Aufl., pp. 137, 138.

14

one should learn the meaning of these ideograms, how would it ever be possible to learn the word itself, or, to speak loosely for the moment, its pronunciation? That was a problem, surely, and the means for its solution did not appear at that time, nor for many days. Botta's work went on, however, without this most desirable knowledge, and he finally picked out the words for king, land, people, and a few others of less importance, but still could not spell the words out in Roman characters. He could set down a sign and say, "There, that means '*land*,' but I absolutely do not know how the Assyrians read it." With knowledge so defective as this Botta naturally did not attempt any complete translations. He had, however, made a useful contribution in positive directions, and a still more useful one negatively by showing how untenable were some of the old alphabetic theories.

Meantime de Saulcy went on with his struggles over the Persepolis and other inscriptions of the Achæmenian kings. He published some papers which unhappily reached no successful result. This has brought him somewhat under the ban of the unthinking, who themselves never dare make a mistake, and hence never accomplish anything. De Saulcy made the mistakes, soon perceived them, and went on cheerfully to repair them. He had also been working at Egyptian, and had learned much in that school of the processes of decipherment. In this he was like Hincks, and

de Longperier seems also to have gained useful
hints in the same school. Now de Saulcy was
ready to take the daring step of attempting to
decipher and translate an entire inscription. This
was the first publication of an entire Assyrian
inscription, with a commentary justifying and explaining the method word by word. In this
paper de Saulcy set down one hundred and
twenty signs the meaning of which he thought he
knew, but the uncertainty was great, and even he
could hardly claim that he had resolved fairly the
difficulties which hung around the repetition of
signs for the same consonant.

What de Saulcy could not accomplish was
achieved by Hincks. In a remarkable paper on
the Khorsabad inscriptions, read June 25, 1849,[1]
Hincks showed how vowels were expressed along
with their consonants in the same sign. There
was, for example, a sign for RA, and another for
RI, and still another for RU. Then there was a
sign for AR, and presumably also for UR and
IR, though he did not fully and perfectly define
the last two. Here was an enormous gain, for to
all these separate signs de Saulcy had assigned
the meaning R. This paper was not fully completed until January 19, 1850, up to which time
Hincks continued to make additions and corrections to it. At its very end he added a few lines
of translation from Assyrian. This was indeed a

---

[1] *Transactions of the Royal Irish Academy*, vol. xxii, "Polite Literature,"
pp. 1, ff.

translation in a sense attained by no other interpreter. It gave first the Assyrian characters, then
an attempted transcription into Roman characters, and finally the almost complete and very
nearly correct translation. It is impossible to
read this paper at this late date without astonish-
ment at its grasp of fundamental principles, its
keen insight into linguistic form and life, and its
amazing display of powers of combination.

The year 1849 had ended well, and the year
1850 had begun with every sign of hope. Now
were even greater things in store. Layard's discoveries at Nineveh had begun to reach London,
where they could not fail to rouse afresh Assyrian
study, just as Botta's had done in France. It
was natural that the first man to avail himself of
the fresh material thus made accessible should be
Sir Henry Rawlinson. No man had suffered so
much in his efforts to secure copies of inscriptions, and now that he was again in London it is
not surprising that he should at once seize upon
the beautiful obelisk which Layard had brought
from the mound of Nimroud. In two papers
read January 19 and February 16 [1] Rawlinson gave
an elaborate and an acute handling of this great
inscription, concluding with a tentative translation
of those parts of it which appeared to his study to
give a reasonable sense. If we compare this work
of Rawlinson with the work of Hincks, it suffers
considerably by the comparison. Rawlinson, it is

---

[1] *Journal of the Royal Asiatic Society*, xii, pp. 401, ff.

true, has often hit the true sense of a passage,
more often he has even presented a smooth translation which late study has gone far to justify.
On the other hand, he did not give text, transcription, *and* translation together, as Hincks had
done, and it was therefore impossible for students
who could not examine the original to criticise,
verify, or disprove the values he assigned to the
characters. It is clear that without this there can
never be definite, determined progress in any work
of interpretation. Nevertheless, though the means
for this had not been given by Rawlinson in his
translation, he had discussed a number of words,
printing the sign with its transcription and translation, and thereby supplying full material for the
use of later workers.

But even after this Rawlinson's great contribution to the decipherment was still to be
given. While scholars in Europe had been strug-
gling over the Persepolis inscriptions he was living alone in Baghdad, seeking every opportunity
to study the rocks at Behistun, and so obtain a
complete copy of the great trilingual inscription
of Darius. He had already published the Persian
part of this text; and Edwin Norris, with his permission, had issued the second (then called Median)
part. The most important part was the Babylonian, and the copy of this Rawlinson still held
in his own possession, laboriously working it over,
and trying to wring the last secret from the complex signs before he ventured upon its issue to

the world. For the length of this delay Rawlinson has been most unjustly blamed and criticised.[1]
That he was jealous of his fame is made clear
enough by the controversial letters of later years,
but in this he was well enough justified. Others
were at work in the effort to decipher these long-
lost records of old world peoples. They were
eager for the phantom of fame for themselves, and
few would be likely to take pains to conserve to
Rawlinson the fame which was justly due his
achievements, as some little compensation for the
loss of ease and for the privations and toils which
he had endured.

At last in 1851 appeared the long-expected,
eagerly-awaited *Memoir*.[2] Rawlinson published
one hundred and twelve lines of inscription in
cuneiform type, accompanied with an interlinear
transcription into Roman characters and a translation into Latin. To this was added a body of
notes in which many principles of grammar and of
interpretation were discussed, together with brief
lists of signs.

This *Memoir* of Rawlinson is justly to be considered an epoch-making production. Here at
last was a long and difficult inscription almost
completely translated, and here was the subject
of the Assyrian language carried even to the point

---

[1] See the allusions made to the subject by F. Max Müller in his *Biographical Essays*, pp. 284, 287, and elsewhere. These and other allusions in the same paper which seemed to reflect upon Rawlinson led to an
animated controversy in the *Athenæum* in 1884.

[2] *Journal of the Royal Asiatic Society*, vol. xiv, entire (1851).

of close disputing about grammatical niceties. It
was indeed the completion of a gigantic task pursued amid great difficulties, with a single eye.
Science and society have too little honored the
man who dared and executed this great task.

But great as was the result of Rawlinson's work
there was a sense in which it brought new difficulties and trials to the patient interpreters of
the texts. It became perfectly clear from his
studies that in Assyrian or Babylonian the same
sign did not always possess the same meaning.
Such signs as these Rawlinson called polyphones.
This was added difficulty upon difficulty. Here,
for example, was a sign which had the syllabic
values *Kal*, *Rib*, *Dan*, etc. This principle seemed
to some of Rawlinson's critics perfectly absurd.
In the popular mind, also, it did very much to
destroy all faith in the proposed interpretation of
the Babylonian inscriptions. "How," one man
would say, "do you know when this sign is to be
read *Kal*, or when *Rib*, or how do you know that
it does not mean *Dan?*" "Yes," adds another,
"how do you expect us to believe that a great people like the Assyrians and Babylonians ever could
have kept record with such a language, or with
such a system of writing as that? The whole thing
is impossible on the face of it." Of course such
criticism could make no impression upon Rawlinson himself; his knowledge had come to him by
painful steps and slow, and was not thus easy to
overthrow. It did, however, have weight in popu-

lar estimation, and the popular estimate cannot be despised or cast aside even by scholars. It had to be reckoned with, as Rawlinson knew well enough. It would be easy after a while to prove that his interpretation was correct—for that day he could wait patiently. It was, however, unfortunate that Rawlinson could not have set forth all his reasons and all his processes, together with all the critical apparatus. In this particular one must feel some disappointment over the great *Memoir*—in this at least it was not equal to the papers of Hincks.

While Rawlinson was now thought by many to have solved the problem in the main points, Hincks never relaxed for a moment his energetic pursuit of interpretation.

In July and August, 1850, he appears to have attended the meeting of the British Association at Edinburgh, where he circulated among the members a lithographed plate containing a number of signs registering forms of verbs. This paper, of which only a brief sketch was published,[1] has been almost overlooked in the history of the progress in Assyrian research. It is, however, of great importance. It shows that Hincks had gone beyond the point of mere guessing at the meanings of sentences, and had reached the point of studying the grammar of the language which was in his

---

[1] *Report of the Twentieth Meeting of the British Association for the Advancement of Science*, held at Edinburgh in July and August, 1850. London, 1851, p. 140, with plate at the end.

hands. In this field he was soon to excel all others, and lay deep and solid foundations of Assyrian grammar.

During the year 1851 Hincks appears to have published nothing, and was then probably engaged in a study of all the material that was accessible. In the next year he published a list of two hundred and fifty-two Assyrian characters, the rules of which he discussed separately.[1] This paper marks an extraordinary advance over all that had gone before. He now applies no longer the old methods of decipherment alone, but adds to this method a new and far more delicate one. He analyzes grammatical forms, and shows how a root appears in different forms according to its use in different conjugations. By this means he is able to test the values proposed and to verify them. In this paper, also, he showed that Assyrian possessed a most elaborate system of writing. There were first signs for single vowels, such as a, i, u. Secondly there were simple syllabic characters, such as ab, ib, ub, ba, bi, bu; thirdly there were complex syllabic characters, such as bar, ban, rab, etc.

Meantime Jules Oppert had returned from Babylonia and soon after visited England to see the British Museum collections. He was present at the meeting of the British Association at Glasgow in 1855, and there heard Sir Henry Rawlin-

---

[1] *On the Assyrio-Babylonian Phonetic Characters*, by the Rev. Edward Hincks, D.D. *Transactions of the Royal Irish Academy*, vol. xxii, part ii, " Polite Literature," pp. 293, ff.

son's account of the excavations at Birs Nimroud,
and himself spoke upon the results of his own
work in Babylonia.[1]
The workers were now increasing in numbers,
for Oppert was a great accession in Paris, after
his two years of absence, and in England there
was a new accession in the person of Fox Talbot,
a remarkably gifted man. But with all the new
workers in Ireland, France, and England, who
gave in their adhesion to the principles and the
results of decipherment, there were many who de-
rided or who doubted the whole matter. Often
before had doubts been expressed about the
translations, and the investigators passed quietly
on and paid no attention. H. Fox Talbot was,
however, in the fresh enthusiasm of his scholastic
life, unwilling longer to hear these doubts without
some effort to dissipate them. He therefore devised a novel and striking plan. Rawlinson was
now about to publish for the trustees of the British Museum lithographic copies of selected Assyrian inscriptions. He had already copied and
had lithographed the contents of a cylinder, which
he asserted contained the name Tiglath-pileser.
An advance copy of this lithograph was sent to
Fox Talbot, who at once made a translation of the
parts which he could readily make out. This
translation he put in a packet, carefully sealed, and

----

[1] *Report of the Twenty-fifth Meeting of the British Association for the Advancement of Science*, held at Glasgow in September, 1855. London, 1856, pp. lxxii, 148, 149.

sent to the Royal Asiatic Society, accompanied
by a letter the purpose of which appears clearly in
the following extracts:

"Having been favored with an early copy of
the lithograph of this inscription by the liberality
of the trustees of the British Museum and of Sir
H. Rawlinson, I have made from it the translation
which I now offer to the society. A few words
will explain my object in doing so:

"Many persons have hitherto refused to believe
in the truth of the system by which Dr. Hincks
and Sir H. Rawlinson have interpreted the Assyrian writings, because it contains many things
entirely contrary to their preconceived opinions.
For example, each cuneiform group represents a
syllable, but not always the same syllable; sometimes one and sometimes another. To which it
is replied that such a license would open the door
to all manner of uncertainty; that the ancient Assyrians themselves, the natives of the country,
could never have read such a kind of writing, and
that, therefore, the system cannot be true, and
the interpretations based upon it must be falla-
cious."[1]

This was the situation as Talbot apprehended it,
and he suggested that his translation be kept sealed
until Sir Henry Rawlinson's should be published,
and then that the two versions be compared. If
then the two were found in substantial agreement,
it would go far to convince the doubting, as each

---

[1] *Journal of the Royal Asiatic Society*, xviii, p. 150.

translation would have been made entirely independently of the other. When this communication was read before the Society Sir Henry Rawlinson moved that measures be taken to carry out Mr. Talbot's plan upon even a greater scale than he had purposed. It was determined to request Sir Henry Rawlinson, Edward Hincks, and Jules Oppert to send to the society, under sealed covers, translations of this same inscription. These translations were then to be opened and compared in the presence of the following committee: The Very Rev. the Dean of St. Paul's (Dr. Milman), Dr. Whewell, Sir Gardner Wilkinson, Mr. Grote, the Rev. W. Cureton, and Prof. H. H. Wilson.

Sir Henry Rawlinson furnished an almost complete version, but neither Dr. Hincks nor Dr. Oppert had had time to complete theirs. They sent in, however, enough for effective comparison. The versions were found indeed to be in closest correspondence, and the committee reported that:

"The coincidences between the translations, both as to the general sense and verbal rendering, were very remarkable. In most parts there was a strong correspondence in the meaning assigned, and occasionally a curious identity of expression as to particular words. Where the versions differed very materially each translator had in many cases marked the passage as one of doubtful or unascertained signification. In the interpretation of numbers there was throughout a singular correspondence."

The examiners then drew up tables of coincidences and of variations, and the Royal Asiatic Society published all four translations side by side.

The effect in Great Britain of this demonstration was great and widespread. It gradually became clear to the popular mind that the Assyrian inscriptions had really been read, and the popular mind in Great Britain is a force in science as in politics. The results of its influence would soon appear.

With this popular demonstration the task of interpreting the Assyrian and Babylonian inscriptions may properly be regarded as having reached an assured position. It was indeed necessary that all the work from the very beginning of Grotefend's first attempts at decipherment of the Persepolis inscriptions should be tested by fresh minds. This testing it secured as man after man came to the fore as a student of Assyriology. The ground was, however, fully gained and completely held. Assyrian study was able to take its place by the side of older sisters in the universities of the world. The material which Botta had sent to Paris was being quickly read, and papers dealing with its historic results were appearing almost weekly. In England the inscriptions which had been sent home from the excavations of Layard, Loftus, Taylor, and especially Rassam, were yielding up their secrets. It could not be long until popular opinion would demand that the excava-

tions be resumed.   At this time, however, workers
were busy securing the results of previous expeditions.

In the midst of all these efforts at decipherment
there began a movement destined to influence
greatly the progress of Assyrian studies in England.   On the 18th of November, 1870, there met
in the rooms of Mr. Joseph Bonomi, Lincoln's Inn
Fields, a company of men summoned by him and
by Dr. Samuel Birch, of the British Museum.
They were bidden " to take into consideration the
present state of archæological research, and, if it
appeared desirable, to institute an association for
directing the course of future investigations, and
to preserve a record of materials already obtained,
an association whose special objects should be
to collect from the fast-perishing monuments of
the Semitic and cognate races illustrations of their
history and peculiarities; to investigate and sys-
tematize the antiquities of the ancient and mighty
empires and primeval peoples, whose records are
centered around the venerable pages of the Bible."
As the result of this preliminary conference a
public meeting was convened at the rooms of the
Royal Society of Literature on the 9th of December, 1870, at which time the Society of Biblical
Archæology was formed.   Dr. Samuel Birch was
chosen president, and Mr. W. R. Cooper, secretary,
while Sir Henry Rawlinson, the Right Hon. W. E.
Gladstone, and Dean R. Payne Smith were vice
presidents.   Among the earliest list of members

were found Edwin Norris, Hormuzd Rassam, W. H. Fox Talbot, Rev. A. H. Sayce, and George Smith. The society was successful from the very beginning of its existence, its influence upon Assyrian and Babylonian study being particularly noticeable. The first volume of *Transactions* was issued in December, 1871, and in it Fox Talbot wrote on " An Ancient Eclipse " (in Assyria), and George Smith contributed an elaborate paper on " The Early History of Babylonia." In a short time the society's publications became the chief depository of investigations made by English scholars in the books of the Assyrians and Babylonians.

CHAPTER VII.

THE DECIPHERMENT OF SUMERIAN [1] AND OF VANNIC.

THE first students who attempted to decipher the ancient Persian inscriptions made much of the difficulty of the cuneiform characters. They were so totally unlike any other form of writing that even while men were busy in the effort to find out their meaning disputes began as to their origin. If the signs had looked like rude pictures of objects, as did Egyptian hieroglyphics, there would have been some clue to their origin, but during the decipherment process no one could discern any such resemblance. When the decipherment of Assyrian began men wondered still more as to the inventors or discoverers of the strangely complicated signs. When Assyrian was finally read it became clear to several investigators almost simultaneously that it belonged to the Semitic

---

[1] The history of the Sumerian discoveries and disputes has been written by Weissbach (*Die Sumerische Frage*, von F. H. Weissbach, Leipzig, 1898) in so masterly fashion that all who now study this interesting and important episode in cuneiform research can hope for nothing more than the position of gleaners, and may be pardoned if they sometimes doubt whether even a single full head of grain remains. It were pedantic to attempt to do the work all over again without drawing upon his unrivaled collection of materials, and this chapter therefore depends very much upon him, and hearty acknowledgment is here made of the fact. It attempts to seize upon the salient points and emphasize them, but students who wish to follow the minute discussions, unsuitable for a book of this character, must have recourse to Weissbach.

family of languages. That discovery intensified the difficulty concerning its method of writing. In 1850 Edward Hincks called attention[1] to the fact that, though Assyrian was a Semitic tongue, yet was its script totally unlike that used by any of the related languages. He suggested that the script was related to the Egyptian, and put forth the hypothesis that it was invented by an Indo-European people, who had been in contact with Egyptians and had borrowed something from their method of writing.

Shortly afterward (1853) Rawlinson wrote to the Royal Asiatic Society[2] announcing the discovery of a number of inscriptions "in the Scythian language," which he thought were related to the Median texts of the Persepolis inscriptions. He pronounced these new inscriptions to be older than the Persepolis inscriptions, and also older than the dynasty of Nebuchadrezzar, and argued that the Scythians were in possession of the western country before the Semites appeared. He was clearly of the opinion that he had found inscriptions written in cuneiform characters, but in a non-Semitic language. He seems, in a word, to be moving toward the idea that these Scythians had invented the cuneiform method of writing. This view was propounded in the

---

[1] *Report of the Twentieth Meeting of the British Association for the Advancement of Science*, 1850. *Transactions of the Sections*, p. 140. See also *Transactions of the Royal Irish Academy*, vol. xxii, "Polite Literature," p. 295 (dated November 24, 1852).

[2] *Athenæum*, 1853, p. 228.

15

very next year by Oppert,[1] who attempted to show how this assumed Scythian script had passed over into the hands of the Assyrians.

Rawlinson was now busily engaged in the investigation of the new problem, and on December 1, 1855, was able to report substantial progress to the Royal Asiatic Society.[2] He had been studying so-called "Scythian" inscriptions as old as the thirteenth century B. C., and he found the same language in the left columns of the Assyrian syllabaries. These syllabaries he explained as consisting of comparative alphabets, grammars, and vocabularies of the Scythian and Assyrian languages. His theory now was that these Babylonian Scythians were known as Accadians. They were the people who had built the cities and founded the civilization of Babylonia. The Semites had merely entered into their labors, and had adopted from them the cuneiform system of writing. The language of the Accadians he thought more closely related to the Mongolian and Manchu type than to any others of the Turanian languages.

Hincks had meantime been studying some small bilingual texts and was prepared to state some of the peculiarities of the newly found Accadian language.[3] He observed, in the first place, that

---

[1] *Athenæum français,* 3, p. 991, ff., October 21, 1854.

[2] *Athenæum,* 1855, p. 1438.

[3] *Zeitschrift der Deutschen Morgenländischen Gesellschaft,* x, p. 516, ff. (1856).

verbs were entirely unchanged in all persons and numbers, while the substantives formed a plural by the addition of *ua* or *wa*. He found also postpositions where we should use prepositions, and this was a resemblance to the Turanian languages, though he would not go so far as Rawlinson in saying to which one of them Accadian seemed most nearly related. A year later Hincks[1] abandoned the name Accadian, preferring to call it by some such name as Old Chaldean. This was his last contribution to the investigation of the inscriptions and the languages which they expressed. On December 3, 1866, he died, leaving behind an imperishable record of painstaking labor, accurate scholarship, and amazing fertility and resourcefulness of mind. To the new science of Assyriology he had made more contributions of permanent value than perhaps any other among the early decipherers. The death of Hincks left Jules Oppert as the leader in the work of unraveling the tangled threads of the new language.

In 1869 Oppert read a learned paper[2] on the origin of the Chaldeans, in which he gave the name Chaldean or Sumerian as the name of the language which Rawlinson had called Accadian. The name Sumerian was judged by many to be more suitable and gradually came into use, though Accadian is even yet used by some schol-

---

[1] *Atlantis*, iv, 57, ff.

[2] *Comptes rendus de la Société française de numismatique et d'archéologie*, i, 73, ff.

ars, while for a short time the phrase Sumero-Accadian was in vogue.

Up to this time the study of Accadian or Sumerian had been carried on very largely along historical and geographical lines. No single text had been studied, expounded, and translated until 1870, when Professor A. H. Sayce[1] devoted to a small inscription of Dungi the most elaborate philological exegesis. The words in Accadian were here compared one by one with words of similar phonetic value in more than a score of languages and dialects, and for the first time Accadian loan words were recognized in Assyrian. This paper marked a distinct advance in the study of Sumerian, at the same time that it indicated the position attained by his predecessors in the new study. Sayce had proved a worthy successor of Hincks in philological insight, and had contributed much to the grammatical study of Sumerian. He was speedily followed in this by Oppert, who contributed more grammatical material in two excellent papers.[2]

Up to this time none had dared to compile a Sumerian grammar, though material was rapidly accumulating. But in 1873 Lenormant began to issue the second series of his *Lettres assyriologiques*,[3] the first part of which contained a com-

---

[1] " On an Akkadian Seal," *Journal of Philology*, iii, 1, ff., 1871.

[2] *Journal Asiatique*, sér. i, 113, ff., and *Mémoires du I Congrès intern. des Orientalistes*, ii, 216, ff. Paris, 1876.

[3] *Lettres assyriologiques*, II Série : *Études accadiennes*, T. i, en 4 parties. Paris, 1874.

plete and systematic grammar of Sumerian. In the section relating to phonetics Lenormant noted the correspondence between *ng* and *m*, and identified *Sumer* (= Sungiri) with *Sennār*, *Shinar* (Gen. x, 10), *Sāmarrah* (Abu 'l-farag, Hist. dyn., ed. Pococke, p. 18), *Sumere* (Amm. Marc. 25, 6). The second part of this book was wholly given up to paradigms, while the third contained an extensive list of cuneiform signs. The fourth and last part was given over to a long discussion of the name of the language, in which Lenormant learnedly opposed Oppert's name of Sumerian, and contended for the older name Accadian. The whole book would in itself make a considerable scholarly reputation, and it was followed by another in an astonishing brief space of time. In this ¹ Lenormant was not directly concerned with the Sumerian language, but in two chapters, entitled " *The People of Accad* " and " *The Turanians in Chaldea and in Western Asia*," he again entered upon the difficult subject. He had now advanced to the view that the Accadian language, as he still insisted upon calling it, must be classified in the Ural-altaic family and considered as the type of a special group. In certain particulars he judged it to have most affinity with the Ugro-finnic, in others with the Turkish languages.

In spite of all that has been achieved by the English and French investigators the subject was

---

¹ Lenormant, *La Magie chez les Chaldéens et les origines accadiennes.* Paris, 1874–75.

still filled with difficulty, and when Eberhard
Schrader, later justly called "the father of Assyriology in Germany," wrote his important book on
the Assyro-Babylonian inscriptions[1] he almost
avoided it. In this book he must needs refer to
the language which appeared in the left column
of the syllabaries, but he did not enter into the
vexed questions in dispute between Lenormant
and Oppert. Two years later, however, in a review[2] of Lenormant he definitely took sides with
him against Oppert and adopted Accadian instead
of Sumerian. In this he was followed by his distinguished pupil, Friedrich Delitzsch,[3] who contributed some further explanations of the syllabaries.

When the year 1873 drew to its close scholars
had reason to feel that the question which had
puzzled Hincks in 1850 was settled. They were
able to say that all scholars were agreed upon two
propositions,[4] namely, 1. The cuneiform method
of writing was not invented by the Semitic Babylonians or Assyrians. 2. It was invented by a
people who spoke a language which belonged to
the agglutinative forms of human speech. There

---

[1] Schrader,Eberhard, Die assyrisch-babylonischen Keilinschriften. Kritische
Untersuchung der Grundlagen ihrer Entzifferung. Zeitschrift der Deutschen
Morgenländischen Gesellschaft, xxvi, pp. 1–392, 1872; also separately.
Leipzig, 1872.

[2] Jenaer Literatur-Zeitung, 1, Rec. No. 200, 1874, quoted by Weissbach.

[3] Assyrische Studien, Heft 1. Assyrische Thiernamen mit vielen Excursen und einem assyrischen und akkadischen Glossar. Leipzig, 1874.

[4] So formulated by Weissbach, op. cit., p. 24.

was indeed still a dispute about the name of the new language whether it should be called Acca-dian or Sumerian, and there were numerous questions concerning its character, age, literature, and history which might occupy the skill and patience of investigators for a long time, but the main question was settled.

But alas for the danger of overassurance! While Oppert and Lenormant were disputing concerning the name of this ancient language, there lived in Paris an orientalist, Joseph Halévy, who held distinguished rank as a scholar in the difficult field of Semitic epigraphy. Halévy was not known as an Assyriologist at all, but he had followed every detail of the process of deciphering Sumerian, had watched every discussion of its grammatical peculiarities, and had never from the beginning believed in its existence! On July 10, 1874, the Académie des Inscriptions listened to the first of a series of papers on the Sumerian question from him. Other papers followed on July 24 and August 14.[1] In these Halévy discussed three questions:[2] 1. Granting its existence, does the Accadian language belong to the Turanian family? 2. May the existence of a Turanian people in Babylonia be conceded? 3. Do these so-called Accadian texts present a real language distinct from Assyrian, or

---

[1] *Comptes rendus de l'Acad. des inscr.*, iv, sér. 2, 201, 209, 215; see also pp. 261-264. The entire paper is published in *Journal Asiatique*, vii, sér. 3, 461, ff., 1874.

[2] So stated by Weissbach, *op. cit.*, p. 25.

merely an ideographic system of writing invented by the Assyrians? As Weissbach has pointed out,[1] the order of these questions is strange and un-methodical. Halévy should have begun with the third question, and then passed on to the other two. But, whatever may be said of the method, there cannot be two opinions as to the consummate ability of the discussion. Halévy's mind was stored with learning philological, historical, and ethno-logical; he was a dialectician superior to Lenor-mant or Oppert; he had the keenness of a ready debater in searching out the weakest places in the arguments of his opponents and the skill of an ex-pert swordsman in puncturing them. It was a most daring act for a man not yet known as an Assyri-ologist to oppose single-handed the united forces of scholarship in the department. Halévy had sought to prove no less a thesis than that all scholars from the beginning of the investigation by Hincks and Rawlinson had been deceived. The signs which they had supposed represented the syllables or words of a language spoken in Babylonia in the very beginning of recorded time were to him but the fanciful product of the fertile minds of Assyrian priests. The cuneiform writing was the invention of Semites, long used by Semites, and the Sumerian words so called were only cryptic signs, invented for mystification and especially used in incantations or religious formulæ.

---

[1] *Ibid.*, p. 25.

When Halévy's papers were published not a single Assyriologist was convinced by them, and only one anonymous writer[1] ventured to accept his conclusions. On the other hand, every Assyriologist of note who had had any share in the previous discussions was soon in the field with papers attacking Halévy's positions or defending the ground which but a short time before had seemed so sure as to need no defense. In a few months Lenormant[2] had written a large volume in opposition, while Schrader was content with an able and much briefer paper.[3] Delitzsch, in a review[4] of Lenormant's book, also ranged himself with them, while Oppert,[5] opposing Halévy with all his learning and acuteness, nevertheless continued to argue for his own peculiar tenets against Lenormant, Schrader, and Delitzsch.

The issue was now squarely joined, and earnest and able though the replies to Halévy had undoubtedly been, nevertheless, it must be said in justice that they had not driven him from the

---

[1] This unknown writer wrote in *Ausland*, Jhg. 47, 941, ff., 1874. I have not succeeded in finding this paper, and quote it on the authority of Weissbach, *op. cit.*, p. 27, footnote 1.

[2] *La Langue primitive de la Chaldée et les idiomes touraniens. Étude de philologie et d'histoire, suivie d'un glossaire accadien*, pp. vii, 455. Paris, 1875.

[3] *Ist das Akkadische der Keilinschriften eine Sprache oder eine Schrift?* Zeitschrift der Deutschen Morgenländischen Gesellschaft, xxix, pp. 1, ff., 1876.

[4] *Lit. Centralblatt*, 1875, column 1075, ff.

[5] *Etudes sumériennes. 1. Sumérien ou accadien? 2. Sumérien ou rien?* Journal Asiatique, vii, sér. 5, 267, ff., 442, ff., 1875.

field. To Lenormant Halévy[1] had replied promptly, and had done much to diminish the effect of that scholar's attack upon his position. The defenders of the existence of the Sumerian language did not agree among themselves on many points, and wherever they differed Halévy skillfully opposed the one to the other in his argument. In 1876 he read before the Académie des Inscriptions, and afterward published, a paper on the Assyrian origin of the cuneiform writing,[2] in which he modified his views somewhat, yet strenuously insisting that the entire system was Semitic. This paper was then reprinted, along with the former publication of 1874, in book form,[3] and with this he began to win some adherents to his views, the earliest being W. Deecke[4] and Moritz Grünwald.[5] That was at least a slight gain, and he was encouraged to press on with fresh arguments.

Meanwhile the lines of those who still believed in the existence of the ancient tongue were closing up. Gradually Oppert's name, Sumerian, was accepted by scholars, foremost among whom were the pupils of Delitzsch, Fritz Hommel, and Paul

---

[1] *La prétendue Langue d'Accad est-elle touranienne?* Réponse à M. F. Lenormant, 31 pp. Paris, 1875. Read before the Académie des Inscriptions November 26, 1875.

[2] *Nouvelle Considérations sur le syllabaire cunéiforme, Journal Asiatique,* vii, sér. 7, 201, ff., 1876.

[3] *Recherches critiques sur l'origine de la civilisation babylonienne,* 268 pp. Paris, 1876.

[4] *Lit. Centralblatt,* 1877, 456, ff.

[5] *Ausland,* Jhg. 49, 584, ff., 1876. Quoted from Weissbach, *op. cit.,* p. 39, footnote 3.

Haupt, while Lenormant conceded a point and called it the language of Sumer and Accad.[1] In 1879 there appeared a small book[2] by Paul Haupt which may truly be said to open a new era in the whole discussion. Haupt was then a young man of extraordinary gifts, and his handling of the Sumerian family laws showed how to treat a bilingual text in a thoroughly scientific manner. There can be no doubt that Haupt had done much to stem the tide which was threatening to set toward Halévy's position. Nevertheless, in 1880, Stanislas Guyard[3] came over to Halévy, and in 1884 Henri Pognon,[4] these being the first Assyriologists to embrace his views. Between these two dates De Sarzec[5] had been carrying on his excavations at Tello, in southern Babylonia, and had been sending to the Louvre most interesting specimens of his discoveries. In 1884 the first part of his book[6] containing copies of the newly found inscriptions appeared. To Sumerian scholars there seemed no doubt whatever that these inscriptions were written in the Sumerian language. Halévy at once began to explain their strangely sounding

---

[1] *Journal Asiatique*, vii, sér. 12, 378, f.

[2] *Die Sumerischen Familiengesetze in Keilschrift, Transcription, und Uebersetzung, nebst ausführlichem Commentar und zahlreichen Excursen. Eine Assyriologische Studie*, von Dr. Paul Haupt, pp. viii, 75. Leipzig, 1879.

[3] *Revue critique*, nouv., sér. ix, 425, ff. (31 Mai, 1880).

[4] *Journal Asiatique*, viii, sér. 2, 413, ff. *Revue crit.*, 1884, ii, 47.

[5] See below, pp. 236, ff.

[6] *Découvertes en Chaldée*. Publ. par les soins de Léon Heuzey. 1. Paris, 1884.

words as in reality Semitic, and in 1883, at the
International Congress of Orientalists in Leiden,
presented a most elaborate paper in which he presented his theory in its fullest and most scientific
form.[1] Halévy was not convinced that his views
were incorrect by any of the arguments already
advanced, neither did the appearance of the De
Sarzec monuments and inscriptions move him.
His efforts became more earnest, and Guyard's
support was likewise full of vigor. Nevertheless,
the cause was not gaining, but in the larger view
really losing. It was significant that the younger
school of Assyriologists were strongly supporting
the Sumerian view. Jensen, who was later to be
known as one of the most eminent Assyriologists
of his time, opposed Halévy's view in his very
first work,[2] as did also Henrich Zimmern[3] whose
first paper was of even greater importance. Carl
Bezold[4] likewise joined with the older school.

But encouragement of the very highest kind
was even now almost in Halévy's hands. In
some notes added to Zimmern's first book[5]

---

[1] *Actes du 6ième Congrès international des orientalistes, tenu en 1883 à
Leide,* ii, 535, ff. Leide, 1885. Halévy's paper is entitled "*Aperçu grammatical de l'allographie assyro-babylonienne.*"

[2] *De incantamentorum sumerico-assyriorum seriei quae dicitur shurbu
tabula VI. Zeitschrift für Keilschriftforschung,* i, 279-322; ii, 15-61;
ii, 306-311; 416-425. *Zeitschrift für Assyriologie,* i, 52-68. Also partly
reprinted as dissertation. Monachii, 1885.

[3] *Babylonische Busspsalmen.* Leipzig, 1885.

[4] *Kurzgefasste Ueberblick über die Babylonisch-Assyrische Literatur.*
Leipzig, 1886.

[5] *Bab. Bussps,* pp. 113, ff.

Delitzsch took occasion to speak in warm terms of Halévy's very important contributions to the subject, and while not yet ranging himself at his side, declared that his view deserved very close examination. Well might the great French orientalist . rejoice over such a promised accession. When the first part of Delitzsch's Assyrian dictionary[1] appeared every page contained proof that in his case Halévy's long and courageous fight had won. Delitzsch had joined the still slender ranks of the anti-Accadians, and when his Assyrian grammar appeared a whole paragraph[2] was devoted to a most incisive attack upon the Sumerian theory. The accession of Delitzsch is the high-water mark of Halévy's theory. The morrow would bring a great change.

Delitzsch's grammar was received with enthusiasm, as it well deserved to be, but the anti-Sumerian paragraph was severely handled by its critics. In like manner the anti-Sumerian position of the dictionary met with a criticism which indicated that even the great name of Delitzsch was not sufficient to increase confidence in Halévy's cause. Sayce, in a review no less remarkable for the range of its learning than for its scientific spirit, protested against Delitzsch's method. Lehmann, in a big book devoted to the inscriptions of

---

[1] *Assyrisches Wörterbuch zur gesammten bisher veröffentlichen Keilschrift-literatur*, u. s. w. 1st part. Leipzig, 1887.

[2] *Assyrische Grammatik.* Leipzig, 1889, § 25. English edition same date.

a late Assyrian king[1] devoted an entire chapter[2] to
the Sumerian question. In it the whole subject was
treated with a freshness and an ability that left
little to be desired. Though some minor criticism
was passed upon it, none but Halévy dared deny
that it marked a step forward in the process of
tearing down his elaborate theories.

In the very same year in which Delitzsch's
grammar appeared Bezold made a brilliant discovery in finding upon an Assyrian tablet the
Sumerian language mentioned.[3] In his announcement of this new fact Bezold writes banteringly,
asking Halévy to permit the language to live, as
the Assyrians had mentioned it by name. Beneath
this humorous phrase there lies, however, a quiet
note of recognition that the mention was important, though not conclusive as to the main
question.

Almost every month after the year 1892
brought some new material to be considered and
related to the ever-debated question. The newer
discoveries of De Sarzec, the wonderful results of
the American expedition to Nippur, the editing of
texts found by previous explorers—all these had
some link with the Sumerian question. In 1897
Professor Delitzsch, borne down by the weight of
fresh evidence, abandoned Halévy's side and once
more allied himself to the Sumeriologists. As he

[1] *Shamashshumukin König von Babylon*, von C. F. Lehmann. Leipzig, 1892.
[2] *Ibid.*, chap. iv, pp. 57–173.
[3] *Zeitschrift für Assyriologie*, iv, pp. 434, f.

had been a great gain, so was he now even a greater loss. Halévy indeed gained others to his side, but none bore so famous a name. The school which he had founded was waning. Though the debate still continues, it has no longer the same intensity. Year by year the question is less and less, " Was there a Sumerian language—were there Sumerians ? " and is more and more, " What was the Sumerian language—who were the Sumerians ? " Every year seems to justify Hincks, Rawlinson, and Oppert, the great masters who laid the foundations in this increasingly fruitful field.

The history of the study of cuneiform inscriptions is complicated by the number of different languages which used the wedge-shaped characters. We have already shown that the cuneiform inscriptions at Persepolis and Behistun were in the Persian, Susian, and Assyrian languages, and we have also set forth at length the long discussion over the question of Sumerian, another language likewise written in the cuneiform characters. The use by four different peoples of wedge-shaped characters may well dispose the mind to accept the statement that still another people wrote their language in similar fashion.

The Armenians have preserved for us among their traditions of Semiramis the statement that she had at one time determined to build a new city in Armenia as the place of summer residence. " When she had seen the beauty of the country, the pureness of the air, the clearness of the fountains of water, and the murmuring of the swift-flowing rivers, she said: 'In such a balmy air, amid such beauty of water and of land, we must build a city and a royal residence that we may spend the one quarter of the year, which is summer, in the comfort of Armenia, and the other three quarters, during the cold weather, in Assyria.'"[1] Even so late as this present century scholars found the name Semiramis full of mystery and attraction, and were anxious to learn more about her great deeds. About the end of June, 1827 Fr. Ed. Schulz departed from Erzeroum determined to suffer any loss in the effort to find the summer city of Semiramis. There is no need to say that he did not find it, but, like many another searcher, found something far more important. As he went along the borders of Lake Van, then almost unknown to Europeans, he turned in at the gates of the fascinating city of Van and began a search through the remains of its former greatness. Beneath the great citadel of Van was found a small chamber approached by a flight of twenty steps. Above these steps he found inscriptions in the cuneiform character carved in the face of the solid rock. When these had been carefully copied he sought elsewhere and was rewarded with the discovery of still

---

[1] *Des Moses von Chorene, Geschichte Gross-Armeniens, aus dem Armenischen übersetzt*, von Dr. M. Lauer. Regensburg, 1869, pp. 31, 32. There is an English translation of the *History of Armenia*, or rather the *Genealogical Account of Great Armenia*, of Moses of Chorene (about 430 A. D.), by Winston, London. 1736 4to, but it is not accessible to me.

others. In other places in the neighborhood he found more, until he had copied no less than forty-two inscriptions. Schulz was murdered, and when his papers were recovered and brought to Paris the inscriptions were splendidly reproduced by lithography, and published in 1840.[1] At this time the Persian decipherment had indeed been well begun, as had also Assyrian, but none were able to read the new inscriptions for which Schulz had given his life. They were exceedingly well copied, when the difficulties are considered, but so soon as an attempt was made to decipher them doubts arose as to their accuracy. It was soon found that three of the inscriptions were written by Xerxes, and were in Persian, Susian, and Babylonian, but the remaining thirty-nine were in some unknown language. In 1840 an inscription in this same language was found by Captain von Mühlbach near Isoglu, on the Euphrates, two hundred and fifty miles west of Van. The copies by Schulz as well as this new text came before the eyes of Grotefend in due course, and he was quick to discern that they did not belong to Assyrian kings. This negative conclusion was of some importance as a guidepost, but Grotefend was able to go no further. In 1847 Sir A. H. Layard found another inscription of the same

---

[1] *Journal Asiatique*, 3éme série, tome ix, 1840, pp. 257–323.

[2] *Monatsberichte über die Verhandlungen der Gesellschaft für Erdkunde zu Berlin*, i, pp. 70–75 ; also in *Original Papers read before the Syro-Egyptian Society of London*, i, 1, pp. 131, ff.

16

kind at Palu,[1] on the eastern bank of the Euphrates about one hundred and eighty miles from Van. It was now clear enough that this new language belonged to a people of some importance in the ancient world, whose civilization or dominion extended over a considerable territory.

There was in these facts an urgent call for some man able to decipher and translate the records and construct a grammar of the language in which they were written. Who should attempt this new problem but that marvelous decipherer of strange tongues, Dr. Edward Hincks? And two papers by him were read before the Royal Asiatic Society, December 4, 1847, and March 4, 1848.[2]

In these papers Hincks determined correctly the meaning of a large number of the characters; found the meaning of such ideographs as "people," "city," and the signification of several words. He further was able to show that the termination of the nominative singular and plural of substantives was "*s*," while the accusative ended in "*n*." He had thus perceived that the language was inflectional, and went on to argue erroneously that it was Indo-European, or Aryan, as he called it. He read the names of the kings as Niriduris, Skuina, Kinuas, and Arrasnis, but very shortly corrected them into Milidduris, Ishpuinish, Minuas, and Argistis, in which the error, chiefly in the

---

[1] Sayce, in *Journal of the Royal Asiatic Society*, new series, xiv, p. 378 (1882).

[2] Both papers are published in the *Journal of the Royal Asiatic Society*, ix, pp. 387–449 (1848).

first name, is very slight. It is difficult to exaggerate the importance of this work, but we may gain some idea of its value by comparing with it Rawlinson's note on the subject published two years later. "There are," says Rawlinson,[1] "it is well known, a series of inscriptions found at Van and in the vicinity. These inscriptions I name Armenian. They are written in the same alphabet that was used in Assyria, but are composed in a different language—a language, indeed, which, although it has adopted numerous words from the Assyrian, I believe to belong radically to another family, the Scythic. There are six kings of the Armenian line following in a line of direct descent. I read their names as: 1. Alti-bari; 2. Ari-mena; 3. Isbuin; 4. Manua; 5. Artsen; 6. Ariduri (?)." In the reading of these names Rawlinson is distinctly behind Hincks, as he was always less keen in the treatment of philological niceties.

For a long series of years Hincks had no successor in the work of decipherment. But every few years new inscriptions[2] were found written in the same language, and each one naturally increased the probability of a successful outcome of the efforts after decipherment.

In 1871 Lenormant[3] took up the task where Hincks and Rawlinson had laid it down. His

---

[1] *Journal of the Royal Asiatic Society*, xii, p. 475 (1850).

[2] A list is given by Sayce, *Journal of the Royal Asiatic Society*, new series, xiv, pp. 380, 381.

[3] *Lettres assyriologiques*, i, pp. 113-164 (1871).

method was scientific, and, like all his work, learned and searching. He first sketched the early history of Armenia, as he had learned its outlines from the Assyrian inscriptions. That was to be the historical basis of his work, and from it he hoped to extract useful geographical material which might help in the securing of names in the Vannic inscriptions. He proposed to call the language Alarodian (Herodotus, iii, 94; vii, 79), and argued that it was non-Aryan, and that its closest modern representative was Georgian. He pointed out that "*bi*" was the termination of the first person singular of the verb, and that *parubi* signified "I carried away."

In the next year Dr. A. D. Mordtmann[1] attacked the question and five years later returned to it again. He determined the meaning of twelve new words, and supplied a most valuable analysis of all the inscriptions, but did not succeed in the translation of a single one of them. Nevertheless, he had made a gain.

The next decipherer was Dr. Louis de Robert[2] (1876), who deliberately cast away all that had been gained by Hincks, Rawlinson, Lenormant, and Mordtmann, and set out afresh upon a totally wrong road. He tried to show that the

---

[1] *Entzifferung und Erklärung der armenischen Keilinschriften von Van und der Umgegend*, von Dr. A. D. Mordtmann. *Zeitschrift der Deutschen Morgenländischen Gesellschaft*, xxvi, pp. 465–696 (1872). *Ueber die Keilinschriften von Armenien. Ibid.*, xxxi, pp. 406–438 (1877).

[2] *Étude philologique sur les inscriptions cunéiformes de l'Armenie.* Paris, 1876.

inscriptions were written in the language of
Assyria. The result was nothing, and the next
worker must return to the methods of the old
masters.

Meantime new inscriptions were constantly coming to light. Bronze shields with the name of
Rusas were found by Sir A. H. Layard, and excavations near Lake Van by Hormuzd Rassam unearthed still more inscribed objects in bronze.
Layard also laid a firmer foundation for future
work by recopying more accurately all the inscriptions for which Schulz had given his life.[1]

On the 9th of April, 1880, M. Stanislas Guyard
presented to the Société Asiatique in Paris[2] "some
observations upon the cuneiform inscriptions of
Van." He had noticed at the end of a good many
of the inscriptions a phrase in which occurred the
word "tablet." He remembered that Assyrian
inscriptions frequently ended with an imprecatory
formula, heaping curses upon whomsoever should
destroy this tablet, and he suggested that here
was a formula exactly the same. When he had
tested this new clew he found that the words
thus secured seemed to fit exceedingly well into
other passages, and his guess seemed thereby confirmed.

It is curious that the very same clew as that
followed by Guyard had also independently been
discovered by Professor A. H. Sayce, who had

[1] *Journal of the Royal Asiatic Society*, xiv, p. 384.
[2] *Journal Asiatique*, 7 sér., tom. xv, pp. 540–543, Mai–Juin, 1880.

been working for several years upon these texts. He had fortunately found out a few more words than Guyard and was able to push on farther as well as more rapidly. The words in which he began to explain his method to the Royal Asiatic Society were strong, but every one was justified by the issue. He says: "The ideographs so freely employed by the Vannic scribes had already showed me that not only the characters but the style and phraseology of the inscriptions were those of the Assyrian texts of the time of Asshur-natsir-pal and Shalmaneser II. I believe, therefore, that I have at last solved the problem of the Vannic inscriptions and succeeded in deciphering them, thereby compiling both a grammar and vocabulary of the language in which they are written. Owing to the number of the texts, their close adherence to their Assyrian models, and the plentiful use of ideographs, it will be found that the passages and words which still resist translation are but few, and that in some instances their obscurity really results from the untrustworthiness of the copies of them which we possess."[1]

The long paper which followed these words began with a survey of the geography, history, and theology of the Vannic people, derived very largely from Assyrian sources, but tested and expanded from the native sources which he had just deciphered. After this followed an account of the method of writing, an outline of the grammar,

---

[1] *Journal of the Royal Asiatic Society*, new series, xiv, pp. 377–732.

an analysis, and a translation of the inscriptions. It was a most remarkable piece of work, as surprising because of its learning as because of its proof of a perfect genius for linguistic combination. It reminds the reader continually of Hincks at his best. The effect of its publication was instantaneous. Guyard[1] reviewed it at length, offering corrections and additions, yet showing plainly enough that the work was successful. Further contributions to the subject were made by Professor D. H. Müller, of Vienna, who had been studying the texts independently both of Sayce and Guyard. More inscriptions also came to light, and in 1888 Professor Sayce was able to review the whole subject, accepting heartily some of the many emendations of his work which had been proposed, rejecting others, and so putting the capstone upon his work. The mystery of the inscriptions at Van was solved. When new texts in the same language should appear men might indeed dispute as to the name of the language whether to call it Vannic or Alarodian or Urartian or Chaldian, but they would at least be able to read it.

So rested the matter of the language of Van until 1892, when Dr. C. F. Lehmann[2] began a series of studies in the inscriptions which Sayce had deciphered, seeking to determine more closely a host of historical and geographical questions which grew out of them. He first demonstrated

---

[1] *Mélanges d'Assyriologie.* Paris, 1883.
[2] *Zeitschrift für Ethnologie*, 1892, pp. 131, ff.

that the people who had written many of these
texts were the same as the Chaldians (Χάλδοι, not
Chaldeans, who are Χάλδαιοι) of the Greeks. The
language was therefore to be called Chaldian, and
another difficulty was cleared up. Beginning in
1895, Dr. Waldemar Belck and Dr. C. F. Lehmann[1]
published a series of papers of great acuteness,
working out the life history of this old people, who
had thus been restored to present knowledge,
clearing up many points previously obscurely or
incorrectly set forth by Sayce.

In further pursuit of the studies thus begun
Drs. Belck and Lehmann[2] departed from Berlin in
the summer of 1898 for a journey through Persian
and Russian Armenia. They visited Van and carefully collated all the inscriptions previously found
by Schulz and others, and found new texts which
had been overlooked by all their predecessors.
New inscriptions of Assyrian kings, especially of
Tiglath-pileser I and Shalmaneser II, were found,
and by these, also, our knowledge of Chaldian history was increased. The results of this valuable
expedition are now being made known, and it
may be regarded as the concluding event in the
history of the decipherment of the Vannic inscriptions.

---

[1] *Ibid.*, 1895, pp. 578–616; 1896, pp. 302–308.

[2] *Sitzungsberichte der Königlich Preussischen Akademie der Wissenschaften zu Berlin*, 1899, pp. 116–120.

Zeitschrift für Ethnologie, 1898, pp. 227, 414–416, 522–527, 568–592;
1899, pp. 411–420.

CHAPTER VIII.

EXPLORATIONS IN ASSYRIA AND BABYLONIA, 1872-1900.

THE first impulse to excavations in Assyria was given by a German scholar who had established himself in Paris. Julius Mohl cheered on Botta to the work of excavation, and kept him encouraged while it dragged along. During all the time that Layard, Loftus, and their coadjutors worked in the field Mohl watched them from afar, and carefully noted their successes. He was now secretary of the Société Asiatique of Paris, and in his annual reports he told the society of all that had gone on in the great valley amid the graves of ancient cities. In his report for the year 1855 his note was distinctively sad. He recorded the fact that every single expedition which had been sent out to dig had laid down the work or had been recalled. That seemed to him a lamentable circumstance, for to his discerning eye the soil was underlaid with monuments recording the whole life of the vast empires which had held sway in Nineveh or in Babylon. He was impatient to have the excavations resumed, and he called on the governments to take steps to this end.

The future was to confirm Mohl's view fully, and even more than confirm it, of the vast treasures that lay buried. The time, however, for their excavation had not come in the year 1855. Neither governments nor free peoples would carry on excavations for antiquities that were mere unmeaning curiosities when they were found. That work must wait until the decipherment had reached a sure result, and until the work of translation had been so far popularized that the results should be generally known. As a former chapter has shown, the period of doubtful translations ended and the period of surely known results began in 1857. It was only necessary that these matters should be popularized, and that would require some time. This popularization was, fortunately, carried on chiefly, at least in England, by the great masters themselves. Rawlinson, Hincks, Talbot, Norris—a remarkable list of names, surely— these were the men who made known in popular papers or by lectures and addresses the great discoveries in Assyria. Some of these papers struck the old note of Shirley, and revealed the importance of Assyrian studies for the light they were sure to shed upon the Bible. That would be certain to arouse interest in Great Britain and, as before, might result in the beginning of more excavations. The sequel will show how wonderfully this very zeal for biblical study operated in the stimulating of Assyrian research.

A boy, George Smith by name, destined for the work of an engraver, read in the short spaces of his crowded days the magic words of Rawlinson and the other pioneers, and was moved to begin the study of Assyrian himself. As he himself witnessess,[1] he was first roused to definite study by the interest of biblical history, and with the purpose of doing something for it, he applied in 1866 to Sir Henry Rawlinson for permission to study the original copies, casts, or fragments of inscriptions belonging to the reign of Tiglathpileser. Rawlinson gladly gave the permission, and Smith went earnestly to work. His success was not great with these, but his industry was rewarded by the discovery of a new inscription of Shalmaneser with the name of Jehu upon it, by which he ascertained the year of Shalmaneser's reign in which Jehu had paid his tribute.[2] In this discovery, the first original work which Smith had done, there was one little hint of use to the Old Testament student. Smith had begun as he was to go on. After this discovery Sir Henry Rawlinson was so struck by the young man's success that he suggested his employment by the British Museum for work in the new Assyrian department. There he was established in the beginning of 1867, and

---

[1] *Assyrian Discoveries*, by George Smith. London, 1875, p. 9.

[2] Smith's report of his first discovery is so interesting in the history of Assyrian study that it is here reproduced entire :

"*Assyrian Inscription.* While examining part of the Assyrian collection in the British Museum I lately discovered a short inscription of Shalmaneser II, king of Assyria, in which it is stated that Jehu, king of Israel, sent him tribute in the eighteenth year of his reign. That he received tribute from Jehu is well known from the black obelisk inscription, but the date of the event has not been previously ascertained. This fact is of chronological interest. I may add that Jehu in this inscription is styled 'Son of Omri,' the same as on the black obelisk." Georg e Smith.—*Athenæum*, No. 2031, September 29, 1866, p. 410.

his success was immediate. In his own survey of his work in the museum Smith remembered most vividly the biblical discoveries, and these were they which gave him his first popular reputation and the opportunities of his life. He found on the texts names and notices of Azariah, king of Judah, Pekah, king of Israel, and Hoshea, king of Israel. These stirred his pulses and drove him on even at the peril of his health. The depletion of vital force through constant and difficult work was probably the ultimate cause of his early death, after the brilliant series of discoveries and explorations which were now before him. Smith possessed in unusual degree a gift for decipherment. While still feeling his way along the intricate mazes of cuneiform decipherment there came to the British Museum some copies of the then undeciphered Cypriote texts. Dr. Birch called his attention to them, and soon he was engaged in an attempt to read them. On November 7, 1871, he read a paper before the Society of Biblical Archæology " On the Reading of Cypriote Inscriptions." [1] The method which he used was similar to the plan of Grotefend, and it was applied with wonderful skill and with surprising results. He had picked out the word for king, though he knew no Greek with which to make comparisons, and had identified forty out of fifty odd characters. A man possessing genius of such order was sure to win fame in the new field of Assyriology.

---

[1] *Transactions of the Society of Biblical Archæology*, i, pp. 129, ff.

From 1867 to 1871 discovery followed discovery until Smith's edition of the Asshurbanapal inscriptions appeared. This volume made clear the immense gain to history from the discovery and decipherment of the Assyrian inscriptions, for it contained the accounts of the campaigns and of the building operations of Asshurbanapal. Yet, great as all this was, its influence fell far short of that of a discovery which Smith made in 1872. In that year, while working among some fragments brought home by Rassam, Smith picked out a broken clay tablet, upon which he soon read unmistakable parallels to the biblical account of the deluge. The piece thus found was soon followed by three duplicates and other lesser fragments. From these he ascertained that the part first found was the eleventh in a series of twelve tablets, and that it gave the history of a great hero whom Smith called Izdubar. He published the announcement of his discovery, and Asshurbanapal was forgotten, few probably thinking of the great king who had made the library out of which these newly found tablets had come. But England did not know how to be calm in the presence of such a discovery as this. When Smith had translated enough of the tablets to make a somewhat connected story of the deluge, as the Babylonians told it, he read a paper on the subject before the Society of Biblical Archæology on December 3, 1872. The meeting was large and enthusiastic. Sir Henry C. Rawlinson pre-sided, Smith presented his translation, and then enthusiasm had sway when it was pointed out by Dr. Birch that this had immense importance for the study of the Bible. Again was struck the old note of Shirley, and again that audience responded. Then Mr. Gladstone spoke, showing how valuable all these discoveries were for the study of the origins of Greek culture, which he said had come from the East by way of Phœnicia. This was appreciated, but it was not exactly what the company most desired to hear, and to that phase Mr. Gladstone's last sentence returned, concluding with the magic word "religion."[1] The cheers broke forth then with a good will, and at a late hour the company went away to spread abroad this marvelous story of the discovery of an early narrative which all thought illustrated, and many believed confirmed and corroborated, the biblical story in Genesis.

The government was urged at once to resume excavations on the site of Nineveh to find more material which might illustrate or confirm the biblical narrative. It did not or could not move instantly, and the public would not wait. The

---

[1] *The Times* (London), December 4, 1872, p. 7. The account of the meeting given above rests chiefly upon the report in *The Times* published the following day. Professor Sayce, however, is inclined to think that the order of addresses in the meeting was somewhat different. Though not present himself at the meeting, he had spent the afternoon with Mr. Smith, and later had a full account of the meeting from Dr. Birch. He believes that it was Mr. Gladstone who emphasized the importance of these discoveries in their bearing upon the Bible, and that Dr. Birch spoke last and not first.

proprietors of the *Daily Telegraph*, a widely circulated journal, moved by the editor, Edwin Arnold, perceived the opportunity and seized it. They offered a thousand guineas to pay the expenses of an expedition to Nineveh on condition that Smith should lead it, and send letters to the paper describing his experience and discoveries. On January 20, 1873, a month after Norris's death, Smith set out upon his enterprise, and on March 2 he reached Mosul, ready to begin excavations. He soon found that delays were the order of the day, and that the firman had not arrived. He therefore made a trip to Babylon, and on his return began small excavations at Nimroud, April 9. The discoveries made were few, and comparatively unimportant, and this mound was therefore abandoned, and excavations undertaken at Kuyunjik on May 7. On May 14 Smith secured from the same room in which Rassam had found Asshurbanapal's library a new fragment of the Deluge story which fitted into the ones previously found. This fact was considered of sufficient moment to be telegraphed to London for publication in the paper. Smith was naturally much pleased with the discovery, but was also in the highest degree gratified by the finding of inscriptions of Esarhaddon, Asshurbanapal, and Sennacherib. Two more fragments of the Deluge tablet were shortly afterward found, and then on June 9 the excavations were stopped, as the proprietors of the *Daily Telegraph* were satisfied with the discovery of the Deluge fragments and did not wish to continue farther the work. Smith was much disappointed at this decision, and reluctantly left for England at once with his treasures.

He was, however, sent out again from London on November 25, 1873, by the trustees of the British Museum, who had set apart one thousand pounds for further excavations at Nineveh. Smith reached Mosul on January 1, 1874, and immediately began excavations at Kuyunjik. These were productive of many inscriptions and of interesting archæological materials, but nothing of startling importance as regards the Bible was found. Smith ceased work and left Mosul on April 4.

When compared with the explorations of Layard and Rassam the work of Smith was comparatively small in amount, but it was valuable in the recovery of much historical material, and its influence upon public feeling and opinion in England was very great. Men were moved by his spirit, no less than by his words and works, to desire that new excavations should be undertaken. Without such inspiration, it is well to remember, the work might have ceased altogether. The British Museum again determined to avail itself of Smith's services, and in October, 1875, he set out for Constantinople to seek to obtain a firman which should permit the resumption of his excavations. He was harried with petty annoyances by Turkish officialdom, but at last secured the coveted permission and returned to England to prepare for his third expedition. In March, 1876, he again set out for the East, and proceeded to Baghdad to inspect some antiquities which were offered for sale. It was then his purpose to begin excavations, but the plague had appeared, the country was unsettled, and there was every possible interference made by natives and by Turkish officials. In previous expeditions he had not learned how to deal with orientals, and alienated their sympathies without impressing them by his power. He was also disturbed more or less by a quarrel with Rassam and his family. Ignorant of the laws of health, by which Europeans are so closely bound in the Orient, he worked too much, rested too little, and was careless in the providing of good food suitable for the climate. At times he rode for days eating only crusts of bread. Beset behind and before with difficulties, and not permitted to excavate, he had to content himself with visits to numerous mounds, which he sketched or planned. On his way back he fell ill of fever, and died at Aleppo, August 19, 1876. Smith's death came to the little world of Assyrian students as a thunderclap out of a clear sky.[1] In England he was looked upon by scholars and people alike almost as a prophet; in Germany,[2]

---

[1] See notices of his life in *The Academy*, x, pp. 265, 266 (by Boscawen). *The Athenæum*, No. 2550, September 9, 1876, p. 338. See also *Transactions of the Society of Biblical Archæology*, vi, p. 574. *The Times*, September 5, 1876, p. 4 c.; September 7, 1876, pp. 10, f.

[2] Professor Delitzsch, who was on very intimate terms with Smith, has

17

where a new and vigorous school of Assyriologists had begun its work, men were thrown into confusion by the severity of the loss which they felt. It was indeed a sore blow to the new study; but science dare not linger. The ranks closed up at the British Museum by the appointment of Mr. W. St. Chad Boscawen, and the trustees sought a man to begin again the excavations which Smith had laid down.

It was natural that they should turn at once to Rassam. It was indeed a long time since he had worked in the field, for he had been absorbed in diplomatic service. He was now living in retirement in England, but responded immediately to the call for service in the same field as that in which his earliest fame had been won.

In November, 1876, Rassam set out for Constantinople to seek a firman—the same errand which had cost Smith so many pangs. After a fruitless wait of four months he returned to England, but went out again when Sir Austen Henry Layard became British ambassador at Constantinople. This was indeed a fortunate appointment for Assyrian studies. Layard would be justly expected to exert himself to secure opportunities for further excavation if that was possible. His representations to the Porte were successful, and in November, 1877, Rassam was back in Mosul,

---

indicated with sufficient clearness his own sense of loss in the reprinting of portions of Smith's last diary in his great geographical treatise (*Wo lag das Paradies?* pp. 266, 267).

where he received by telegraph the news that the firman was granted. His choice of a site for excavations was most happy. The natives had been finding at the hitherto unexplored mound of Balawat, about fifteen miles east of Mosul, fragments of bronze plates, some specimens of which had been sent to him in England. These he had shown to Professor Sayce, who found the name of Shalmaneser upon them, discovered their importance, and advised Rassam to begin diggings at that site. Sayce had thus come into a relation to Rassam similar to that held by Mohl in earlier days to Botta. The result was most successful. Rassam discovered in this mound, from which the fragments had come, the beautifully inscribed and adorned bronze plates which had covered at one time the palace gates of Shalmaneser.

He also, however, began excavations at Kuyunjik and at Nimroud, where small numbers of interesting inscriptions were found. Rassam further made extensive journeys over portions of Babylonia, and among other results identified the site of Sippara. He visited Babylon and made some small excavations there, returning then by way of Van to England. Though not so rich in results as his former expedition, this last venture of Rassam helped on the national collections of the British Museum, and thereby added to the knowledge of ancient history.

While Rassam was busy a new discoverer appeared in the East and very quietly began his

work. M. Ernest de Sarzec was appointed French
consul at Bassorah, on the Persian Gulf, and entered upon his duties in January, 1877. He had
been in Abyssinia and had served in Egypt. He
knew the desert and its people, and he carried to
his new post strong enthusiasm for archæological
work. Two months after he entered Bassorah
de Sarzec had begun excavations at Telloh—
a mound four miles in length, lying in the
great alluvial plain of southern Babylonia, about
five miles from the banks of the Schatt-el-Hai,
and sixty miles north of Mugheir. On this mound
de Sarzec worked from March 5 to June 11, 1877,
and again from February 18 to June 9, 1878. In
July, 1878, he returned to Paris and found himself
famous. He went again and worked in the mound
from January to March, 1880, and also November
12, 1880, to March 15, 1881. His work was thus
prolonged over a considerable period, and instead
of merely running trenches hither and thither, he
dug systematically over a large part of the mound.
The results were full of surprises to the guild of
Assyrian students, and were indeed almost revolutionary. He uncovered a fine temple, whose outer
walls were one hundred and seventy-five feet long
and one hundred feet broad, erected upon a vast
mound from sixteen to twenty feet high. The
outer wall was five feet thick, built of great baked
bricks one foot square, bearing the name Goudea.
These bricks were tightly fastened together by
bitumen. In the interior he found thirty-six

rooms, chiefly small in size, though one was fifty-
five by sixty-five feet. In almost every room there
were found objects of interest or of instruction
for the study of the history of early Babylonia.
In one room alone there were found no less than
eight diorite statues, from an early period of
Babylonian art, which had been unfortunately
mutilated by some later barbarians, for all were
headless. The valuable inscriptions were, however, in perfect preservation. In another part of
the mound during the very first season there
were found two beautiful terra cotta cylinders,
each twenty-four inches in length by twelve in
diameter. Each of these contained no less than
two thousand lines of inscription, forming thus
the longest inscriptions from an early period then
known. De Sarzec's work was done in masterly
fashion, and when the inscriptions and objects of
art were brought to Paris and deposited in the
Louvre, it was felt that indeed a new era had
opened for French archæological study. Quarters
were fitted up in the Louvre, and these objects
found a place beneath the great roof, together
with the discoveries of Botta, the pioneer. They
did not receive the same acclaim as Botta's discoveries had done in France, or Layard's in England, but they were even of greater value scientifically. From the inscriptions the early language
of the Sumerians was more perfectly learned, and
from the statues and reliefs some faint idea was
first conceived of the appearance of the great

people who had laid the foundations of civilization in southern Babylonia. That was a distinguished service which de Sarzec had rendered. It alone was sufficient to give him high place on the roll of those who had made Babylonia live again.

Again and again since 1881 has de Sarzec resumed his work at Telloh, and every year has he brought forth from the same mounds fresh discoveries of moving interest. In 1894 the spades of his workmen struck into a chamber from which were taken no less than thirty thousand tablets— a vast hoard of archives mostly of a business character and relating to trade, commerce, agriculture, and industry, with a goodly number of temple documents and religious notices. The mass of tablets was so great that it was not possible to protect them from the thieving propensities of the natives, and many thousands were stolen, to be sold and scattered all over the world both in public museums and in private hands. While this is to be deplored, it is perhaps safe to expect that in the end very few of them will be lost to science. With this exception de Sarzec has been successful in securing for the Louvre an important part of the brilliant results of his explorations, and the end of his work is not yet.

During all this long period of exploration and excavation, carried on by almost all the nations of Europe, there have been developing in America schools of students of the languages, history, and religions of the ancient Orient. It was natural that in America, also, men should begin to talk of efforts to assist in the great work of recovering the remains of Babylonian and Assyrian civilization. In 1884, at meetings of the American Oriental Society and of the Society of Biblical Literature and Exegesis, conferences were held upon this subject in which Professor John P. Peters, of Philadelphia, the Rev. Dr. William Hayes Ward, Professor Francis Brown, and Professor Isaac H. Hall, of New York, and Professors C. H. Toy and D. G. Lyon, of Harvard University, were participants. These and other gentlemen finally formed an organization, afterward connected with the Archæological Institute of America, for the purpose of raising funds to send out to Babylonia an expedition to explore the country and see where excavations might profitably be undertaken. Miss Catherine Lorillard Wolfe, of New York, gave five thousand dollars to defray the expenses of this preliminary exploration, and on September 6, 1884, the Wolfe expedition to Babylonia departed from New York.[1] The personnel of this expedition consisted of Dr. William Hayes Ward, Mr. J. H. Haynes, then an instructor in Robert College, Constantinople, and Dr. J. R. S. Sterrett. They trav-

---

[1] See "Report on the Wolfe Expedition to Babylonia, 1884-85," by William Hayes Ward, *Papers of the Archæological Institute of America,* Boston, 1886, and also "The Wolfe Expedition," by Rev. W. H. Ward, D.D., LL.D., *Journal of the Society of Biblical Literature and Exegesis,* June to December, 1885, pp. 56-60. The diary of Dr. Ward is published in part by Dr. Peters in *Nippur,* vol. i, Appendix F, pp. 318-375.

eled over much of the land of Babylonia, visiting
sites where excavations had previously been made,
as well as scores of mounds that had not yet been
examined by archæologists. Upon his return, in
June, 1885, Dr. Ward earnestly recommended
that an expedition be placed in the field to engage in the actual work of excavation. He advised that Anbar be the site chosen for this
purpose,[1] but spoke with enthusiasm of the opportunities in other places, among them at Niffer,
then erroneously identified with ancient Calneh, of
which he said, "There nothing has been done;
it is a most promising site of a most famous
city."[2]

The report of Dr. Ward bore no immediate
fruit, but the leaven was steadily working, and
efforts were proceeding in several directions to
secure funds to undertake excavations. The labors
of Dr. John P. Peters at last bore fruit, and
an expedition was sent out by the University of
Pennsylvania which departed from New York
June 23, 1888. Of this company Dr. Peters was
director, and Professors Hermann V. Hilprecht,
of the University of Pennsylvania, and Robert F.
Harper, of the University of Chicago, were Assyriologists, Mr. Perez Hastings Field, architect, and J.

---

[1] *Journal of the Society of Biblical Literature*, p. 60. On this mound
of Anbar compare a most interesting note by Sir Henry Rawlinson quoted
in *Nippur* by John P. Peters. New York, 1897, vol. i, pp. 178, 179.
Rawlinson reached the negative result that Anbar could not be identified
with any Assyrian or Babylonian site.

[2] *Papers of the Archæological Institute*, Report of Dr. Ward, p. 29.

H. Haynes, business manager, commissary, and photographer. It was, however, long ere the expedition could come to its work. There were the usual delays in securing permission from the Imperial Ottoman government; there were difficulties in the gathering of equipment and in the assembling of the staff; there was a shipwreck of part of the expedition on the island of Samos, and perils of health and of life during the long journey overland to southern Babylonia.[1]

At last, on February 6, 1889, excavations were begun on the mount of Nuffar, or Niffer, the site of ancient Nippur, and continued until April 15, with a maximum force of two hundred Arabs. The difficulties were enormous, for there were constant struggles with some of the native tribes, with many individuals among them, and with sundry Turkish officials. But in spite of all this the expedition made a trigonometrical survey of all the mounds and won from them more than "two thousand cuneiform tablets and fragments (among them three dated in the reign of King Ashuretililani of Assyria), a number of inscribed bricks, terra cotta brick stamp of Narâm-Sin, fragment of a barrel cylinder of Sargon of Assyria, inscribed stone tablet, several fragments of inscribed vases (among them two of King Lugalzaggisi of Erech), door socket of Kurigalzu, about twenty-five Hebrew bowls, a large number of stone and terra cotta vases of various sizes and

---

[1] See the lively narrative of Peters, *Nippur*, vol. i, pp. 1–241.

shapes, terra cotta images of gods and their ancient moulds, reliefs, figurines, and toys in terra
cotta, weapons and utensils in stone and metal,
jewelry in gold, silver, copper, bronze, and various
precious stones, a number of weights, seals, and
seal cylinders." [1] It is an excellent record, yet
to Dr. Peters it seemed that the first year's work
"was more or less of a failure, so far at least
as Nippur was concerned." [2] This judgment is
probably influenced by the great difficulties with
the Arabs which embittered the last days of the
work.[3] It was successful, though far surpassed in
importance by that which was to follow.

From January 14 to May 3, 1890, the University of Pennsylvania expedition was again at work
at Nippur, with Dr. Peters as director, and Mr.
Haynes as business manager, and with a maximum force of four hundred Arabs. During this
season about eight thousand inscribed tablets
were taken from the ruins as well as antiquities of
other kinds in large numbers.[4] It was a brilliantly
successful year in every particular, being also less
disturbed by troubles with the Arabs than the
former. All these antiquities were sent to Constantinople for the Imperial Museum, though later

---

[1] This summary of the year's operation is quoted from Hilprecht, *Old
Babylonian Inscriptions, Chiefly from Nippur*, vol. i, part ii. Philadelphia,
1896, p. 8.

[2] Peters, *Nippur*, vol. i, p. vii.

[3] See Peters, *ibid.*, vol. i, chap. xii; *The Catastrophe*, pp. 279, ff.

[4] See the summary by Hilprecht in *Old Babylonian Inscriptions*, vol. i,
part ii, p. 8, and compare the full and entertaining narrative of Peters,
Nippur, vol. ii, *passim*.

considerable portions of them were presented to the
museum of the University of Pennsylvania as a
personal gift of the sultan. This gracious act
arose directly out of the dignified and generous
course pursued by the authorities of the University of Pennsylvania. They had honestly handed
over the antiquities to the Constantinople authorities, as indeed they had promised to do, but had
gone much further than this. Professor Hilprecht
was sent to Constantinople to catalogue these
same collections for the Imperial Museum. This
work was done with great skill, but also with
such tact as to call forth expressions of gratitude
from all who were connected with the museum.
By gifts of antiquities to the museum in Philadelphia, of which Professor Hilprecht was himself
a curator, the sultan aimed to repay the University of Pennsylvania for this free gift of his
services.

For a time excavations at Nippur were inter-
mitted, but on April 11, 1893, the University of
Pennsylvania had another expedition in the field
under the directorship of Mr. J. H. Haynes. Then
began one of the most important of all the long
series of expeditions in Babylonia or in Assyria.
Haynes remained steadily on the ground at work
until February 15, 1896, with a short break from
April 4 to June 4, 1894. Never before had a
European ventured to carry on excavations through
a hot season. Professor Hilprecht has not spoken
too cordially in saying that " the crowning success

was reserved for the unselfish devotion and untir-
ing efforts of Haynes, the ideal Babylonian explorer. Before he accomplished his memorable
task, even such men as were entitled to an independent opinion, and who themselves had exhibited unusual courage and energy, had regarded
it as practically impossible to excavate continuously in the lower regions of Mesopotamia. On
the very same ruins of Nippur, situated in the
neighborhood of extensive malarial marshes, and
' among the most wild and ignorant Arabs that can
be found in this part of Asia,'' where Layard himself nearly sacrificed his life in excavating several
weeks without success,' Haynes has spent almost
three years continuously, isolated from all civilized
men, and most of the time without the comfort of
a single companion. It was indeed no easy task
for any European or American to dwell thirty-
four months near these insect-breeding and pestif-
erous Affej swamps, where the temperature in
perfect shade rises to the enormous height of
120° Fahrenheit (= c. 39° Réaumur), where the
stifling sandstorms from the desert rob the tent
of its shadow and parch the human skin with the
heat of a furnace; while the ever-present insects
bite and sting and buzz through day and night;
while cholera is lurking at the threshold of the
camp and treacherous Arabs are planning robbery

---

¹ Layard, *Nineveh and Babylon*, p. 565.

' Layard, *l. c.*, pp. 556–562. "On the whole I am much inclined to
question whether extensive excavations carried on at Niffer would produce
any very important or interesting results " (p. 562).

and murder—and yet during all these wearisome hours to fulfill the duties of three ordinary men. Truly a splendid victory, achieved at innumerable sacrifices, and under a burden of labors enough for a giant; in the full significance of the word a *monumentum aere perennius.*" [1]

During the third campaign of the University of Pennsylvania about twenty-one thousand cunei-form tablets and fragments were taken out of the mound, and besides these there were found large numbers of antiquities of other kinds, all of great importance in the reconstruction of the past history of Babylonia. Among these were large numbers of vases and fragments of vases from the very earliest period of history, drain tiles, water cocks, brick stamps, beautiful clay coffins glazed in tile fashion and finely preserved, and diorite statues and fragments. [2]

After a brief and necessary interruption, the Philadelphia expedition began work again in February, 1899, with Dr. J. H. Haynes as manager and Messrs. Geere and Fisher as architects. In January, 1900, Professor Hilprecht reached Nippur and took charge as scientific director. Under his direction "an extensive group of hills to the southwest of the temple of Bel" were systematically excavated. From the same location about twenty-five hundred tablets were taken in

---

[1] Hilprecht, *Old Babylonian Inscriptions*, vol. i, part ii, p. 10.

[2] Compare the summary in Hilprecht, *ibid.*, p. 9. An account of this expedition by Mr. Haynes himself has not yet appeared, though it is understood that one is in contemplation.

the first campaign, and later excavations had increased the number to about fifteen thousand.
Within six weeks "a series of rooms was exposed
which furnished not less than sixteen thousand
cuneiform documents, forming part of the temple
library during the latter half of the third millennium B. C."[1]

From these four campaigns had come a vast
store of literature of all kinds; here were letters
and dispatches, chronological lists, historical
fragments, syllabaries, building and business inscriptions, astronomical and religious texts, votive
tablets, inventories, tax lists, and plans of estates.
No expedition had ever been more successful and
none had ever been more warmly supported at
home. Fortunate in its directors at home, rich in
the scientific directorate of Professor Hilprecht,
the results attained have been worthy of all the
expenditure of energy, life, and treasure.

Alone among the greatest of the modern nations
Germany had done very little in the field of exploration while other peoples had been so busy.
German scholarship had made the highest contributions to decipherment and to the scientific
treatment of texts unearthed by the patient explorers sent out by others. It were strange if
Germany should not also seek to find new tablets as
well as to read them. Professor Friedrich Delitzsch,
long an exponent of the science of Assyriology

---

[1] Hilprecht, "Latest Research in Bible Lands," *Sunday School Times*,
May 5, 1900, p. 276.

and one of the most eminent scholars of modern times, urged the formation of the German Orient Society,[1] which was finally constituted early in 1898.

Even before the proposed society was organized a "commission for the archæological investigation of the lands of the Euphrates and Tigris " prepared to secure direct information concerning the various sites which seemed to promise the best results when excavated. To this end Professor Eduard Sachau, of the University of Berlin, accompanied by Dr. Robert Koldewey, departed for the East October 23, 1897. They thoroughly explored Babylonia and Assyria,[2] and brought back abundant information for the use of the new society, which was now fairly started. To it scholars gave their aid, the German Emperor made a grant of funds, and in the end of the year an expedition was sent to the East with Dr. Koldewey as director and Dr. Bruno Meissner, of Halle, as Assyriologist. The latter, after very useful service, retired and was succeeded by Dr. E. Lindl, of Munich. In the spring of 1899 work was commenced in the great mound of El-Kasr, Babylon, beneath which were the remains of the palace of Nebuchadrezzar. Success was had in a measurable degree from the very beginning in

---

[1] See Friedrich Delitzsch, *Ex Oriente Lux !* Ein Wort zur Förderung der Deutschen Orient-Gesellschaft. Leipzig, 1898.

[2] *Am Euphrat und Tigris.* Reisenotizen aus dem winter 1897–1898, von Eduard Sachau, mit 5 Kartenskizzen und 32 Abbildungen. Leipzig, 1900, pp. 160.

the discovery of a new Hittite inscription[1] and
of many tablets of the neo-Babylonian period.
The future work, which must continue for a number of years, is in good hands, for German patience
and persistence will be certain to continue it to
the end.

In 1888 there was made in Egypt a most surprising discovery of letters and dispatches written
for the most part in the Babylonian script and
language. A peasant woman, living in the
wretched little mud village of Tell-el-Amarna,[2]
on the Nile, about one hundred and eighty miles
south of Memphis, was searching for antiquities
among the sand and stones by the mountain side
some distance back from the river. Little did she
know that beneath this rubbish lay all that remained of the temple and palace of the great
heretic king of Egypt, Amenophis IV, or, as he
called himself, Akh-en-Aten. Her concern was
only to find some bits of *anteeka*, which might be
sold to those strange people from Europe and
America, who buy things simply because they are

[1] *Wissenschaftliche Veröffentlichungen der Deutschen Orient Gesellschaft.*
1 Heft. *Die Hettitische Inschrift gefunden in der Königsburg von Babylon am 22. August* 1899 *und veröffentlicht* von Dr. Rob. Koldewey.
Vorwort von Prof. Dr. Friedrich Delitzsch. Leipzig 1900.

[2] There is a dispute as to whether the name of the place should be Tell-
el-Amarna or simply El-Amarna. Winckler has adopted the latter on the
basis of a private communication from Professor Maspero, who asserts
that El-Amarna is alone heard from the lips of the natives on the spot.
To this view also Steindorff is inclined, for he writes " Tell el-'Amarna (or
better, El- 'Amarna) " (Baedeker's *Egypt*, Leipzig, 1898, p. 193). On the
other hand, Petrie (*History of Egypt*, ii, p. 205), Budge (*The Tell-El-*

old. Out of the mound she took over three hundred pieces of inscribed tablets, some of them
only $2\frac{1}{8}$ inches by $1\frac{11}{16}$ inches, while others are $8\frac{3}{4}$
inches by $4\frac{7}{8}$ inches and even larger. One hun-
dred and sixty of these, many of them fragments,
were acquired by Herr Theodore Graf, of Vienna,
and were purchased from him by Herr J. Simon,
of Berlin, and presented to the Royal Museum in
the latter city. Eighty-two were bought for the
trustees of the British Museum by Dr. E. A.
Wallis Budge; sixty came into the possession of
the Gizeh Museum in Cairo, and a few into private hands.

The documents thus restored to the world are
to be reckoned with the most important of cuneiform discoveries. They consist of letters and
dispatches which passed between Amenophis III
and Amenophis IV on the one hand, and on
the other various monarchs, princes, and govern-
ors of western Asia, among whom were Kadashman-Bel of Babylonia, Asshur-uballit of Assyria,
Dushratta of Mitanni, Rib-Adda of Byblos, Abi-
milki of Tyre, Abdi-Kheba of Jerusalem, and
many others. Their historical value is great not
only because of the chronological material deduci-
ble from them, but also because they give a note-

Amarna Tablets in the British Museum, passim), and Sayce, all of whom
know the place well, unite in reading Tell-el-Amarna. Professor Sayce
says in a personal note to the writer: "There is no place called El-Amarna,
which is the Egyptian name of a Bedâwin tribe (El-Amarân). But there is
a Tel el-Amarna and a Dêr el-Amarna, some miles to the south of the Tel."

18

worthy side light upon the entire social relations of the time.[1] During the long series of years that excavation had been carried on in the East by Europe and America but little interest in the subject was aroused in Turkey, in whose great empire all these finds were made. But during the latter part of the period there came a great revival of enthusiasm for antiquity in Turkey itself, due almost entirely to the wisdom, patience, and learning of one man. Trained in Europe, a man of fine natural taste and of great personal enthusiasm, Hamdy Bey was admirably fitted for the post of director-general of the Imperial Ottoman Museum. He has transformed it and all its arrangements and made certain a great future for it. Ably seconded by his brother, Halil Bey, he gave great and continued help to the Philadelphia expedition, and magnificently has his museum profited thereby. It remained only that this museum, the best situated in all the world to gain thereby, should itself undertake excavations. Hamdy Bey succeeded in interesting the sultan himself in the matter and inducing him to provide a sum of money from his private purse to undertake excavations at Abu-Habba, the site of ancient Sippar.

---

[1] On the Tell-el-Amarna discoveries in general consult the valuable bibliography in *The Tell-el-Amarna Tablets in the British Museum with Autotype Facsimiles*, London, 1892, pp. lxxxvii, ff., and add to that especially Winckler, *Der Thontafelfund von El-Amarna*, Berlin, 1889, seq., and also *Keilinschriftliche Bibliothek*, vol. v. A useful summary of the general historical results is given by Carl Niebuhr, *Die Amarna Zeit*. Liepzig, 1899.

The director of the expedition was the French
Dominican, Father Scheil, a distinguished Assyriologist, who was accompanied by Bedry Bey, who
had been Turkish commissioner to the Philadelphia expedition, and therefore knew by experience
the best method of exploration. The expedition
was completely successful, and in the short space
of two months, at a cost of only three thousand
francs, gathered a fine store of over six hundred
and seventy-nine tablets and fragments, mostly
letters and contracts dated in the reign of Samsu-
iluna, the son and successor of Hammurabi, as well
as many vases and other objects similar to those
found by the expedition at Nippur.[1] Scheil was
naturally supported by all government officials in
the most loyal fashion, and his success is an interesting promise for the future. The Turkish government is able to control its own representatives in
the neighborhood of the mounds, and if it is once
thoroughly aroused to the interest and importance
of excavating its untold buried treasures of art,
science, and literature, scarcely any limits may be
set to the great results that may be expected for
our knowledge of ancient Babylonia.

Besides these great expeditions other smaller
and less conspicuous undertakings have frequently
been made to secure the archæological treasures

[1] On this expedition and its results see Notes by Scheil in *Recueil de
Travaux relatifs a la Philologie et a l'archéologie Egyptiennes et Assyriennes*,
vol. xvi, and especially Extrait d'une lettre du P. Scheil, *ibid.*, p. 184, and
compare the survey by Hilprecht, *Recent Research in Bible Lands*. Philadelphia, 1897, pp. 81, ff.

of Babylonia and Assyria. The most successful among these are doubtless the repeated oriental visits of Dr. E. A. Wallis Budge, of the British Museum. He has gone quietly into various parts of the East and, with a thorough understanding of the natives, has been able year by year to increase the collections of the museum. No public account of his work has been made, and no narrative of his labors can therefore be given here.

Here rests for a time the story of expeditions to uncover the buried cities of Babylonia and Assyria. For a short time only in all probability, for the gain has been so large, the rewards so great, that new expeditions must ever seek an opportunity to labor in the same fields.

While great expeditions have their periods of labor and their periods of rest one form of exploration goes on all the time in spite of many efforts to prevent it. The natives of the district have learned that antiquities may be sold to Europeans and Americans for gold. The traffic in them in Turkey is forbidden by law, and their export from the country is interdicted. But the native digs on surreptitiously and smuggles the results into the hands of merchants, who market them in Baghdad, London, and elsewhere. This practice brings into the possession of museums and so into the hands of scholars hundreds of tablets that otherwise might long remain hidden. Yet it is greatly to be deplored, for much is thus broken by careless and ignorant handling, and the source or origin, a point of great importance, is unknown or concealed from fear of the government. It is therefore on many accounts to be hoped that the Turkish government may ultimately succeed in preventing it, and may secure for its own rapidly growing museum more of the objects that are found by chance.

All that has been found yet is but a small part of that which doubtless lies buried beneath the mounds. Therein is an urgent call to men of wealth, to learned societies, and to governments to continue the work that has already been so marvelously successful. The gaps that yet remain in our knowledge of ancient Assyria and Babylonia may in large measure be easily filled up by the same methods that have given us our present acquaintance with that mighty past.

CHAPTER IX.

THE SOURCES.

THE sources for the history of the Babylonians and Assyrians may be grouped under four main heads : I. The monumental remains of the Assyrians and Babylonians themselves; II. The Egyptian hieroglyphic texts; III. The Old Testament; IV. The Greek and Latin writers.

Of these four by far the most important in every particular are the monumental remains of the Babylonians and Assyrians.

I. *The Monuments of Babylonia and Assyria.* From the mounds that cover the ancient cities of Babylonia and Assyria there has come a vast store of tablets, which now number certainly not less than one hundred and sixty thousand in the various museums of the world. These tablets contain the literature of the two peoples, a literature as varied in form and content as it is vast in extent. In the end all of this literature may be considered as sources for history. Every business tablet is dated, and from these dates much may be learned for chronology, while even in the tablets themselves there is matter relating to the daily life of the people, all of which must ultimately be valuable in the reconstruction of the so-

cial history. So also are all religious texts, all
omens and incantations, sources for the study of
the history of religious development. But as we
are here concerned chiefly with political history,
the primary sources are the so-called royal inscriptions. These royal inscriptions begin very early
in Babylonian history, and then chiefly as mere
records of names and titles. These early kings
caused their names and titles to be written in
some way upon all their constructions. Even
little statuettes and vases bear the royal mark,
while the bricks used in the erection of large
buildings were stamped with the king's name and
the names of the lands over which he ruled. Simple and uninteresting though these often are, they
give the political relations of lands and, in connection with other materials, enable us to trace
out the line of political development. This style
of name and title writing continues down to the
fall of the Babylonian empire. Alongside of it,
however, there was early developed a narrative
form of royal inscription, giving an account of the
campaigns and conquests of the royal arms. These
narrative inscriptions are of three kinds : 1. Annals ;
2. Campaign inscriptions; 3. General votive inscriptions.

In the annalistic inscriptions the deeds of the
king are arranged in chronological order by years
of reign. Of all the ancient sources these are by
far the most important, for from them we learn
the exact order of events, often a matter of first-

rate importance. Besides these texts the kings
have left many inscriptions in which the events
are arranged in campaigns. While this second
class is just as important as the first for the mere
statement of events, it is, nevertheless, much less
valuable to us. From the arrangement of campaigns it is sometimes difficult to ascertain the exact order of events in time, and hence the sequence
of conquests or of defeats. The general or votive
inscriptions begin usually with a most elaborate
ascription of titles, and with all manner of boasting
phrases concerning the king's prowess. They
then set forth the king's conquests, arranged in
groups, and usually after a geographical plan.
The order often widely departs from a chronological one, and as some kings have left us only texts
of this kind, it is impossible to understand the
sequence of events during certain reigns.

The royal inscriptions which describe battle,
siege, and conquest are almost exclusively Assyrian. The inscriptions of Babylonian kings
which have come down to us are almost without
exception peaceful in tone and matter. They record little else than the erection of temples and
palaces or the restoration of those which had
fallen into partial or complete decay. For the
order of events in their campaigns against other
peoples as well as for the events themselves we
must rely almost entirely upon non-native sources.

In addition to these historical sources the
Babylonians and Assyrians have left a great mass

of chronological material to which we must give attention later (see Chapter XII).

In respect of their value as sources of knowledge these monumental remains can only be said to be as valuable as the records of other ancient peoples. They bear for the most part the stamp of reasonableness. Often, indeed, do they contain palpable exaggerations of kingly prowess, of victories, and of conquests. They therefore require sifting and rigid criticism. But in most cases it is possible to learn from the issue of the events the relative importance of them, and so be able to check the measure of extravagance in the narrative. When subjected to the same tests and tried by the same canons of criticism the Assyrian and Babylonian monuments yield as just and true a picture of their national history as the sources of Greek and Roman history to which the world has been so long accustomed.

The second source is of far less importance than the first, yet is at times exceedingly valuable.

II. *Egyptian Hieroglyphic Texts* are of very slight importance as direct sources of knowledge concerning the political history of Babylonia and Assyria, but they contain many place and personal names useful in the elucidation of corresponding names in Assyrian texts.

The third source, while more important than the second, is still not so valuable as the primary monumental source.

III. *The Old Testament*. The gain of the Old

Testament has been greater from Assyrian studies than the reverse, though the apologetic value of monumental testimony has often been greatly exaggerated. Nevertheless, it must not be forgotten that it was interest in the Old Testament which inspired most of the early explorers and ex· cavators and some of the earlier decipherers and interpreters, and that from the historical notices in the Old Testament came not a few points for the outworking of details in the newly discovered inscriptions. The historical portions of the Old Testament which are still of importance as sources for Assyrian and Babylonian history are especially 2 Kings, while of even greater importance, in many instances, are the prophets Isaiah, Nahum, Jeremiah, and Ezekiel.

IV. *The Greek and Latin Writers.* As sources the Greek and Latin writers once held first place, but are now reduced to a very insignificant position by the native monumental records. Nevertheless, they still retain some importance, and need constantly to be used to check and control the native writers as well as to assist in the ordering of their more detailed materials.

First in importance among all the classical writers stands Berossos, or Berosos, for so the name is also transliterated into Greek. He was a Babylonian by origin, and a priest of the great god Bel. The date of his birth and of his death are equally unknown, but it is clear that he was living in the days of Alexander the Great (356–

323 B. C.),[1] and continued to live at least as late as Antiochus I Soter (280–261 B. C.). He wrote a great work on Babylonian history, the title of which was probaby *Babyloniaca*, though it is also referred to under the title of *Chaldaica* by Josephus and Clemens. It was dedicated to his patron, Antiochus I Soter. The *Babyloniaca* was divided into three parts, of which the first dealt with human history from the chaos to the flood, the second from the flood to Nabonassar, and the third from Nabonassar to Alexander. The first two consisted only of lists of kings without any proper historical narrative, while with the third began the real story of events.

Both lists and narrative of Berossos could not fail to be of considerable moment to us, if we had them in even fairly well preserved form. Unhappily, however, the original work has perished, and all that remains are excerpts which have come to us after much copying and many transfers from hand to hand. The history of these fragments is a very curious example of book making in antiquity. In the Mithradatic war a certain Alexander of Miletus was taken prisoner and carried to Rome as the slave of Lentulus, from whom he received the name of Cornelius. In 82 B. C. he received the Roman citizenship and lived in Rome with some distinction as a man of letters. There he wrote an enormous number of books relating to ancient history, and on that account received the name of

---

[1] See Eusebius, *Chronica*, ed. Alfred Schoene. Berlin, 1875, p. 11.

Polyhistor.[1] The period of his greatest distinc·
tion and productivity was between 70 and 60 B. C.
His historical works were simply excerpts from
the writings of his predecessors, and in this man·
ner he compiled a history of Assyria, the exact title
of which is not now known. This history was
made up of extracts from Berossos, Apollodoros,
Chronica, and the third book of the Sibyllines, and
was worked over into pseudo-Ionic Greek by Aby·
denos. It came also into the hands of Josephus and
of Eusebius. Josephus was seeking especially those
parts of the history which illustrated the history
of the Jews, and naturally took from Alexander
only those parts which were suitable for his pur·
pose. In like manner, also, Eusebius copied only
portions. By this process we have preserved in
Josephus, *Antiquities of the Jews,* and in Euse·
bius, *Chronica,* small parts of the great work of
Berossos, while the dynasties have come down to
us from George the Synkellos. Wherever we can
secure enough of Berossos to compare with the
native monumental sources we find most remarka·
ble agreement with them. From Berossos but
little is to be learned of direct value, but the sup·
port which we gain from these fragmentary re·
mains for the general course of the history is very

---

[1] On the life of Alexander Polyhistor compare J. Freudenthal, *Hellen·*
istische Studien, Heft I, *Alexander Polyhistor und die von ihm erhaltenen*
Reste jüdischer und samaritanischer Geschichtswerke. Jahresbericht des
jüdisch-theologischen Seminars, Breslau, 1874, p. 17, and the further ref·
erences there given in footnote, especially Rauch, *De Alexandri Polyhistoris*
vita atque scriptis. Heidelberg, 1843.

great. As will later appear, chronological material of much complexity and difficulty is obtained from certain parts of these fragments. The next Greek writer who comes before us as a possible source is Ktesias. He was a contemporary of Xenophon, and was born of the family of the Asclepiadæ at Cnidus. He wandered thence in B. C. 416 to the court of Persia and became body physician to King Artaxerxes Mnemon, whom he cured of a severe wound received in the battle of Cunaxa, B. C. 401. In 399 he returned to his native city, and in the ease thus achieved proceeded to work up into historical form the materials he had collected. He wrote in twenty-three books a history of Persia (Περσικά) in the Ionic dialect. The first six books treated the history of Assyria, and the rest the history of Persia down to his own time, in which he claims to have used the royal annals of the Persian kings (διφθέραι βασιλικαί). His work was extensively used in the ancient world,[1] and wherever quoted became at once the object of sharp controversy. He was accused of being untrustworthy and indifferent to truth, and the charges and the controversy continue until to-day. The severity of the judgments[2] against him probably arise partly out of

---

[1] Gilmore, *The Fragments of the Persika of Ktesias*, London, 1888, pp. 2, 3, names no less than thirty-four writers, among them Strabo, Plutarch, and Xenophon, who have preserved portions of Ktesias.

[2] As a specimen of a sharp modern judgment upon him, both personally and as an author, one may refer to Marcus v. Niebuhr, *Geschichte Assur's*

the acrimonious manner in which he attacked
Herodotus, and partly out of the fact that he used
Persian sources for his history. In the years
of his Persian residence he had so completely
absorbed the Persian point of view as to seem
hardly just to the Greek conception of their history in its relations to the Persians. If we subject
to modern criticism the fragments of his history
that remain, our judgment must be that the first
six books, relating to the early history of Assyria,
are valueless. Whether this was due to the fact
that he was unable himself to read the sources
which he used, and was therefore obliged to rely
upon the word of others to tell him the story
found in them, or that he must be accused of
actually inventing and setting forth as history an
entertaining mass of empty fables, will probably
never be decisively determined. The books themselves have perished. Only fragments of them
survive in the quotations by Diodorus and Eusebius and others, and in an epitome by Photius.'
For our purposes they scarcely come into the question at all.

<hr>

und Babel's. Berlin, 1857, pp. 289, ff. While as a specimen of a more
favorable judgment see Sayce, *The Ancient Empires of the East,* Herod.
otus, i-iii, London, 1883, p. xxxiii: "It is certain that he (Ktesias) was
justified in claiming for his history the authority of Persian documents,
and that many of the charges of falsehood brought against him must be
laid not upon him, but upon his Eastern friends. His history of Assyria
is much like the Egyptian history of mediæval Arab writers, clothed only
in a Greek dress;" and also Paul Rost, *Untersuchungen zur altorientalischen Geschichte,* pp. 109, 110. Mittheilungen der Vorderasiatischen
Gesellschaft, 1892, 2, Berlin.

¹ See Gilmore, *op. cit., passim.*

Last of all among the classical writers we come to Herodotus, the father of history. Of the value of his works as a source very diverse opinions have been and are still held. From him surely much was expected. Born in Halicarnassus, in Caria, B. C. 484, he had associations with the greatest men of his time, and apparently planned his history with skill and care. He desired to tell of the famous events in the struggle between the Greek and the barbarian, and of the causes which led to the Persian war. He traveled extensively in the East, and there is some reason to believe that these journeys were undertaken with a view to the gathering of materials for his history. Egypt he visited, but there is doubt whether he traversed the whole country from the Mediterranean to Elephantiné. There is still more doubt concerning his travels beyond the confines of Egypt. He certainly attempts to leave the impression, even when he does not specifically so state, that he also visited Tyre, on the Syrian coast, that he penetrated to Babylon and thence to Nineveh, to Ecbatana, and perhaps even to Susa. Professor Sayce has attempted to prove, with much learning and great acuteness, that " he never visited Assyria and Babylonia," [1] and asserts that " he stands convicted of never having visited the district he undertakes to describe," [2] and concludes with the statement that " the long contro-

---

[1] Sayce, *Ancient Empires of the East*, p. xxviii.
[2] *Ibid.*, p. xxix.

versy which has raged over the credibility of
Herodotus has thus been brought to an end by
the discoveries of recent years."[1]   That Professor
Sayce has proved upon Herodotus a host of in-
accuracies, some travelers' tales, and has effectually
disposed of his claims to rank as an independent
source of ancient history there can be no doubt.
Yet that in this case, as in other similar modern
judgments, there is an excess of skepticism is perhaps no less true.   There is good reason for believing that Herodotus had really visited Babylon,
for the topographical details which he gives bear
frequently the stamp of an eyewitness.[2]   The main
fact, however, remains that from Herodotus but
little of historical value may be learned, save as
every single fact is checked by the explicit statements of native monumental historians.[3]

After these there remain among classical writers few who deserve to be mentioned as sources.
The chronological materials left by some of them,
as, for example, the earlier parts of Berossos and

---

[1] *Ibid.*, p. xxxiii.

[2] See, for example, Baumstark in Pauly-Wissowa, *Real Encyclopädie der
class. Wissenschaft,* Stuttgart, n. d., col. 2689. "Seine Angaben über B.
sind die einzigen unmittelbar und vollständig auf uns gekommen aus
der gesamten griechischen Litteratur vorchristlicher Zeit. Dass sie im
wesentlichen auf Augenschein beruhen, wäre besser niemals bestritten
worden."

[3] For a careful assembling of the valuable references in Herodotus and a
comparison of the native sources see J. Nikel, *Herodot und die Keilschriftforschung,* Paderborn, 1896, and add also *Herodotus and the Empires of the
East,* based on Nikel's *Herodot und die Keilschriftforschung,* by Herbert
Cushing Tolman, Ph.D., and James Henry Stevenson, Ph.D. New York,
n. d. (1899).

the exceedingly valuable Canon of Ptolemy, will have to be estimated later (see Chapter XII).

From a few other less-known writers, such as Kleitarchos, Arrian, Hieronymos of Kardia, and an unknown writer concerning Alexander the Great (Onesikritos), certain topographical details are learned.

Our judgment of all the classical writers must be that their value is entirely subordinate to the native sources, and not so valuable as the notices in the Old Testament or the brief words from the Egyptian hieroglyphic texts.

19

CHAPTER X.

THE LANDS OF BABYLONIA AND ASSYRIA.

THE Babylonian and Assyrian peoples had their seat in a great valley with but one distinct and sharp natural boundary. This clear boundary was the Persian Gulf upon the south, which said to all landsmen, "Thus far shalt thou come and no farther." That boundary these peoples respected and never ventured out on the troubled and mysterious waters. On the east the boundary between them and their next neighbors was fluctuating and uncertain. The natural boundary would seem to be the mountains of Elam, but these mountains slope gradually westward to the plain, and do not rise precipitously from it. Down these slopes poured hordes of men in all ages, and there was no sharp line of defense to keep them from the valley, while on the other hand the people of the valley were often filled with conquering power sufficient to extend their border far up the slopes into Elam. On the north, also, the boundary was almost equally uncertain. The mountains of Armenia might be regarded as the natural border on the north, but these are intimately connected with the great valley, for they belong to the drainage system of the Euphrates and the Tigris, and, like the mountains of Elam, slope more gently toward than from the valley. On the north, therefore, as on the east, the lands of Assyria and of Babylonia were open to incursion from the outside, or to raids from within outward. The western border was still more indefinite. In the northwest the valley land swept away in a gentle rise from the Euphrates to the plateau of Aram, and over it even to the Mediterranean. While upon the southwest the desert formed the only barrier between the valley and Arabia or the lands of the Jordan valley. Nomadic peoples passed over this barrier with ease, and became powerful factors in the history of the Babylonians. On the other hand, however, the Babylonians did not readily pass the broad line of the desert.

Within this roughly bounded country two great empires existed for centuries, and the dividing line between them moved up and down the valley as the power of either became stronger than that of the other. Nature had set no boundary between them, for the whole valley lay open from north to south. Yet, though this is true, there have existed from remote times separate provinces in the valley, with more or less definite boundaries between them. If we begin in the south, these separate provinces may thus be described: Close to the Persian Gulf was a small country, the country of the Sea Lands, the influence of which was marked in the early history of the whole

valley.   The country of the Sea Lands was entirely alluvial, and small in extent.   Through it
in early times the Tigris and   the   Euphrates
passed by separate estuaries into the Persian Gulf.
Later, though at what time is unknown, the two
rivers united and began to flow through one
channel into the sea.   This alluvial territory is
now growing by the river deposits at the rate of
about a mile in seventy years, and there is good
reason for believing that its average growth in
historic time has been not less than a mile in thirty
years.   If the ratio of increase has been as high
as this, the country of the Sea Lands was a very
small land during the period 4000–600 B. C.
Above it geographically lay the land of the
Kaldi, likewise alluvial, and extending northward
nearly to the city of Babylon.   It has also no line
of clear separation from the Sea Lands, nor from
Babylonia to the north.   As kings from the Kaldi
country later ruled in Babylon and had control
over the whole vast empire, of which it was the
capital, the name of Chaldea was extended by
Greek and Roman historians so as to include the
whole of Babylonia.   Next above the land of the
Kaldi was Babylonia itself, which extended northward along the valley, with two exceptions, to
the Armenian mountains.   These exceptions were
the original lands of Assyria and Mesopotamia.
Assyria, in its original geographical and historical
sense, was the small triangular-shaped land lying
between the Tigris and the Zab Rivers and the

Median mountains. When the Assyrians gained in power and numbers they soon extended their dominion beyond these very narrow boundaries, and with their dominion went likewise the geographical name, so that even in early times the name Assyria had been carried westward to the Euphrates and southward as far as Hit, while to the Greeks and Romans it covered the entire valley.[1] The other separate land or province was the small country included between the Euphrates and the Khabur Rivers and the mountains of Armenia. This was the land known as Nahrina, the Aram-Naharaim[2] of the Hebrews, and the Mesopotamia of the Greeks and Romans. Unhappily this name of Mesopotamia was extended to cover the territory between the Tigris and Euphrates southward even to the Persian Gulf. This completely destroys the historical nomenclature, and introduces a confusion that does not appear in any of the records of either the Assyrians or Babylonians.

For this country between the Tigris and Euphrates, including Assyria, Mesopotamia, Babylonia, Chaldea, and the Sea Lands, the ancient inhabitants had no general geographical name.

---

[1] That ἡ Ασσυρία means the whole of the valley, including Babylonia, appears from its regular use by Herodotus (for example, i, 178, 185; iii, 92, and iv, 39). It is used in the same manner also by Xenophon (*Cyropædeia*, ii, 1, 5.)

[2] Gen. xxiv, 10; Deut. xxiii, 5. There seems good reason for the view that it ought to be written Aram-Naharim, that is, plural not dual. (See W. Max Müller, *Asien und Europa nach altägyptischen Denkmälern*, Leipzig, 1893, pp. 249–255, and compare Budde, *Das Buch der Richter*, on Judg. iii, 8, and Moore on same passage.)

The geographical terminology varied with the rise and fall of political power. There were, however, certain clear exceptions to this general rule. For example, the name Assyria was never extended so as to cover Babylonia proper, though it is extended so far westward. On the other hand, the name Babylonia is carried so far north as almost to include Assyria, though the small original land of Assyria appears always to be kept sharply distinguished. The general term of the Assyro-Babylonian valley may properly be used to cover all the country.

Though the word Mesopotamia was never applied by either Assyrians or Babylonians to their country, yet it is in a real sense the product of two rivers, in a sense almost as complete as that Egypt is the product of the Nile.

The Tigris and the Euphrates have their sources upon opposite sides of the same mountain range. This is the highest ridge between the Black Sea and the great valley, and the only one which has peaks bearing perpetual snow—hence known to the ancient Greeks as the Niphates. From its western side the Euphrates flows westward to Malatiyeh, as though to lose itself in the Mediterranean. But at Malatiyeh the course is suddenly changed to the southeast, passing within a few miles of the source of the Tigris at Lake Göljik, thence forcing its way through the mountains in a tortuous course. Thence its course is generally southeast until opposite Baghdad, where it approaches to within twenty miles of the Tigris, and the rivers appear about to form a junction. Both, however, again separate, and only make their final union at last after a very sharp convergence. The estimated length of the Euphrates is seventeen hundred and eighty miles. It is navigable for a distance of twelve hundred miles above its mouth. During its whole course it is an imposing river—among the greatest rivers of the world. Like most mountain streams, its early course is swift and its bed rocky. Its first great tributary is the Kara Su—that is, the Black Water—at Keban-Maaden, a few miles west of Kharpoot. Its next affluent is the Sajur, received from the right, or west. This is followed by the Balikh, which, in a course of only one hundred and twenty miles, brings the water from Mount Masius. The next is the Khabur, also received from the left, which brings another considerable body of water also from the lower slopes of Mount Masius. From this point, for eight hundred miles until the junction with the Tigris, the Euphrates receives no tributaries whatever. It has been well said that the "upper region of the Euphrates resembles that of the Rhine, while its middle course may be compared with that of the Danube, and its lower with the Nile." [1]

The Tigris is formed by the junction of two

[1] Colonel Chesney says, " In some respects the scenery of the Euphrates reminded me of that of parts of the Nile, though far exceeding the latter in picturesque effect " (*Narrative of the Euphrates Expedition.* London, 1868, p. 76).

small head streams, the eastern rising near Bitlis, not far from the western bank of Lake Van, while the western comes from the neighborhood of Kharpoot. Unlike the Euphrates, the Tigris receives many important tributaries, which flow down from the Zagros and Elmatine mountains. The first important one of these is the Eastern Khabur, after which in rapid succession follow the Upper Zab, the Lower Zab, the Adhem, and the Diyaleh. This constant accession of fresh water gives the Tigris a character entirely different from the Euphrates. The Euphrates continually decreases in size and flows ever in a more sluggish stream. When it receives the Khabur it is four hundred yards wide and eighteen feet deep; at Irzah or Werdi, seventy-five miles lower down, it is three hundred and fifty yards wide and of the same depth; at Hadiseh, one hundred and forty miles below Werdi, it is three hundred yards wide, and still of the same depth; here its current is four knots per hour in the flood season, but this speed diminishes within the next fifty miles; at Hit, fifty miles below Hadiseh, its width has increased to three hundred and fifty yards, but its depth has been diminished to sixteen feet; at Felujiah, seventy-five miles from Hit, the depth is twenty feet, but the width had diminished to two hundred and fifty yards. From this point the contraction is very rapid and striking. The Saklowijeh Canal is given out upon the left, and some way further down the Hindiyeh branches off upon the right, each carrying, when the Euphrates is full, a large body of water. The consequence is that at Hillah, ninety miles below Felujiah, the stream is no more than two hundred yards wide and fifteen feet deep; at Diwaniyeh, sixty-five miles further down, it is only one hundred and sixty yards wide; and at Lamlun, twenty miles below Diwaniyeh, it is reduced to one hundred and twenty yards wide, with a depth of no more than twelve feet. Soon after, however, it begins to recover itself. The water, which left it by the Hindiyeh, returns to it upon the one side, while the Schatt-el-Hai and numerous other branch streams flow in upon the other; but still the Euphrates never recovers itself entirely, nor even approaches in its later course to the standard of its earlier greatness. The channel from Kurnah to El Khitr was found by Colonel Chesney to have "an average width of only two hundred yards, and a depth of about eighteen or nineteen feet, which implies a body of water far inferior to that carried between the junction of the Khabur and Hit."

The Tigris and the Euphrates have both flood seasons and carry their waters over a wide extent of country, exactly as the Nile. This fact is so perfectly clear that there can be no doubt concerning it, though Herodotus directly asserts the contrary, saying, "The river does not, as in Egypt, overflow the corn lands of its own accord, but is spread over them by the help of engines."[1] The

---

[1] Herodotus, i, 193.

rise is indeed not so prolonged as the rise of the Nile, but its influence is, nevertheless, distinctly to be seen. The rise in the Tigris is due to the melting of the snows on the mountains, and as it drains the southern slopes, and the Euphrates the northern slopes, the Tigris rises more rapidly. The Tigris usually begins to rise early in March. By the first or second week in May the highest point is reached, and the river then declines rapidly and reaches its level at about the middle of June. As the course of the Tigris during the entire upper part of its course is between banks of considerable height, the river rarely overflows. On its lower course, however, and especially between the thirty-second and thirty-first parallels, it covers a wide extent of country. The inundation of the Euphrates is much more regular and extensive. The melting of snow on the northern slopes is slower, and the river begins to swell very slowly about the beginning of March, and gradually increases until the highest point is reached about the end of May, when the waters stand about thirteen feet above low water.[1] At this point the river remains, for about a month, sinks slightly toward the middle of July, and then more rapidly till September. The Euphrates begins to overflow its banks much higher up than the Tigris, and even at its junction with the Khabur is de-

---

[1] Colonel Chesney found the increased depth to be thirteen and a half feet (*Expedition for the Survey of the Rivers Euphrates and Tigris.* London, 1850, vol. i, p. 61).

scribed as "spreading over the surrounding country like a sea." From Hit downward the river spreads over both banks, but with a strong tendency to flow farther and more deeply over the western bank. The slow and regular rise of the river made it exceedingly valuable for irrigation, and the Babylonian people fully availed themselves of this great opportunity. Along its banks were constructed brick walls provided with break-waters to divert and control the swift current at the rise. Sluice gates controlled the rise so that the eastern bank received an inundation equal to the west, while canals almost innumerable diverted the retreating waters, and prevented the flow from damaging the cultivable area. Furthermore, the water was retained in sufficient quantity to supply an irrigation system far back from the river for the grain harvest, after the fall of the river. This entire system is now a vast ruin. The river rises and falls as it wills, and sweeping far over the western bank, turns the country into a morass. The harm of this is both negative and positive. It makes impossible any such great ingathering of grain as existed when this great valley was the world's granary, and it fills the land with a dangerous miasma, which produces fevers and leaves the inhabitants weak and sickly. There are few instances in the world of a sadder waste of a beautiful and fertile country.

In the lower alluvial country the Tigris and Euphrates have made numerous changes in their

river beds. These changes have often begun in
the spring and summer floods and then continued.
The branch streams which are thus formed per-
petually vary, being sometimes so large as to be
navigable and again left absolutely dry. Yet, on
the whole, with the exception of the great change
produced by the union of the Tigris and Euphrates at their mouths, the general course of the
rivers remains about the same throughout the
historic period.

Of the changes in branch streams by far the
most important are on the side of Arabia. There
branches off near Hit a wide, deep channel, which
skirts the Arabian rocks and passes into the Persian Gulf by an entirely distinct channel. This
conveys a considerable body of Euphrates water,
and keeps back the encroachment of the desert,
thus extending considerably the arable part of
Chaldea and the Sea Lands. There is some
doubt as to its age, and as to whether or not it was
in the beginning partly or wholly artificial.

Besides the two rivers neither Assyria nor Babylonia has any supplies of water beyond one single
fresh-water lake, on the Arabian side of the Euphrates fifty miles south of the ruins of Babylon,
and twenty-five or thirty miles from the river.
It does not appear to have been well known or
counted of importance by the ancient inhabitants,
for no mention of it has yet been found in any
Assyrian or Babylonian texts; it was known to
the Romans as *Assyrium Stagnum*, and is now

called Bahr-i-Nedjif. It lies in a basin forty miles long and from ten to twenty miles broad, inclosed on three sides by limestone hills varying from twenty to two hundred feet in height. On the remaining side there is a ridge of rock which separates it from the Euphrates basin. At the season of the inundation the Euphrates pours water into this lake and then it appears to be a part of the inundation. The water is then sweet and good. When the river returns to its original level the lake remains with but very slight change in volume, but the water becomes so disagreeable as to be unpotable. It has been supposed that this may be due to its connection with rocks of the gypsiferous series.

The great valley has a climate which appears little fitted to produce men of energy and force, for the temperature over its entire surface is very high in the summer season. In the far south, along the Persian Gulf, and in the near-by regions, the atmosphere is moist and the heat is of the same character as that of Hindustan or Ceylon. Records do not exist to show the range of the thermometer, but the passing traveler states the simple fact that the temperature is higher than at Baghdad. In Baghdad the average maximum daily temperature indoors during June and July is set down as 107° Fahrenheit, and it often goes up to 120° or 122°.[1] At present this high tem-

---

[1] *The Bedouins of the Euphrates*, by Lady Anne Blunt, ii, p. 278. "In July, 1889, the average daily maximum temperature at Baghdad was

perature is also reached in the north as far up at
least as Mosul. It is now also rendered much
more oppressive by hot winds, which arise suddenly and filled with impalpable sand drive about
in eddying circles or sweep in vast clouds over a
wide extent of country. This dust becomes at
times so thick as to completely shut off near objects from the vision, as though by a fog. The
gleaming particles of sand shine beneath the swel-
tering sun, the sand enters nostrils or mouth and
seems to choke the very lungs. Death itself sometimes alone terminates the suffering experienced in
these terrible visitations. It is, however, altogether probable that in the period of the ancient
history neither the heat nor the sand was such a
menace.¹ Then the whole land in the south was
one vast network of canals. The presence of the
body of water thus everywhere spread abroad
greatly modified the temperature, so that the
sudden change which now exists from the heat of
the day to the cool of the night could not have
been so great. Besides this these canals made
the land a cultivated garden, free almost entirely
from the incursion of yellow sand. These sands
properly belong to the Arabian desert, from which
they yearly come in increasing quantities into the
plain and valley. During the period of the glory

114° in the shade, and in 1890 we encountered the same temperature more
than once in June." Peters, *Nippur*, ii, p. 310.

¹ The reference here is to the period of Babylonian occupation. That
great heat was experienced in the Greco-Roman period is well evidenced.
See, for example, Theophr., *de vent.*, 25, and Plutarch, Alexander, 35.

of Babylon these sand waves had certainly not
gone beyond the Euphrates, and they could
hardly have reached it. At present from May
to November the sky is usually without a single
cloud. In November the clouds gather, and in
December and January there are heavy rains.
These flow rapidly off into the rivers, for there is
no canal system to retain the water for use in agriculture. There is no cold weather in all the land in
the sense understood in the temperate zone. There
is in midwinter an occasional sign of frost, sufficient to whiten the dew upon the grass in early
morning, and in rare cases ice has been known to
form in the marshes. So mild, indeed, are the
winters that Persian kings made Babylon their
winter residence to avoid the bitter cold of their
own highlands. In recent times native Indians,
expelled for state reasons from their own country,
fix their residence in Bassorah or Baghdad to enjoy
the mild winter climate.

The whole alluvial plain of Babylonia was prover-
bially fertile in the ancient world. Herodotus began
the chorus of praise in the west, and it has continued with greater or less emphasis down the ages.
He begins his praise in the oft-quoted words : " Of
all countries that we know, there is none that is so
fruitful in grain. It makes no pretension, indeed,
of growing the fig, the olive, the vine, or any
other tree of the kind ; but in grain it is so fruitful as to yield commonly two hundredfold, and
when the production is at the greatest, even three

hundredfold. The blade of the wheat plant and of the barley plant is often four fingers in breadth. As for the millet and the sesame, I shall not say to what height they grow, though within my own knowledge; for I am not ignorant that what I have already written concerning the fruitfulness of Babylonia must seem incredible to those who have not visited the country." [1] The same note exactly is struck by Theophrastus in his statement: " In Babylon the wheat fields are regularly mown twice, and then fed off with beasts to keep down the luxuriance of the leaf; otherwise the plant does not run to ear. When this is done the return in lands that are badly cultivated is fiftyfold; while in those that are well farmed it is a hundredfold." [2] Strabo follows in the same strain, saying: " The country produces barley on a scale not known elsewhere, for the return is said to be three hundredfold. All other wants are supplied by the palm, which furnishes not only bread, but wine, vinegar, honey, and meal;" [3] and Pliny says that the wheat crop, where the land is well farmed, is a hundred and fiftyfold.

In estimating these tributes to the productiveness of the land it is perhaps well to remember that Herodotus had an affluent imagination and was inclined to exaggerate for effect. Theophrastus is more reliable when speaking of such mat-

---

[1] Herodotus, i, 193.

[2] Theophrastus, *Historia Plantarum*, viii, 7 (ed. Fredericus Wimmer, p. 135, line 2, ff.).

[3] xvi, p. 742 (ed. Carolus Müllerus, p. 632, line 26, ff.).

ters, but probably leaned somewhat on the tradition of Herodotus. The other statements must be exaggerations. To the modern husbandman in this valley the yield of wheat and barley is from thirty to fortyfold. When all allowance is made for the poor methods now followed, and for changed conditions, it is still unlikely that the ancient average yield greatly exceeded sixtyfold.

Modern travelers hardly equal the ancient in their estimate of the fertility of the soil, especially when compared with that of Egypt. Rich, who was a most careful observer and accurate reporter, says, "The soil is extremely fertile, producing great quantities of rice, oats, and grain of different kinds, though it is not cultivated to above half the degree of which it is susceptible." Chesney, who knew the land from much experience during survey work, is even more strong in the statement: "Although greatly changed by the neglect of man, those portions of Mesopotamia which are still cultivated, as the country about Hillah, show that the region has all the fertility ascribed to it by Herodotus." Loftus adds to this the comparative statement that "the soil is not less bountiful than that on the banks of the Egyptian Nile."[1] This statement is, however, of very slight value indeed, for when it was written Loftus had never been in Egypt. Probably the soundest modern estimate is that of Olivier, who knew both Egypt and Baby-

---

[1] *Travels and Researches in Chaldaea*, p. 14.

Ionia, and adjudged the former to be somewhat more fertile than the latter.[1]

It is commonly believed that wheat and barley are indigenous to the plains of the Euphrates, and that thence, after a period of cultivation, they spread westward over Syria and Egypt and on to Europe. If this be true, the land might well be expected to yield a good harvest of native cereals.

But the productivity of the land did not stop with the great cereals. The inhabitants had a wide range of vegetables for food, among which are pumpkins, kidney-beans, onions, vetches, egg plants, cucumbers, "gombo" lentils, chick-peas, and beans.

Above the vegetables and cereals of the land rose its trees, of which the variety was great, both of those that yielded fruit and of those that added merely to the beauty of the land; among these were the apple, fig, apricot, pistachio, vine, almond, walnut, cypress, tamarisk, plane tree, and acacia. But valuable and beautiful though they all were, none was equal in utility, in song, or in story with the palm. From the most ancient of days down to the present all the Orient has rung with the praises of the palm. In Babylon it found a suitable place for its development. It was cultivated with extreme care. Even in early times the process of reproduction had been discovered, and was facilitated by shaking the flowers of the male palm

---

[1] Olivier, *Voyage dans l'Empire Othoman*, etc., ii, p. 423.

over those of the female. From the products of this tree the peasantry were able almost to support life. The fruit was eaten both fresh and dry, forming in the latter case almost a sweetmeat. If decapitated, the tree gave a juice which might be used as a wine, and was "sweet and headachy," in the opinion of Xenophon. The Greeks even assert that the Babylonians derived from the palm bread, wine, vinegar, honey, groats, string and ropes of all kinds, firing, and a mash for fattening cattle.

The fauna of the land was as rich and as varied as its flora. The rivers swarmed with fish. In their slow-flowing waters the barbel and carp grew to large size and were most highly esteemed. But the eel, murena, silurus, and gurnard were also used for food, and found in abundance.

By the waters and amid the great reeds which almost seemed to wall in the rivers were birds in extraordinary variety, among them pelicans, cranes, storks, herons, gulls, ducks, swans, and geese. On land were found the ostrich, the bustard, partridge, thrush, blackbird, ortolan, turtledove, and pigeon, together with birds of prey like eagles and hawks. A few snakes are found, of which only three varieties are known to be poisonous, but none of these are so dangerous as many found in adjoining lands.

The larger animals were numerous, but of all the varieties that existed wild only the ox, ass, goat, and sheep were domesticated at an early period and made useful to man. To these were added the domestic hog, which seems, however, to have remained in a semi-wild state. In a later period the horse and camel were brought into use.

But if the domesticated animals were comparatively few, the wild animals were of extraordinary number. At the head of all of them, in the estimation of the Assyrians and Babylonians, stood the lion. He is not so fierce as his namesake of Africa. In size he is not much larger than a St. Bernard dog, and his Assyrian name originally meant big dog. The modern representative in the same regions is not deemed formidable by Europeans, for he never attacks men save when brought to bay in a position from which there is absolutely no chance of escape, when he will fight desperately. The natives, however, hold them in dread, and never make a fight against one which may be seen in the very act of slaying sheep. There are two varieties, one without a mane and the other with a mane of thick, tangled black hair. It is the latter which excites most fear in the native breast. The Assyrian and Babylonian kings hunted lions in the chase, and made great boast of the number that they had slain. The chase of the lion was, indeed, the royal sport, and fills a large share of the numerous monumental illustrations of hunting.

In very early times the elephant wandered at will over the middle Euphrates country, but it disappeared certainly before the thirteenth century,

and was henceforward only an object of curiosity,
when received by kings as presents in distant
wars. Like the elephant, other beasts of chase or
prey early disappeared, or ceased to be objects of
interest because of their rarity. Among these
were the urus, leopard, lynx, wild-cat, hyena,
porcupine, beaver, and the ibex. During at least
a large part of the history the wild ass and on-
ager roamed in small herds over much of the
country and especially between the Balikh and
the Tigris. The beauty and swiftness of the wild
ass have long been celebrated in the Orient, and
the Assyrians admired and represented them
in their monuments. It appears that they attempted to tame them for the drawing of chariots, but met with poor success. Modern attempts to make them serviceable have been
equally futile. The natives frequently capture foals
and rear them on milk in the tent. They become
docile and affectionate, but are delicate in captivity
and useless for labor. Two varieties of deer appear in monumental representation, the one apparently representing the gray deer, which still exists in the country, and the other the fallow
deer, which is now entirely unknown. The
hare, also, is frequently exhibited as the object of
chase.

While both Babylonia and Assyria were exceed.
ingly rich in flora and fauna, they are both, and
especially the former, exceedingly poor in mineral
wealth. The alluvium is absolutely destitute of

metals and of stone. This had an important re-
flex influence upon the civilization of the country.
As stone was not procurable close at hand, the
early builders who would have it for utility or
decoration sought it at great distances. From
Arabia came probably the earliest stone utilized
in the country. This had to be transported long
distances overland. The skill required for this
in the overcoming of engineering difficulties pushed
forward the development of the people in mechan-
ical pursuits, and hence reacted upon civilization.
But even as early as 3000 B. C. stone was brought
from the Lebanon and the Amanus. This was
rafted down the Euphrates, after a considerable
land journey to its upper waters. And herein was
cause for the study of problems in river transportation and in the construction of navigable rafts.
Such problems as these would be insoluble by
natives in the same district at present, but they
were successfully carried out on a large scale in
early times, as the great buildings and the inscriptions describing them abundantly witness. But,
though the Babylonians did thus acquire stone,
they could hardly have secured enough to house
the entire population as well as for royal resi-
dences and the homes of the gods. The need for
a permanent and less costly building material was
solved in another way. There was beneath their
feet an inexhaustible supply of the best qualities
of clay. This was readily molded into bricks.
Some of these were dried in the sun, and were

then deemed sufficient for the filling in of the in-
teriors of walls. Others were baked in kilns, and
with these the walls were faced. In the excel-
lence of materials used, and in the perfection of
form, texture, and solidity, and in the great size
of their bricks the Babylonians have probably
never been excelled. The same material was
used for the manufacture of books or tablets.
These were made even more carefully, and were
almost indestructible. For records the ancient
world knew nothing their superior and perhaps
nothing equal. The papyrus of ancient Egypt
was so fragile and so easily destroyed by either
fire or water that it bears no comparison with the
brick which resisted both almost equally well.
The clay tablet has preserved through the centuries a vast literature, much of it uninjured,
while untold portions of the literature of the
more cultured Egyptians have hopelessly perished.

In the erection of buildings the bricks were
joined together in three different ways. They
are found simply set together in the interior of
walls, without any substance to form a close junction. More commonly they were united by bitumen, which was found in several parts of the
country, but especially at Hit. Here are inexhaustible springs which have supplied the whole
surrounding country for untold centuries, and
form the subject of repeated references in the literature not only of Babylonia, but of Egypt,

Greece, and Rome as well.[1] Slime and mud were also used, and with these calcareous earths appear to have been mixed, the whole forming a solid and extremely tenacious mortar.

From the bitumen pits petroleum is now taken, and may have been known to the ancients. But here ends the very brief catalogue of the mineral products of Babylonia. The land could hardly be poorer in this respect.

In mineral wealth Assyria was incomparably superior to Babylonia. Stone of excellent quality, and in many varieties, such as limestone, conglomerate, and sandstone, is found on every hand, while other stones were easily accessible. A soft and beautiful alabaster, readily cut into slabs, abounds on the eastern banks of the Tigris. This beautiful material was extensively used for wainscoting in Assyrian palaces, and its outer surfaces were then richly carved in bas-reliefs. The progress thus made in the art of sculpture was noteworthy, and is to be numbered among the greatest triumphs won by this warlike people in the arts of peace. The mountains of Kurdistan, easily reached by the rivers or water courses above the great cities, supplied many beautiful forms of marble; while Mount Masius offered a fine quality of dark-colored basalt of great fineness and hardness. These stones were indeed not used

---

[1] See, for example, Herodotus, i, 179; Pliny, *Nat. Hist.*, vi, 129, ff., 152; Strabo, xvi, 743. The pits are described by Chesney (*Narrative of Euphrates Expedition*, p. 280; comp. also p. 76) and by Rich (*Narrative of a Journey to the Site of Babylon*, London, 1839, pp. 101, 102).

for the walls of buildings. The colonists of Assyria retained the custom of Babylonia, from which they had come, and built their houses, temples, and palaces of brick, and later ages continued to follow their example. Like Babylonia, Assyria had extensive bitumen pits, located at Kerkuk,[1] in the territory between the Lesser Zab and the Adhem, while another source is found in the bed of the Shor-Derreh torrent, near Nimroud. Salt is also obtainable in the former district.

The lands which were thus rich in flora and fauna and sufficiently supplied with minerals for man's ordinary use maintained a great population, largely settled in cities, in which the real political life of the land began. The cities which play important parts in the later history may here be set down, with just enough of color and description to make them real in the story of their political life.

In the far south lay the city of Eridu, which played but a small part in all the history of Babylonia, unless indeed it had importance in a period still more ancient than that known to us. The site is now known as Abu-Shahrein,[2] and has not

---

[1] See Ainsworth, "Journey to Constantinople," in Chesney's *Narrative of Euphrates Expedition*, p. 497 : "There are several wells from which considerable quantities of naphtha and petroleum are obtained. From eight to ten gallons were said to be collected from each well per diem."

[2] See Loftus, "Notes on Abu-Shahrein and Tel-el-Lahm," in *Journal of the Royal Asiatic Society*, xiv, pp. 412, ff. "We found . . . . that the name Abu-Shahrein had vanished, and Nowawis taken its place as the present designation of the ancient ruins of Eridu." Peters, *Nippur*, ii, p. 96.

yet been adequately studied. The remains of the city, so far as they have been excavated, appear to contain a large temple, which was probably the home of the god Ea, who here received special veneration.

West of Eridu stood the great city Ur, which occupied from the earliest times down to the beginning of Babylon's hegemony a position of distinguished influence in the land, and even thereafter continued to be the most important city in the south. The chief god of the city was Sin, the moon god, here worshiped under the name of Nannar. The moon god always exerted profound influence over the minds of the people, and Ur therefore was early adorned with a large temple for the worship of Sin, which was frequently restored down the centuries to the days of Nabonidus. The ruins of the city have been but slightly explored, and will almost certainly give a rich treasure, at some future day, to a complete examination of them. The mound is now called El-Mugheir [1]—the place of bitumen—for the inhabitants have used it for centuries as a place to secure bitumen, which they dug from between the bricks of Babylonian buildings.

At the modern town of Senkereh,[2] on the left

---

[1] Loftus, *Travels and Researches in Chaldæa and Susiana*, London, 1857, pp. 127, ff.; Peters, *Nippur*, ii, pp. 196, ff. (with photograph of the Ziggurat).

[2] Loftus, *op. cit.*, p. 256. See especially Sachau, *Am Euphrat und Tigris*, pp. 66–68. Sachau believes that the mound contains not only remains of temples and palaces, but also of the dwellings of the inhabit-

bank of the Shatt-en-Nil Canal stood the next chief city, Larsa. This was also one of the most ancient cities of the land. The sun god held the chief position in Larsa, and here the early kings Ur-Gur and Dungi built a temple in his honor. This temple found restorers in Hammurabi, Burna-buriash, Nebuchadrezzar, and Nabonidus, and so remained a venerated spot unto the very end of Babylonian history. The city early played an important political part, and retained its place at the head of a small state even down to the reign of Hammurabi. It was the last city to succumb to him and yield allegiance to the conquering might of Babylon.

Somewhat north of Larsa, probably at the mound of Tell-Id, was the city of Girsu, which is mentioned as early as the reign of Dungi, and was the chief city of at least one petty king (Urkagina) in the early period. Its influence was, however, small in comparison with those farther south or when compared with the city of Uruk (Erech, Orchoë), which is but a short distance from it. Uruk was a border city between northern and southern Babylonia, and long remained the center of a small independent kingdom. It was the place of worship of the goddess Nana of the

ants. "In diesen babylonischen Städten Senkere und Warkâ scheinen ausser den Tempeln und Palästen auch noch die Wohnungen der Bürger unter dem Schutt erhalten zu sein ähnlich wie in Pompeji, während in Ninive ausser den beiden Königsburgen, Kojunjik und Nebi Jûnus, der Mauer und den Thoren alle übrigen Wohnungen spurlos von der Erdober-fläche verschwunden sind. Aehnliches gilt auch von dem Weichbild von Babylon." *Ibid.*, p. 67.

Sumerians, with whom the Semitic inhabitants identified their goddess Ishtar. The temple dedicated to the goddess and called E-Anna (house of heaven) was built by Ur-Gur and Dungi and often restored. It now forms the ruin of El-Buwarije, while the general mass of ruins is called Warka,[1] which has unhappily not been dug up. The city had independence at an early period, and is coupled by Hebrew tradition[2] with the earliest centers of the land, and Babylonian records go far to prove that this is correct. It was, however, much more than a mere center of power. It was a seat of learning and must have had a library at a very early period. Many books in the library of Asshurbanapal, and especially religious hymns, bear colophons which show that they were copied from originals at Uruk. Strabo adds to this fact the statement that at Orchoë there was a school of Chaldeans, that is in his use of the word "astrologists." This would indicate that culture was still resident in this city, though it had vanished from other more ancient centers. The political, literary, and religious history of the city all make it of so great interest and importance that it is especially a matter for regret that it has never been properly excavated.

On the banks of the canal Shatt-el-Hai, which unites the Tigris and Euphrates, is a mound

---

[1] Loftus, op. cit., pp. 159, f. It has been visited by Ward (see Peters, Nippur, i, pp. 349, 350) and by Sachau (op. cit., pp. 61–64), who has well described its present appearance.

[2] Gen. x, 10.

Telloh,[1] from which have come vast stores of inscribed tablets of every description. It marks, in all probability, the site of the ancient city of Lagash, which had a long history as a separate state, though with many fluctuations of power.

The next city in our progress northward was Isin, of which, unhappily, very little is known. It was linked in the title of the kings who made Nippur, its near-by neighbor, the chief city of the land, but its history was swallowed up in the greater history of the places about it, and its ruins have not been certainly identified.[2]

Nippur, on the other hand, is now the best known city in all Babylonia. The greatest discoveries yet made beneath the soil of the entire land were made here by the University of Pennsylvania expedition. Nippur was the oldest center of the worship of the god Bel, and may be the oldest city of all Babylonia of which there is any known record. As Ur was the city of the moon god, and Sippara the city of the sun god, so was Nippur the home of Bel, and as these three were the greatest of the gods of Babylonia, so their cities outranked all others in early political history, until dethroned by force; after which they continued to be the chief places of veneration in all the empire. Nippur was rich in build-

---

[1] Heuzey-de Sarzec, *Decouvertes en Chaldée, passim* ; Peters, *Nippur*, i, pp. 268, 269 ; ii, 291. The visit by Ward is described in his diary (Peters, *Nippur*, i, pp. 337–339, 342).

[2] Peters suggests Bismya as the probable site of Isin (*Nippur*, ii, 272).

ings devoted to religion and to royal residence, and its great ruin mound, Niffer or Nuffar, has yielded an extraordinary mass of ancient treasures.

But great as all these cities were in age, and rich though they continued to be in religious as· sociations, they were all surpassed in influence by the city of Babylon. They were forgotten of men when the dust and sand settled upon them, but the glory and the shame of Babylon re· mained. Even the name of the city lived on in the ruin heap Babil.[1] The chief ruins of Baby· lon lie near the modern village of Hillah, and cover such a great extent of country that until very recently no men have been found bold enough to attempt the exploration of the entire mound. The city laid no claim to great age, and was probably not very ancient when Hammurabi made it the chief city over all the land and dis· placed the more ancient seats of power. The re· ligious glory of the city was also in a sense ficti· tious. Its chief god had been Marduk (the bibli· cal Merodach), and to him fitting worship was paid for generations. But Marduk's own position in the pantheon was not great enough to bring to

---

[1] There is still some doubt about the identification of various mounds near Hillah with the parts of ancient Babylon. There is a learned and exhaustive review of the matter by Baumstarck in Pauly-Wissowa, *Real-enc. der class. Alterthumswissenschaft*, ii (1899), and an outline of the problems by the writer in the *Jewish Encyclopædia, sub voce.* There is a good plan of the sites in *Encyclopædia Biblica* (Cheyne), i, facing cols. 417, 418. The mounds are well described by Peters (*Nippur*, i, pp. 212; ii, 53) and by Sachau (*op cit.*, pp. 37, ff.).

the city a religious primacy, and he was therefore identified with the great god Bel, and under that name was worshiped in Babylon. To him was erected a great temple in pyramidal form rising to seven stories, and known as E-sagila. Kings vied with each other to make this the largest and most beautiful shrine in the empire, and in it all rulers must needs "take the hands of Bel" before their authority was deemed valid. So came the city to possess political power, dominion over the hearts and consciences of men, and wealth unapproach-able. To Babylon in the days of Nabonidus was joined another city, Borsippa, which may have been as old as the capital itself. In it stood the temple of E-zida, now Birs Nimroud,[1] dedicated to Nabu (the biblical Nebo), on which kings lavished almost as much labor and wealth as upon E-sagila. The two cities were linked also in their religious festivals, for on the first day of Nisan (March–April), the beginning of a new year, the god Nabu left his temple in solemn procession to visit his father, Marduk, in Babylon. Of so great im-portance was this festival that the king was required to share in it, no matter where he might be at the time, whether on business or pleasure bent, under the penalty of forfeiting for the com-ing year the title of king of Babylon. It is easy to see that this gave enormous power to the priesthood, for it was they alone who repre-

---

[1] Oppert, *Expedition en Mesopotamie*, i, pp. 200, ff.; Peters, *op. cit.*, i, pp. 213, ff.

sented these great deities in the eyes of all the people.

Five hours (about fifteen miles) northeast of Babylon lay Kutha, now a mound and village called Tell-Ibrahim,[1] once the leading city of northern Babylonia before the rise of the city of Babylon. The chief god of the city was Nergal, whose temple was called E-shid-lam, at which passing kings were wont to pay honors and offer sacrifices. From Kutha a profound influence passed into the world's history by the act of one of the Assyrian kings. Sargon deported thence a number of inhabitants to Samaria on the fall of the northern kingdom of Israel, who introduced the worship of Nergal and then engrafted upon it features derived from the religion of Jehovah. In close relation with Kutha stood the near-by city of Kish, somewhat as Borsippa stood to Babylon.

In the extreme northern part of Babylonia, and nearly opposite to the present Baghdad, lies the mound Akerkuf,[2] which marks the site of Dur-Kurigalzu (Kurigalzuburg), a city named after a Babylonian king, but the influence of which in history was slight. Much the same may be said of the city of Upi (Opis) during most of the period of Babylonian history, with this exception, that it appears to have had some influence during the Hammurabi period.

---

[1] Rassam, *Asshur and the Land of Nimrod.* New York, 1897, p. 396.
[2] On the mound see Chesney, *Narrative of Euphrates Expedition*, p. 83, and Rich, *Narrative of Journey to the Site of Babylon*, pp. 2, 3.

The cities of Assyria were not so ancient as those of Babylonia, and their general character was commercial rather than religious, military rather than peaceful and culture-loving. Their temples were indeed large and imposing, for the Assyrians had amassed great wealth in war, and they believed, no less than the Babylonians, that the gods had led them to victory. They also boasted great piles devoted to the residence of kings, in which, however, libraries were not so common as in Babylonia.

The first city of Assyria in age was Asshur, whose site is now marked by the mound of Kalah Shergat,[1] on the right bank of the Tigris. It was originally a colony and dependency of Babylonia, but its kings spread their power over the adjoining country, which they named Asshur, after their city. It was the home of the great god Asshur, whose temple E-kharsag-kurkurra was erected by the earliest rulers of whom we know anything, and frequently restored by later monarchs. When Calah became the capital of the kingdom Asshur lost its dignity and decreased in size, but retained a certain reverence as the ancient site of the most revered national god, and as the mother city of the kingdom.

A little farther north, but on the eastern bank of the Tigris and at its junction with the Upper

---

[1] Rassam, *Asshur and the Land of Nimrod*, pp. 256, 257. Sachau, *op. cit.*, pp. 91, f., and 104, with two illustrations of the mounds. Ainsworth, *Journal of the Geographical Society*, xi, p. 5.

21

Zab, Shalmaneser I built the city of Calah, which he made the capital of Assyria. It remained the royal residence down to the age of Sargon. The mound Nimroud[1] marks its site, and this has been fairly but not completely dug over. The city was not an ancient and venerated shrine of any deity, but worship was paid to Asshur in its temple.

A little farther up the eastern bank of the Tigris the ruin heaps and squalid villages of Kuyunjik[2] and Neby Yunus mark the site of Nineveh, which Sennacherib made the capital of the empire. The city was, however, much older than this, and may almost certainly be accounted one of the most ancient cities in the kingdom. It was the center of the worship of Ishtar, who was called Ishtar of Nineveh to distinguish her from Ishtar of Arbela. Ishtar of Nineveh was worshiped in a great temple on which generation after generation lavished extraordinary plunder. It was the dream of Sennacherib to make Nineveh surpass Babylon in size and magnificence, and, though he did not reach that ideal, he did make it a fine city, second only to the ancient mother city by the Euphrates. To all the world Nineveh stood as the representative city of the hated Assyrian empire, and that made its name a by-word among the peoples.

---

[1] Layard, *Nineveh and its Remains*, New York, 1849, i, pp. 28, 44, etc. Sachau, *op. cit.*, p. 105. Rassam, *op. cit.*, pp. 9, 225 (with plan and illustration of ruins).

[2] Layard, *op. cit.*, i, p. 98, etc.

North of Nineveh, at the foot of the mountains, Sargon planted a new city, to which he gave his own name, Dur-Sharrukin (that is, Sargon'sburg), which he probably designed not only to make a royal residence, but also the capital of the country and a rival of Nineveh. The remains of the city at Khorsabad[1] were the first Assyrian ruins excavated, and these have shown that he made the city magnificent with a palace and other buildings, but it never became even an equal of Nineveh.[2] It apparently did not long outlive its founder, but sank away into insignificance.

Far more important than this creation of the fancy of an Assyrian king was the city of Arbaïlu. How old this city was is not known. There is not in all the inscriptions any evidence that the Assyrian kings paid any attention to it. It certainly received at their hands no great palaces and no temples. It had no political weight in the development of Assyrian power, though it must have had an Assyrian populace. It lived a quiet life apart from the great tides of war or commerce during the Assyrian period, and survived the ruin which overwhelmed the empire. It was still an important city in Persian days, and continued to exist when the city of Nineveh was un-

---

[1] M. Botta's letters on the discoveries at Nineveh, translated from the French by C. T[obin]. London, 1850, *passim*. Rassam, *op. cit.*, p. 295. Sachau, *op. cit.*, pp. 106, 121.

[2] The site was a very poor one, as has often been pointed out (see, for example, Sachau, *l. c.*); for it was badly supplied with water, and lay apart from the great lines of communication.

known save as a name in the memory. A great mound marks its site, and its name is retained in the modern Erbil.[1] The mound has not yet been excavated, and may very probably contain important memorials of the city's long career.

Outside the strict limits of Assyria lay the city of Naçibina. It lay upon the Kharmis, a tributary of the Khabur, at the foot of the mountains. It was the center of an Assyrian province, and continued to live under the name of Nisibis after the empire had ended. Hadrian ceded it to the Parthians, but it returned to Roman rule and was flourishing at the time of Septimius Severus (Septimia Colonia Nisibis). Under the Seleucids it still continued prosperous and bore the name of Antiochia Mygdoniæ. Its modern representative, a miserable collection of huts, has returned to the ancient name and is called Nisibin.

Farther west, on the left bank of the Balikh, was Harran, or Road-Town, through which passed the great highways from south and east toward the west. Harran was the center for the worship of Sin, the moon god, in the north, as Ur was in the south, and perhaps no sacred city in the land ever held so tenaciously to its ancient belief. When Christianity overran Mesopotamia this city remained the last center of paganism, and under the Mohammedan sway the sect of Sabeans here continued the worship of the moon. The history of Harran runs so far back that its origin is lost

---

[1] Sachau, *op. cit.*, pp. 111–113 (with picture of the mound).

in the mists that surround the very beginnings of
civilization. During the continuance of Assyrian
power it was a constant factor in the life of the
empire, and when Nineveh had ceased to vex
mankind it was still a powerful city. The Parthians made a stronghold of it, and there Crassus
was defeated. It later formed part of the Chris-
tian kingdom of Abgar, and became a city of the
Roman empire. The mounds[1] which mark its
site must certainly contain memorials of its long
history, but they have not been excavated. The
classical name was Carrhæ (which evidently contains a reminiscence of the ancient name), and it has
still some importance as a road town.

---

[1] Ainsworth, *Euphrates Expedition*, i, p. 203.

CHAPTER XI.

THE PEOPLES OF BABYLONIA AND ASSYRIA.

THE civilization of Assyria and Babylonia and their great sweep of history were not made by one people. Men of several different stocks contributed to the result, and here, as often afterward in the world's history, the history bears the stamp not of a unity but of a diversity of races. Even in modern times, with all the resources at our command, it is often difficult to distinguish the different strains of races and to trace their influence in the movements of history. We need, therefore, feel no surprise that there should be great difficulty in tracing out the racial affinities of the peoples who made history in Assyria and Babylonia.

At the earliest period to which direct monumental records go back we find a people in possession of Babylonia who are called by us Babylonians. Their written records are found to be in part a Semitic language, a language closely related in forms and vocabulary to the northern branch of the Semitic family, of which Hebrew and Aramaic are well-known examples. But when these earliest records are all gathered together it appears that large numbers of them are bilingual; that is to say, side by side with the Semitic Babylonian is found another language. This other language appears in these inscriptions in the form of two dialects, one called "the language of the land of Accad" and the other "the language of the land of Sumer." As the latter contains the older forms it is now called the Sumerian language, and the other is regarded as a dialect of it. In this Sumerian language, written though it be in part at least by Semitic Babylonians, lies the proof of the existence of a Sumerian people. They belong distinctly, as yet, to the prehistoric period in Babylonian life. Of their racial connections we know only the single negative fact that they were not Semites. Their language is agglutinative, and they have been connected on linguistic grounds both with Indo-Europeans and especially with Turanians. But the evidence is slight in itself and of doubtful weight even if it were more extensive, for language is, after all, proof not of race but of social contact.[1]

But, though we are unable to say who these Sumerians were, we are in a position to aver some

---

[1] The theory that the Sumerians were Mongols has been strongly supported by Hommel, Lenormant, and others, and as strongly denied by Halévy, Paul Haupt, and Donner. In recent times attempts have been made by Hermann (*Ueber die Sumerische Sprache*, Russian Archæological Congress, Riga, 1896), in a paper which I have not seen, to show that there is a connection between Sumerian and the Ugro-Finnish member of the Ural-Altaic family. (See A. H. Keane, *Man Past and Present*, Cambridge, 1899, pp. 273, ff.) The solution of the question is not yet found.

facts concerning their work in the world and their relations to the Semitic Babylonians. It was they who invented the cuneiform system of writing, a cumbrous and artificial system indeed, and yet a wonderful advance upon the still more cumbrous picture writing out of which it was developed. When the Semitic Babylonians conquered the Sumerians and possessed their lands they adopted at once this system of writing and took over with it the literature which it enshrined. This literature was especially devoted to the setting forth of forms of worship, of hymns of praise to gods, of prayers for forgiveness from sins, and of incantations for delivery from disease. It was natural that the Babylonians should desire to retain this religious material in its ancient tongue, as it was not to be expected that it would be so efficacious if translated into their own Semitic speech. There arose, therefore, a custom of providing these religious texts with interlinear translations into the Semitic speech. Sumerian had now come into the same position as did Latin in the religious life of the Middle Ages. It remained only that it should advance into a position similar to that held by Latin in general life in the same period. This also came about, for not only were religious texts so written, but also historical texts as well. Gradually this custom ceased and the Sumerian language was no longer mentioned or used; but the system of writing which the Sumerians had devised continued in full use to the fall of the Babylonian commonwealth, and even lived on in the hands of the Indo-Europeans who came after them.[1]

The Babylonians had indeed conquered the Sumerians, but in a higher sense they had been conquered by them, and their civilization in general and their religion in particular owed a deep debt to this strange, almost unknown people who stand on the very confines of human history.

At about the beginning of the fourth millennium before Christ the Sumerian people, who had already attained a high civilization, found their land invaded by a vast horde of barbarians, for so these must have appeared to them. These were Semites, closely related in blood to the Arabs who once overran Spain and the Hebrews who once came pouring across the Jordan into Canaan. Whence these invaders came is not certain. It has been thought by some that they came from the northeast through the passes of the Kurdistan mountains, and that Babylonia was the land in which they had their first national development and from which they spread over western Asia to make great careers as Arabians, Canaanites, and

---

[1] A great controversy has raged about the question of this Sumerian language. It has been asserted by some that the view taken here is wholly erroneous, and that we have in these bilingual texts not two languages, but simply two forms of writing. According to this view the so-called Sumerian language was simply a cabalistic method of sacred writing, invented for their own purposes by Semitic priests. This view, first proposed in this form by Halévy, in the beginning secured some converts, but has latterly lost ground. To the present writer the facts seem wholly opposed to it. See Chapter VII.

Aramæans.[1] This view, once stated and supported with surpassing learning, is now almost
abandoned, and but few great names may be
cited among its modern adherents. A second
view finds the original home of the Semites in
Africa, either in the northeastern[2] or northwestern part of the great continent.[3] It were idle
to deny that strong linguistic support for this
view may be found in the recognized affinity between the Semitic languages and Egyptian, Coptic,
Berber, and the Kushite (Bisharee, Galla, Somali,
etc.) languages. But when all has been said in
favor of this view there still remain more potent

---

[1] The northern origin of the Semites was adopted by Renan, *Histoire
générale des langues sémitiques*, 2d edit., p. 29, but the strongest argument
for it is presented by J. Guidi, *Della Sede primitiva dei Popolo Semitici*,
in the *Memorie della R. Accademia dei Lincei*, 3d series, vol. iii. (Some
additions are made to the evidences of Guidi by Jacob Krall, *Grundriss der
altorientalischen Geschichte*, I Theil, Wien, 1899, p. 31.) To this same view
adheres Hommel, who has devoted much learning to its exposition and
defense; for example, *La Patrie originaire des Sémites*, in the *Atti del IV
Congresso Internationale degli Orientalisti*, vol. i, pp. 217–228, Firenze,
1880; *Die Namen der Säugethiere*, Leipzig, 1879, pp. 496, ff.; *Die Semitischen Völker und Sprachen*, pp. 7, 11, 12, 59–63, 95, ff.; *Die Sprach-
geschichtliche Stellung des Babylonisch-assyrischen* (Études archéologiques
linguistiques et historiques dédiées à C. Leemans, Leide, 1885, pp. 127–129)
and *Geschichte Babyloniens und Assyriens*. Berlin, 1885, p. 267.

[2] Nöldeke, Theodor, *Die Semitischen Sprachen*, 2te Auflage. Leipzig,
1899, p. 11. Nöldeke puts forward this view very tentatively and only as
an hypothesis, and admits " dass die Herkunft aller Semiten aus Arabien
sehr wohl denkbar wäre " (p. 13).

[3] Professor D. G. Brinton, of Philadelphia, has suggested northwestern
Africa as the primitive seat of the Semites, and has supported it with
many arguments, chiefly ethnological. His paper, read before the Philadelphia Oriental Club, has been printed together with a criticism by Professor Jastrow, who inclines to Nöldeke's view rather than to Brinton's. *The
Cradle of the Semites*, by Daniel G. Brinton, M. D., and Morris Jastrow, Jr.,
Ph.D., Philadelphia, 1890.

considerations in favor of a third view, that the original home of the Semites was in Arabia,[1] out of which they came in successive waves of migration to find larger and more bountiful lands in Babylonia, Mesopotamia, and even in the far western land of Canaan. This latter view seems ever to win new adherents and may be said now to be generally accepted by modern scholars. The Babylonians conquered the Sumerians, drove some of them out, destroyed others, and assimilated the rest. During the long course of their history they remained as unchanged and unchangeable as the Egyptians. They were powerful in warfare at first, but gradually cast aside the warlike spirit and became so devoted to the arts of peace as to be unable to defend their country from invasion, which happened again and again during their long history. Yet so great was their vitality and so marked their racial individuality that they always triumphed in the end and absorbed their conquerors. Just as their type, the distinctive Semitic type, prevailed over the Sumerian, so also did it prevail over the Kassites, Elamites, and that long line of lesser peoples who conquered them in part or settled among them peaceably.

---

[1] Sayce, *Assyrian Grammar for Comparative Purposes*, 1st ed., p. 13. E. Schrader, *Die Abstammung der Chaldaer und die Ursitze der Semiten*, in the *Zeitschrift der Deutschen Morgenländischen Gesellschaft*, xxvii, pp. 397, ff. Tiele, *Babylonisch-Assyrische Geschichte*, pp. 106, 107. Ed. Meyer, *Geschichte des Altertums*, i, pp. 207, ff. Keane, *Man Past and Present*, pp. 490, 491. Winckler, *Die Völker Vorderasiens.* Leipzig, 1899, p. 10. Winckler states the general movements and the general relationships of the Semitic peoples very admirably in this brief tract.

The Babylonians were devoted chiefly to religion and to literature, as their remains would seem to indicate. It was they who erected the largest temples that the world has ever seen, and as the materials used were perishable, ever reerected and restored them. It was they who provided these temples with books, liturgies, hymns, and prayers, and heaped up thousands of tablets recording all these building operations and giving glory and honor to the gods who had inspired the work.

Out of the Babylonian people sprang the Assyrians, for Assyria was colonized from Babylonia. Though of the same blood, the Assyrians gradually became a very different people. Less exposed to invasion during a large part of their history than the Babylonians, they remained of much purer Semitic blood. In religion, in language, and in literature they continued to the end ever dependent upon the southern people. Their climate belonged to the temperate rather than to the subtropical zone, and the inclemency of winters over at least part of their little kingdom served to toughen their fiber, while their early efforts at conquest gradually hardened them into the form which they bore during all their history. They became a military people on the one hand, and a commercial people on the other. Early accustomed to blood and fire, they became totally unlike the peace-loving Babylonians, and their history is filled with deeds of almost unparalleled savagery. Wherever their armies marched women were ravished, men were mutilated or flayed alive, houses and cities and fields of grain were given to the torch, and desolation and ruin were left behind. Yet out of this conquest they achieved empire, and sobered by its burdens, learned to govern as well as to destroy, and devised methods of subjection and of rule, which were afterward applied by a people who in certain respects much resembled them, the Romans. Along with this development in the arts of war and the practice of government there went a great growth in trade. The Assyrian traders invaded the whole East and took gain both from buying and from selling, from transport and from storage. They influenced the king to conquest in more than one instance that the field of their operations and the extent of their money getting might be increased. That they contributed to civilization by their barter and trade there is no doubt, and this result affords a bright contrast to the weary details of blood and fire which otherwise would fill the whole canvas. Yet, though thus given over in large measure to war and commerce, the Assyrians knew their lack and ever looked with envy to the superior civilization of Babylonia. Some of their kings imitated the Babylonians in the founding and storing of libraries with books of religion and literature and not merely with boastful narratives of bloody conquest. Others bore witness to the attractiveness of the Babylonian culture by conquering parts of that country that they might worship at its ancient shrines and add to their names royal titles, bestowed by an hereditary priesthood, which had come down from an immemorial past. Thus were mixed up in the Assyrian nature elements both of barbarism and of civilization, and now one and now the other is manifested in the work which they did in the world. But when the whole history is surveyed, as in a panorama, the barbarism must be admitted to prevail over the civilization and the total impression to be less favorable than that which the Babylonians make upon us.

Long after the Babylonians and Assyrians had risen to power in the world the great valley came to know another people who called themselves Kaldu, and were known to the Hebrews as Kasdim, to the Greeks as Chaldaioi (Χαλδαῖοι), from whom we have called them Chaldeans. They were undoubtedly Semites,[1] for not only are their names purely Semitic, but their religion, manner of life, and adaptation to Semitic usages all bear the same stamp as those of the Semitic Babylonians. The origin of the Chaldeans is, like that of the Babylonians, lost in the past. They also probably came out of the heart of Arabia and settled first along the western shore of the Persian Gulf, pushing gradually northward until they held the country about the mouths of the Tigris and Euphrates.

[1] Jensen has suggested that they were "Semitized Sumerians," and Lehmann appears to agree with him (Lehmann, *Shamashshumukin*, p. 173), but at best the opinion is merely a guess and has no direct support in the inscriptions.

From that district they begin the long series of incursions which finally won for them the control of Babylonia, and made them the heirs of the Babylonian people in civilization and in empire. In the beginning they were nomads and tillers of the soil, but became men of the city and formed little city kingdoms similar to those which had existed in the early days of Babylonian civilization. The lines of their development were, however, more similar to those of the Assyrians than to those of the Babylonians. They developed military prowess and founded a great empire by the sword. Its extension toward the west was marked by bloodshed and the destruction of ancient centers of civilization. But later the objects of civilization were furthered by them and their kings became patrons of learning. In this latter stage they are perhaps to be regarded as having lost their national life and character and as transformed by the Babylonian civilization which they had conquered.

The Sumerians, the Babylonians, the Assyrians, and the Chaldeans—these were the peoples who wrought out the history here to be narrated. Besides these there were many other lesser peoples who contributed to the movements which are to be told, but their characterization may best be left to the time of their appearance in the narrative, as they were secondary rather than primary actors in the great drama.

CHAPTER XII.

THE CHRONOLOGY.

UNLIKE the Egyptians, both the Assyrians and Babylonians, but especially the latter, gave much attention to chronology, seeking in a number of different ways to preserve the order of events and to construct a backbone for their historical recollections. The chronological material thus produced must have been very extensive, for the portions which have come down to us are silent witnesses of the yet unrecovered or totally destroyed materials of which they were but fragments. Our chronology of the history of these people must be based primarily upon their own chronological materials, but from certain of the Greek writers useful material is secured. All this material may here be grouped in order, accompanied by notes upon its value and use, as sources for chronology.

A.—BABYLONIAN AND ASSYRIAN MONUMENTS.

I. *Babylonian Chronological Materials.* The Babylonian priests, historiographers and chronographers have left us an enormous mass of chronological materials, all now in a fragmentary state, but showing clearly how much importance was attached by them to the arrangement of historical facts in due order of time. These original sources may thus be arranged:

1. *The Babylonian King List A.* A brief list of the names of the kings of several Babylonian dynasties, now badly broken, with many names missing. By the side of each king's name is given the number of years of his reign, and at the end of each dynasty also a summation of the years of reign of all the kings of that dynasty.[1]

2. *The Babylonian King List B.* A list of Babylonian kings, containing the names and years of reign of the kings of the first and second dynasties, with the years of reign of each one, and also the summation as before.[2]

3. *A Babylonian Chronological Tablet of Dynasty I* (cited here as C).[3] There has recently been discovered in the collections of the British Museum an extremely valuable chronological tablet, dated in the reign of Ammi-sadugga,

---

[1], [2] These two King Lists have been repeatedly copied, collated, and verified. The chief literature upon them is as follows: (a) *Proceedings of the Society of Biblical Archæology*, 1884, pp. 193–204 (Pinches). (b) *Sitzungsberichte der Berl. Ak. der Wissenschaften*, 1887, pp. 579–607 (Schrader). (c) *Assyrische Gebete an den Sonnengott*, I u. II, Leipzig, 1894 (Knudtzon). (d) *Proceedings of the Society of Biblical Archæology*, 1888, pp. 22, ff. (Pinches). (e) *Keilinschriftliche Bibliothek*, Berlin, 1890, vol. ii, pp. 286, ff. (Schrader). (f) *Zwei Hauptprobleme der altorientalischen Chronologie und ihre Lösung*, Leipzig 1898 (Lehmann).

[3] (a) The text is catalogued in British Museum as BU. 91–5–9, 284, and is published in *Cuneiform Texts from Babylonian Tablets*, etc., in the British Museum. Part VI, edited by E. A. W. Budge. London, 1898 (copied by Pinches). (b) The new Babylonian Chronological Tablet (BU. 91–5–9, 284, with translation). *Proceedings of the Society of Biblical Archæology*, January, 1899 (Sayce). (c) King, *Hammurabi*, ii and iii.

22

giving lists of important events in the years of reign of all the kings of the first dynasty down to Ammi-sadugga. At the end of each list of events is given the number of years that each king reigned. The disturbing fact about this list is that the figures given in it do not tally with those given in tablets A and B. For example, in A and B, Sumuabi reigns 15 years, but here 14, so also for Sumu-la-ilu is here given 36 years instead of 35, for Sin-muballit 20 instead of 30, for Hammurabi 43 instead of 55, and for Samsu-iluna 38 instead 35 years. Previous to the discovery of this tablet lists A and B had been followed as closely as possible by all chronologists. This procedure must now be changed and the new tablet considered, for it was written while this dynasty was still on the throne, and the summaries agree exactly with the yearly lists of principal events.

4. *Fragments of a Babylonian Chronicle (A, cited by some as S).*[1] A badly broken tablet, containing originally six columns, of which only column V nearly complete, and parts of columns II and IV now remain. It contains in brief chronicle fashion mention of certain important events in the reigns of Babylonian kings of the dynasties of the Sea Lands and of Bazi.

5. *The Babylonian Chronicle (B).*[2] A large

---

[1] First discovered and published by George Smith, *Transactions of the Society of Biblical Archæology*, iii, pp. 361, ff. The text is republished by Winckler, *Untersuchungen*, p. 153.

[2] See the following publications. (a) *Proceedings of the Society of Biblical Archæology*, vi, pp. 193, ff. (Pinches). (b) *Zeitschrift für Assyriologie*,

tablet containing one hundred and seventy-six lines of writing, dated in the twenty-second year of Darius I, and containing brief chronicles of the chief events in the reigns of Babylonian kings from Nabonassar to Saosduchinos, and of Assyrian kings from Tiglathpileser III to Asshurbanapal.

6. *Fragments of a Babylonian Chronicle of Nabonidus (Nab. Chron).*[1] A small broken tablet containing a chronicle of events of the last years of the reign of Nabonidus and the taking of Babylon by Cyrus.

7. *Fragments of a Babylonian Chronicle (cited as P).*[2] An unbaked tablet, originally about eight inches square, containing accounts of expeditions made by some of the early Babylonian kings against external enemies. Less than one third of the tablet is preserved. That which remains begins in the reign of Kadashman-Kharbe, son of Karakhardash. The style of this chronicle is so similar to that of one of the Assyrian lists that it is probable the latter was copied from this.

Besides these direct statements made in inscrip-

---

ii, pp. 148, ff. (Winckler). (c) *Journal of the Royal Asiatic Society,* xix, pp. 655, ff. (Pinches). (d) Abel-Winckler, *Keilschrifttexte,* pp. 47, 48.

[1] (a) On a Cuneiform Inscription relating to the capture of Babylon by Cyrus, and the events which preceded and led to it. *Transactions of the Society of Biblical Archæology,* 1881, vii, 139, ff. (Pinches). (b) *Untersuchungen zur altoriental. Geschichte,* pp. 154, 155 (Winckler).

[2] (a) *Journal of the Royal Asiatic Society,* October, 1894, pp. 807, ff. (Pinches.) (b) *Records of the Past,* new series, vol. v, pp. 106, ff. (Pinches.) (c) *Alttestamentliche Untersuchungen,* Lepzig, 1893–97, pp. 115, 116, 122, 124, and 297, ff. (Winckler).

tions for purely chronological purposes the Baby. lonian texts of other kinds, both historical and contract, contain numerous allusions to dates, synchronisms, and the like. The more important of these may here be grouped together with the necessary comments upon their meaning or bearing.

8. *A Boundary Stone Dated the Fourth Year of King Bel-nadin-apli.*[1] In this text it is stated that from Girkishar, king of the Sea Lands, to Nebuchadrezzar I there were six hundred and ninety-six years. This does not seem like a round number, and if we could bring it to bear upon some fact already known to us, it would be extremely valuable. But the only king known to us (who is known as king of the Sea Lands) is Gul-ki-shar (or kur?) the sixth king of the second dynasty. The names are not identical, though they are judged to mean the same person by several scholars.[2] Where so great doubt exists it is hardly safe to lay much stress upon the chronological statement here made. Future investigation will probably clear the matter of all doubt.

9. In an inscription of Nabonidus occurs this statement with reference to one of the early kings:

---

[1] Hilprecht, *Old Babylonian Inscriptions*, vol. i, part i, pl. 30, text 83.

[2] For example, by Hilprecht, *Assyriaca* (Boston, 1894), pp. 20, ff., and also by Hommel in Hastings, *Bible Dictionary*, i, pp. 223, 224, and in *Expository Times*. On the other hand, Winckler (*Altorientalische Forschungen*, i, p. 130, footnote 3, and also p. 267), Rost (*Untersuchungen zur Altorientalischen Geschichte*, in Mittheilungen der Vorderasiatischen Gesellschaft, 1897, p. 16), and Lehmann (*Zwei Hauptprobleme*, pp. 17, 18) are against this view. Lehmann is of the opinion, also, that the name in the King List is not Gulkishar, but perhaps Gulkikur (??) (*op. cit.*, p. 17).

"The name of Hammurabi, one of the old kings, who seven hundred years before Burnaburiash had built E-barra and the temple pyramids on the old foundations, I saw therein and read." [1]

Like the preceding notice, this, also, is of doubtful application and therefore of doubtful weight. Two kings by the name of Burnaburiash are known to us, but as they reigned very close together, the choice between them makes little difference. They were contemporaries of Amenophis III, king of Egypt, and are to be located about 1400 B. C. If we reckon seven hundred years backward from this date, we get 2100 B. C. as the period of Hammurabi. This date is, however, irreconcilable with the Babylonian King Lists, according to which Hammurabi must be placed about 2300 B. C. No solution which meets the situation is yet proposed for this difficulty. The most tempting way out would be to change the length of dynasty III, given as five hundred and seventy-six years and nine months, for which Rost [2] would suggest three hundred and ninety-six, but if this be done, we have simply altered our sources, and are reduced to conjecture. It seems wiser for the present to abide by the King Lists, and permit this round number of seven hundred years to stand as unexplained.

10. In another text of Nabonidus there occurs again a chronological hint:

"E-DU-BAR, his temple in Sippar-Anunit, which

---

[1] I. R. 69, b. 4-8 (British Museum 85, 4-30, 2, col. ii, 20-26).
[2] *Orientalistische Zeitschrift*, iii, col. 145 (1900).

no king had built for eight hundred years, since Shagarakti-Buriash, king of Babylon, son of Kudur-Bel. His foundation inscription I sought, found, and read."[1] Nabonidus reigned 555–539 B. C., if we count backward eight hundred years, we reach for Shagarakti-Buriash the period about 1355 B. C. The difficulty now appears of deciding who this king is. He must clearly belong to the Kassite dynasty (dynasty III), and since the name of Ku-dur Bel has been identified as No. 26 on the King List there seems little doubt that the king here meant is Shagarakti-Shuriash,[2] some of whose in-scriptions have come down to us. In the tentative chronology here given this king is located 1298–1286, which approximates with sufficient close-ness to the date given by Nabonidus.

11. In the same inscription of Nabonidus[3] there is given still further a chronological note which carries us far back into the past:

".... the foundation stone of Naram-Sin, which no king before me had found for 3,200 years— [this] Shamash the great Lord of E-barra . . . showed to me."

If we accept this, we are carried back to 3750 B. C. for the date of Naram-Sin, and therefore to about 3800 B. C. for his father, Sargon I. Over this date there rages a ceaseless controversy. It was at first generally accepted, for example, by

---

[1] V R. 64, c. 27–30, Comp. *Keilinschrift. Bibl.*, iii, 2, p. 107.

[2] This is the solution to which Rost is attached (*Untersuchungen*, pp. 15, 51, 52).

[3] V R., 62 b. 57–60. Comp. *Keilinschrift. Bibl.*, iii, 2, p. 105.

Oppert,[1] Tiele,[2] Hommel,[3] and Delitzsch.[4] Of these Hommel afterward became persuaded that the date was too high and proposed to reduce it to 3400 B. C.[5] Lehmann has argued learnedly for a reduction of Naram-Sin to 2750 B. C.,[6] and Winckler[7] has expressed doubt about the matter. Positive proof on either one side or the other has not yet come to light, and for the present it seems best to hold the date 3800 B. C. tentatively, pending further light on the subject. It is indeed hardly probable that the historiographers of Nabonidus had before them lists which carried the dates backward to the exact number 3,200. It looks like a round number and was probably intended to be so taken. To cast it away altogether is, however, to leave us in the dark without a single definite point for reckoning.

12. Asshurbanapal in his narratives of victorious campaigns in Elam has also provided us with a chronological note. He brought back to its place of origin a statue of a goddess carried away to Elam by Kudur-nankhundi 1,635 years before—[8] that is, about 2285 B. C. This appears to be a

---

[1] *Journal Asiatique* (1883), i, p. 89.

[2] *Geschichte*, p. 114.

[3] *Ibid.*, pp. 166, 167.

[4] Delitzsch-Mürdter, *Geschichte Babyloniens und Assyriens*, 2d ed., pp. 72, f.

[5] Hastings, *Bib. Dict.*, i, p. 224.

[6] Lehmann, *Zwei Hauptprob.*, pp. 172, ff.

[7] *Untersuchungen*, p. 44, f.

[8] III R. 38, 1 a. 12-18. Comp. George Smith, *Asshurbanipal*, pp. 250, ff., and *Keilinschriftliche Bibliothek*, ii, p. 209, foot of the page.

valuable indication of time, for the numeral does not look like a round number, and there is no reason to doubt its substantial accuracy. Neither is there any special difficulty in attaching it to the other historical and chronological facts.

13. Sennacherib also has left a very definite date in one of his inscriptions. He says:

"Adad and Shala, the gods of Ekallate, whom Marduk-nadin-akhe, king of Accad, in the time of Tiglathpileser, king of Asshur, had taken away and brought to Babylon, after a lapse of four hundred and eighteen years, I have taken out of Babylon and restored to Ekallate their place."[1] This, also, like the preceding, appears to be not a round number, but the result of some careful calculation or to rest directly upon early documents. It has, nevertheless, been much doubted in quite recent times. Rost[2] proposes to read 478 in order to bring it better into relation with what seems to him to be the order of events demanded by other chronological facts. On the other hand, Lehmann[3] proposes to read 318 instead of 418, because that figure appears better to fit the situation as demanded by the other facts. Neither of these attempts seems to be well founded. It is better to accept a number like this as final, even though it appears to be in conflict with the other facts in our very limited knowledge of ancient

---

[1] III R., 14, 48–50. Comp. *Keil. Bibl.*, ii, p. 119.

[2] *Untersuchungen*, p. 16.

[3] *Zwei Hauptprobl.*, p. 98, ff.

Babylonia. It appears on the face of the matter to be more worthy of credence than such round numbers as 600, 700, 800, and 3,200. If we accept it tentatively, it brings out our reckoning in this way : Sennacherib has dated the four hundred and eighteen years from the destruction of Babylon by himself. This took place in 689, and we should therefore be carried back to 1107 as a date during the reign of Marduk-nadin-akhe. To this date may be added another fact of importance for this reign. On a boundary stone of Marduk-nadin-akhe[1] there is mention of a victory over Assyria in the tenth year of his reign. It is most natural to connect this victory with the removal of the statues to which Sennacherib refers. This would make 1107 the tenth year of the reign, and therefore 1117 or 1116 the first year of his reign.[2] This is a date that ought not lightly to be set aside, and the arguments brought against it by Rost and Lehmann do not seem to be decisive.

These are all the notices in Babylonian historical inscriptions which may be made directly applicable to the question of chronology. It has appeared in each case that they are not always to be reconciled with each other without some sort of forcing. Every chronological scheme that has been proposed has in some way made accommodations, either by altering the figures or by rejecting some of them altogether.

[1] III R. 43, col. i, 5, 27, 28.

[2] So Hilprecht, *Old Babylonian Inscriptions*, i, part i, p. 43, and Hommel in Hastings, *Bible Dictionary*, i, p. 224.

In addition to these King Lists, chronicles, and references in historical inscriptions the chronologist secures some aid from genealogical details. Thus a king often gives his father's name, and upon his father's inscription is found the name of the grandfather. By such simple means a whole dynasty may be arranged in correct order.

Even more important than this are external indications of age, and these may be divided into two parts: (1) The approximate date of an inscription, and hence of a king in whose reign it was written, may sometimes be obtained from palæographical indications. A study of the forms of characters and the manner of their writing gives at times an indication of the period. Likewise, also, (2) the position in which an inscription is found within a mound is at times an approximate indication of age. Sometimes the finding of a text beneath the pavement of known age may be conclusive, but in general this kind of evidence, as also that drawn from palæography, is rather precarious, being subject to too many possible interpretations in the hands of different persons. The greatest value of palæography and of archæology is found when they lend additional weight to direct statements in lists or in chronological texts.

If now we turn from Babylonia to Assyria, we shall find that this people, also, gave great attention to chronological details, and partly because we are nearer to them and partly because their monumental remains have reached us in a rather better condition we are able to come to conclusions rather more satisfactory than in the case of Babylonia.

II. *Assyrian Chronological Material.*

1. The Assyrians early constructed an *Eponym Canon*, in which were set down the names of the chief officers of the state in regular yearly succession. In this list the name of a new king was always entered in the year of his accession. There was thus provided an admirable method of preserving order in references to the past, and historical inscriptions, especially in a colophon at their conclusion, often mention the *limmu* or eponym of a certain year, just as they give the name of the king who was reigning. These eponyms were used therefore for dating, exactly as in later times the Greeks used archons and the Romans, consuls. A number of copies of the eponym canons must have existed, for numerous fragments have come down to us. These it has been possible to piece together in the correct order largely by means of the Canon of Ptolemy, to be mentioned below. When so arranged the parts which have come down to us extend from B. C. 902, when the eponym was Asshurdan, to B. C. 667, when the eponym was Gabbaru.[1]

---

[1] See on the Eponym Canon in general, Schrader, *Keilinschriften und Geschichtsforschung*, Giessen, 1878, pp. 299–356, where the references to the original texts are given.

2. *The Assyrian Expedition Lists.* In addition to the Eponym Canon, which is characterized by lists of names only, the Assyrians drew up supplementary lists in which the names of eponyms were also given, and by the side of each name were added short notices of important events that fell in his year, such as expeditions to certain countries for the purpose of conquest. The fragments of this list which have come down to us begin during the reign of Shamshi-Adad IV (B. C. 824–812), and brief though they are, have proved of immense importance. On one of these fragments, by the side of the Eponym Pur(ilu) Sa-gal-e, there is mentioned an eclipse of the sun under these words, "In the month of Sivan there was an eclipse of the sun." Astronomical investigations have shown that a total eclipse of the sun occurred at Nineveh June 15, 763 B. C., lasting two hours and forty-three minutes, with the middle of the eclipse at 10:05 A. M. This astronomical calculation gave a fixed date for the year of that eponym and thereby fixed every year in the entire canon.[1]

3. *Synchronistic History.* In addition to these important lists we have also lists of the synchronisms between Babylonia and Assyria, beginning with the peace treaties between Karaindash, king of Babylon, and Asshur-bel-nisheshu, king

[1] On these Expedition Lists see again Schrader, *op. cit.,* and also Winckler, *Keilinschriftliches Textbuch zum Alten Testament,* Leipzig, 1892, pp. 61–67. Also Schrader, *Cuneiform Inscriptions and the Old Testament,* ii, pp. 178, ff.; *Keilinschriftliche Bibliothek,* Berlin, 1889, vol. i, pp. 204, ff.

of Assyria. This synchronistic history is written in the style of brief chronicles, and is, also, unhappily fragmentary.[1]

Besides these lists and chronicles which were made for chronological purposes, there have also come down to us in historical inscriptions certain references which are valuable for chronological purposes. These may be conveniently enumerated as follows:

4. The statement made by Sennacherib (see under Babylonia No. 13, pp. 320, f.), from which we recovered the date 1107 in the reign of Marduk-nadin-akhe, is useful, also, for the chronology of Assyria, for from it we obtain the date 1107 as falling in the reign of Tiglathpileser I.

5. From the inscriptions of Sennacherib, and from the same period of his reign, there has come to us a note that assists in locating an early Assyrian king. At Babylon Sennacherib found a seal of Tukulti-Ninib with a brief inscription, to which he added an inscription of his own, so that the whole stood as follows:

"Tukulti-Ninib, king of the world, son of Shalmaneser, king of Asshur, conqueror of the land of Kardu. Whoever alters my writing and my name, may Asshur and Adad destroy his name and land. This seal is presented, given, from Asshur to Accad.

"Sennacherib, king of Asshur, after six hundred

---

[1] The synchronistic history is first published entire by F. E. Peiser and Hugo Winckler in *Keilinschriftliche Bibliothek*, i, pp. 194, ff.

years conquered Babylon and brought it away from the possessions of Babylon." [1]

If we add to 689, the date of the destruction of Babylon, this six hundred years, we get the date of 1289 as falling somewhere within the reign of Tukulti-Ninib.

6. In the inscriptions of Tiglathpileser I appears this note concerning two of the early Assyrian rulers:

"At that time the temple of Anu and Adad, the great gods my lords, which in former times Shamshi-Adad, *isshakku* of Asshur, son of Ishme-Dagan, *isshakku* of Asshur, had built, for six hundred and forty-one years had been falling down. Asshurdan, king of Assyria, son of Ninib-apal-esharra, king of Assyria, had torn down that temple, but had not rebuilt it; for sixty years its foundations had not been laid." [2]

If now the date of Tiglathpileser is correctly determined above under No. 4, the addition of sixty years to it will give the date 1167 as falling within the reign of Asshurdan and 1808 as falling in the reign of Shamshi-Adad. As the date from which Tiglathpileser reckoned backward is not certainly known, these dates may vary a few years in either direction, but will probably be a little higher.

With these dates the special allusions in As-

---

[1] III. R. 4, 2. Com. *Keilinschriftliche Bibliothek*, i, p. 11, No. 1.

[2] I. R. 15, col. vii, lines 60–70. Com. *Keilinschriftliche Bibliothek*, i, p. 43, and *Records of the Past*, new series, i, p. 117.

syrian historical inscriptions, which are important for our purpose, come to an end.

It remains now only that we turn to those sources outside of the Babylonian and Assyrian inscriptions, which contain chronological material, which may be of importance in its bearing upon the native sources. Of these the first in importance which comes to us from the Greeks is in reality simply Babylonian, for it is based upon Babylonian documents originally.

B.—GREEK WRITERS.

I. *Berossos.* We have given attention above to the use of Berossos as a source for the history, and we must now turn to his chronological tables. In this is found one of the most difficult problems with which the chronologist has to deal. As has already been shown, the *Babyloniaca* of Berossos was divided into three books. The first book described the origin of the world and of man and continued down to the deluge. The second described the deluge and perhaps came down into the historical period; and the third book was devoted to the historical period.

The manner in which Berossos has come down to us has been already described, and that mistakes could easily creep in during such a process may easily be seen. In no particular would mistakes be more likely to appear than in the lists of figures in his chronological lists, and as a matter of fact the mistakes are indeed very evident. If we take up these books in order, we shall speedily see what material, if any, of value may be found in them. According to Berossos there reigned before the flood ten kings during a period of one hundred and twenty sars. The sar is 3,600 years; that is, these kings reigned 432,000 years. As these statements have come down to us both in Eusebius and in the Syncellus, they may be regarded as certainly coming from Berossos.

Book I. 10 kings = 120 sars = 432,000 years.[1]

If we turn to Book II, we find that there is a difference between the sources in which Berossos has been preserved for us.

According to the Syncellus (ed. Dindorf, p. 147, line 12) there were 86 kings who ruled 34,080 years, to which is added also the explanation 9 sars at 3,600, 2 ners at 600, and 8 sos at 60 = 34,080. On the other hand, Eusebius (*Chron.*, ed. Schoene, i, p. 26) says that these 86 kings ruled 33,091 years, which is, in all probability, simply a mistake for 34,091. There is therefore exactly eleven years difference between the Syncellus and Eusebius in this report, which would correspond to the difference between the death of Alexander the Great (323 B. C.) and the beginning of the Seleucid era (312).[2]

How are these figures to be interpreted? The most probable explanation is that first suggested, and later amplified and corrected by Alfred von

---

[1] Eusebius, *Chron.*, ed. Schoene, i, p. 9; Syncellus, ed. Dindorf.

[2] So Rost, *Untersuchungen*, p. 9.

[3] v. Gutschmid's first paper appeared in the *Rheinisches Museum für Philologie*, Neue Folge, Band viii (1853), pp. 252-267. It is reprinted in

Gutschmid,[1] that the Babylonians had grouped their kings of the post deluge period in a cycle of 36,000 years. If now we take from this number the number 34,080 preserved by the Syncellus, we have left exactly 1,920 years for the historical list of kings.

If we could find the point at which these 1,920 years terminated, we shall arrive at the point at which Babylonian history begins. Many have been the views on this subject, but a consensus of opinion is now gradually forming as the result of a suggestion first offered by Peiser.[1] There is preserved in Abydenus, according to Eusebius, this sentence, "*Hoc pacto Chaldaei suae regionis reges ab Aloro usque ad Alexandrum recensent;*" that is, "In this manner the Chaldeans reckon the kings of their land from Aloros to Alexander." By the word *Chaldaei* is here meant doubtless Berossos, and from this we learn that Berossos had continued his history to Alexander, and the king here meant is certainly Alexander, son of Alexander the Great. Do the 1,920 years end here? It is probable that

---

Kleine Schriften, von Alfred von Gutschmid, herausgegeben von Franz Rühl (Leipzig, 1890), ii, pp. 97–114. Much of this paper was withdrawn by von Gutschmid in a review of Brandis, *Ueber den hist. Gewinn aus der Entzifferung der assyr. Inschriften* in *Neue Jahrbücher für Philologie*, Band lxxiii (1856), pp. 405–421 (reprinted *Kleine Schriften*, ii, pp. 115, ff.), and was modified later in *Beiträge zur Geschichte des Alten Orients* (1858), pp. 18, ff., and in *Neue Beiträge zur Geschichte des Alten Orients* (Leipzig, 1876), pp. 115, ff.

[1] *Zeitschrift für Assyriologie*, vi, pp. 264, ff. This suggestion had previously been made by Floigl, v., *Die Chronologie der Bibel des Manetho und Beros*. Leipzig, 1880, p. 259, *Geschichte des semitischen Altertums in Tabellen*, Leipzig, 1882, p. 7, but had escaped the attention of scholars generally. Peiser's suggestion was independent of Floigl.

23

they do. It is indeed most probable that they extended down to the Seleucid era in 312, for Berossos would surely be glad to pay such a compliment to these rulers, to one of whom he had dedicated his book.[1] If now we date backward from 312 (or 311, the date of Alexander's death), we arrive at 2232 or 2231 as the year of the beginning of Babylonian history according to Berossos. But immediately that we attempt to determine where to place this date in our Babylonian chronology difficulties begin. Lehmann would locate it during the reign of Hammurabi as the year when all Babylonia was united under one scepter and Bel-Marduk became the national deity. On the other hand, Rost would accept it as the date of the beginning of the first dynasty. There is no decisive argument in favor of either view, and it is easy to imagine that it may refer to some other event of consequence. It were folly to accept it to the exclusion of the dates which have come down to us from original Babylonian sources.

It is believed by some scholars (Lehmann, Rost, Marquart) that the date 2232–2231 is confirmed from another Greek source, and this must be considered.

Simplicius in his commentary upon Aristotle's treatise, Περὶ οὐρανοῦ (De Caelo), says that Callisthenes had been asked by Aristotle to send to Greece any records of astronomical observations

---

[1] So Rost, *Untersuchungen*, p. 4. Lehmann agrees with this (*Zwei Hauptprobl.*, p. 107) on slightly different grounds.

which he might find in Babylon. This Callisthenes did, after entering Babylon with Alexander the Great in the autumn of 331 B. C. Upon the authority of Porphyrius, Simplicius avers that Callisthenes found such observations extending back for 31,000 years.[1] There is, however, grave doubt about this figure. A Latin translation by Moerbeka (about 1271 A. D.) reads 1903, which is in itself more reasonable. Furthermore, the reading 31,000, assuming it to be an error, can readily be explained on palæographical grounds.[2] Lehmann therefore insists that the reading 1903 is original, and proposes to use it as dating backward from 331 B. C., which would yield 2233 B. C. as the date of the beginning of the observations. This would agree remarkably well with Berossos, and so confirm it from the astronomical side. But the difficulty about the text is fatal to confidence in it. The figure 31,000 is actually in our only original witness to the text, and it cannot be proved that 1903 was actually in the codex which Moerbeka used.[3] The numeral 31,000 indeed is just such a number as is afforded by other of the Greek writers. Pliny states that the num-

---

[1] *Simplicii in Aristotelis " De Caelo " commentario.* Consilio et autoritate Academiae Litterarum Regiae Borussicae editit J. S. Heiberg, Berlin, 1894, p. 506, line 14.

[2] See the discussion in Lehmann, *Zwei Hauptprob.*, p. 109, and especially the palæographical observations of Professor Diels on p. 110, and the Nachträge on p. 210.

[3] Rost (*Untersuchungen*) has worked out the same comparison as Lehmann in practically the same way, but independently of him.

ber of years given by Berossos was 490,000,' and Diodorus makes it 473,000.² The numerals in all these copyists of Berossos seem in a hopeless tangle, and it is useless to attempt to build any solid chronological structure upon them.

Having failed in this search for a starting point of Babylonian chronology by means of Berossos and Simplicius, we must search still further to see if there be left anywhere else in Berossos even one single point that might be useful in connection with the native sources. Schwartz has lately subjected the whole of the fragments of Berossos to a searching examination and arrives at the conclusion that the following scheme may be regarded as certain:³

I. 10 Kings before the flood			
120 Sars =	432,000		
II. 86 Kings after the flood..	34,090		
8 Median Usurpers.....	224	[2448-7 B. C.—2224-3]	
11 Kings..............	248	[2224-3	—1976-5]
49 Chaldean Kings......	458	[1976-5	—1518-7]
9 Arabian Kings.......	245	[1518-7	—1273-2]
45 Kings..............	526	[1273-2	—747-6]
III. From Nabonassar to Cyrus	206	[747-6	—538-7]
Total.............	468,000 = 130 Sars		
From Cyrus to Alexander's			
Death................	215	[538-7	-323-2]
Grand Total	468,215		

<hr>

[1] Pliny, *Nat. Hist.*, vii, 57 (ed. Mayhoff, Teubner, ii, p. 49).

[2] Diodorus, ii, 31 (ed. Dindorf, Lips., 1828, i, p. 181).

[3] Schwartz in Pauly-Wissowa, *Real-Encyclopädie der class. Altertums-wissenschaft*, ii, p. 314.

It is utterly impossible to reconcile this scheme
with that which has been preserved for us by the
Babylonian King Lists and Chronicles. We do not
find the same divisions of dynasties in the latter,
nor do we understand who are meant by the
Median, Chaldean, and Arabian usurpers and
kings. The learned and ingenious efforts made by
Hommel[1] to reconcile them are not generally regarded as at all successful, nor have later attempts
been any more fruitful. Like a number of other
problems, this must be left unsolved, at least for
the present.

II. *The Canon of Ptolemy.* Among the works
left by Claudius Ptolemæus, an eminent Egyptian
astronomer, mathematician, and geographer who
lived in the second century A. D., is a Κανὼν
βασιλέων (Canon of Kings), a catalogue of Babylonian,
Persian, Greek, and Roman kings. It is impossible now to determine the origin of this remarkable
list. When tested by the native monuments it
has in every case stood the test, and was extremely
valuable in the early work of the decipherment,
for by its use the order of the kings was first
established. It begins with Nabonassar and extends to Alexander the Great. It was plainly
made for astronomical and not for historical purposes, and therefore only contains the names of
those kings who began to reign with the begin-

---

[1] Hommel, *Semiten*, i, pp. 329, ff. Compare in opposition to these attempts
Tiele, *Geschichte*, i, p. 109, and Winckler, *Untersuchungen z. altorientalische
Geschichte*, 3, ff.

ning of a year and continued to its end. Kings who came to the throne after the beginning of the year and reigned but a few months are not named at all. For purposes of comparison the Canon of Ptolemy, with the Babylonian names, may here be set down.

THE BABYLONIAN CANON OF RULERS IN CLAUDIUS PTOLEMÆUS.[1]

Length of Reign.	Greek Forms of Names.	Babylonian Forms of Names.	Years B. C.
14	Ναβονασσάρου	Nabu-nasir	747
2	Ναδίου	(Nabu)-nadin-(zir)	733
5	Χίνζηρος καὶ Πώρου	Ukinzir. Pulu	731
5	Ἰλουλαίου	Ululai	726
12	Μαρδοκεμπάδου	Marduk-apal-iddin	721
5	Ἀρκεάνου	Sharrukin	709
2	ἀβασιλεύτου πρώτου	. . . .	704
3	Βηλίβου	Bel-ibni	702
6	Ἀπαραναδίου	Ashur-nadin-shum	699
1	Ῥηγεβήλου	Nergal-ushezib	693
4	Μεσησιμορδάκου	Mushezib-Marduk	692
8	Ἀβασιλεύτου δευτέρου	. . . .	688
13	Ἀσαριδίνου	Ashur-akh-iddin	680
20	Σαοσδουχίνου	Shamash-shum-ukin	667
22	Κινιλαναδάνου	Kandalanu	647
21	Ναβοπολασσάρου	Nabu-apal-usur	625
43	Ναβοκολασσάρου	Nabu-kudurri-usur	604
2	Ἰλλοαρου-δάμου	Amel-Marduk	561
4	Νηρικασολασσάρου	Nergal-shar-usur	559
17	Ναβοναδίου	Nabu-na'id	555

This single brief list far exceeds in value all that remains of Berossos, and indeed all the chronological material in all the other Greek sources.

---

[1] For this list see primarily *Table Chronologique des Regnes . . . des C. Ptolémée*, etc., par M. l'Abbé Halma, *Ouvres de Ptolemée*, tom. iii, Paris, 1819, p. 3, and comp. Georgius Syncellus, ed. Dindorf, Bonn, 1829, vol. i., pp. 390, ff., and *Keil. Bibl.*, ii, pp. 290, 291. Winckler, *Keilinschriftliches Textbuch zum Alten Testament*, p. 68.

C.—Egyptian Inscriptions.

From the Egyptian inscriptions scarcely anything of value may be obtained for chronological purposes. The light which the Assyrian and Babylonian inscriptions has brought to the Egyptian texts is indeed far more useful than the converse.

D.—The Old Testament.

Practically the same statement is true with reference to the Old Testament, the chronological materials of which were first set in their proper light through Assyrian and Babylonian discoveries.

If now from all these sources we essay the making of a chronological table for Babylonia and Assyria, it must be admitted that with respect to the former, at least, the result is not encouraging. Every effort to make all the facts which have come down to us dovetail accurately together has failed. These facts can only be reconciled by supposing error somewhere. Every investigator differs from every other as to the place in which he finds the errors, yet each feels confident that he has found the correct solution. For the present it seems unwise to attempt to draw up a hard and fast list of kings in the early centuries by means of a system which rests on the acceptance of figures from some ancient documents and the rejection of figures from others. The only scientific course would seem to be to decline to force these figures into agreement, but simply to put down those which seem reasonably well attested, and to indicate those places in which they are in conflict with other figures. This we proceed to do, accompanying the dates in some cases with references to the sources enumerated above, and with explanations of the discrepancies. We begin here with the earliest known period.

TABLES.

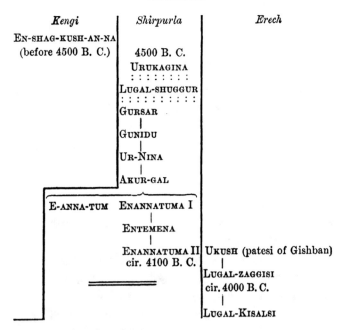

Kengi	*Shirpurla*	*Erech*
EN-SHAG-KUSH-AN-NA (before 4500 B. C.)	4500 B. C. URUKAGINA : : : : : : : : LUGAL-SHUGGUR : : : : : : : : : : GURSAR GUNIDU UR-NINA AKUR-GAL	
E-ANNA-TUM	ENANNATUMA I ENTEMENA ENANNATUMA II cir. 4100 B. C.	UKUSH (patesi of Gishban) LUGAL-ZAGGISI cir. 4000 B. C. LUGAL-KISALSI

First Dynasty of Ur.
LUGALKIGUBNIDUDU   cir. 3900 B. C.
LUGALKISALSI.

Agade	Shirpurla (Lagash)
SHARGANI-SHAR-ALI cir. 3800 B. C. (Sargon I)	LUGAL-USHUMGAL cir. 3800 B.C. (vassal of Sargon I)
NARAM-SIN cir. 3750 B. C.	· · ·
BINGANI-SHAR-ALI	· · ·
	· · ·
	UR-BAU cir. 3200 B. C.
	NAMMAGHANI
	· · ·
Second Dynasty of Ur cir. 3000 B. C.	· · ·
URGUR	GUDEA cir. 3000 B. C.
DUNGI I	URNINGIRSU (vassal of Dungi I)
	· · · ·
	· · · ·
	AKURGAL II ⎫
	· · · · ⎬ ? order
	LUKANI ⎭
	GHALA-LAMA

Dynasty of Isin cir. 2500 B. C.

	Third Dynasty of Ur	ISHBIGARRA ⎫ order LIBIT-ISHTAR ⎬ PUR-SIN I ⎬ unknown UR-NINIB ⎭

Third Dynasty of Ur	
DUNGI II cir. 2400 B. C.	ISHME-DAGAN
GUNGUNU	EN-AN-NA-TUM
PUR-SIN II	(vassal of Gungunu)
GAMIL-SIN	
INE-SIN	

Kingdom of Larsa.

SIN-IDDINAM.

NUR-ADAD.

KUDUR-NANKHUNDI (? about 2285 B. C.).

CHEDORLAOMER.

KUDUR-MABUG.

ERI-AKU (Arioch).

Kingdom of Babylon.

First Dynasty.

		Length of Reign According to King List.
		Years.
1. SUMUABI.	2454–2440	15
2. SUMU-LA-ILU	2439–2405	35
3. ZABU	2404–2391	14
4. APIL-SIN	2390–2373	18
5. SIN-MUBALLIT	2372–2343	30
6. HAMMURABI.	2342–2288	55
7. SAMSU-ILUNA.........	2287–2253	35
8. ABESHU' (EBISHUM)...	2252–2228	25
9. AMMISATANA.........	2227–2203	25
10. AMMISADUGGA........	2202–2182	21
11. SAMSUSATANA	2181–2151	31

The order of these names is taken from Babylonian King Lists A and B. The years of reign are those given in the King List. It is possible that some of the differences between these and the numbers given in Chronological Tablet C may be explained on the basis suggested by Sayce (*Proceedings Soc. Bib. Archæology*, xxi, p.18), that in A and B allowance is made for rival princes who were deemed illegitimate and hence not mentioned by name, while in C we have naturally only the names and the years of legitimate rulers. For confirmation of this theory we shall have to await the discovery of new material.

Second Dynasty.

		Length of Reign.
1. An-ma-an..........	2150–2091	(60)
2. Ki-an-ni-bi.........	2090–2035	(56)
3. Dam-ki-ilu-shu......	2034–2009	(26)
4. Ish-ki-bal..........	2008–1994	(15)
5. Shu-ush-shi........	1993–1970	(24)
6. Gul-ki-shar........	1969–1915	(55)
7. Kir-gal-dara-bar...	1914–1865	(50)
8. A-dara-kalama	1864–1837	(28)
9. A-kur-ul-an-na	1836–1811	(26)
10. Melam-kur-kur-ra.	1810–1803	(8)
11. Ea-ga-mil.	1802–1783	(20)

These names with the numerals attached are found in Lists A and B. The length of several of the reigns seem exceedingly high, and there is reason to doubt whether they are correct. It is also impossible to reconcile the total period of three hundred and sixty-eight with the facts learned from other sources, respecting the period which has elapsed between certain kings of dynasty I and dynasty II; as, for example, between Hammurabi and Burnaburiash (see above, I, 9, p. 316). Many efforts have been made to relieve these difficulties. Hommel at one time attempted to prove that this second dynasty really preceded dynasty I;[1] he then later took the view that the second dynasty and the first were contemporaneous,[2] and that the second dynasty, so called, was

---

[1] *Geschichte*, i, p. 169.

[2] Hommel, *The Ancient Hebrew Tradition as Illustrated by the Monuments*, London, 1897, pp. 125, ff.

really "entirely apocryphal."[1]   He has since come
to the conclusion that "the first six and possibly,
also, the last king (Ea-gamil, twenty years) should
be retained, and the seventh to the tenth wholly
rejected."[2]   It does not appear that there is any
good reason for rejecting all or any part of these
names as apocryphal, but the figures which are
attached to them may easily be wrong in whole or
in part, just as the discovery of List C has shown
that there are errors or, at least, irregularities in
the Lists A and B respecting dynasty I.   For the
present the only safe position is one of doubt and
uncertainty.

We may now turn with rather more confidence
to the next dynasty.   In it we come, for the first
time, to a period in which native documents have
preserved for us fractions of years.   For this and
other reasons the chances of error are reduced and
a higher degree of probability in the result may be
expected.

Third Dynasty.   Kassites.

		Length of Reign.
1. GANDISH.............cir.	1782–1767 B. C.	16
2. AGUM-SHI	1766–1745	22
3. BIBEIASHI..............	1744–1723	22
4. DUSHI	1722–1714	9 (?19)
5. ADUMETASH	1713–	
6. TASHZIGURMASH.		
7. AGUM-KAKRIME.		

[Perhaps about six unknown kings.]

---

[1] *Op. cit.*, p. 126.

[2] Hommel, "The True Date of Abraham and Moses," *The Expository Times*, x, p. 211 (February, 1899).

KARAINDASH, cir. 1450.

KADASHMAN-BEL [formerly called Kalimma-Sin]. cir. 1430.

BURNABURIASH I, cir. 1420.

KURIGALZU I, cir. 1410.

BURNABURIASH II [son of Kurigalzu], cir. 1400.

KARAKHARDASH, cir. 1370.

KADASHMAN KHARBE I.

[SHUZIGASH or NAZIBUGASH, Usurper], cir. 1360.

KURIGALZU II, son Kadashman-Kharbe I, cir. 1350.

NAZIMARUTTASH, son of Kurigalzu II, cir. 1340.

KADASHMAN-TURGU, son of Nazimaruttash.

KADASHMAN-BURIASH.

		Length of Reign.
26. KUDUR-BEL ....about 1304–1299		6
27. SHAGARAKTI-SHURIASH cir. 1298–1286		13
[800 years before Nabonidus.]		
28. BIBEIASHU ....cir. 1285–1278		8
29. BEL-SHUM IDDIN	cir. 1277–1275	1 year 6 mos.
30. KADASHMAN-KHARBE II		1 year 6 mos.
31. ADAD-SHUM-IDDIN ......cir. 1274–1269		6
32. ADAD-SHUM-USUR ......cir. 1268–1239		(30)
33. MELISHIPAK ....cir. 1238–1224		15
34. MARDUK-APAL-IDDIN....cir. 1223–1211		13
35. ZAMAMU-SHUM-IDDIN ...cir. 1210		1
36. BEL-SHUM-IDDIN........cir. 1209–1207		3

The names in this list still offer many difficulties to the historian and chronologist. The names from No. 1 to No. 6 are drawn from the Babylonian King List A, as are also the years of reign assigned to the first four. The provisional date for Gandish (1782 B. C.) is also assigned on the basis of the same list, which assigns five hundred and seventy-six years and nine months as the length of this dynasty. If now the date of the end of the dynasty be set at 1207 B. C., on a reckoning of the following dynasty (see below), and this year 1207 be the five hundred and seventy-sixth year, it follows that the dynasty must have begun in 1782 (1207 + 575 = 1782). The dates of the first four kings of the dynasty are computed on the basis of the length of their reigns given in the same list.

The kings from No. 26 to 36 are also put down as they are found in the same list, together with the years of reign computed in the same manner.

The arrangement of the kings from No. 7 to No. 25, inclusive, is in several cases extremely doubtful. They rest largely upon inscriptions belonging to several of the kings found chiefly at Nippur, and the reasons for the order here adopted are given for the most part in the history proper which follows, and usually in the footnotes or in the references contained in them. At the best the order, and in some instances the names themselves, must remain doubtful until cleared up by monumental evidence.

Fourth Dynasty. Dynasty of Isin.

1. MARDUK (?)................cir. 1206–1189 B. C. (18)
2. ....⎫ cir. 1188–1183 B. C. (6)
3. ....⎪
⎬ Four unknown kings.
4. ....⎪
5. ....⎭
6. NEBUCHADREZZAR I, cir. 1135 B. C.
7. BEL-NADIN-APLI, cir. 1125 B. C.

8. MARDUK-NADIN-AKHE, cir. 1117–1096 B. C. (22)
9. [MARDUK-AKHE-IRBA?] 1095. (1 year 6 mos.)
10. MARDUK-SHAPIK-ZER-MATI 1094–1083. (12)
  [ADAD-APAL-IDDIN, usurper, not mentioned in King
    List.]
11. NABU-SHUM (or-nadin), cir. 1082–1075 (8)

For the arrangement of the fourth dynasty our materials are exceedingly scanty. The King List A is badly broken and but little can be made out of it. The first name is almost entirely destroyed, but the number of years is certainly fixed at 18. The numeral 6 attached to the second king appears also to be certain. From a monument of his own Nebuchadrezzar I is known, and Bel-nadin-apli from a boundary stone. Marduk-nadin-akhe is known from Assyrian synchronisms, and the years of reign, 22, appear upon the King List A. The location of Marduk-akhe-irba is exceedingly doubtful, but the numeral 1 year and 6 months is on the King List, as are also the numerals 12 and 8 which follow. The reasons for the location of the remaining kings are given below in the history.

The length of this dynasty has usually been given, on the basis of the King List, as 72 years and 6 months, but by a simple calculation Peiser proved that this was impossible, and suggested that it must be 132 years.[1] After an examination of the passage he became convinced that it must be 132, and with this Knudtzon[2] agrees, as does also

---

[1] ZA vi, 268, ff.
[2] Knudtzon, *Assyrische Gebete*, i, p. 60; ii, p. 277.

Lehmann, though the latter thinks that 133 is possible.[1] The date of Marduk-nadin-akhe is made clear by the allusion of Sennacherib (see above, I, 13, p. 320), and from that date it is possible to reckon downward to the end of the dynasty at 1075 and forward to its beginning (1075 + 131=1206 B. C.), though the latter figure is to be regarded only as tentative.

Fifth Dynasty.   Dynasty of the Sea Lands.

			Length of Reign.
1. SIBARSHIPAK	cir. 1074–1057	(18)
2. EA-MUKIN-ZER	cir. 1057	(5 mos.)
3. KASSHU-NADIN-AKHE cir. 1056–1054	(3)

Both names and length of reign are taken from King List A.

Sixth Dynasty.   Dynasty of Bazi.

1. EULBAR-SHAKIN-SHUM	1053–1037	(17)
2. NINIB-KUDUR-USUR	1036–1034	(3)
3. SILANIM-SHUKAMUNA	1033	(3 mos.)

Both names and length of reign are taken from King List A.

Seventh Dynasty.   The Dynasty of Elam.

1. *An Elamite* [name unknown]   1032–1027   (6)

The length of reign is given in King List A, but the name is broken off, and has not yet been recovered from any other source.

From this point onward there is a considerable gap in our knowledge of the Babylonian kings, and even the length of the gap cannot be definitely ascertained.

---

[1] Lehmann, *Zwei Hauptprobl.*, pp. 14, 15.

Eighth Dynasty.   *The Dynasty of Babylon.*

NABU-KIN-ABLI	1026–991	(36)
Unknown King	990	8 mos. and 10 days

Several unknown kings, possibly four or even six.

SHAMASH-MUDAMMIK	cir. 910
NABU-SHUM-ISHKUN	cir. 900
NABU-APAL-IDDIN	cir. 880 [at least 31 years]
MARDUK-NADIN-SHUM	
MARDUK-BALATSU-IKBI	cir. 812
BAU-AKH-IDDIN	cir. 800
⋯⋯⋯⋯⋯⋯⋯	⎱ *Probably two*
⋯⋯⋯⋯⋯⋯⋯	⎰ *missing names*
NABU-SHUM-ISHKUN	

NABU-NASIR	747–734	
NABU-NADIN-ZER	733–732	(2)
NABU-SHUM-UKIN	731	(1 mo. and 12 days)

Our knowledge of the chronological order of the kings of this dynasty is exceedingly slight. The Babylonian King List A gives the length of reigns in a few instances, and these are set down. The position of the kings from Shamash-mudammik to Bau-akh-iddin is determined by the Assyrian synchronisms (see history). When Nabu-nasir is reached we come to the exact chronological material of the Ptolemaic Canon, which gives us the definite dates 747 and 733.

Ninth Dynasty.

UKIN-ZER, 731–730.
PULU (= TIGLATH-PILESER III, of As- ⎱ Canon of Ptolemy
syria), 729–727. ⎰ five years.
ULULAI (= SHALMANESER IV, of Assyria), 727–722   (5)
MARDUK-APAL-IDDIN (Merodach-baladan), 721–709   (12)

24

Sharrukin, 709–705. (5.)
Sin-akh-erba (Sennacherib), 705–703.
Marduk-zakir-shum, 703.
Marduk-apal-iddin (Merodach-baladan), 703-702.
Bel-ibni, 702–700. (3.)
Ashur-nadin-shum, 699–694. (6.)
Nergal-ushezib, 693. (1.)
Mushezib-Marduk, 693–690. (4.)
Sin-akh-erba (Sennacherib), 689–682.
Asshur-akh-iddin (Esarhaddon), 681–668.
Shamash-shum-ukin, 667–647.
Kandalanu (= Ashur-ban-apal), 647–626.
Nabu-apal-usur (Nabopolassar), 625–605.
Nabu-kudurri-usur (Nebuchadrezzar), 604–562.
Amel-Marduk (Evil-Merodach), 561–560.
Nergal-shar-usur, 559–556.
Labashi-Marduk, 556.
Nabu-na'id (Nabonidus), 555–539.

For this period the chronological material is abundant and extraordinarily accurate. The dates may be regarded as fixed with as much definiteness as may be expected in the history of the ancient Orient.

The Chronology of Assyria.

Ishakkus of Asshur.

Ishme-Dagan, cir. 1830.
Shamshi-Adad I, cir. 1810.
Igur-kapkapu,
Shamshi-Adad II,
Khallu, (?)
Irishum, (?)

Kings of Assyria.

BEL-KAPKAPU, cir. 1700 B. C.

.   .   .   .   .   .

ASSHUR-BEL-NISHESHU, cir. **1450** B. C.

PUZUR-ASHUR, cir. 1420.

ASSHUR-NADIN-AKHE, cir. 1380 B. C.

ASSHUR-UBALLIT, cir. 1370.

BEL-NIRARI, his son, cir. 1350.

PUDI-ILU, his son.

ADAD-NIRARI I, his son, cir. 1345.

SHULMANU-ASHARID I, his son (SHALMANESER I), cir. 1330.

TUKULTI-NINIB, his son, cir. 1290.

ASSHUR-NAZIR-PAL I, cir. 1280.

ASSHUR-NARARA.

NABU-DAIAN.

BEL-KUDUR-USUR, cir. 1240.

NINIB-APAL-ESHARRA, cir. 1235 B. C.

ASSHUR-DAN, cir. **1210**.

MUTAKKIL-NUSKU, cir. 1150.

ASSHUR-RISH-ISHI, cir. 1140.

TUKULTI-APAL-ESHARRA (TIGLATHPILESER I), cir. 1120.

ASSHUR-BEL-KALA, cir. 1090.

SHAMSHI-ADAD I, cir. 1080.

ASSHUR-NAZIR-PAL II, cir. 1050.

ERBA-ADAD.

ASSHUR-NADIN-AKHE.

.   .   .   .   .   .

ASSHUR-ERBI.

TUKULTI-APAL-ESHARRA (TIGLATHPILESER II), cir. 950.

ASSHUR-DAN II, his son, cir. 930.

ADAD-NIRARI II, his son, 911–891.

TUKULTI-NINIB II, his son, 890–885.

ASSHUR-NAZIR-PAL III, his son, 884–860.

SHULMANU-ASHARID (SHALMANESER II), 859–825.

SHAMSHI-ADAD II, 824–812.

ADAD-NIRARI III, 811–783.

SHULMANU-ASHARID (SHALMANESER III), 782–773.
ASSHUR-DAN III, 772–755.
ASSHUR-NIRARI II, 754–745.
TUKULTI-APAL-ESHARRA (TIGLATHPILESER III = PULU),
745–727.
SHULMANU-ASHARID (SHALMANESER IV), 726–722.
SHARRUKIN (SARGON), 721–705.
SIN-AKH-ERBA (SENNACHERIB), 704–681.
ASSHUR-AKH-IDDIN (ESARHADDON), 680–668.
ASSHUR-BAN-APAL, 668-626.
ASSHUR-ETIL-ILANI, 625–622 (?).
SIN-SHUM-LISHIR (? date).
SIN-SHAR-ISHKUN, 621(?)–607.

BOOK II:

THE HISTORY OF BABYLONIA.

CHAPTER I.

THE HISTORY OF BABYLONIA TO THE FALL OF LARSA.

THE study of the origins of states is fraught with no less difficulty than the investigation of the origins of animate nature. The great wall before every investigator of the beginnings of things, with its inscription, "Thus far shalt thou come and no farther," stands also before the student of the origins of the various early kingdoms of Babylonia. It may always be impossible to achieve any picture of the beginnings of civilization in Babylonia which will satisfy the desire for a clear and vivid portrayal. Whatever may be achieved by future investigators it is now impossible to do more than give outlines of events in the dim past of early Babylonia.

If we call up before us the land of Babylonia, and transport ourselves backward until we reach the period of more than four thousand five hundred years before Christ, we shall be able to discern here and there signs of life, society, and government in certain cities. Civilization has already reached a high point, the arts of life are well advanced, and men are able to write down their thoughts and deeds in intelligible language and in permanent form. All these presuppose a long period of development running back through millenniums of unrecorded time. At this period there are no great kingdoms, comprising many cities, with their laws and customs, with subject territory and tribute-paying states. Over the entire land there are only visible, as we look back upon it, cities dissevered in government, and perhaps in intercourse, but yet the promise of kingdoms still unborn. In Babylonia we know of the existence of the cities Agade, Babylon, Kutha, Kish, Gishban, Shirpurla (afterward called Lagash), Guti, and yet others less famous. In each of these cities worship is paid to some local god who is considered by his faithful followers to be a Baal or Lord, the strongest god, whose right it is to demand worship, also, from dwellers in other cities.[1] This belief becomes an impulse by which the inhabitants of a city are driven out to conquer other cities and so extend the dominion of their god. If the inhabitants of Babylon could conquer the people of Kutha, was it not proof that the stronger god was behind their armies, and should not other peoples also worship him? But there were other motives for conquest. There was the crying need for bread—the most pressing need of all the ages. It

---

[1] Winckler, *Untersuchungen*, Leipzig, 1889, p. 65.

was natural that they who had the poorer parts of the country should seek to acquire the better portions either to dwell in or to exact tribute from. The desire for power, a thoroughly human impulse, was also joined to the other two influences at a very early date. The ruler in Babylon must needs conquer his nearest neighbor that he may get himself power over men and a name among them. Impelled by religion, by hunger, and by ambition, the peoples of Babylonia, who have dwelt apart in separate cities, begin to add city to city, concentrating power in the hands of kings. Herein lies the origin of the great empire which must later dominate the whole earth, for these little kingdoms thus formed later unite under the headship of one kingdom and the empire is founded.

At the very earliest period whose written records have come down to us the name of Babylonia was Kengi—that is, " land of canals and reeds." [1] Even then the waters of the river were conveyed to the fields and the cities in artificially constructed canals, while the most characteristic form of vegetable life was the reed, growing in masses along the water courses. More than four thousand five hundred years before Christ there lived in this land of Kengi a man who writes his name En-shag-kush-ana,[2] who calls himself lord of Kengi. We know

---

[1] Hilprecht, *Old Babylonian Inscriptions*, i, part ii, p. 47, and p. 38, foot-note 9.

[2] The inscriptions of this king are published by Hilprecht, *op. cit.*, Nos. 90–92. See further Hilprecht's notes on p. 51.

very little indeed of him, but it seems probable that his small dominion contained several cities, of which Erech was probably the capital, and Nippur was certainly its chief religious center. Even at this early time there was a temple at Nippur dedicated to the great god En-lil, over which there was set a chief servant of the god, who controlled the temple worship, protected its sanctity if necessary, and was accounted its ruler. The title of this ruler of the temple, this chief priest, was *patesi*.[1] Naturally enough the man who held such an important religious post often gained political power. If the god whom he represented was a god whose power had been shown in the prosperity of his worshipers in war or in trade, it was natural enough that neighboring cities should come under his glorious protection, and that his *patesi* should stand in the relation of governor to them. Now En-shag-kush-ana was the *patesi* of En-lil, and the honor of that god was in his keeping. We do not know of what race he was. He may have been Sumerian, he may have been a Semite, or he may have been of mixed race, for that mixture of blood had already begun is shown clearly enough by contemporary monuments. But whatever his own blood was his people were Sumerians and the civilization over which he ruled was likewise

---

[1] There has been a long dispute over the meaning of the word. See especially Winckler, *Altorientalische Forschungen*, vol. i, part iii, pp. 232, ff.; Hilprecht, *op. cit.*, p. 49, and especially footnote 1 ; Rost, *Untersuchungen*, p. 31, footnote 3 ; Jensen, *Zeitschrift d. Deut. mörgenl. Gesellschaft*, xxxxviii, 254, ff. The view set forth above owes much to Hilprecht.

Sumerian. But even at this early time the Sumerian vitality was dying out, and the day was threatening when a new and more virile people would drive the Sumerians out of their heritage and possess it in their room. Some individuals of this race were already settled in the Sumerian territory in the south, and others of them already possessed the great northern domain, which once had belonged to the Sumerians. Out of this period to which En-shag-kush-ana belongs we hear several echoes of the conflict that was already begun for the possession of all Babylonia. To about this period there belongs a little broken inscription written by another lord of Kengi, who has been trying to reconquer part of northern Babylonia which was already in the possession of these new invaders. These invaders were Semites, whose original home was probably Arabia, but who were now for some time settled northwest of Babylonia and probably in Mesopotamia. They coveted the rich alluvial soil on which the Babylonians were living as well as the fine cities which already dotted it here and there. The Sumerians had probably once possessed this very land in which they were now dwelling, but had been driven from it by their resistless advance. It seems probable that the city of Gishban was one of their earliest possessions, and that to it they later added Kish, which became the chief city of their growing kingdom. While En-shag-kush-ana was lord over the Sumerian kingdom in the south the kingdom of Kish was threatening to overwhelm the whole of Babylonia. It was a successor of his, or perhaps a predecessor, who attacked Enne-Ugun, the king of Kish. Victory came to the Sumerians, and the king, whose name is yet unknown, came home, bearing with him the spoil of the conquered Semite—"his statue, his shining silver, the utensils, his property" [1]—and set them up as an offering in the sanctuary of the great god En-lil, who had given him the victory. Well might the king of Kengi boast of a victory which must for a time at least stay the progress of the invading Semite.

It was, however, only a temporary reverse for this people. The Semites had the fresh power of a new race, and soon produced a leader able to strike the one blow needed to destroy forever the Sumerian commonwealth. There was a *patesi* of Gishban, called Ukush, and it was his son Lugalzaggisi who, when he had come to the rule over Kish and Gishban, went down into southern Babylonia and overwhelmed it. It was probably easily accomplished, for the work of the Sumerians was done. Yet theirs had been a noble career, and the people who had invented a system of writing that served their conquerors for thousands of years were a people who had left a deep impress on the world's history. About 4000 B. C. Lugalzaggisi made Erech the capital of the now united Babylonia, and Nippur readily became the chief center of its religious life. The language of the Sumerians was used by their conqueror in which to cele-

---

[1] Hilprecht, *Old Bab. Ins.*, vol. i, part ii, p. 50.

brate his conquest, and to their gods did he give thanks for his victories. It was they who had called him to the rule over Kengi and appointed unto him a still greater dominion. His words glow with feeling as he says: " When En-lil, lord of the lands, invested Lugalzaggisi with the king-dom of the world, and granted him success before the world, when he filled the land with his power, (and) subdued the country from the rise of the sun to the setting of the sun—at that time he straightened his path from the lower sea of the Tigris and Euphrates to the upper sea, and granted him the dominion of everything (?) from the rising of the sun to the setting of the sun, and caused the countries to dwell in peace." [1] Lugalzaggisi made a small empire at one stroke, and his boast-ful inscription begins with a long list of titles: "Lugalzaggisi, king of Erech, king of the world, priest of Ana, hero of Nidaba, son of Ukush, patesi of Gishban, hero of Nidaba, he who was favorably looked upon by the faithful eye of Lu-galkurkura (that is, En-lil), great patesi of En-lil." [2] The power of his name extended even to the shores of the Mediterranean, though, of course, he did not attempt to rule over so vast a territory.

Lugalzaggisi was succeeded on the throne by his son, Lugal-kisalsi, [3] and it appeared for a time as though the Sumerian kingdom was blotted out

---

[1] Hieprecht , *Old Bab. Ins.*, i, part ii, p. 53
[2] *Ibid.*, p. 52.
[3] *Ibid.*, plate 42, text No. 89.

forever, and that no more than peaceful absorption into the Semitic life could await it. But a kingdom slowly built up during the ages often makes more than one effort to retain its life, and this was to be the case with the Sumerian kingdom.

Perhaps while Lugal-kisalsi was still alive a reaction began. The nucleus for it was found in an ancient kingdom, the kingdom of Shirpurla, whose chief city was Sungir,[1] in southern Babylonia. Who had laid the foundations of either city or kingdom is unknown to us. We come upon them both in full power and dignity, about 4500 B. C. Urukagina then is king of Shirpurla, and he is engaged in the building and restoration of temples and the construction of a canal to supply his city with water.[2] But it is only a glimpse that we catch of his operations in the far distant past, and then he disappears and for some time, perhaps a generation or more, we hear nothing of his city or kingdom. Then there appears a new king in Sungir, Ur-Nina. Like Urukagina, he also was a builder of temples, for which he brought timber all the way from Magan—the Sinaitic peninsula. There is no mention in any of his little inscriptions of war, and in his time

---

[1] Sungir (formerly read Gir-su) later becomes Sumer and gives its name to the whole of southern Babylonia. It appears in Hebrew in the form Shinar (שִׁנְעָר), Gen. xi.

[2] See translations of the inscriptions of Urukagina by Amiaud, *Records of the Past*, new series, i, pp. 68, ff., and Jensen, *Keilinschrift. Bib.*, iii, part i, p. 10.

uninterrupted peace seems to have prevailed.[1] He was succeeded by his son, Akurgal, none of whose inscriptions have come down to us. After him came his son, Eannatum,[2] who felt sorely the increasing pressure of the Semitic hordes, and determined to strike a blow against Gishban and its domination of Babylonia. The Sumerians won, and the bloody battle remained long famous in the annals of a dying people. Upon his return, covered with honor, Eannatum set up in the temple of his god Nin-Sungir a splendid stele[3] in commemoration of his victory. Upon one of its white limestone faces stand two goddesses, before whom lies a great heap of weapons and of booty taken from the Semites. Above them is the totem, or coat of arms of the city—a double-headed eagle above two demi-lions placed back to back. On the other side of the stele is Eannatum standing upright in his war chariot, with a great spear in

---

[1] The inscriptions of Ur-Nina are published in Heuzey-Sarzec, *Découvertes en Chaldée*, pl. 1, No. 2; pl. 2, Nos. 1, 2; pl. 31. They are well translated by Amiaud (*Records of the Past*, new series, vol. i, pp. 64–66) and by Jensen, *Keilinschrift. Bibl.*, iii, part i, pp. 11–15.

[2] The name was originally read Edingiranagin. See now Hilprecht, *Old Bab. Ins.*, vol. i, part ii, p. 42, note 1, and *Zeitschrift für Assyriologie*, xi, p. 330, note 2. Thureau-Dangin, *Revue d'Assyriologie*, iv, 70, note 6.

[3] This is the well-known stele of the Vultures, now in the Louvre. Most of our knowledge of it is due to Heuzey, who has given much time to its study. It has been the subject of some controversy, but Heuzey has been for the most part vindicated. See Heuzey, *Études d'Archæologie Orientale*, i, pp. 49–82, and *Comptes Rendus de l'Académie des Inscriptions*, 1892, vol. xx, pp. 262–274, and *Découvertes en Chaldée*, pl. 3, 4. The whole monument is well described by Maspero, *Dawn of Civilization*, pp. 606, ff., and by Hilprecht, *Recent Research in Bible Lands* (Philadelphia, 1897), pp. 76, ff.

his hand, followed by his troops and charging upon the enemy. The plain is covered with the bodies of his enemies, and vultures fight with each other and devour the mangled heads, legs, and arms of the defeated enemy. Rude though it undoubtedly is, yet the execution bears witness to high civilization, for such execution could only be the result of long practice in the plastic art. By this one stroke Eannatum had freed Ur and Uruk from the Semitic invader and had imparted a fresh lease of life to the almost expiring Sumerian commonwealth. The new energy of victory was shown at once. Elam was invaded and Sumerian supremacy almost entirely reestablished over the whole of Babylonia and its tributary lands. The simple records of his deeds makes Eannatum one of the greatest conquerors of the far distant past. He was succeeded by his brother, En-anna-tuma I, and he by his son, Entemena, who has left us a beautiful silver vase with a brief inscription as well as fragments of vases which he presented to the great god En-lil at Nippur. After him came his son, En-anna-tuma II, who remains up to this time but a shadowy personality before us. With him we lose sight of the little kingdom of Shirpurla for a considerable period, and all our interest is transferred again to Semitic kingdoms in the north.

At about 3800 B. C. we catch a glimpse of another conqueror in Babylonia. At Nippur [1] there

---

[1] By the expedition of the University of Pennsylvania (see Hilprecht, *Old Bab. Ins.*, i, part i, p. 19).

have been found sixty-one fragments of vases bearing the name of the king Alusharshid.[1] From the fragments of these vases a complete inscription has been made out, which reads: "Alusharshid, king of the world, presented (it) to Bel from the spoil of Elam when he had subjugated Elam and Bara'se." This inscription makes known the important fact that a king, living probably at Kish, had conquered part of the land of Elam and the unknown land of Bara'se (or Para'se), from which he brought back fine marble vases and dedicated them to the gods of Babylonia. It is significant that these vases are dedicated to gods at Nippur and Sippar,[2] for in this we find indications of a kingdom which included northern Babylonia, Nippur, Sippar, and extended its influence even over the land of Elam. And with these few faint rays of light from the north and its kingdom darkness again closes in upon early Babylonia.

Once more, at about the same period, do we get sight of a bright light in the gray dawn of history, and this time it is not from Babylonia, but from Guti, the mountain country of Kurdistan, from which the Tigris and Euphrates Rivers came down to Assyria and Babylonia. Here reigned a

---

[1] The signs with which the name is written are URU-MU-USH, the reading of them as Alusharshid as well as the translation of the inscription belongs to Hilprecht (op. cit., p. 20).

[2] Inscriptions of Alusharshid have also been found in Sippar (Academy, September 5, 1891, p. 199, P. S. (see Hilprecht, op. cit., p. 21), and still others are in the possession of the British Museum, Cuneiform Texts from Babylonian Tablets, etc., in the British Museum, part vii, London, 1899, Nos. 12,161, 12,162.

king whose words are thus read: "Lasirab (?) the mighty king of Guti, . . . has made and presented (it.) Whoever removes this inscribed stone and writes (the mention of) his name thereupon his foundation may Guti, Ninna, and Sin tear up, and exterminate his seed, and may whatsoever he undertakes not prosper." [1] In itself brief and unimportant, this little text introduces us to another land under Semitic influences at a very early period.

Manishtusu,[2] another king of the same period, has left us a mace head and a stele as memorials of his sovereignty, yet we have few clews to his personality.

Far away also from northern Babylonia, in the mountain country of the northeast, there existed at about this same period another Semitic kingdom, of which Anu-banini was king. His was the kingdom of Lulubi, and he a Semitic ruler. At Ser-i-Pul, on the borderland between Kurdistan and Turkey, his carved image has been found with an inscription calling down curses on whomsoever should disturb "these images and this inscribed stone." [3]

---

[1] The credit of publishing the text of the inscription here referred to belongs to Winckler (*Zeitschrift für Assyriologie*, iv, p. 406), but he misunderstood and wrongly dated it at about 1600 B. C. (*Geschichte*, p. 82). Hilprecht correctly translated and located it on palæographical evidence (*Old Bab. Inscrip.*, i, part i, pp. 12, 13).

[2] *Altbabylonische Keilschrifttexte*, von Hugo Winckler, Leipzig, 1892, No. 67, p. 22.

[3] The inscription was found February 28, 1891, by J. de Morgan, and is published by Scheil (*Recueil de Travaux relatifs a la Phil. et Archéolol.*

Here, then, are several signs of Semitic power and culture in northern Babylonia and its neighboring lands. Some one of these centers of influence might become the center of a great kingdom that should again attack the Sumerians in the south. But this was reserved for a city which had up to this time produced no great conqueror. Out of the city of Agade came a man of Semitic stock great enough to essay and accomplish the task of ending finally the political influence of the Sumerians. His name is Shargani-shar-ali, but he is also called Shargina, and is best known to us as Sargon I. Most of that which is told of him comes to us in a legendary text—hardly the place to which one would commonly go for sober history. But a little sifting of this source speedily reveals its historic

Egypt. et Ass., vol. xiv, liv. 1 & 2, pp. 100, ff.). See also Hilprecht, *Old Bab. Insc.*, vol. i, part i, p. 14, and Hommel, *Proceedings of the Society of Bib. Archæology*, xxi, pp. 115, 116. The inscription had, however, been known long before it was seen by De Morgan. Sir Henry Rawlinson knew it, and, indeed, correctly understood it, save only that he made a slight error in reading the name. This anticipation of later work by the great explorer and decipherer is made plain in the following words extracted from an unpublished letter written under date of September 17, 1880, by Rawlinson to Professor Sayce: "Many thanks for your references, which I believe, however, were all duly entered in my notebooks. I am afraid we don't take quite the same view of the Geography of the Inscriptions. My own idea is that, at any rate until the time of Sargon, the Assyrians hardly penetrated beyond the outer range of the Perhim plateau. I think I can trace all the early campaigns (and can identify many of the names) along the western side of the great range from Sulimanieh to Susa. Instead of Nizir being at Alwend I place it at *Bend-i-Nuh*, Noah's ridge, the culminating range of Zagros. The inscription at Sir Pul belongs to Kannubanini, king of the *Lulubini*, thus fixing their locality and showing them to be identical with the modern Luri or Luli."

basis. The text,[1] two mutilated copies of which are in existence, belongs to a much later date than that of the king himself. It was probably written in the eighth century B. C., and purports to be a copy of an inscription which was found upon a statue of the great king. The story begins in this way: "Shargina, the powerful king, the king of Agade am I. My mother was poor, my father I knew not; the brother of my father lived in the mountains. My town was Azupirani, which is situated on the bank of the Euphrates. My mother, who was poor, conceived me and secretly gave birth to me; she placed me in a basket of reeds, she shut up the mouth of it with bitumen, she abandoned me to the river, which did not overwhelm me. The river bore me away and brought me to Akki, the irrigator. Akki, the irrigator, received me in the goodness of his heart. Akki, the irrigator, reared me to boyhood. Akki, the irrigator made me a gardener. My service as a gardener was pleasing unto Ishtar and I became king, and during . . . four years held royal sway. I commanded the blackheaded people and ruled them." In the fragmentary lines which follow the king mentions some of the important places conquered in his reign, and among them names Dur-il and Dilmun, the latter an island in the Per-

---

[1] Published III R. 4, No. 7. It has been frequently translated, for example, by George Smith, *Transactions of the Society of Bib. Arch.*, i, pp. 46, 47; by Fox Talbot, *Records of the Past*, first series, vol. v, pp. 1, ff.; by Delitzsch, *Paradies*, pp. 208, 209; and by Winckler, *Keilinschrift. Bibl.*, iii, 1, pp. 100–103.

sian Gulf. Unhappily this account does not enable us to construct a very clear idea of his campaigns, and we are forced to fall back upon a source which at first sight seems even less likely to contain veritable historical material than the legendary tablet which we have just cited. This is an astrological tablet[1] in which the writer tries to prove by historical examples that portents are valuable as indicating the issue of some campaign. Each campaign was preceded by some portent, and after it is told the writer explains that Sargon invaded Elam and conquered the Elamites, or that he marched into the west and mastered the four quarters of the world; or that he overcame an uprising of his own subjects in Agade. The fact that these details occur in an astrological text makes one wary of placing much reliance upon them. On the other hand, they are perfectly reasonable in themselves, and we should accept them at once from any other inscription.

It has been maintained by some that Shargina, or Sargon, and his great deeds are purely legendary,[2] and by others that his deeds have been simply projected backward[3] from some later king,

---

[1] First published by George Smith in *Transactions of the Society of Biblical Archæology*, i, pp. 47–51, and IV R. 34. See partial translations by Hommel (*Geschichte*, pp. 304–306) and Winckler (*Keilinschrift. Bibl.*, iii, part i, pp. 102–107). The text is republished in IV Rawlinson, second edition, plate 34.

[2] So, for example, Winckler, *Geschichte Bab. und Assyriens*, p. 38.

[3] Hommel supposed the existence of another king Sargon, whom he located about 2000 B. C., whose conquests he believed were ascribed to the earlier king (*Geschichte*, Berlin, 1885, p. 307, note 4). He has, how-

and have therefore no historical value. There is, however, no valid reason for doubting the main facts concerning the king's achievements. That he actually existed is placed beyond all doubt by the discovery of several of his own inscriptions.[1] One of these reads thus: "Shargani-shar-ali, son of Itti-Bel, the mighty king of Agade and of the . . . of Bel, builder of Ekur, temple of Bel in Nippur,"[2] and so bears witness not only to his historical existence, but also to his work as a builder. Of that tangible evidence has been found at Nippur. Far down in the mound is found the remains of a "pavement consisting of two courses of burned bricks of uniform size and mold. Each brick measures about fifty centimeters square and is eight centimeters thick."[3] Most of the bricks in this pavement are stamped, and a number of them contain the inscription of Shargani-shar-ali, who is thus shown to have laid down this massive construction, in which later his son also participated. No good reason for doubting that he was a great conqueror, east, south, and west, has been brought forward. On the other hand, when these same omen tablets refer to his son and

ever, since accepted the historical character of this king (art. "Babylonia," *Dict. of the Bible*, Hastings, i, p. 225, art. "The Oldest History of the Semites," *Expository Times*, December, 1896, vol. viii, pp. 103, ff.). Maspero believes that it is Sargon II (722–705 B. C.), who is projected backward (*Dawn of Civilization*, Eng. trans., New York, 1885, p. 599).

[1] Published by Winckler, *Altbabylonische Keilschrifttexte*, p. 22, and by Hilprecht, *Old Babyl. Ins.*, vol. i, part i, plates 1–3.

[2] Hilprecht, *Old Babyl. Ins.*, vol. i, part i, p. 15.

[3] *Op. cit.*, vol. i, part ii, p. 19.

successor they can be tested by texts of the king referred to, and prove to be worthy of credence. The allusions to these expeditions show that they were raids intended to gain plunder with which to increase the wealth and beauty of his home cities. It is not to be supposed that he succeeded in extending his dominion over lands so distant as northern Syria, but that the securing of great cedar beams from the Lebanon was the chief object of that expedition. A use for these cedar beams was soon found in buildings. The great temple of Ekur to the god Bel in Nippur and the temple of Eulbar to the goddess Anunit in Agade were built by him.[1] Other allusions to buildings erected by him are also to be found in later inscriptions. In warlike prowess he was the model for an Assyrian king who bore his name centuries later; in building skill he was emulated by a long line of Babylonian kings even unto Nabonidus, who sought diligently to find the foundation stones which he had laid. In the omen tablet there is evidence of credulous faith in the signs of heaven, but that is surely no reason for doubting all that is told therein of Sargon. A lonesome figure he is, in the dull gray dawn of human history, stalking across the scene, bringing other men to reverence the name of Ishtar, and making his own personality dreaded.

Sargon was succeeded by his son, Naram-Sin

---

[1] I R., 69, col. ii, line 29 (*Keilinschrift. Bibl.*, iii, 2, pp. 84, 85, tr. by Peiser).

(about B. C. 3750), who seems to have maintained in large degree the glory of his father's reign. The records of his reign are fragmentary, but every little piece bears witness to its importance. He is asserted to have invaded the city of Apirak, and to have carried the people into slavery after he had killed their king, Rish-Adad.[1] His chief warlike expedition known to us was into the land of Magan,[2] which appears to lie in Arabia, near the Peninsula of Sinai. But he was still more famous as a builder, for he rebuilt temples in Nippur [3]and in Agade, and erected at his own cost the temple to the sun god in Sippar.[4] Besides these temples this great king laid the foundations and erected the enormous outer wall of Nippur—the great wall Nimit-Marduk. He first dug for his foundations about five meters below the level of the ground down to the solid clay. Upon this he "built of worked clay mixed with cut straw and laid up *en masse* with roughly sloping or battered sides to a total height of about 5.5 meters. Upon the top of this large base, which is about 13.75 meters wide, a wall of the same enormous

---

[1] This fact comes from the astrological tablet, discussed above under Sargon, col. ii, lines 12-14.

[2] *Ibid.*, lines 15-16. Comp. I· R. 3, No. 7 (on an object brought from Magan).

[3] Brick stamps of this king have been found at Nippur bearing the legend, "Naram-Sin, builder of the temple of Bel." Hilprecht, *Old Babylonia Ins.*, i, part i, p. 18.

[4] V R., p. 64, col. ii, lines 57-60 (trans. by Peiser in *Keilinschrift. Bib.*, iii, part ii, p. 105.

width "[1] was raised. The bricks were "dark gray in color, firm in texture, and of regular form. In quality they are unsurpassed by the work of any later king."[2] Each of these bricks bore the stamped name and titles of the king. A king who could and did construct such massive fortifications must have possessed a kingdom of great political importance, of whose extent, however, it is now impossible to form a very clear idea. His chief city, or at least his original home city, was Agade, but he calls himself King of the Four Quarters of the World, in token of the world-wide dominion which he deemed himself to have attained. It is small wonder that a king who had thus won honor among men as a builder of mighty works and an organizer of a great kingdom should be deified[3] by his followers and worshiped as a creator. Nothing is known of the successors of Naram-Sin except of his son, Bingani-shar-ali. The kingdom of Sargon and his son vanishes from our view as rapidly as it came, leaving not even a trace of its effects.

Sargon I had had as one of his vassals Lugal-

---

[1] Hilprecht, *Old Bab., Inst.*, vol. i, part ii, p. 20.

[2] This is the judgment of Haynes, who dug down this wall. See Hilprecht, *op. cit.*, p. 21.

[3] Cesnola found at Curium in Cyprus a seal with this inscription, " Apal-Ishtar (?) son of Ilu-bana, servant of the god Naram-Sin " (see Tomkins, *Abraham and His Age*, London, 1897, plate x, and p. xxviii). This would seem to show that Naram-Sin had been deified. See also M. Thureau Dangin (in *Revue d'Assyriologie*, vol. iv, No. iii, p. 76), who quotes the legend, "The god Naram-Sin, god of Agade, Sharru-Ishdagal, the scribe, thy servant."

ushumgal,[1] *patesi* of Shirpurla, and it seems quite probable that after the end of the dynasty of Sargon and Naram-Sin the hegemony returned to the famous old city which had once stood at the head in the earlier day of the entire Sumerian domination. Whether that be the case or not, when we next get a clear view of Babylonia, long after the days of the kings of Agade, it is Shirpurla that we find in the chief place. Of the *patesis* of Shirpurla at this early date two are known to us as men of power and distinction, Ur-Bau (about 3200 B. C.) and Gudea (about 3000 B. C.). We possess a long inscription of the former, containing six columns,[2] engraved upon the back of a small statue of the king, which has been wrought with considerable skill out of dark green diorite. Like other inscriptions of the same period, it contains but little material for historical purposes. There is no word of battle and war; all is peace serene in these ancient texts. It is not, however, to be supposed that the lot of these kingdoms was thus happy. It must always be remembered that even unto the end the kings of Babylonia did not write accounts of their wars. From other sources we know well that Nebuchad-

---

[1] Heuzey, *Comptes Rendus de l'Académie des inscriptions et belles-lettres* (séance du 28 aout, 1896).

[2] Published by Heuzey in De Sarzec, *Découvertes en Chaldée*, plates 7, 8, copied and translated by Amiaud, in the same work. See also Y. Le Gac in *Zeitschrift für Assyriologie*, vii, pp. 125, ff., and Jensen, *Keil. Bib.*, iii, part i, pp. 19, ff. *Revue d'Assyriologie et d'Archéologie Orientale*, ii, pp. 124–135, and iii, pp. 42–48.

rezzar was a great soldier, but in only a single one of his own inscriptions does he speak of aught else but building of palaces and temples and dedications to the gods. Ur-Bau had, doutless, his fair share of the tumults of a very disturbed age.

The inscriptions of Gudea are similar to those of Ur-Bau in their subjects, but they give us incidentally a glimpse into a wider field. Ur-Bau was succeeded on the throne by Nammaghani, his son-in-law, who was, perhaps, followed by Ur-ningal, and then comes a break in the list to be filled by one or more kings yet unknown to us. After this lacuna comes the mighty Gudea, a king great enough to prove that even yet the Sumerian factor could not be eliminated from the world's history. Like Ur-Bau, he was a great builder, and of his wonderful work his inscriptions are full. In the building of his temples Gudea was directed by a divine vision. The goddess Nina appeared to him in a dream and showed him the complete model of a building [1] which he should erect in her honor. In the execution of this plan he brought from Magan (northeastern Arabia) the beautiful hard dolerite out of which his statues were carved. From the land of Melukhkha (northwestern Arabia and the Peninsula of Sinai) were brought gold and

---

[1] Gudea A, published by Amiaud in De Sarzec, *Découvertes*, etc., p. iv, plates 20 and 13, and page 134. The credit of first explaining the exceedingly difficult expressions in this text which refer to the dream belongs to Zimmern (*Traumgesicht Gudea's*, in *Zeitschrift für Assyriologie*, iii, pp. 232–235). See now Price, *The Great Cylinder Inscriptions of Gudea*, part i. Leipzig, 1899.

precious stones. These lands were not far from
his own, but it is more surprising to read that he
brought from Mount Amanus, in northwestern Syria, great beams of cedar, and in other neighboring
mountains quarried massive stones for his temples.
All these facts throw a bright light upon the civilization of his day. That was no ordinary civilization which could achieve work requiring such skill
and power as the quarrying or the cutting of
these materials and the transportation of them over
such distances. A long period for its development must be assumed. Centuries only and not
merely decades would suffice as the period of
preparation for such accomplishments. But it is
also to be observed that the securing of these materials must have involved the use of armed force.
The sturdy inhabitants of the Amanus would not
probably yield up their timber without a struggle.
One little indication there is of Gudea's prowess in arms, for he conquered the district of
Anshan, in Elam.[1] This single allusion to conquest
is instructive, for it was probably only representative of other conquests by the same builder and
warrior. But in spite of this inference the general
impression made by his reign is one of peace, of
progress in civilization, of splendid ceremonial in
the worship of the gods, and of the progress of the
art of writing. As a warrior he is not to be compared with Sargon of Agade; as an exponent of

---

[1] Gudea B, col. vi, 64–66. Comp. Jensen, *Keilinschrift. Bibl.*, iii, part
1, p. 38, note 9.

civilization he far surpasses him. The successor of Gudea was Urningirsu, himself followed after an interval by Akurgal II, Lukani, and Ghalala-ma.[1] But these later *patesis* were no longer free to do their own will as Gudea had been. With him had again passed away the independence of the ancient kingdom of Shirpurla.

The civilization of Shirpurla was, as we have seen, a high one. From the indications which we possess at present it would seem a far higher civilization than that of Agade, which had overcome it for a time. But it was not a Semitic civilization. All these inscriptions of the kings and of the *patesis* of Shirpurla are written in the Sumerian and not in a Semitic language. This also would seem to point to the conclusion that the Semites entered Babylonia from the north and not from the south.

From Shirpurla the power passed to Ur,[2] a city admirably situated to achieve commercial and historical importance. The river Euphrates flowed just past its gates, affording easy transportation for stone and wood from its upper waters, to which the Lebanon, rich in cedars, and the Amanus were readily accessible. The wady Rummein

---

[1] Lukani and Ghalalama are known to us from an inscription of the latter upon a fragment of a statue now in the Louvre. See Heuzey, *Revue Archéologique*, 1886, pl. vii, No. 1., and also in De Sarzec, *Découvertes*, pl. 21, No. 4 ; Jensen, *Keilinschrift. Bibl.*, iii, part 1, pp. 70, 71.

[2] The ruins of Ur, now called Mugheir, have long been known. They were first explored by Taylor and Loftus. The early references to Ur and its commerce have been collected by Hommel (*Die Semitischen Völker u. Sprachen*, pp. 204–211, and *Geschichte*, pp. 212–218, 325–329).

came close to the city and linked it with central and southern Arabia, and along that road came gold and precious stones, and gums and perfumes to be converted into incense for temple worship. Another road went across the very desert itself, and, provided with wells of water, conducted trade to southern Syria, the Peninsula of Sinai, and across into Africa. This was the shortest road to Africa, and commerce between Ur and Egypt passed over its more difficult but much shorter route than the one by way of Haran and Palestine. Nearly opposite the city the Shatt-el-Haî emptied into the Euphrates, and so afforded a passage for boats into the Tigris, thus opening to the commerce of Ur the vast country tributary to that river. Here, then, were roads and rivers leading to the north, east, and west, but there was also a great outlet to the southward. The Euphrates made access to the Persian Gulf easy. No city lay south of Ur on that river except Eridu, and Eridu was no competitor in the world of commerce, for it was devoted only to temples and gods—a city given up to religion.

In a city so favorably located as Ur the development of political as well as commercial superiority seems perfectly natural. Even before the days of Sargon the city of Ur had an existence and a government of its own. To that early period belong the rudely written vases of serpentine and of stalagmite which bear the name and titles of Lugal-kigub-nidudu [1] (about 3900 B. C.), king

---

[1] Published by Hilprecht, *Old Bab. Ins.*, vol. i, part ii, No. 86.

of Erech, king of Ur. We know nothing of his work in the upbuilding of the city, nor of that of his son and successor, Lugal-kisalsi. They are but empty names until further discovery shall add to the store of their inscribed remains. After their work was done the city of Ur was absorbed now into one and now into another of the kingdoms, both small and great, which held sway over southern Babylonia.

About a thousand years after this period the city of Ur again seized a commanding position through the efforts especially of two kings, Ur-Gur[1] and Dungi. The former has left many evidences of his power as well in inscriptions as in buildings. Most probably by conquest Ur-Gur welded into one political whole the entire land of northern and southern Babylonia, and assumed a title never borne before his day. He calls himself king of Sumer and Accad. In that title he joined together two words each of which contained a history extending far back into the past. The word Sumer, derived from Sungir, as we have already seen,[2] stood for the ancient Sumerian civilization, while Accad had come from Agade,[3] the city that was once the

---

[1] The reading of the name of this king has long been a bone of contention. It has been read Urukh, Urkham, Orkham, Urbagas, Urbabi, Likbabi, Amilapsi, Urea, Likbagas, Urbau, etc. Recently the form Ur-Gur has seemed likely to prevail. Inscriptions of this king are published I R. 1, and translated by Winckler, *Keilinschrift. Bibl.*, iii, part i, pp. 77, ff.

[2] See above, p. 205.

[3] The identification rests in the beginning upon a statement of George Smith: " I have only recently discovered the identity of Akkad with the capital of Sargon " (*Assyrian Discoveries*, p. 225), based on the finding of

leader in the new Semitic movement which was to supersede it. In this new kingdom we may see the first clear move made toward the formation of the great empire that was to come later.

All over this kingdom which he had thus formed did Ur-Gur build great structures for protection, for civil use, or for the worship of the gods. In his own chief city of Ur he built the great temple to the moon god; in the city of Erech he erected a temple to the goddess Nina. At Larsa also there are found unmistakable evidences that it was he who built there the shrine of the sun god. When these cities are dug up in a systematic fashion we shall be able to obtain some conception of his activity in this matter. At present we are able to form a more complete picture of his works in Nippur than in Ur. In Nippur he built a great *ziggurat*, or pyramidal tower, whose base was a "right-angled parallelogram nearly fifty-nine meters long and thirty-nine meters wide. Its two longest sides faced northwest and southeast respectively, and the four corners pointed approximately to the four cardinal points. Three of these stages have been traced and exposed. It is scarcely possible that formerly other stages existed above. The lowest story was about six and a third meters high, while the second (receding a little over four meters

---

Agade in a Sumerian text with the interlineal transcription Accad in Assyrian. Comp. Delitzsch, *Paradies*, p. 198, and Hilprecht, *Old Babylonian Inscrip.*, i, part ii, p. 58. On the other hand, Tiele, (*Geschichte*, p. 76), and Lehmann (*Shamashshumukin*, p. 73) argue against the view.

from the edge of the former) and the third are so utterly ruined that the original dimensions can no more be given. The whole *ziggurat* appears like an immense altar." [1] The defensive walls of Ur were also built by Ur-Gur, who seemed to be building for all time. Of his wars and conquests we hear no word, but, as has been said before in a similar instance, it is not probable that his reign was thus peaceful. It was probably built by the sword, and to the sword must be the appeal perhaps in frequent instances.

Ur-Gur was succeeded by his son, Dungi, [2] who was also indefatigable in building operations. He completed the temple of the moon god in Ur, and built, also, in Erech, Shirpurla, and Kutha. These two names of Ur-Gur and Dungi are all that remain of what was perhaps a considerable dynasty in Ur. Their buildings and their titles would seem to indicate that they held at least nominal sway over a considerable part of Babylonia. It is probable, however, that they were contented with the regular receipt of tribute, and did not attempt to control all the life of the cities subject to them. Each of these cities had its own local ruler, who submitted to the superior force of a great king, who was to him a sort of suzerain, but on the least show of weakness any one of these rulers was ready to set up his own independence, and, if he were strong

---

[1] Hilprecht, *Old Bab. Ins.*, vol. i, part ii, pp. 17, 18.

[2] The inscriptions of Dungi are published I R. 2, and translated by Winckler, *Kesilinschrift. Bibl.*, iii, part i, pp. 81, ff.

enough compel also his neighbors to accept him as suzerain. When the dynasty of Ur-Gur and Dungi was no longer able to maintain its position in Babylonia there were not wanting men strong enough to seize it.

After some time, when we again are able, by the means of monumental material, to see the political life of Babylonia we find that the supremacy has passed into the hands of the city of Isin. The kings of Isin whose names have come down to us are Ishbigarra,[1] Ur-Ninib,[2] Libit Ishtar,[3] Bur Sin I,[4] and Ishme-Dagan,[5] who ruled about 2500 B. C. The chief title used by them is king of Isin, but some of them use the greater title, king of Sumer and Accad. All of them use the names of other cities in addition to that of Isin, such as Nippur, Ur, Eridu, and Erech. Their inscriptions give no hint of the life of these cities or of the never-ending struggles for supremacy that must have been going on. To their titles they add only an occasional allusion to building or to restoration. Ishme-Dagan is the last man of this dynasty to bear the title of king of Sumer and Accad; his son, En-annatuma,[6] acknowledges his dependence upon a

---

[1] IV R. 35, 7, line 9.

[2] The name used to be read Gamil-Ninib (Hilprecht, *Old Bab. Ins.*, i, part i, p. 27); for his inscriptions comp. also IV R. 35, 5 (*Keilinschrift. Bibl.*, iii, part i, p. 85).

[3] The name is also read Libit-Anunit (Hilprecht, *Old Bab. Ins.*, i, part i, p. 27. Comp. also I R. 3, No. xviii (*Keilinschrift. Bibl.*, iii., part i, p. 87).

[4] Hilprecht, *op. cit.*, p. 27.

[5] I R. 2, No. 5, 1 and 2 (*Keilinschrift. Bibl.*, iii, part i, p. 87).

[6] I R. No. 6, sub. 1 and 2 (*Keilinschrift. Bibl.*, iii, part i, p. 87).

king of Ur who begins a new dynasty in that famous old city.

The third dynasty of Ur consists of Dungi II, Gungunu, Bur Sin II, Gamil Sin, and Ine-Sin.[1] They began to reign about 2400 B. C. as kings of Ur, and to that add the curious title "King of the Four Quarters (of the world)." Where was the Kingdom of the Four Quarters of the World, and why do the kings use such a title? It appears much earlier in an inscription of Naram-Sin, and is applied also to Sargon after his three campaigns in the west, while an inscription of Dungi bears the same curious legend. Again and again in later centuries is the title borne by kings of Babylonia and Assyria. It has been thought to be the name of some kingdom with a definite geographical location and a capital city. It has been located at several places in northern Babylonia, but without satisfactory reason. The title is rather the claim to a sort of world-wide dominion. Well indeed might Sargon use it after he had made expeditions into the west and laid the whole civilized world tributary at his feet. The use of the title by these kings may also imply some successful raids in the far west.[2] If there were any such, no account of them has come down to us.

---

[1] On the inscriptions of these kings see Hilprecht, *Old. Bab. Ins.*, i, part i, p. 27, and compare *Keilinschrift. Bibl.*, iii, part 1, pp. 87–91. See also Sayce, *Proceedings of the Society of Bib. Arch.*, vol. xxi, pp. 19, ff. F. Thureau-Dangin, *Revue Semitique*, 1897, pp. 72, ff.

[2] On this title, King of the Four Quarters (shar kibrat irbitti), see especially Lehmann, *Beiträge zu Assyriologie*, ii, p. 618; Hilprecht, *Old Bab. Ins.*, vol. i, part i, p. 25.

26

Besides the usual records of their building we have from this dynasty only hundreds of contract tablets, now scattered in museums nearly all over the world. These tablets, uninteresting in themselves, are yet the witnesses of an extraordinary development in commercial lines. The land of Babylonia was waxing rich and laying the foundations for great power in the world of trade when its political supremacy was ended. The end of the dynasty, and with it the end of the dominion of Ur, is clouded in the mists of the past.

At about this same period there was also in existence a small kingdom called the kingdom of Amnanu,[1] with its chief city Erech. The names of three of its sovereigns have come down to us upon brief inscriptions,[2] the chiefest of them being apparently Sin-gashid. Unlike the kingdoms founded in Ur and in other cities, this kingdom of Amnanu seems to have exerted but small influence upon the historical development of the country. The name of the kingdom disappears, and is attached to no later king until it is suddenly used again by Shamashshumukin (667–647 B. C.),[3] but apparently without any special significance,[4] and rather as a reminiscence of ancient days.

---

[1] Comp. Winckler, *Altorientalische Forschungen*, i, pp. 231, 232.

[2] I R. 2, No. viii, 1, 2. IV R. 35, 3, Brit. Mus., 82, 7–14, 181, copied by Peiser. All these are translated by Winckler, *Keilinschrift. Bibl.*, iii, part i, pp. 82-85.

[3] V R. 62, No. 2, line 2. Comp. Lehmann, *Shamasshshumukin*, ii Theil, Tafel i and ii.

[4] See Winckler as above and comp. Lehmann, *op. cit.*, i Theil, p. 75.

After Ur, in the progress of the development of empire in Babylonia, came the dominion unto Larsa, the modern Senkereh, on the bank of the canal Shatt-en-Nîl. The names of two of the chief kings of this dynasty are Nur-Adad[1] and his son, Sin-iddin,[2] but the order in which they stand is still uncertain. Both of these kings built in Ur, and Sin-iddin also founded a temple to the sun god in Larsa, and dug a new canal between the Tigris and the Shatt-en-Nîl. This work of canal building, which became so important and so highly prized in the later history, begins therefore at this early period. The king who built canals saved the land from flood in the spring and from drought in the summer and was a real public benefactor. The names of the other kings who ruled in Larsa and had dominion in Babylonia at this time are either wholly unknown to us or are exceedingly difficult to place in correct order.

The times were sorely disturbed and it is easy to understand why the Babylonian records are in such disorder as to make it difficult to understand the exact order of events. At this time a new factor in Babylonian history was making itself felt. Babylonia had long been the battle ground between the ancient Sumerians and the Semites. The day had now come when a new people the

---

[1] His inscriptions are published, I R. 2, No. iv, and translated by Winckler, *Keilinschrift. Bibl.*, iii, part i, p. 91.

[2] Inscriptions of this are published, I R. 5, No. xx (*Keilinschrift. Bibl.*, iii, part i, pp. 92, 93), and by Delitzsch in *Beiträge zur Assyriologie*, pp. 301, ff. (see also *Keilinschrift. Bibl.*, iii, part i, pp. 90, 91).

Elamites must enter the lists for the possession of the deeply coveted valley. The rulers of
Elam appear to have made many attempts to get
a hold upon parts of Babylonia. One of them was
Rim-Anum,[1] who actually did get control at about
this time of some parts of the country, and was referred to in business documents as Rim-Anum the
king. As no historical texts have come down to
us from his reign, it is impossible to say how long he
ruled or what influence he had upon the country.

To this same period of Elamite invasions belongs Kudur-Nankhundi,[2] who made a raid into
Babylonia 2285 B. C., reached Erech and plun-
dered its temples, carrying away into captivity a
statue of the goddess Nana. His influence upon
the land was apparently very slight, for apparently
no documents exist which are dated in his period.
It is probable that he was not successful in estab-
lishing any dominion over the country at all.
But his failure would not daunt other princes; the
prize was great and men would not fail in its winning for want of a trial.

Probably soon after Kudur-Nankhundi the successful raid was made. The Babylonian inscriptions have preserved for us no mention of the
king's name who swept down into the valley

---

[1] For business documents in his reign comp. Sayce, *Proceedings of the
Society of Biblical Archæology*, xix, p. 73, and Scheil in *Recueil de Travaux
relatif à la Phil. et archéol. Egypt et Ass.*, xx, pp. 64, 65. Comp. further
Lehmann, *Zwei Hauptprobleme*, p. 207.

[2] III R. 38, 1 a. 12–18. See above, p. 319. The name appears in the
form Kudur-Nakhkhunte in old Susian.

and carried all before him. The Hebrews among their traditions preserved the name of Chedorlaomer [1] (Kudur-Lagamar) as the Elamite who invaded the far west. To him or to other Elamite invaders the weak kingdom of Sumer and Accad was able to offer no effectual resistance, and the kings of Larsa were quickly dispossessed. The Elamites in a few short years had swept from east to west, destroying kingdoms whose foundations extended into the distant past. Their success reminds one of the career of the Persians in a later day.

Under the rule of these Elamite conquerors Kudur-Mabuk [2] was prince of E-mutbal, in western Elam. His authority and influence were extended into Babylonia, and perhaps even farther west. He built in Ur a temple to the moon god as a thank offering for his success.

He was succeeded by his son, Eri-Aku, [3] who was still more Babylonian than his father. He extended the city of Ur, rebuilding its great city walls "like unto a mountain," restored its temples, and apparently became a patron of that city rather than of Larsa, though he still calls himself king

---

[1] See further on Chedorlaomer below, p. 390. A very similar view of the events is now taken by Winckler (in Helmolt's *Weltgeschichte*, iii, p. 96).

[2] An inscription of Kudur-Marbuk is published I R. 2, No. iii, *Keilinschrift. Bibl.*, iii, part i, pp. 92, 93.

[3] Inscriptions of Rim Sin—that is, Eri-Aku—are found I R. 5, No. xvi, 3, No. x, *Mittheilungen des Akad-Orient-Vereins zu Berlin*, i, p. 16, and are translated by Winckler, *Keilinschrift. Bibl.*, iii, part i, pp. 94, 95. On the reading of the name as Eri-Aku see Schrader in *Sitzungsberichte K. Preuss. Ak. Phil.-hist. Classe*, 24 Oct., 1895, xli.

of Larsa. The Elamite people were now become in the fullest sense masters of all southern Babylonia. Eri-Aku calls himself "exalter of Ur, king of Larsa, king of Sumer and Accad," and so claims all the honors which had belonged to the kings of native stock who had preceded him. This invasion and occupation of southern Babylonia by the Elamites prepared the way for the conquest of southern Babylonia by the north and the establishment of a permanent order of things in the land so long disturbed.

With Larsa ends the series of small states, of whose existence we have caught mere glimpses, during a period of more than two thousand years. As Maspero has well said: "We have here the mere dust of history rather than history itself; here an isolated individual makes his appearance in the record of his name, to vanish when we attempt to lay hold of him; there the stem of a dynasty which breaks abruptly off, pompous preambles, devout formulas, dedications of objects or buildings, here or there the account of some battle or the indication of some foreign country with which relations of friendship or commerce were maintained—these are the scanty materials out of which to construct a connected narrative." But, though we have only names of kings of various cities and faint indications of their deeds, we are able, nevertheless, out of these materials to secure in some measure an idea of the development of political life and of civilization in the land.

As has been already said, the civilization of southern Babylonia, in the period 4000–2300 B. C., was at the foundation Sumerian. But during a a large part of this time it was Sumerian influenced by Semitic civilization. The northern kingdom even about 3800 B. C. was Semitic. Intercourse was free and widely extended, as the inscriptions of Sargon and Naram-Sin and the operations of Gudea have conclusively shown. The Sumerian civilization was old, and the seeds of death were in it; the Semitic civilization, on the other hand, was instinct with life and vigor. The Semite had come out of the free airs of the desert of Arabia and had in his veins a bounding life. It was natural that his vigorous civilization should permeate at first slowly and then rapidly into the senile culture of the Sumerians. The Sumerian inscriptions early begin to give evidence of Semitic influence. Here it is a word borrowed from the Semitic neighbors, there it is a name of man or god. This influence increased. Toward the end of the period the Semitic words are frequent, the Semitic idiom is in a fair way to a complete peaceful conquest, and political contest would bring about the final triumph of Semitism, though not the extermination of Sumerian influence. It remained until the very end of Babylon itself, and the rise of the Indo-European world powers. The conservatism of religious customs gave to the old language and the old literature, now become sacred, a new life. The temples still bore Sumerian names when Baby-

lon's last conqueror entered the magnificent
gates.

Concerning the political development we know
altogether too little for dogmatic conclusions. The
whole may be summed up in the following manner:
The earliest indications show us the city as the
center of government. The chief man in the city
is its king, or, if there be no title of king, he is
called *patesi*. When the surrounding country is
annexed his title remains the same; he is still
king of the city. But after a time a new custom
comes into vogue. Ur-Ba'u is king of Ur, but he
is more, he is also king of Sumer and Accad. By
that expression we are introduced to the conception
of a government which controlled not only segre-
gated cities, but a united country, northern and
southern Babylonia. The position of the capital
was indeed fluctuating. The capital depends altogether on the king and his place of origin. The
kingdom has its governmental center in Ur, but
Ur is not its permanent capital. The capital is
later found in Isin, and the kings of Isin are then
kings of Sumer and Accad when they have conquered and bear rule in the north and south. This
old title lives on through the centuries, and later
kings in other cities are proud to carry it on
their inscriptions.

This union of all Babylonia under one king was
not the means of creating a national unity strong
enough to resist the outside invader. Sumerian
civilization seemed to have reached the end of its

development as a political factor. The raids of the Elamites scattered and broke its power, and the time was ready for a man strong enough to conquer the petty kings of Larsa, take the title of king of Sumer and Accad and make a strong kingdom.

CHAPTER II.

THE FIRST AND SECOND DYNASTIES OF BABYLON.

THE origin of the city of Babylon is veiled in impenetrable obscurity. The first city built upon the site must have been founded fully four thousand years before Christ, and it may have been much earlier. The city is named in the Omen tablet of Sargon,[1] and, though this is no proof that the city was actually in existence about 3800 B. C., it does prove that a later tradition assigned to it this great antiquity. At this early date, however, it seems not to have been a city of importance. During the long period of the rise of the kingdom of Sumer and Accad no king in the south finds Babylon worthy of mention, though Babylon must have been developing into a city of influence during the later centuries of the dominion of Isin and Larsa. From about 2300 B. C. the influence of this city extends almost without a break to the period of the Seleucides. No capital in the world has ever been the center of so much power, wealth, and culture for a period so vast. It is indeed a brilliant cycle of centuries upon which we enter.

The name of the first king of Babylon is given

---

[1] IV R. 34, obverse l. 8. *Keilinschrift. Bibl.*, iii, part i, pp. 102, 103.

in the Babylonian King Lists as Sumu-abi (about 2454-2440 B. C.),[1] of whom we know nothing. We have likewise no historical inscriptions of his immediate successors, and our only knowledge of their reigns is to be obtained from the fragmentary notes of contract tablets, which sometimes give indications of the life of the people. From the inscriptions of later kings we also get word of some building operations of two of them. These kings are Sumu-la-ilu (about 2439-2405 B. C.), who built six strong fortresses in Babylon, and Zabu (about 2404-2391 B. C.), who erected in Sippar of Anunit the temple of Edubar to the city's deity. After Zabu there was apparently an attempted revolution, for we get hints that a certain Immeru[2] attempted to ascend the throne. His name does not appear on the King List, and it is probable that he was not able to gain a secure position in the kingdom.

The next rulers are Apil-Sin (about 2390-2373

---

[1] The dates which are set down with the names of the kings of this dynasty must in all cases be taken as approximate only and as subject to the greatest doubt. They rest in all cases upon the original sources, but these sources contain numerous contradictions and discrepancies, and it is idle to attempt to make from them a chronology that may lay any claim to accuracy. See above, p. 338.

[2] The name Immeru occurs on a number of contract tablets, but without being called king. Events are, however, dated by his name, just as though he were king. (See Meissner, *Beiträge zum altbab. Privatrecht*, Leipzig, 1893, Nos. 10 and 38; Peiser, *Keilinschrift. Bibl.*, iv, pp. 8, 9.) His exact position is difficult to fix. He is located after Zabu by Meissner (*op. cit.*, p. 4), and this has found considerable acceptance (so Lehmann, *Zwei Hauptprob.*, p. 31, and King, art. "Babylonia" in Cheyne & Black, *Enc. Biblica.*). Sayce, however, says he was a contemporary of Sumu-la-ilu, and perhaps . . . a vassal king of Larsa (*Early Israel and the Surrounding Nations*, London, 1899, p. 281).

B. C.) and Sin-muballit (about 2372–2343 B. C.),
whose reigns are likewise unknown to us.

It is a noteworthy fact that in the large numbers of business documents which have come
down to us out of the period of this first dynasty
of Babylon, none of these rulers down to Apil-Sin
is called king and Sin-muballit only in the form of
a passing allusion in one single tablet. It is difficult to explain this fact unless we accept the view
that the real kingdom of Babylon did not begin
until Hammurabi had driven out the Elamites and
so won for himself the title borne by the old kings
of Ur, Isin, and Larsa.

The son and successor of Sin-muballit was Hammurabi (about 2342–2288 B. C.), with whom begins a new era. It is the chief glory of his name
that he made a united Babylonia, and that the
union which he cemented remained until the scepter passed from Semitic hands to another race.
In this he far exceeded the success of Sargon and
Lugalzaggisi, whose empires were of but short
duration. Yet he had even greater difficulties to
meet than they. The Elamites were firmly fastened in the country, and would hardly give it up
without a struggle. The activity displayed by
these Elamite princes in building was an indication of how much they valued their new possessions. We are not yet in possession of facts enough
to enable us to follow the movements of Hammurabi in his conquest of the country. The
struggle was probably brief and without distinction.

The people of the kingdom of Sumer and
Accad had no genuine national life, no divine
patriotism. When one king passed they cared
not, and as willingly paid taxes to another, if only
he made them no heavier. The Elamites were
soon driven out of Babylonia, and Hammurabi
assumed the titles of king of Sumer and Accad,
king of the Four Quarters of the World, as well
as the old title, king of Babylon. The ready ac-
quiescence of the people in the new rule of Hammurabi and the new leadership of the city of Babylon is shown conclusively by the entire absence of
any uprising or of any attempt to throw off the
yoke. The time was ripe for the overturning of the
old Sumerian state, and in Hammurabi was found
the man for the new era. The manner of the conquest is unknown to us, and in the knowledge of
the fact we must rest content.

We know very little about the government of
the country which Hammurabi had thus organized
into a consolidated kingdom or empire. That he
had petty princes or viceroys under him is made
clear by sundry letters and dispatches to such officials which have come down to us.[1] But it is still
impossible so to order these little fragments as to
gain complete or satisfying pictures of his relation
to them. If Hammurabi be the same person as
Amraphel, who is mentioned in the Hebrew traditions (Gen. xiv), and many suppose, with consid-

---

[1] See *The Letters and Inscriptions of Hammurabi*, by L. W. King, M.A.,
three volumes, London, 1898, ff.

erable reason, that he is,[1] we have there evidence
that he was deemed in a later period to have had
a considerable body of allies with whom he was
associated in campaigns in the west. Of these
who are thus mentioned Chedorlaomer has not yet
been identified on any Babylonian inscription of
an early date, though the name may well correspond with a form Kudur-lagamar,[2] for both parts
of which there is ample support. On an inscription of late date (about 300 B. C.) a name has been
found which, whether it be read Kudur-nuchgamar,
or Kudur-lugkgamar, or what not, almost certainly

---

[1] See, for example, Hommel (*The Ancient Hebrew Tradition*, London,
1897, p. 193, and elsewhere), Sayce (*Early Israel*, p. 213). Driver (*Authority and Archæology*, p. 39) says, "There is little doubt" that Amraphel "is
a corrupt representation of Khammurabi." But the name can scarcely be
called "corrupt" in view of the form Ammu-rabi. Comp. Zimmern, *Theol-
ogische Rundschau*, i, p. 321.

[2] Kudur appears frequently in these Elamite names. Lagamar occurs as
the name of an Elamite deity in an Assyrian text (V R. vi, col. 6, 33), and
also in the inscriptions of Anzan-Shushinak (F. H. Weissbach, *Anzanische
Inschriften, Abh. d. phil. hist. Classe. der k. Sächs. Ges. d. Wissenschaften*,
xii, p. 125. Leipzig, 1891). Unfortunately a sharp controversy has occurred over the name Chedorlaomer which was thought to appear in some
texts of the period of the Arsacidæ (see Pinches, *Journal of the Transactions of the Victoria Institute*, xxix, 1897, pp. 56, ff.), and Father Scheil
thought that he also had found the name in early tablets (*Revue Biblique*,
v, October, 1896, pp. 600, f.; *Recueil de Travaux relatif . . . Egypt. et Ass.*,
xix, 4, ff.). In the latter case King (*Letters and Inscriptions of Hammurabi*, London, 1898, p. xxix) has shown conclusively. that the text was
misread by Scheil and that the name Chedorlaomer does not occur on it.
He has further demonstrated that the reading of Mr. Pinches is very
doubtful. Keen and successful though his criticism is, it can hardly be
denied that beneath all the obscurity there lies a real reference to the Chedorlaomer of Gen. xiv. Such, for example, is the view of Zimmern (*Theolo-
gische Rundschau*, i, pp. 320, 321) and Driver (*Authority and Archæology*,
pp. 42, 43). See, for a learned discussion of the whole matter, the article
"Chedorlaomer," by Thiele and Kosters, in *Encyclopædia Biblica* (ed. Cheyne
& Black), i, cols. 732-734.

represents Chedorlaomer. The name of Tidal,
king of Goïim, has not yet been certainly identified; but in this same inscription a certain "Tud.
chula, son of Gazza," appears to be mentioned, who
possibly represents Tidal.[1] Arioch, king of Ella-
sar, is certainly to be identified with Eri-Aku, son
of Kudur-Mabuk, the well-known king of Larsa.
The narrative of their campaigns in the west ac-
cords well with what we know of the general situation, but forms only an episode in Babylonian
history, and cannot now be satisfactorily related to
the general movements of the time.

As soon as the conquest of Sumer and Accad
was completed Hammurabi showed himself the
statesman even more than the soldier. He displayed extraordinary care in the development of
the resources of the land, and in thus increasing
the wealth and comfort of the inhabitants. The
chiefest of his great works is best described in his
own ringing words—the words of a conqueror, a
statesman, and a patriot: "Hammurabi, the powerful king, king of Babylon, . . . when Anu and
Bel gave unto me to rule the land of Sumer and
Accad, and with their scepter filled my hands, I
dug the canal Hammurabi, the Blessing-of-Men,
which bringeth the water of the overflow unto the
land of Sumer and Accad. Its banks upon both
sides I made arable land; much seed I scattered
upon it. Lasting water I provided for the land of
Sumer and Accad. The land of Sumer and Ac-

---

[1] See Pinches, King, and Driver, as above cited, on Chedorlaomer.

cad, its separated peoples I united, with blessings and abundance I endowed them, in peaceful dwellings I made them to live." [1] This was no idle promise made to the people before the union of Sumer and Accad under the hegemony of Babylon, but the actual accomplishment of a man who knew how to knit to himself and his royal house the hearts of the people of a conquered land. There is a world of wisdom in the deeds of this old king. No work could possibly have been performed by him which would bring greater blessing than the building of a canal by which a nearly rainless land could be supplied with abundant water. After making the canal, Hammurabi followed the example of his predecessors in Babylonia and carried out extensive building operations in various parts of the land. On all sides we find evidences of his efforts in this work. In Babylon itself he erected a great granary for the storing of wheat against times of famine—a work of mercy as well as of necessity, which would find prompt recognition among oriental peoples then as now. The temples to the sun god in Larsa and in Sippar were rebuilt by him; the walls of the latter city were reconstructed "like a great mountain"—to use his own phrase—and the city was enriched by the construction of a new canal. The great temples of E-sagila in Babylon and E-zida in the neigh-

---

[1] The Louvre Inscription Col. I 1–II 10. See, for full references to the original texts, Jensen in *Keilinschrift. Bibl.*, iii, part i, p. 123, and comp. also translation by Winckler (*Geschichte*, p. 64).

boring Borsippa showed in increased size and in beauty the influence of his labors. There is evidence, also, that he built for himself a palace at the site now marked by the ruin of Kalwadha, near Baghdad.

But these buildings are only external evidences of the great work wrought in this long reign for civilization. The best of the culture of the ancient Sumerians was brought into Babylon, and there carefully conserved. What this meant to the centuries that came after is shown clearly in the later inscriptions. To Babylon the later kings of Assyria look constantly as to the real center of culture and civilization. No Assyrian king is content with Nineveh and its glories, great though these were in later days; his greatest glory came when he could call himself king of Babylon, and perform the symbolic act of taking hold of the hands of Bel-Marduk. Nineveh was the center of a kingdom of warriors, Babylon the abode of scholars; and the wellspring of all this is to be found in the work of Hammurabi.

But if the kings of Assyria looked to Babylon with longing eyes, yet more did later kings in the city of Babylon itself look back to the days of Hammurabi as the golden age of their history. Nabopolassar and Nebuchadrezzar acknowledged his position in the most flattering way, for they imitated in their inscriptions the very words and phrases in which he had described his building, and, not satisfied with this, even copied the exact

27

form of his tablets and the style of their writing. In building his plans were followed, and in rule and administration his methods were imitated. His works and his words entitle him to rank as the real founder of Babylon.[1]   Hammurabi reigned fifty-five years according to the King Lists, but forty-three years according to a native document which comes to us from his own dynasty.

When the long reign was ended the son of Hammurabi entered into his father's labors.   Samsu-iluna (about 2287–2253) seems to have followed closely in the footsteps of Hammurabi.   He tells us of building in Nippur and in other cities—some of them still unknown to us—of increasing the size of Babylon itself, and of continuing the works upon canals.[2]   The profound peace which Hammurabi achieved by arms continues through his reign and into the reigns of his successors.   We have no historical inscriptions, for the records which have come down from their reigns are the so-called contract or business tablets, from which no connected story has yet been made out.   From them we learn of the high civilization of the country and of its continued prosperity.   The names of these kings, with their approximate dates, can only be set down until some future discovery reveals records with a historical meaning.

---

[1] See Winckler, *Geschichte*, pp. 63, 64.

[2] The text of Samsu-iluna here referred to is published by Winckler (*Untersuchungen*, p. 140) and translated by him, *Keilinschrift. Bibl.*, iii, part i, pp. 131, ff.

Abeshu' (Ebishum), about...... 2252–2228 B. C.
Ammisatana, about.......... 2227–2203 B. C.
Ammisadugga, about......... 2202–2182 B. C.
Samsusatana, about.......... 2181–2115 B. C.

The names of the kings of this dynasty are very peculiar when one thinks that they are set down as native rulers over the city of Babylon. The origin of Zabu and its meaning are very doubtful, Apil-Sin and Sin-muballit are good Babylonian names, but the other eight are most certainly not Babylonian at all. This at once raises the question as to the nationality or race of these kings. The names would seem to suggest that the men who bore them were not Babylonian, but had come from some other branch of the great Semitic family. This seems now to be quite probable. Their names are for the most part to be connected with the Canaanite branch of the Semitic family, and it seems probable that they owe their origin to an invasion of Babylonia by the same race that peopled the highlands of Canaan. How and when they settled in Babylon remains obscure.

According to the King Lists this dynasty was followed immediately by the second dynasty, which in all things must have been very like its predecessor. It is called the dynasty of Uru-Azag,[1] and it has been conjectured that this refers to a district of the city of Babylon. This

---

[1] Winckler reads Uru-azagga and supposes this to be a part of the city of Babylon (*Geschichte*, pp. 67, 68, 328). See on this Hilprecht's criticism (*Assyriaca*, pp. 25–27, 103), who reads simply Shish-khu and believes in the non-Semitic origin of the dynasty. To this Winckler replies in *Altorien-*

would make this dynasty consist of native princes, who had originated in a separate part of the city, by which they are named. The names of these kings and the length of their reigns are here given:

1.	An-ma-an, about	2150–2091	(60)
2.	Ki-an-ni-bi	2090–2035	(56)
3.	Dam-ki-ilu-shu	2034–2009	(26)
4.	Ish-ki-bal	2008–1994	(15)
5.	Shu-ush-shi	1993–1970	(24)
6.	Gul-ki-shar (? kur)	1969–1915	(55)
7.	Kir-gal-dara-bar	1914–1865	(50)
8.	A-dara-kalama	1864–1837	(28)
9.	A-kur-ul-an-na	1836–1811	(26)
10.	Me-lam-kur-kur-ra	1810–1803	(8)
11.	Ea-ga-mil	1802–1783	(20)

368 years.

We owe this list of kings and the length of each reign to the Babylonian historians.[1] It is certainly a surprising list of years of reign. As our confidence in the length of reigns given to kings in the first dynasty has been somewhat shaken by the discovery of the Babylonian Chronicle, in which Hammurabi receives forty-three years instead of fifty-five years, we may feel a reasonable doubt as to the accuracy of these long reigns. No inscriptions of any of these kings have yet been found,

talische Forschungen, vol. i, pp. 275–277. Sayce has supposed Uruazagga to be represented by "a part of the mounds of Tello or its immediate vicinity" (Records of the Past, new series, i, p. 13), but later reads Sisku (Early Israel, p. 281.) Hommel has attempted to connect the first king of his dynasty with Prince An-a-an of Erech (Proceedings of the Society of Biblical Archæology, xvi, pp. 13–15), but without success (see Hilprecht, Assyriaca, pp. 101, ff.).

[1] See further above on the Chronology, p. 339.

and no business documents dated in their reigns have come to light. It is not therefore to be argued that the kings had no existence. Inscriptions of theirs may readily be supposed to be still in existence in the vast stores yet unearthed, or reasons may easily be found for supposing that a systematic effort had been made to destroy all their records. It has been supposed that during, perhaps, the latter part of this term the disturbances and movements began which resulted in the removal of all rule from the hands of the Babylonians and the transfer of it to invaders from the Kassite country. However that may be, a long period elapsed from the days of Hammurabi until the passing of power into the hands of foreigners. Hammurabi had indeed builded well. North and south together acknowledged the dominion of his successors. Peace at home and abroad gave leisure for the pursuit of literature, art, and science. This great silent period gives the necessary time for the progress in all these things, which is evidenced by the works no less than the words of the following centuries. From the peace and stability which his genius achieved we must now turn to the turmoil which ensued when his influence was finally overcome. Yet it was overcome in part only; the city of Babylon, which he had made great, so continued. Its supremacy there was none to question. It was only the constant effort of men to possess it and all that its traditions covered and contained.

CHAPTER III.

THE KASSITE DYNASTY.

At about the year 1783 ends the long period of stable peace, during which Babylonia was ruled by kings of native blood. This land of great fertility had tempted often enough the hardy mountaineers of Elam, even as in later centuries the fair plains of northern Italy were coveted by the Teutons, who surveyed them from the mountains above. As long as the influence of Hammurabi and the other founders of the united kingdom of Babylonia remained the country was able to defy any invader. But the development of the arts, the progress of civilization, and the increase of trade and commerce had weakened the military arm. Babylon was becoming like Tyre of later days, whose merchants were always willing to pay tribute to a foreign foe rather than run the risk of a war which might injure their trade. At this time, however, Babylon still possessed patriotism and national pride, and there is no reason to believe that the foreigner seated himself upon the proud throne of the Babylonians without difficulty. It is indeed unlikely that the conquest of Babylon was achieved by a definitely organized army, led by a commander who purposed making himself king of Babylon, while still continuing to reign in his own country. It is rather the migration of a strong, fresh people which here confronts us. This people is called the Kasshu, and their previous seat was in Elam, but it is difficult to localize them more perfectly. It seems probable that they stood in some relation to the people dwelling along the banks of the Zagros, who became famous in later times under the name of the Kossæans [1] (Κοσσαῖοι), and it has even been suggested that they are, in some way, to be connected with another people, the Kissians (Κίσσιοι), who were at one time settled in the country of Susiana,[2] but are also believed to be mentioned in Cappadocia.[3] In the present state of our knowledge we are not justified in identifying them positively

---

[1] Delitzsch believes that these are all one people (*Die Sprache der Kossäer*, p. 4). But see for reasons to the contrary Oppert (*Zeitschrift für Assyriologie*, iii, pp. 421, ff., and v, pp. 106, f.) and also Lehmann (*ibid.*, vii, pp. 328, ff.; *Zeitschrift der Deutsche Morgenländische Gesell.*, 1895, p. 306; *Zwei Hauptprobl.*, pp. 211, 212). Lehmann identifies the Kasshu with the Kissians, and against this view may be quoted Rost, *Untersuchungen*, pp. 43, 44. The name Kassite, which we have here adopted, is colorless and leaves the question undecided until more light has been obtained. It was proposed by Sayce (*Records of the Past*, new series i, p. 16), but he, nevertheless, identifies them with the Kossæans (*ibid.*, note 7). Kassite is now in general use (for example, by Winckler, *Geschichte*, pp. 78, 79, and Hilprecht (Cassite), *Old Bab. Ins.*, vol. i, part i, p. 28; McCurdy (Kasshites), *History, Prophecy, and the Monuments*, i, p. 143).

[2] λέγονται δὲ καὶ Κίσσιοι οἱ Σούσιοι. Strabo, *Geographica*, xv, 2 (ed. Augustus Meineke, vol. iii, p. 1014). Sennacherib (Taylor Cylinder, col. i, line 64, tr. by Rogers in *Records of the Past*, new series, vi, p. 86) found the Kashshi in the Kossæan mountains. Comp. Billerbeck, *Das Sandschak Suleimania*, Leipzig, 1898, p. 126, who locates them in the " *Luti-Bagtsche* Bergland."

[3] Ptolemæus, v, 6, 6, quoted by Rost, *Untersuchungen*, p. 44.

with either or both of these peoples. It will be safer simply to call them Kassites, and thus leave their racial affinity an open question. Certain indications there are which seem to show that they did not come direct from their ancient home into Babylonia, but were settled first in the far south, near the Persian Gulf. They entered Babylon probably as roving bands, then in increased numbers overran the land and gained control, so that they set up a foreign dynasty in place of the previous native Babylonian rule.

Concerning this Kassite dynasty our knowledge is very unsatisfactory. The Babylonian historians preserved in their King Lists the names of all these kings, but unhappily this list, in the form in which we possess it, is badly broken and many of the names are lost. The list assigns to this dynasty five hundred and seventy-six years and nine months.[1] On this representation the Kassites must have ruled from about 1782 B. C. to about 1207 B. C. During this long period the Kassites naturally did not remain foreigners, but were rapidly assimilated to Babylonian culture as well as to Babylonian usages. They naturally wrote inscriptions, as their predecessors had done; they built buildings and worshiped the Babylonian gods. But their rule did not bring forth so rich a fruit as Hammurabi's had done, and the records that have come down to us are much more fragmentary. Of only one king in this

[1] See above pp. 340-342.

dynasty do we possess any long historical inscription, and his name does not appear upon the King List, but stood where the list is broken beyond hope of restoration. The correspondence of some of the kings with kings of Egypt has been preserved, and by it a most welcome light is shed upon the obscure period. We possess only contract tablets of other kings, the number of which will be largely increased by the publication of tablets that have been found at Nippur.

The names of the first kings in the list are:

			Length of Reign.
1. Gandish [1]	...... Perhaps about	1782–1767 B. C.	16
2. Agum-shi......	"	" 1766–1745 B. C.	22
3. Bibeiashi [2].....	"	" 1744–1723 B. C.	22
4. Dushi [3]........	"	" 1722–1714 B. C.	(9)(19?)
5. Adumetash [4]....	"	" 1713–	
6. Tashzigurumash. [5]			

---

[1] The name of this king is also abbreviated into Gande (Hilprecht, *Old Bab. Ins.*, i, part i, pp. 28, ff.), and even into Gan (*ibid.*, p. 30). It also appears in the form Gaddash on an inscription published by Pinches (*Babylonian and Oriental Record*, i, pp. 54, 78; comp. *Academy*, 1891, p. 221). The inscription is in the British Museum (84–2–11, 178), and is published by Winckler (*Untersuchungen*, p. 156, No. 6). Also Hilprecht, *Zeitschrift für Assyriologie*, vii, p 309, note 4, and *Old Bab. Ins.*, i, part i, p. 30, n. 3.

[2] This name is written Guyashi by Pinches and Winckler. Delitzsch discovered another sign before the GU (*Assyriologische Miscellen*, Sonderabdruck aus den Berichten der phil-his. classe der K. Sächs Gesell. der Wiss. Sitzung vom 8 Juli, 1893, p. 184). Knudtzon reads Bibeiashi, and avers that the reading is certain after a new collation (see Lehmann, *Zwei Hauptprob.*, p. 19).

[3] The reading of the name is doubtful. It is sometimes read Ush-shi. Knudtzon (*Assyrische Gebete*, i, p. 60) reads Du; while Delitzsch suggests that it may be AD. Rost (*Untersuchungen*, p. 24) reads Abu (?) makhru.

[4] Reading doubtful. Delitzsch and Winckler read Adumetash, and so also Lehmann. Rost is doubtful and suggests a comparison with Attametu.

[5] Reading doubtful, though the signs are reasonably clear. Winckler reads Tash-shi-gurumash, because in the text of Agumkakrime the latter

To us these names convey no real meaning. They are only shadows of men. The name of the first king also appears in a votive tablet under the form Gande, and in still another little fragment as Gaddash. He gives honor to the great god Bel, and wrote his name and titles on the door sockets set up by former Babylonian kings. But his name is not written in the same skillful manner as of former worthies. The rude workmanship is eloquent of the change which had come through a ruder race. The world's progress was put back when the Kassites come to rule in Babylon.

But, though we know so little about this king Gandish, we know even less about his followers for a long time. These six kings fill a blank space in the history which had been all aglow with life and color in the days of the first dynasty.

After the sixth name the Babylonian King List is hopelessly broken, and no names can be read for a considerable space. It seems probable that Tash-zi-gurumash may be the same as the king from whom Agum-kakrime claims descent. If this be true, we may have found by this means the name of the next king on the list. There belonged to the library of Asshurbanapal a long inscription [1] in

---

calls himself a son of Tash-shi-gurumash, a name so like this that they may, without violence, be thought the same (Delitzsch, *Assyriologische Miscellen*, p. 185).

[1] This text was first published II R. 38, No. 2, and repeated in more perfect form V R. 33. It was collated by Delitzsch and then translated in *Kossäer*, pp. 55, ff. It was again collated by Bezold and, upon his contributions, translated by Jensen (*Keilinschrift. Bibl.*, iii, part i, pp. 134, ff.). For further literature see Bezold (*Ueberblick*, p. 57).

Assyrian characters which purports to be a copy
of an inscription of an early king of Babylon. Certain peculiarities of the Assyrian text make it
much more probable that it is a translation from
Sumerian.[1] The king whose deeds it recounts was
Agum-kakrime. In this text he calls himself the
son of Tashshigurumash. It is very tempting to
connect this Tashshigurumash with the sixth name
in the list of kings, and this is now generally done.
It is probably right, yet it must be admitted that
it is still somewhat doubtful. If Agum-kakrime
were really the son of *King* Tashshigurumash, it is
natural to suppose that with his father's name in
his inscription would stand the title of king, which
is not the case. The entire inscription sounds
rather like the text of an usurper who is attempting to bolster up his claims to the throne by sounding titles and genealogical connections, as was done
in certain cases in later times.[2]

Whether Agum-kakrime was the next name in
the list or not, it seems almost certain that he
must have belonged to this same period and his
name must have followed very shortly upon the
list. In his inscription, after giving all his connections of blood and all his ties to the gods, he
sets forth the lands of his rule in these words:
"King of Kasshu and Accad; king of the broad
land of Babylon; who caused much people to set-
tle in the land of Ashnunnak; king of Padan and

---

[1] Winckler (*Geschichte*, p. 79).
[2] So, for example, by Sargon II and Tiglathpileser III.

Alvan; king of the land Guti, wide extended peoples; a king who rules the Four Quarters of the World am I." This is a remarkable list of titles. It is at once noteworthy that the titles do not follow the usual Babylonian order. Usually a Babylonian king would write the title in this fashion: "King of Babylon, king of the Four Quarters of the World, king of Sumer and Accad, king of Kasshu." The titles "king of Padan and Alvan, king of Guti, etc.," would hardly have been used in this form at all. The Babylonian kings would seem to feel that they could not bear direct rule over a land lying outside of the rule of the Babylonian gods who alone could give the title to a king in Babylon. Rather would such a king have called himself "King of the kings of Padan, Alvan, and Guti," which lands he would thus rule through a deputy appointed by himself. It is to be observed that later Kassite kings conformed very carefully to this custom.[1] That Agum-kakrime violated it is another proof that he belongs to the earlier kings of the dynasty, in a time before the Kassites had accommodated themselves to the customs of their conquered land.

But the titles of Agum-kakrime serve another and larger purpose for us than the furnishing of a confirmation of the position we have assigned him in the dynasty; they furnish us with a view of the extent of territory governed from Babylon

---

[1] These distinctions are due to the keenness of Winckler (*Geschichte*, pp. 80, 81).

during his reign. His kingdom covers all Babylonia, both north and south, which belonged to the
ancient empire of Hammurabi; but it far exceeded
these bounds. Agum-kakrime still continued to
rule the land of Kasshu, and the land of Ashnunnak. Guti also, a land of which we have heard
nothing since the days of Lasirab, was also subject to him, as well as Padan, the land of Mesopotamia between the Euphrates and the Balikh, and
Alvan (modern *Holwan*), which was contiguous to
Guti and lay in the mountains of Kurdistan. As
there is no indication in the inscriptions of the
previous dynasties that so large a territory had
been added to Babylonia since the days of Hammurabi, we are shut up to the view that the Kassites had themselves achieved it. This would
make them greater conquerors than even the
mighty founder of Babylon's greatness.

The major part of this inscription of Agum-kakrime deals with the restoration to Babylon of
some gods which had been carried away in a previous raid upon the country. Agum-kakrime says
that he sent an embassy to the far away land of
Khani,[1] which was probably located in the mountain country east of the Tigris, and south of the

---

[1] The location of Khani is now fairly well settled. Asshurnazirpal (I R.
28, col. I, 18, comp. *Keilinschrift. Bibl.*, i, 124) alludes to "Mount Khana on
the side of the lands of the Lullumi," and Billerbeck (*Sanschak Sul.*, p. 8)
would identify this mountain with the "Karadagh oder das Bergland zwis-
chen diesem und dem Hamrin." See further, Sayce, *Proceedings Soc. Bib.
Arch.*, January, 1899, pp. 13, ff., who locates "the country of Khana on
the eastern side of the Babylonian frontier."

Lower Zab, to bring back to Babylon the statues of
Marduk and Zarpanit.   In order to understand
this move on his part it must be remembered that,
from the Babylonian point of view, there could be
no legitimate king in Babylon unless he had been
appointed to his rule by Marduk, patron god and
real ruler of the city.   But Marduk had been carried away by the people of Khani.   It was all important, therefore, for the stability of the throne
that this god, at least, be immediately restored.
If Agum-kakrime had had sufficient troops at his
command, he would probably have taken the god
by force from this captors ; as Nebuchadrezzar I
and Asshurbanapal did in later times.   He did
not do this, but sent an " embassy."   In this expression we may see an euphemism for the purchase
or ransom of the gods by actual payment of gold
or silver.   When these gods were taken away
we do not know.   Perhaps we shall not go far
astray if we locate this event in the later reigns
of the kings of the second dynasty, at which time
we have also placed the beginnings of the Kassite
influence.   The gods must have been removed by
a destructive invasion, for Agum-kakrime follows
the story of their restoration with the statement
that he placed them in the temple of Shamash, and
provided them with all the necessities for their
worship, because Marduk's own temple, E-sagila,
had to be restored before it was fit for his
occupancy.   This ruinous state of Babylon's great
state temple points backward to a period of

great weakness, to the period when Babylon was tottering from the proud position to which Hammurabi had brought it, and was already an easy prey for the foreigner.

The remaining lines of this important inscription deal with temple restorations, and thus add the name of Agum-kakrime to the list of great builders who have already passed in review before us. No other events in his reign are known to us, nor is its length preserved. The indications which remain would seem to show that he must have reigned long and peacefully.

After the reign of Agum-kakrime there is a sharp break in the chain of our information concerning the history of this dynasty. It will be necessary to make clear the reason for this break, and to set forth briefly the means adopted for the partial repair of the breach.

In giving the names of the kings of this dynasty from Gandish to Agum-kakrime we have simply followed the lists made by the Babylonian scholars in ancient times. If the list were perfectly continued, we should have an easy task in following out the kings of the dynasty, and in setting forth something of their activity by means of other historical material. Unhappily the tablet containing the list is broken off just after the name of Tashshigurumash. The list is then resumed after some distance by the name Kudur-Bel, alongside of whose name stands the numeral VI as the number of years of his reign. Following the name Kudur-

Bel there are found the names of ten kings of
the Kassite dynasty. There are thus preserved
the names of sixteen kings, to which we may add
that of Agum-kakrime, making seventeen in all.
At the bottom of the list it is stated that there
were thirty-six kings in the dynasty, and that the
sum of the years of their reigns was five hundred
and seventy-six years and nine months. For the
completion of the list we therefore need the
names of nineteen kings. How many of these
names can be obtained? In the present state of
investigation it is safe to say that of these nineteen
missing names twelve have been secured with
reasonable certainty, and for the most part they
can be arranged accurately in order in the dynasty. These names have been secured in some
instances from contract tablets dated in their
reigns; in others from their own inscriptions; in
others from the so-called Synchronistic History—
an original Assyrian document giving very briefly
the early relations between Babylonia and Assyria—in others from letters and dispatches which
passed between the courts of Babylonia, Assyria,
and Egypt.

Before proceeding with the history of the remaining kings of this dynasty it will be necessary
to say something by way of preface of the conditions of political life prevailing elsewhere, in order
to the better understanding of the facts which we
possess with reference to these reigns.

More than one hundred years before the begin-

ning of the Kassite dynasty a new state, destined
to a splendid career of dominion among men, was
showing the beginnings of its life along the eastern bank of the Tigris. The land of Assyria in
its original limits was a small land inclosed within
the natural boundaries of the Tigris, the Upper
and the Lower Zab, and the Median mountain
range. Its inhabitants at this time were Semites,
and apparently of much purer blood than their
relatives the Babylonians, who had intermarried
with the Sumerians—a custom afterward continued with the Kassites and with many other peoples. The chief city of this small Assyrian state
was Asshur, in which were ruling, at the period
of the beginning of the Kassite dynasty, Semitic
Ishakkus, who were the beginners of a long and
distinguished line. Their land was admirably furnished by nature. In it lived a people who were
not enervated by luxury nor prostrated in energy
by excessive and long-continued heat, but accustomed to battle with snowdrifts in the mountains
and to conserve their physical force by its constant
use. It is no wonder that under such favorable
conditions this people should have risen rapidly
to power. In a short time we shall find them
able to negotiate treaties with the kings of Babylonia, and soon thereafter the main stream of history flows through the channels they were now
digging. It is for these reasons that we have here
touched lightly upon the beginnings of their
national life.

28

Two other lands require brief mention before we can properly understand the movement of races during the period of the Kassite dynasty.

In the northwestern part of the great valley between the Tigris and Euphrates lay a small country whose two chief limits were set by the river Euphrates and its tributary the Balikh. In the Egyptian inscriptions of the eighteenth and nineteenth dynasties it is called Naharina—that is, the river country—but it was called Mitanni by its own kings. How long a people had lived within its borders with kings of their own and a separate national existence remains an enigma. No inscriptions of the people of Mitanni, save letters written to kings of Egypt, have been found. We should indeed hardly know of the land at all but for the discovery of the royal archives of the kings Amenophis III and Amenophis IV, the kings of Egypt who had diplomatic intercourse with it. From these letters and dispatches we have learned the names of several of the kings of Mitanni, among them Artatama, Artashuma, Sutarna, and Dushratta. Their chief god was Tishup, whose name as well as the names of his worshipers is not Semitic, but what their racial ties may be we do not know. At the time when these kings were writing dispatches to the kings of Egypt their land was in some sort of union with Khanigalbat, a land later known as Melitene and situated much farther north and west in the mountains. Between the kings of Mitanni and the kings of Egypt there

were bonds of marriage, the kings of Egypt having married princesses from the far distant "river
land." The fact that the proud kings of Egypt
were anxious to ally themselves to the kings of
Mitanni would seem to indicate that the land
was sufficiently wealthy or influential to make it
worthy of the attention of Egypt. The letters of
Mitanni were written chiefly in the Semitic language of Babylonia, and in the cuneiform characters, with which we are familiar in the native inscriptions. One of these letters, however, preserved in the Royal Museum in Berlin,[1] is written
in the language of Mitanni, which has thus far not
yielded to the numerous efforts made to decipher
it.[2] The kingdom of Mitanni must take its place
among the small states which have had their
share in influencing the progress of the world,
but whose own history we are unable to trace.
But, though we cannot do this, we may at least observe that it seems to have been largely under
Semitic influences, for its method of writing was
borrowed from its powerful neighbors.

The last land to which our attention must be
diverted, before proceeding with the main story is
the land of Kardunyash.[3] Originally the word

---

[1] VA. Th. 422.

[2] Attempts to decipher this language have been made by Sayce (*Academy*,
vol. xxxvii, 1890, p. 94 ; *Zeitschrift für Assyriologie*, v, pp. 260–274), by
Jensen (*Zeitschrift für Assyriologie*, v, pp. 166–208 ; vi, pp. 34–72), and
by Brünnow (*ibid.*, v, pp. 209–259).

[3] Winckler (*Untersuchungen*, pp. 135, 136 ; *Geschichte*, pp. 86, 87). For
references to the El-Amarna letters from Kardunyash see below.

Kardunyash seems to be applied to a small territory in southern Babylonia close to the Persian
Gulf. The termination, " ash " is Kassite, and it
has been supposed, with good reason, that the
Kassites first settled in this land by the Persian
Gulf, and used it as a base from which to overrun
and conquer Babylonia. Whether this be true or
not, it is at least certain that the name Kardunyash comes to be used by the Kassite kings as a
sort of official name for the land of Babylonia.

We are now able to return to the Kassite dynasty after a long excursus; the better prepared
to gather together such little threads of information as link them with their neighbors.

As we have seen above, the Babylonian King
List is so broken after the name Tashshigurumash
that some names are lost. Of these missing names
we have already secured the name of Agum-
kakrime. After him there lived six kings whose
names, together with all their words and works,
are lost.

The next king of the Kassite dynasty of whom
we have knowledge is Karaindash (about 1450
B. C.). Like his predecessors and successors, he
was a builder, as his own brief words make
plain : "To Nana, the goddess of E-Anna, his
mistress, built Karaindash, the powerful king,
king of Babylon, king of Sumer and Accad,
king of Kasshu, king of Kardunyash, a temple in
E-Anna." In this brief inscription the king
places Babylon first in his list of titles, and the

two Kassite titles, Kasshu and Kardunyash, at the very last. This can only be due to a following of the immemorial Babylonian usage. The old land soon absorbed the peoples who came to it as conquerors, and by the potency of its own civilization and the power of its religion compelled adherence to ancient law and custom. The Kassites had conquered Babylonia by force of arms; already has Babylonian culture conquered the Kassites and assimilated them to itself.

In the reign of Karaindash we meet for the first time evidence of contact between the still youthful kingdom of Assyria and the empire of Babylonia —even then hoary with age. Our knowledge of these relations between the two kingdoms comes from the Assyrians, who made during the reign of Adad-nirari III (811–783 B. C.) a list of the various friendly and hostile relations between Babylonia and Assyria from the earliest times down to this reign. The original of this precious document has perished, but a copy of it was made for the library of Asshurbanapal by some of his scholars, to whom our knowledge of the ancient Orient owes so much. This copy is now in the British Museum, and, though badly broken, fully half of it may be read.[1] It has been named the Synchronistic History, and, though it is not a history in

---

[1] Published II R. 66, and III R. 4, 3. See also Delitzsch, *Kassäer*, pp. 6, ff., and the valuable translation by Peiser and Winckler (*Keilinschrift. Bibl.*, i, pp. 194, ff.), which is based on a new collation by Winckler. See also above, p. 324.

any strict sense, it is convenient to retain this appellation. The very first words upon it which may be read with certainty relate to Karaindash, and are as follows : "Karaindash, king of Karduny-ash and Asshurbelnishishu, king of Assyria, made a treaty with one another, and swore an oath concerning this territory with one another." This first entry evidently refers to some debatable land between the two countries, concerning which there had been previous difficulty. The two kings have now settled the boundary line by treaty. This shows that Assyria was already sufficiently powerful to claim a legitimate title to a portion of the great valley, and it was acknowledged by Babylon as an independent kingdom. It is not long before this small kingdom of Assyria begins to dispute with Babylonia for the control even of the soil of Babylonia itself. With this first notice of relations between the two kingdoms begins the long series of struggles, whether peaceful or warlike, which never cease till the bloodthirsty Assyrian has driven the Babylonian from the seat of power and possessed his inheritance.

We are unhappily not in a position to be very certain as to the order of succession of the followers of Karaindash, but his immediate successor was probably Kadashman-Bel.' No historical inscription of this king and no business documents dated

---

[1] The name was formerly read Kallima-Sin (Winckler, *The Tell-el-Amarna Letters*, i, pp. 2, ff.), but see for the correction Knudtzon, *Zeitschrift für Assyriologie*, xii, pp. 269, 270.

in his reign have yet come to light in Babylonia.
We should be at a loss to locate him at all were it
not for the assistance to be obtained from the
archives of the Egyptians. As in the case of the
land of Mitanni, so also here are we in possession
of some portions of a correspondence with Amenophis III, king of Egypt. The British Museum
possesses a letter written in Egypt by Amenophis
III to Kadashman-Bel, and the Berlin Museum
has three letters from Kadashman-Bel to Amenophis III. The first letter is probably a copy of
the original sent to Babylonia. It begins in this
stately fashion: "To Kadashman-Bel, king of Kardunyash, my brother; thus saith Amenophis, the
great king, the king of Egypt, thy brother: with
me it is well. May it be well with thee, with thy
house, with thy wives, with thy children, with thy
nobles, with thy horses and with thy chariots,
and with thy land may it be well; with me may
it be well, with my house, with my wives, with
my children, with my nobles, with my horses,
with my chariots, with my troops, and with
my land, may it be very well."' The letter
then discusses the proposed matrimonial alliance
between Egypt and Babylonia and urges that
Kadashman-Bel should give to him his daughter
to wife. The letter further announces the sending
to Kadashman-Bel of an ambassador to negotiate
a commercial treaty between the two states, by
which certain imports from Babylonia into Egypt
were to pay a customs duty. The letters pre-

served in Berlin seem to relate to the same correspondence and deal chiefly with the proposed marriage of the daughter of Kadashman-Bel to Amenophis III, to which friendly consent was finally given. Both the daughter and the sister of Kadashman-Bel were thus numbered among the wives of Amenophis III—full proof of the very intimate relation which now subsisted between the two great culture lands of antiquity, Babylonia and Egypt. To find letters passing between Babylon and Egypt about 1400 B. C., and ambassadors endeavoring to negotiate commercial treaties, does, indeed, give us a wonderful view into the light of the distant past. This all witnesses to a high state of civilization; to ready intercourse over good roads; to firmly fixed laws and stable national customs. It gives us, however, no light upon the political history of Babylonia, which is the object of our present search, and we must pass from it. Kadashman-Bel had a long reign and was succeeded by Burnaburiash I.

The Synchronistic History [1] sets down this king as contemporary with Puzur-Asshur, king of Assyria, with whom he seems to have had a hostile demonstration concerning the boundaries between the two lands. As the Assyrian writer alludes only euphemistically to their relation as unfriendly, and says nothing of an Assyrian victory, it is safe perhaps to conclude that Burnaburiash was successful. Little else of his reign is known, though he

---

[1] Col. i, lines 5-7.

was also in a measure a builder of temples, for a brick brought from the temple ruins at Larsa shows that he had erected there a temple to the sun god.[1]

Of the next king, Kurigalzu I, about 1410 B. C., son of Burnaburiash I, our knowledge is also very unsatisfactory. It is known from the letters of Burnaburiash II that he stood in friendly relations with Amenophis III, king of Egypt, and it is probable that his relations with the Assyrians were friendly. The few inscriptions[2] of his which remain record simply the usual building operations. The titles which he uses in his texts are "King of Sumer and Accad, king of the Four Quarters of the World," to which in one instance he adds the title "shakkanak (that is, governor) of Bel," and in another case uses this latter title only. The title of king of Babylon, which we might have expected, is not used by him at all. This may be because he was not officially made king by the use of all the solemn ceremonies which the priesthood had devised. The city of Dur-Kurigalzu (Kurigalzuburg) derived its name from him, but it does not appear whether he was its founder or only a benefactor and rebuilder. The compiler of the Synchronistic History found no events in his reign in connection with the contemporary Assyrian king, Asshur-nadin-akhe,

---

[1] I R. 4, xiii, *Keilinschrift. Bibl.*, iii, i, p. 153.

[2] I R. 4, Lehmann in *Zeitschrift für Assyriologie*, v, 417, and Hilprecht, *Old Bab. Ins.*, i, part i, pl. 20, etc.

which were worthy of narration, and he is therefore passed by without a word. His reign was probably short, and at its conclusion, about the year 1400, he was succeeded by his son, Burnaburiash II, whose reign was long and prosperous, though no Babylonian memorials of it have been preserved.

Four letters written by this king to Amenophis IV (*Napkhuriya, Akh-en-Aton*), king of Egypt, are preserved in the Berlin Museum,[1] and two more are in the British Museum.[2] No historical material of great moment is offered in these letters. They reveal a period of relative peace and prosperity, and deal, in considerable measure, with the little courtesies and amenities of life. It is, for example, curious to find the Babylonian king reproving the king of Egypt for not having sent an ambassador to inquire for him when he was ill.[3] When kings had time for such courtesies, and could only excuse themselves for failing to observe them on the ground of their ignorance of the illness and the great distance to be covered on the journey, there must have been freedom from war and from all distress at home and abroad.

The successor of Burnaburiash II appears to have been Karakhardash (about 1370 B. C.), who had for his chief wife Muballitat-Sherua, daughter of

---

[1] VA. Th. 149, 150, 151, 152. *Der Thontafelfund von El-Amarna,* Heft i.

[2] Bu. 88-10-13, Nos. 21, 46, and 81.

[3] VA. Th. 150, 10, ff., translated by Zimmern, *Zeitschrift für Assyriologie,* v, p. 139.

Asshur-uballit, king of Assyria, so that the custom of intermarriage which prevailed between the royal houses of Egypt and Babylon at this period had also its illustration between the houses of Assyria and Babylonia. This alliance made for peace between the two royal houses, but did not establish peace between the peoples of the two countries. When Karakhardash died his son, Kadashman-Kharbe I, came to the throne. His mother was Muballitat-Sherua, and so it happened that an Assyrian king had his grandson upon the throne of Babylon. This king conducted a campaign against the Sutu, whom he conquered and among whom he settled some of his own loyal subjects. Upon his return from this expedition he found himself confronted by a rebellion of the Kassites, who were probably jealous of the growth of Assyrian influence, and he was killed. The rebels then placed upon the throne Nazibugash (also called Shuzigash, about 1360 B. C.), a man of humble origin and not a descendant of the royal line. As soon as the news of this rebellion reached Assyria Asshuruballit, desiring to avenge his grandson, marched against Babylonia, killed Nazibugash, and placed upon the throne Kurigalzu II, a son of Kadashman-Kharbe.[1] Kurigalzu II (about

---

[1] These facts are found in the Babylonian Chronicle P, first published in translation by Pinches, *Records of the Past*, new series, v, pp. 106, ff., and retranslated more accurately by Winckler, *Altorientalische Forschungen*, pp. 115, f. With this chronicle is to be compared the Synchronistic History, in which there appear to be some errors. Comp. Winckler, *ibid.*, and also Rost, *Untersuchungen*, p. 54, etc.

1350 B. C.) was probably made king while still young, and his reign was long. We cannot follow its events in detail, but may get a slight view of some of its glories. Many centuries before his day, when Kudur-nakhundi of Elam ravaged in Babylonia, he carried away a small agate tablet, which was carefully preserved in the land of Elam. This happened about 2285 B. C., and now, about 1350 B. C., Kurigalzu II invades Elam and conquers even the city of Susa itself. The little agate tablet is recovered, and the victorious Kurigalzu II places it in the temple of E-kur at Nippur, with his own brief inscription engraved on its back: "Kurigalzu, king of Karadunyash, conquered the palace of Susa in Elam and presented (this tablet) to Belit, his mistress, for his life." [1] It is to this campaign that the Babylonian Chronicle probably refers in its allusion to the campaign of Kurigalzu against Khurbatila, king of Elam, which resulted so victoriously. After the invasion of Elam the victorious Kurigalzu II also fought with Bel-nirari, king of Assyria, and worsted him, as the Babylonian Chronicle narrates the story, though the Assyrian Synchronistic History claims the victory in the same conflict for the Assyrians. [2]

Nazi-Maruttash (about 1340 B. C.), son of Kurigalzu II, the next king, also fought with the As-

---

[1] Hilprecht, *Old Bab. Inscrip.*, vol. i, part i, p. 31.

[2] Comp. Chron. P, iii, 20–22, with Synchronistic History, i, 18, ff., and see Winckler, *Altorientalische Forschungen*, i, pp. 122, 123, and Rost, *Untersuchungen*, p. 54, note 1. Chronicle P has here read Adad-nirari incorrectly for Bel-nirari.

syrians, led by their king, Adad-nirari I, who defeated him signally, and gained some Babylonian
territory by pushing the boundary farther south.
This is the Assyrian account; what the Babylonian story may have been we do not know, for
the Babylonian Chronicle is broken at this point.
Of the son of Nazi-Maruttash who succeeded him
under the name of Kadashman-Turgu we know
nothing, and of his successor, Kadashman-Buriash
(about 1330 B. C.), we only know that he was at
war with Shalmaneser I, king of Assyria,[1] without
being able to learn the outcome. These constantly
recurring wars with Assyria are ominous, and indicate the rapid increase of Assyrian power. They
point toward the day of destruction for Babylon,
and of glory for the military people who were beginning to press upon the great city.

The following reigns are almost entirely unknown to us. The names of the kings awaken no
response in our minds, and we can only set them
down as empty words; they are Kudur-Bel (about
1304–1299 B. C.) and Shagarakti-Shuriash (about
1298–1286 B. C.), though in their cases the Babylonian King List has supplied us with the length
of their reigns, and we know definitely and certainly their order in the dynasty.

The Babylonian Chronicle now again comes to
our aid, and with rather startling intelligence.
Tukulti-Ninib, king of Assyria, has invaded Baby-

---

[1] III R. 4, No. 1. Comp. Delitzsch, *Kossäer*, p. 10, and Hilprecht, *Old Babylonian Inscriptions*, vol. i, part i, p. 31.

lon. We do not know what steps led to this
attack. Perhaps the old boundary disputes had
once more caused difficulty, perhaps it was only
the growing Assyrian lust for power and territory.
But whatever the cause this was no ordinary invasion intended chiefly as a threat. The Assyrian
king enters Babylon, kills some of its inhabitants,
destroys the city wall, at least partially, and, last
and worst of all, removes the treasures of the temple, and carries away the great god Marduk to Assyria.[1] Here was a sore defeat indeed, and the
end, for the time at least, of Babylonian independence. The line of kings is continued during the
period of war and invasion with the names of
Bibeiashu (about 1285–1278 B. C.), during whose
reign the invasion probably occurred; Bel-shum-
iddin, and Kadashman-Kharbe II, who together
reigned but three years (about 1277–1275), and
Adad-shum-iddin (about 1274–1269 B. C.). But the
last three of these kings must have been only vassals of Tukulti-Ninib, who was the real king of
Babylon for seven years, even though he was represented by these as his deputies.[2] Here is the
city of Hammurabi, glorious in its history, ancient
in its days, ruled by a king of the small and rela-
tively modern state of Assyria. But the old spirit
was not quite dead, and after seven years of this
domination the Babylonians rose in rebellion, drove

---

[1] Chronicle P, col. iv, 3–6.

[2] See Hommel's acute suggestions for removing the chronological difficulties in Winckler, *Altorientalische Forschungen*, i, pp. 138, 139.

the Assyrians from Babylon, and made Adad-shum-usur (about 1268–1239 B. C.) king, while Tukulti-Ninib returned to Assyria only to find a rebellion against him headed by his own son.[1] In this his life was lost, and he went down with the decline of his once brilliant fortunes. On the other hand, the reign of Adad-shum-usur was at once the token and result of better fortunes in Babylonia. In his reign the power of Babylon again began to increase. He attacked Assyria itself, and the Assyrians were scarce able to keep the victorious Babylonians out of their country. Their king, Bel-kudur-usur, was slain in battle, and in the overturning Babylonia made gains of Assyrian territory. The reign of Meli-Shipak (about 1238–1224 B. C.) was also a period of Babylonian aggression against the Assyrian king Ninib-apal-esharra,[2] and to such good purpose that the next Babylonian king, Marduk-apal-iddin (about 1223–1211 B. C.), saw the Assyrians once more confined to their narrow territory, stripped of all their conquests, and was able to add to his own name the proud titles "king of Kishshati, king of Sumer and Accad,"[3] in token of the extension once more of Babylonian dominion over nearly the whole of the valley.

But this change was too great and too sudden to last, and the power of Assyria must soon re-

[1] Chronicle P, iv, 7–11.
[2] Synchronistic History, ii, 3–8.
[3] VI R. 41, i, 20.

turn and then again continue to develop. When
Asshur-dan became king of Assyria, and this was
probably while Marduk-apal-iddin was still reigning, there was another reversal of fortunes, though
this time the change was neither so sudden nor so
great. Asshur-dan fought with the next Babylonian king, Zamamashumiddin (about 1210 B. C.),
and succeeded in winning back some of the cities in
the ever-debatable land between Assyria and
Babylonia,[1] and thus gave proof that the Assyrian
power was again waxing strong. The next Kassite king, Bel-shum-iddin (about 1209–1207 B. C.),
reigned also but a short time, and the very brevity
of these reigns may, perhaps, as often, indicate that
the period was filled with strife. Assyria was certainly threatening the Babylonian empire, for the
long reign of Asshur-dan gave time for the carrying out of extensive plans, and the power to realize
them was plainly not wanting. The failure of the
Kassites to hold inviolate the territory of Babylonia resulted in a Semitic revolution in which the
dynasty that had ruled so long in the queenly city
ended. Its advent was heralded by war and by
internal dissensions in the last preceding dynasty;
and its approaching end was indicated in like
manner.

---

[1] Synchronistic History, iii, 9–12.

CHAPTER IV.

THE DYNASTY OF ISIN.

THE cause of the downfall of the great Kassite dynasty is unknown to us. It may have been due to an uprising of the Semites against foreign domination, with the war cry of "Babylonia for the Babylonians;" a cry which in various languages has often resounded among men and won many a national triumph.

The Babylonian King List names the new dynasty, the dynasty of Isin,[1] but its origin is still doubtful. It has been suggested that it began in Babylon and is named after a section of the city known as Isin,[2] but it is still possible that it originated in the city of Isin, whose influence had been marked at an earlier period of the history. This dynasty reigned in Babylon a period of one hundred and thirty-two years. The list is so badly broken that but few of the names have been retained, and we are once more forced to seek the means of restoring the names from notices in other documents. There were eleven kings in this dynasty who were regarded by the Baby-

---

[1] Jensen reads Isin (*Zeitschrift für Assyriologie*, xi, p. 90), and Craig (*American Journal of Semitic Languages and Literatures*, xiii, pp. 220, 221), supports him. Comp. also Rost (*Untersuchungen*, p. 10, note 2).

[2] So, for example, Rost, *l. c.*

29

lonian historians as legitimate, and of these four
or five are entirely unknown to us.

The names of the first two kings of the dynasty,
who reigned eighteen and six years respectively
(about 1206–1189 B. C. and 1188–1183 B. C.), are
lost and cannot yet be restored; so, also, are the
names and the regnal years of the next three
kings. The sixth king of the dynasty was Nebuchadrezzar I [1] (about 1135 B. C.). This king ex-
hibits once more the spirit almost of a Hammurabi. His victories are brilliant, and his defeats
only evidence the hopelessness of the cause of
Babylonia and the vigor of his efforts to save the
state. When he began to reign Mutakkil-Nusku
was probably king of Assyria, and in him lived
the traditions of the glorious reign of Asshur-dan,
who had once more carried the Assyrian arms to
victory. Assyria was preparing to contest with
Babylonia the possession of the whole of the valley, and the older land had need of a man of force
and character. In the reign of the next Assyrian
king, by name Asshur-rish-ishi, came the first great
contest, the beginning of the struggle for supremacy between the two great nations. Nebuchadrezzar took the initiative and entered Assyria, but
was met by Asshur-rish-ishi, defeated and forced

---

[1] Hilprecht has tried, with great learning and acuteness, to prove that
Nebuchadrezzar I was the first king of this dynasty (*Old Babylonian Inscriptions*, i, part i, pp. 38–44), but without success. Delitzsch has shown
that the name of Nebuchadrezzar could not have stood in the first place on
the King List (*Assyriologische Miscellen*, p. 186), and Winckler has proved
that this view cannot be reconciled with Assyrian chronology (*Untersuchungen*. pp. 28, 29, and *Altorientalische Forschungen*, i, p. 131).

to retreat in a veritable rout, having burned even his baggage to lighten his return to Babylonia. Having collected reinforcements, he returned to the contest, but was met by superior forces, again defeated and forced to retreat, having lost forty of his chariots. This terrible reverse found a counterbalancing success elsewhere, for Nebuchadrezzar conquered the Lulubi, punished Elam on the east,[1] and, most important of all, swung fearlessly and successfully his flying columns into the far west, even into Syria,[2] that goal of such mighty endeavor in the distant past. In one of his inscriptions Nebuchadrezzar calls himself "sun of his land, who makes his people prosperous, the protector of boundaries." Well might he make the boast, for, though unsuccessful against the Assyrians, he had maintained a kingdom, which without him had probably fallen before the new and already almost invincible Assyrian power.

Nebuchadrezzar I was succeeded by Bel-nadin-apli (about 1125 B. C.), whose reign furnishes no event of importance known to us. In the reign of his successor, Marduk-nadin-akhe (about 1117–1096 B. C.), the Assyrians displayed in a still clearer light the power which was finally to put the destinies of all western Asia in their hands. The throne of Assyria was now occupied by

---

[1] V R. 55–57, and Hilprecht, *Freibrief Nebuchadrezzar's.* See also S. A. Smith, *Assyrian Letters*, iv, and Meissner in *Zeitschrift für Assyriologie*, iv, pp. 259, ff. (by latter mistakenly ascribed to Nebuchadrezzar II).

[2] *Proceedings of the Society of Biblical Archæology*, 1882, p. 10, and comp. Hilprecht, *Old Babylonian Inscriptions*, i, part i, p. 41.

Tiglathpileser I, one of the greatest warriors of antiquity. Against his kingdom Marduk-nadin-akhe at first had some success, for he carried away from Ekallati the images of the gods Adad and Sala. These remained away for centuries, and were only restored to their place by Sennacherib. But such successes only nerved Tiglathpileser to greater efforts. He invaded Babylonia and captured a number of cities in its northern half and even took Babylon itself. Herein is the first great blow against Babylonian independence. The Assyrians did not hold the captured city, but Tiglathpileser I was the grand monarch of western Asia, and the Babylonian king ruled only by sufferance.

The next Babylonian king was probably Marduk-akhe-irba, who ruled only one year and six months and then gave place to Marduk-shapik-zer-mati (about 1094–1083 B. C.), with whom there began again a brief period of stable peace. The Assyrians under king Asshur-bel-kala had given over for the present the policy of crushing Babylonia, and had adopted rather the plan of making an ally and friend of the ancient commonwealth. After the death of Marduk-shapik-zer-mati, a man of unknown origin, Adad-apal-iddin, came to the throne. Usurper though he was, Asshur-bel-kala continued the same friendship to him, and even gave him a daughter in marriage. The last king of this dynasty was Nabu-shum (or -nadin), about 1082–1075 B. C., of whose reign no tidings have yet come down to us.

During the latter part of this dynasty the Assyrians were chiefly occupied in the internal strengthening and solidifying of their kingdom, while the Babylonians were unable to undertake any extensive campaigns. After this period our direct Babylonian information becomes more and more fragmentary, and even in some cases of doubtful meaning. The Babylonian state had lost the key to western Asia and the Assyrians had found it. Neither state was for the moment making any great efforts, but the future belonged to Assyria for centuries at least, and the sun of Babylonia had suffered a long eclipse. From now onward we must turn away from Babylon to see the main stream of history flowing through its rival's dominions.

We have followed the fortunes of the Babylonian cities from the gray dawn of antiquity down the centuries, through good report and evil report. We have watched the cities grow into kingdoms and have seen the kingdoms welded into a mighty empire. We have followed its advance to the very zenith and have seen its decline into subjection. It is a noble history, and even in outline has enough of the rich color of the Orient to make a glowing picture for the mind. From its contemplation we must now turn to look upon the development and progress of the kingdom of Assyria.

All Audio and Video Tapes Available Now • Call 1 (800) 952-LOST For Our Free Catalog

ANCIENT MYSTERIES OF NORTH AMERICA, by Tédd St. Rain. This in-depth slide presentations, which is based on his forthcoming book *Mystery of America*, outlines some of the most perplexing ancient mysteries and other anomalies that have been found in North America. Explore the evidence for Arabian, Celtic, Chinese, Egyptian, Greco-Roman, Hindu, Irish, Mesopotamian, Minoan, Nordic, Pacific Islander, Phoenician, Viking, Welsh, and West African voyages to the New World. Other topics include runestones and tablets found in the East; prehistoric mines near Lake Superior; Roman relics found in Arizona; enigmatic beehive structures, ancient coins unearthed in the Midwest; elephant slabs found in New Mexico; ground and rock petroglyphs in the Southwest; Egyptian hieroglyphics and Chinese characters; ancient footprints fossilized in rock; a 14-inch mummy found in Wyoming; human teeth found in coal deposits; red-headed giants that lived in Nevada; underground cities in the Grand Canyon; evidence for an advanced civilization; and many more anomalous finds discovered in North America. AMNA-01a • 110 min Audio Tape • $12.00 / AMNA-01 • 110 min VHS Video Tape • $19.95 Inquire on availability of other videos in St. Rain's *"Mystery of the World"* series.

REMOTE VIEWING TRAINING SESSIONS: DISCOVERING YOUR INTUITION, with Prudence Calabrese and TransDimensional Systems. Prudence Calabrese is the Director of TransDimensional Systems, www.largeruniverse.com, which provides information solutions to government, corporations and individuals using an array of services including remote viewing, knosomatics, intuitive counseling, technology transfer, consciousness mapping, physical profiling and other techniques. This seven-part, 13 hour, video program includes training in Basic Remote Viewing and Knosomatics, the Collector, Use of the Matrix and Advanced Post-Matrix Exercises. Included as a bonus is a discussion and explanation of techniques in Remote Healing and use of Remote Viewing for everyday purposes and career choices. Actual in-class results are shared, sessions are examined and the entire process is revealed. Join Prudence Calabrese and her staff as she leads another class into the unknown world and the Larger Universe. RVT-00a • 13 Hours on 7 Audio Tapes • $60.00 postpaid / RVT-00 • 13 Hours on 7 VHS Video Tapes • $110.00 postpaid / Introduction only • RVT-01 • 2 hours • VHS Video Tape • $19.95

THE COSMIC ORIGINS OF MAN, with Father Charles Moore. Father Charles Moore graduated from Stanford University with a degree in law, was admitted to the California Bar and then was elected District Attorney of Santa Cruz County in 1954. He was ordained a Roman Catholic Priest in 1964. Father Charlie is a local spiritual leader, historian and scholar who speaks about our history, spirituality, ancient cultures and modern society. His broad grasp on human nature, our origins, organized religions, legends and myths make this presentation a fascinating and informative exposé of our ancient political and religious practices. With his incredible knowledge he gives new dimensions and deeper understandings to topics we thought we already knew. He has traveled extensively in search of the roots of religious practice. His quest has taken him to Britain, Europe, Hawaii, Alaska, Mexico, and India as well as he homelands of several Native American tribes where he has studied over a dozen languages. He shares with us his highly unconventional views about human genetic, religious and cultural origins. BACN-01a • 105 min Audio Tape • $12.00 / BACN-01 • 105 min VHS Video Tape • $19.95

SCIENCE, POLITICS AND THE NEW MILLENNIUM, with Dr. Nick Begich. Best selling author and lecturer Dr. Nick Begich presents an overview of the HAARP (High Frequency Active Auroral Research Program) transmitter and antenna in Alaska. His countless years of research help to provide a glimpse of new technological achievements that can help better the environment and reshape mankind in the future. Pulling from an array of extensive documentation from government, academic and media sources, Begich is able explain the big picture in terms that anyone can understand. On the eve of the 2000 presidential election, Nick discussed science and politics in the new millennium. He discussed differences between the two major parties and what is going behind the scenes. He also gave an update on the latest research activities including new technologies, health and earth science related issues. There was a citywide power loss shortly after Begich began his presentation, but through the use of a quickly replaced battery pack, only a few moments of this valuable presentation were lost. BACN-05a • 120 min Audio Tape • $12.00 / BACN-05 • 120 min VHS Video Tape • $19.95

TECHNOLOGY OF THE GODS, with David Hatcher Childress. David Hatcher Childress is a real-life Indiana Jones. He has written a series of books about his journeys and research into lost cities and ancient mysteries of Africa, Arabia, China, Central Asia, India, South America Ancient Lemuria, Central America, Atlantis, Europe, as well as other locations. He is recognized as an expert not only on ancient civilizations and technology, but also on free energy, anti-gravity and UFOs. In his lecture, he presents fascinating information on the advanced technology and anomalous architecture of our predecessors from around the globe. David Hatcher Childress provides a qualified presentation about his search for Atlantis, megalithic cultures and ancient technology. From the Hittite empire of the Middle East to the mountains of South America and the plains of Central America, records of ancient civilizations of an advanced nature are found throughout the world. In this presentation, Childress explores the massive cities high in the Andes and their links to Atlantis and Mu. A full two hours with over 200 slides from his travels around the world. Visit www.wexclub.com for more info. BACN-07a • 120 min Audio Tape • $12.00 / BACN-07 • 120 min VHS Video Tape • $19.95

BIGFOOT / UFO CONNECTION, with Jack "Kewaunee" Lapseritis.. Kewaunee Lapseritis is a social scientist, applied anthropologist and health care professional who has thoroughly researched the Bigfoot/Sasquatch phenomenon for the last 45 years. In 1979, Kewaunee received the shock of his life when both a Bigfoot and ET simultaneously communicated with him telepathically. Since that time, he has documented 95 percipients, including a college professor, a government administrator and a whole array of people who have had similar psychic close encounters. Unlike many researchers looking for hard evidence of this elusive creature, Lapseritis has concentrated more on documenting the "experience" of the phenomenon, and gathering first-hand accounts of contacts. That is, after hearing dozens of accounts of Sasquatch contact from witnesses who tell similar stories it is impossible for him not to accept the truth of these experiences. His findings are chronicled in his book, The Psychic Sasquatch and Their UFO Connection. BACN-08a • 105 min Audio Tape • $12.00 / BACN-08 • 105 min VHS Video Tape • $19.95

PARADIGM POLITICS, with Daniel Sheehan. Daniel Sheehan is a social activist who has spent virtually his entire life working on progressive social programs and initiatives. As the Legal Counsel on such nationally-recognized investigative cases involving government as The Karen Silkwood Case, The Iran/Contra Case, The Pentagon Papers Case, The Watergate Burglary Case, and The American Sanctuary Movement Case, Dan brings to the issue of Extraterrestrial Intelligence and the UFO Phenomenon a unique background in investigating and exposing the world of American governmental covert operations, "black budget" operations,
mind control programs, government disinformation projects, covert warfare an
clandestine operations. Recently Daniel served as Director of "The Strategi
Initiative to Identify the New Paradigm" for the State of the World Forum. He cu
rently teaches World Politics at UC Santa Cruz and acts as General Counsel to D
Stephen Greer's Disclosure Project. BACN-12a • 120 min Audio Tape • $12.00
BACN-12 • 120 min VHS Video Tape • $19.95

FORBIDDEN ARCHEOLOGY, with Michael Cremo. Michael Cremo is on th
cutting edge of science and culture issues. In the course of a few months' time h
might be found on pilgrimage to sacred sites in India, appearing on a national tel
vision show, lecturing at a mainstream science conference, or speaking to an alte
native science gathering. As he crosses disciplinary and cultural boundaries, he pre
ents to his various audiences a compelling case for negotiating a new consensus o
the nature of reality. In his talk, Michael shows some of the more spectacular exam
ples of what have been called out-of-place artifacts and outlines the extreme antic
uity of humanity. He also explains how he was inspired by the ancient Sanskrit wri
ings of India and other wisdom traditions. BACN-14a • 120 min Audio Tape
$12.00 / BACN-14 • 120 min VHS Video Tape • $19.95

TALKING TO THE OTHER SIDE, with Mark Macy. Mark Macy was a
agnostic until a brush with colon cancer set him on a spiritual search in the 1980
Then he learned about the miracles of Instrumental TransCommunication (ITC
personal letters planted mysteriously in computers by invisible hands, images fro
other realms flashing across TV screens, and actual phone calls from angels. Thes
researchers use contemporary electronic technology – from audio and vide
recorders to personal computers – for documenting what they claim are commun
cations from their friends and associates on "the other side." His mission is simpl
to present graphic evidence that the worlds of the dead and the living are comin
closer together. BACN-15a • 105 min Audio Tape • $12.00 / BACN-15 • 105 m
VHS Video Tape • $19.95

ANCIENT EGYPTIAN HI-TECH, with Christopher Dunn. Christopher Du
has an extensive background as a master craftsman, starting as a journeyman lat
turner in his hometown of Manchester, England. Recruited by an American aer
space company, he immigrated to the United States in 1969. The author's pyram
odyssey began in 1977 when he read Peter Tompkins' book Secrets of the Gre
Pyramid. His immediate reaction to the Giza Pyramid's schematics was that this ed
fice was a gigantic machine. Discovering the purpose of this machine and doc
menting his case has taken the better part of twenty years of research. In 1998,
published the groundbreaking book The Giza Power Plant: Technologies of Ancie
Egypt, which proposed that the Great Pyramid of Giza was actually a large acous
cal device that produced energy. BACN-20a • 120 min Audio Tape • $12.0
BACN-20 • 120 min VHS Video Tape • $19.95

**THE INTERCEPTION: Roswell Crash Site Metal Recovery with Denn
Balthaser.** Dennis Balthaser, concentrates his research on the 1947 Rosw
Incident, Area 51 and Underground Bases. At the 2002 Aztec Symposium he w
talk about his Interception experience. While still affiliated with the Internation
UFO Museum in Roswell, NM, in 1997 as the UFO investigator, he was contact
by a gentleman in Oklahoma claiming his father had been a military policeman
the Roswell crash site and had a piece of the metal from the crashed vehicle. In t
lecture Balthaser gives a detailed account of the events that transpired from the ori
inal phone call through the current investigation, which is still on-going. Balthas
was in the United States Army in an Engineering Battalion. He moved to Rosw
NM in 1996, to pursue his 25 year interest in UFOlogy and particularly the Rosw
Incident, Underground Bases and Area 51. Aztec-01a • 2 Hour Audio Tape • $12.
/ Aztec-01 • 2 Hour VHS Video Tape • $19.95

CRITIQUE OF THE ROSWELL CRITICS with Stanton Friedman. Stant
T. Friedman was born in New Jersey on July 29, 1934. He was named valedicto
an of his 1951 Linden, New Jersey, high school class and spent two years at Rutg
University in New Brunswick, New Jersey before switching to the University
Chicago in 1953. He received BS and MS degrees in Physics from UC in 1955 a
1956, where Carl Sagan was a classmate. Since 1967 he has lectured on the to
Flying Saucers Are Real at more than 600 colleges and over 100 professional grou
in fifty states, nine Canadian provinces, England, Italy, Germany, Holland, Fran
Finland, Brazil, Australia, Korea, Mexico, Turkey, Argentina, and Israel. Stan is t
original civilian investigator of the Roswell Incident, who co-authored Crash
Corona and instigated the Unsolved Mysteries Roswell program. Aztec-05a
2 Hour Audio Tape • $12.00 / Aztec-05 • 2 Hour VHS Video Tape • $19.95

**AZTEC 1949-1950: New Information on the Aztec UFO Crash with Lin
Moulton Howe.** Linda Moulton Howe, Emmy Award-winning TV producer, inv
tigative reporter and writer, will present eyewitness accounts and documents ab
a "dog fight" of silver discs in the sky over Aztec followed by a crash and retrie
of one disc from Hart Canyon in March 1949; multiple disc flyovers by the hu
dreds the next year on March 17, 1950 reported in The Denver Post and T
Farmington Daily Times; and alleged government knowledge and cover-up of
Aztec disc crash and subsequent disc flyovers. Linda Moulton Howe is a gradu
of Stanford University with a Masters Degree in Communication. She has devo
her documentary film, television and radio career to productions concerning s
ence, medicine and the environment. She also produces, writes and reports for te
vision segments. Aztec-06a • 2 Hour Audio Tape • $12.00 / Aztec-06 • 2 Hour V
Video Tape • $19.95

**HOW THE WAR ON TERROR INTERRUPTED ET CONTACT, with J
Marrs.** A native of Fort Worth, Texas, Mr. Marrs has worked for several Te
newspapers, including the Fort Worth Star-Telegram, where beginning in 1968
served as police reporter. Since 1980, Mr. Marrs has been a freelance writer and p
lic relations consultant. Since 1976, Mr. Marrs has taught a course on the assass
tion of President John F. Kennedy at the University of Texas at Arlington. In 19
his book, , was published to critical acclaim and within three years had gone int
eighth printing in both hardbound and softbound editions. Crossfire reached
New York Times Paperback Non-Fiction Best Seller list in mid-February 1992
remained there for more than six weeks. Aztec-07a • 2 Hour Audio Tape • $12.
Aztec-07 • 2 Hour VHS Video Tape • $19.95

Ordering Information

**For Audio/Video Tapes Only: To order individual tapes add $5
shipping and handling for the first item and $1.00 for each ad
tional item. Send your check or money order to (CA residents a
8.25% sales tax): Lost Arts Media, Post Office Box 150
Long Beach, CA 90815. Visit www.lostartsmedia.com
to order by credit card call 1 (800) 952-LOST or 1 (562) 596-AR**

ALL BOOKS ARE 6 X 9 AND TRADE PAPER

STAGE MAGIC AND TRICKS

AFTER-DINNER SLEIGHTS AND POCKET TRICKS, by C. Lang Neil. ISBN 1-59016-011-8 • 92 pages • illustrated • GB£7.95 • US$11.95

BOOK OF TRICKS AND MAGIC: Containing a Choice Selection of Tricks and Games for Parlor Entertainment, edited by Professor Svengarro. ISBN 1-59016-079-7 • 88 + 12 pages • illustrated • GB£7.95 • US$11.95

FIFTY NEW CARD TRICKS: A Comprehensive Description of the Continuous Front and Back Hand Palm with Cards, by Howard Thurston. ISBN 1-59016-239-0 • 83 + 12 pages • illustrated • GB£7.95 • US$11.95

GILBERT COIN TRICKS FOR BOYS AND GIRLS, by Alfred C. Gilbert. ISBN 1-59016-283-8 • 60 + 42 pages • illustrated • GB£7.95 • US$11.95

MAGIC FOR HOME AND STAGE, by the Shrewesbury Publishing Company. ISBN 1-59016-502-0 • 150 pages • illustrated • GB£9.95 • US$14.95

MODERN CARD EFFECTS AND HOW TO PERFORM THEM, by George DeLawrence and James "Kater" Thompson. ISBN 1-59016-523-3 • 80 + 12 pages • illustrated • GB£7.95 • US$11.95

MODERN CARD TRICKS WITHOUT APPARATUS, by Will Goldston. ISBN 1-59016-524-1 • 109 pages • illustrated • GB£7.95 • US$11.95

NEW BOOK OF COIN TRICKS, by Professor Svengarro. ISBN 1-59016-557-8 • 92 pages • illustrated • GB£7.95 • US$11.95

NEW BOOK OF PARLOR TRICKS AND MAGIC, by Hernandez. ISBN 1-59016- 558-6 • 61 + 47 pages • illustrated • GB£8.95 • US$12.95

PARLOR BOOK OF MAGIC AND DRAWING ROOM ENTERTAINMENTS, edited by Signor Blitz. ISBN 1-59016-638-8 • 214 pages • illustrated • GB£12.95 • US$17.95

PROFESSIONAL MAGIC TRICKS REVEALED, by George Milburn. ISBN 1-59016-679-5 • 64 + 44 pages • illustrated • GB£7.95 • US$11.95

THE SECRETS OF HOUDINI, by J. C. Cannell. ISBN 1-59016-759-7 • 279 pages • illustrated • GB£15.95 • US$20.95

TRAGIC MAGIC: Compromising Magical Sketches and a Number of Original Tricks, by Harry Leat. ISBN 1-59016-860-7 • 122 pages • illustrated • GB£8.95 • US$12.95

TRICKS WITH CARDS, by Professor Hoffman. ISBN 1-59016-866-6 • 145 pages • illustrated • GB£9.95 • US$13.95

TRICKS AND MAGIC MADE EASY, by Edward Summers Squire. ISBN 1-59016- 867-4 • 188 pages • illustrated • GB£11.95 • US$15.95

TRIX AND CHATTER, by W. Dornfeld. ISBN 1-59016-864-X • 286 pages • illustrated • GB£15.95 • US$21.95

TWENTY MAGICAL NOVELTIES, by Bagshawe. ISBN 1-59016-875-5 • 80 pages • illustrated • GB£7.95 • US$11.95

FOLKLORE AND MYTHOLOGY

BOOK OF RUSTEM: Retold From the Shah Nameh of Firdausi, by E.M. Wilmot-Buxon. ISBN 1-59016-077-0 • 240 + xii + 10 illustrated pages • illustrated • GB£13.95 • US$19.95

CLASSIC MYTH-LORE IN RHYME, by Cary Blair McKenzie. ISBN 1-59016-125-4 • 104 + ii pages • illustrated • GB£7.95 • US$11.95

CLASSIC MYTHS IN ENGLISH LITERATURE AND IN ART: Volume One, by Charles Mills Gayley. ISBN 1-59016-126-2 • 276 + xxxxiv + 10 illustrated pages • illustrated • GB£17.95 • US$23.95

CLASSIC MYTHS IN ENGLISH LITERATURE AND IN ART: Volume Two, by Charles Mills Gayley. ISBN 1-59016- 127-0 • 319 + iv + 7 illustrated pages • illustrated • GB£17.95 • US$23.95

DICTIONARY OF MYTHOLOGY: Of Characters Found in Grecian and Roman Mythology, by John H. Bechtel. ISBN 1-59016-167-X • 221 pages • illustrated • GB£12.95 • US$17.95

FOLK TALES FROM THE FAR EAST, by Charles H. Meeker. ISBN 1-59016-251-X • 254 + xii pages • illustrated • GB£14.95 • US$19.95

FRIDTHJOF'S SAGA: A Norse Romance, by Esaias Tegnér. Translated from Swedish. ISBN 1-59016-257-9 • 213 + viii pages • GB£15.95 • US$12.95

FORTY MODERN FABLES, by George Ade. ISBN 1-59016-253-6 • 303 + viii pages • GB£8.95 • US$22.95

GREEK AND ROMAN MYTHOLOGY, by Jessie M. Tatlock. ISBN 1-59016-292-7 • 370 + xxxiv pages • heavily illustrated • GB£20.95 • US$26.95

ON THE TRACK OF ULYSSES, by W. J. Stillman. ISBN 1-59016-611-6 • 106 + xii pages • illustrated • GB£8.95 • US$12.95

PAN AND HIS PIPES AND OTHER TALES FOR CHILDREN, by Katherine Dunlap Cather. ISBN 1-59016-635-3 • 84 pages • illustrated • GB£7.95 • US$11.95

STORIES OF NORSE GODS AND HEROES, by Annie Klinggensmith. ISBN 1-59016-782-1 • 101 + ii pages • illustrated • GB£7.95 • US$11.95

THE STUDENT'S MYTHOLOGY, by C. A. White. ISBN 1-59016-814-3 • 315 + iv pages • GB£16.95 • US$22.95

WINE, WOMEN AND SONG, by John Addington Symonds. ISBN 1-59016-918-2 • 180 + viii pages • GB£11.95 • US$15.95

THE YOUNG FOLK'S BOOK OF MYTHS, by Amy Cruse. ISBN 1-59016-965-4 • 265 + xiv + 42 illustrated pages • heavily illustrated • GB£16.95 • US$22.95

ARCHAEOLOGY

THE ROMANCE OF EXCAVATION, by David Masters. ISBN 1-59016-736-8 • 191 + xiv + 25 illustrated pages • illustrated • GB£12.95 • US$17.95

ARCHAEOLOGY OF THE DELAWARE RIVER VALLEY, by Max Schrabisch. ISBN 1-59016-037-1 • 181 + viii pages • illustrated • GB£11.95 • US$16.95

MAGIC SPADES, by R. V. D. Magoffin and Emily C. Davis. ISBN 1-59016-504-7 • 348 + xiv pages • illustrated • GB£18.95 • US$24.95

THE STONE, BRONZE AND IRON AGES, by John Hunter-Duvar. ISBN 1-59016-778-3 • 285 +xvi pages • illustrated • GB£15.95 • US$21.95

SUSSEX ARCHAEOLOGICAL COLLECTIONS, compiled by the Sussex Archaeological Society. ISBN 1-59016-819-4 • 215 + vi + 16 illustrated pages • illustrated • GB£13.95 • US$18.95

ANCIENT HISTORY

THE BIBLICAL STORY OF CREATION, by Giorgio Bartoli. ISBN 1-59016-064-9 • 155 + iv + 2 illustrated pages • illustrated • GB£9.95 • US$14.95

A BRIEF HISTORY OF ANCIENT TIMES, by James Henry Breasted. ISBN 1-59016-083-5 • 320 pages • illustrated • GB£16.95 • US$22.95

DARIUS THE GREAT: Ancient Ruler of the Persian Empire, by Jacob Abbott. ISBN 1-59016-152-1 • 286 pages • illustrated • GB£15.95 • US$20.95

THE DAWN OF HISTORY: An Introduction to Pre-Historic Study. Edited by Charles Francis Keary. ISBN 1-59016 155-6 • 240 + viii pages • illustrated • GB£13.95 • US$18.95

AN ANCIENT HISTORY FOR BEGINNERS, by George Willis Botsford. ISBN 1-59016-029-0 • 492 + xxii + 36 maps/illustrated pages • illustrated • GB£25.95 • US$34.95

HEROES AND CRISES OF EARLY HEBREW HISTORY, by Charles Foster Kent. ISBN 1-59016-309-5 • 251 + xvi pages • GB£14.95 • US$19.95

OUTPOSTS OF CIVILIZATION, by W. A. Chalfant. ISBN 1-59016-623-X • 193 pages • GB£11.95 • US$16.95

RASSELAS: PRINCE OF ABYSSINIA, by Samuel Johnson. ISBN 1-59016-704-X • 263 + iv pages • GB£14.95 • US$19.95

STORIES FROM THE EARLY WORLD, by R. M. Fleming. ISBN 1-59016-779-1 • 162 + xii + 11 illustrated pages • illustrated • GB£11.95 • US$15.95

THE UPANISHADS: Translated into English with a Preamble and Arguments by G.R.S. Mead and Jagadīsha Chandra Chattopādhyaya ISBN 1-59016-883-6 • 137 pages • illustrated • GB£9.95 • US$13.95

MESOPOTAMIAN RELIGION

ASSYRIA: Its Princes, Priests and People, by Archibald Henry Sayce. ISBN 1-59016-047-9 • 166 pages • illustrated • GB£10.95 • US$14.95

THE RELIGION OF BABYLONIA AND ASSYRIA, by Theophilus G. Pinches. ISBN 1-59016-708-2 • 126 pages • illustrated • GB£8.95 • US$13.95

RELIGIOUS AND MORAL IDEAS IN BABYLONIA AND ASSYRIA, by Samuel A. B. Mercer. ISBN 1-59016-711-2 • 129 + xiv pages • illustrated • GB£9.95 • US$13.95

MESOPOTAMIAN HISTORY

ANCIENT ASSYRIA, by C. H. W. Johns. ISBN 1-59016-025-8 • 175 + 2 illustrated pages • illustrated • GB£10.95 • US$15.95

ANCIENT BABYLONIA, by C. H. W. Johns. ISBN 1-59016-026-6 • 148 pages • illustrated • GB£9.95 • US$14.95

THE ANCIENT EMPIRES OF THE EAST, by Archibald Henry Sayce. ISBN 1-59016-032-0 • 303 + xxiv illustrated pages • illustrated • GB£16.95 • US$23.95

BABYLONIAN LIFE AND HISTORY, by Ernest Alfred Thompson Wallis Budge. ISBN 1-59016-054-1 • 168 pages • illustrated • GB£10.95 • US$15.95

BOOK OF HISTORY: Volume IV, The Middle East: India, Ceylon, Burma, Siam and Central Asia, by W. M. Flinders Petrie, et al. ISBN 1-59016-074-6 • 434 + vi pages • illustrated • GB£21.95 • US$28.95

THE CIVILIZATION OF BABYLONIA AND ASSYRIA: Volume One, by Morris Jastrow, Jr. ISBN 1-59016-120-3 • 236 + xx + 31 illustrated pages • illustrated • GB£15.95 • US$21.95

THE CIVILIZATION OF BABYLONIA AND ASSYRIA: Volume Two, by Morris Jastrow, Jr. ISBN 1-59016-121-1 • 277 + xx + 45 illustrated pages • illustrated • GB£17.95 • US$23.95

HISTORY OF BABYLONIA, by George Smith. ISBN 1-59016-320-6 • 192 pages • illustrated • GB£11.95 • US$16.95

HISTORY OF BABYLONIA AND ASSYRIA, by Hugo Winkler. ISBN 1-59016-321-4 • 352 + xii pages • illustrated • GB£18.95 • US$24.95

A HISTORY OF BABYLONIA AND ASSYRIA: Volume One, by Robert William Rogers. ISBN 1-59016-316-8 • 429 + xx + 2 illustrated pages • illustrated • GB£21.95 • US$29.95

A HISTORY OF BABYLONIA AND ASSYRIA: Volume Two, by Robert William Rogers. ISBN 1-59016-317-6 • 418 + xvii pages • illustrated • GB£21.95 • US$28.95

HISTORY OF EGYPT, CHALDEA, SYRIA, BABYLONIA AND ASSYRIA: Volume Six, by Gaston Maspero. ISBN 1-59016-324-9 • 446 + xiv pages • illustrated • GB£22.95 • US$29.95

LIFE IN ANCIENT EGYPT AND ASSYRIA, by Sir Gaston Camille Charles Maspero. ISBN 1-59016-463-6 • 374 + xviii pages • illustrated • GB£19.95 • US$26.95

MESOPOTAMIA: The Babylonian and Assyrian Civilization, by L. Delaporte. ISBN 1-59016-516-0 • 369 + xxii pages • illustrated • GB£19.95 • US$26.95

MESOPOTAMIAN ARCHAEOLOGY, by Percy S. P. Handcock. ISBN 1-59016-518-7 • 421 + xxii + 31 illustrated pages • illustrated • GB£22.95 • US$30.95

MYTHS AND LEGENDS OF BABYLONIA AND ASSYRIA, by Lewis Spence. ISBN 1-59016-547-0 • 410 + 22 illustrated pages • illustrated • GB£21.95 • US$28.95

POPULAR DICTIONARY OF ASSYRIAN AND BABYLONIAN TERMINOLOGY, by F. C. Norton. ISBN 1-59016-655-8 • 201 pages • illustrated • GB£11.95 • US$16.95

A SMALLER ANCIENT HISTORY OF THE EAST, by Philip Smith. ISBN 1-59016-766-X • 316 pages • illustrated • GB£16.95 • US$22.95

STORIES OF ANCIENT PEOPLES, by Emma J. Arnold. 1-59016-784-8 • 232 + ii illustrated pages • illustrated • GB£13.95 • US$18.95

THE STORY OF CHALDEA, by Zénaïde A. Ragozin. ISBN 1-59016-787-2 • 381 + xxii pages • 56 illustrations • GB£20.95 • US$26.95

THE STORY OF EXTINCT CIVILIZATIONS OF THE EAST by Robert E. Anderson. ISBN 1-59016-790-2 • 213 pages • illustrated • GB£12.95 • US$17.95

THE SUMERIANS: A Civilization in 3,500 B.C., by C. Leonard Woolley. ISBN 1-59016-818-6 • 198 + x + 24 illustrated pages • illustrated • GB£12.95 • US$18.95

VOICES OF THE PAST: From Assyria and Babylonia, by Henry S. Roberton. ISBN 1-59016-892-5 • 219 + 24 illustrated pages • illustrated • GB£14.95 • US$19.95

TRANSLATIONS FROM THE PAST

ARMENIAN LITERATURE, with a Special Introduction by Robert Arnot. ISBN 1-59016-038-X • 142 + x + 1 illustrated pages • illustrated • GB£9.95 • US$14.95

ASSYRIAN AND BABYLONIAN LITERATURE, with Critical Introduction by Robert Francis Harper. ISBN 1-59016-044-4 • 480 + lxxxvi + 4 illustrated pages • illustrated • GB£26.95 • US$35.95

BABYLONIAN LITERATURE, with a Special Introduction by Epiphanius Wilson. ISBN 1-59016-055-X • 309 + viii + 3 illustrated pages • illustrated • GB£16.95 • US$22.95

EGYPTIAN HISTORY

ANCIENT EGYPT FROM THE RECORDS, by M. E. Monckton Jones. ISBN 1-59016-028-2 • 244 + x + 13 illustrated pages • illustrated • GB£14.95 • US$19.95

EGYPTIAN HISTORY AND ART, by A. A. Quibell. ISBN 1-59016-203-X • 178 + xii + 15 illustrated pages • illustrated • GB£11.95 • US$16.95

EGYPTIANS OF LONG AGO, by Louise Mohr. ISBN 1-59016-204-8 • 154 pages • illustrated • GB£9.95 • US$14.95

AN EXCURSION IN THE LEVANT: 1903 by Colonel Thomas Innes. ISBN 1-59016-222-6 • 82 + 31 illustrated pages • illustrated • GB£8.95 • US$12.95

KINGS AND GODS OF EGYPT, by Alexandre Moret. ISBN 1-59016-438-5 • 290 + xii + 16 illustrated pages • illustrated • GB£16.95 • US$22.95

OUR INHERITANCE IN THE GREAT PYRAMID: Volume One, by Piazzi Smyth. ISBN 1-59016-614-0 • 296 + xviii + 23 illustrated pages • illustrated • GB£17.95 • US$23.95

OUR INHERITANCE IN THE GREAT PYRAMID: Volume Two, by Piazzi Smyth. ISBN 1-59016-615-9 • 328 + vi pages • illustrated • GB£17.95 • US$23.95

TUTANKHAMEN AND THE DISCOVERY OF HIS TOMB, by G. Elliot Smith. ISBN 1-59016-870-4 • 133 pages • illustrated • GB£8.95 • US$13.95

GREEK HISTORY

EPOCHS OF ANCIENT HISTORY: The Greeks and The Persians, by G. W. Cox. ISBN 1-59016-214-5 • 218 + xxii + 4 illustrated pages • illustrated • GB£13.95 • US$18.95

GREEK ARCHITECTURE AND SCULPTURE, by T. Roger Smith and George Redford. ISBN 1-59016-294-3 • 145 pages • illustrated • GB£9.95 • US$13.95

GREEK TRAGEDY, by J. T. Sheppard. ISBN 1-59016-296-X • 160 + viii pages • illustrated • GB£10.95 • US$14.95

THE HEROES OR GREEK FAIRY TALES, by Charles Kingsley. ISBN 1-59016-310-9 • 208 pages • GB£10.95 • US$15.95

HISTORY OF THE SCIENCES IN GRECO-ROMAN ANTIQUITY, by Arnold Reymond. ISBN 1-59016-330-3 • 245 + x pages • illustrated • GB£13.95 • US$19.95

OLD GREEK LIFE, by J. P. Mahaffy. ISBN 1-59016-596-9 • 101 pages • illustrated • GB£7.95 • US$11.95

POMPEII: ITS LIFE AND ART, by August Mau. ISBN 1-59016-652-3 • 558 + xxii + 18 illustrated pages • illustrated • GB£26.95 • US$35.95

THE STORY OF THE GREEKS, by H. A. Guerber. ISBN 1-59016-804-6 • 288 pages • illustrated • GB£15.95 • US$21.95

ROMAN HISTORY

HISTORY OF NERO, by Jacob Abbott. ISBN 1-59016-328-1 • 321 pages • 12 illustrations • GB£16.95 • US$22.95

ANCIENT ROME: From The Earliest Times Down to 476 A.D., compiled by R. F. Pennell. ISBN 1-59016-031-2 • 206 + iv pages • illustrated • GB£12.95 • US$17.95

HISTORICAL TALES: ROMAN TIMES, by Charles Morris. ISBN 1-59016-312-5 • 340 + ii + 11 illustrated pages • illustrated • GB£18.95 • US$24.95

AN INTRODUCTION TO ROMAN HISTORY LITERATURE AND ANTIQUITIES, by A. Petrie. ISBN 1-59016-370-2 • 126 pages • illustrated • GB£8.95 • US$12.95

RAMBLES IN ROME, by S. Russell Forbes. ISBN 1-59016-702-3 • 368 + xxx pages • illustrated • GB£20.95 • US$26.95

A SHORT HISTORY OF ROME AND ITALY, by Mary Platt Parmele. ISBN 1-59016-763-5 • 276 + xvi pages • GB£15.95 • US$21.95

STORIES IN STONE FROM THE ROMAN FORUM, by Isabel Lovell. ISBN 1-59016-781-3 • 258 + x + 14 illustrated pages • illustrated • GB£15.95 • US$20.95

HISTORY OF THE AMERICAS

AMERICA NOT DISCOVERED BY COLUMBUS, by Rasmus B. Anderson. ISBN 1-59016-018-5 • 164 pages • illustrated • GB£10.95 • US$14.95

THE STORY OF EXTINCT CIVILIZATIONS OF THE WEST by Robert E. Anderson. ISBN 1-59016-791-0 • 195 pages • illustrated • GB£11.95 • US$16.95

ANCIENT CIVILIZATIONS OF MEXICO AND CENTRAL AMERICA, by Herbert J. Spinden. ISBN 1-59016-027-4 • 270 pages • illustrated • GB£14.95 • US$20.95

AZTECS AND MAYAS, by Thomas J. Diven. ISBN 1-59016-049-5 • 248 pages • illustrated • GB£13.95 • US$19.95

DISCOVERIES OF AMERICA TO 1525, by Arthur James Weise. ISBN 1-59016-170-X • 378 + xiv + 21 illustrated pages • illustrated • GB£20.95 • US$27.95

HISTORY OF LATIN AMERICA, by Hutton Webster. ISBN 1-59016-326-5 • 243 + xiv + 36 illustrated pages • illustrated • GB£15.95 • US$21.95

THE SPANISH CONQUERORS, by Irving Berdine Richman. ISBN 1-59016-771-6 • 238 + iv pages • GB£13.95 • US$18.95

THE STORY OF THE PANAMA CANAL, by Logan Marshall. ISBN 1-59016-808-9 • 286 + 72 illustrated pages • illustrated • GB£18.95 • US$24.95

AMERICAN HISTORY

THE CONSTITUTION OF THE UNITED STATES: A Historical Survey of Its Formation, by Robert Livingston Schuyler. ISBN 1-59016-141-6 • 211 + viii pages • GB£12.95 • US$17.95

HISTORIC SHRINES OF AMERICA, by John T. Faris. ISBN 1-59016-314-1 • 419 + 40 illustrated pages • GB£21.95 • US$29.95

HISTORY OF CALIFORNIA, by Helen Elliott Bandini. ISBN 1-59016-323-0 • 302 pages • GB£15.95 • US$21.95

THE HISTORY OF THE UNITED STATES, by John Clark Ridpath. ISBN 1-59016-332-X • 218 + viii + 9 illustrated pages • illustrated • GB£13.95 • US$18.95

ONE HUNDRED YEARS OF THE MONROE DOCTRINE by Robert Glass Cleland. ISBN 1-59016-607-8 • 127 pages • GB£8.95 • US$12.95

THE SOUTHERN MOUNTAINEERS, by Samuel Tyndale Wilson. ISBN 1-59016-770-8 • 202 + xiv pages • GB£12.95 • US$17.95

THE STORY OF THE CONSTITUTION, prepared by Sol Bloom. ISBN 1-59016-802-X • 192 pages • illustrated • GB£11.95 • US$16.95

THE TRANSFORMATION OF JOB: A Tale of the High Sierra by Frederick Vining Fisher. ISBN 1-59016-865-8 • 214 + xviii pages • heavily illustrated • GB£12.95 • US$18.95

THE WAR MYTH IN THE UNITED STATES, by C. H. Hamlin. ISBN 1-59016-902-6 • 92 + iv pages • GB£7.95 • US$11.95

EUROPEAN HISTORY

THE GREAT HISTORIANS, by Kenneth Bell and G. M. Morgan. ISBN 1-59016-288-9 • 349 + xvi pages • GB£18.95 • US$24.95

A PRIMER OF HERALDRY FOR AMERICANS, by Edward S. Holden. ISBN 1-59016-676-0 • 106 + x + 24 illustrated pages • illustrated • GB£9.95 • US$13.95

THE QUEST OF THE COLONIAL, by Robert and Elizabeth Shackleton. ISBN 1-59016-691-4 • 443 + xv pages • illustrated • GB£21.95 • US$28.95

TEN FRENCHMEN OF THE NINETEENTH CENTURY, by F. M. Warren. ISBN 1-59016-832-1 • 265 + vi + 9 illustrated pages • illustrated • GB£15.95 • US$20.95

GENERAL HISTORY

EPOCHS OF MODERN HISTORY, by William Stubbs. ISBN 1-59016-215-3 • 300 + viii + 2 illustrated pages • illustrated • GB£16.95 • US$22.95

ICE AGES: The Story of the Earth's Revolutions, by Joseph McCabe. ISBN 1-59016-352-4 • 134 + x + 4 illustrated pages • illustrated • GB£9.95 • US$14.95

THE LOST CITIES OF CEYLON, G. E. Mitton. ISBN 1-59016-482-2 • 256 + xiv + 34 illustrated pages • illustrated • GB£15.95 • US$21.95

THE REVOLUTIONARY SPIRIT PRECEDING THE FRENCH REVOLUTION, by Félix Rocquain. ISBN 1-59016-717-1 • 186 + xii pages • GB£11.95 • US$16.95

WORLD HISTORY

HENRY VIII AND HIS COURT, Herbert Beerbohm Tree. ISBN 1-59016-308-7 • 117 + vi pages • illustrated • GB£8.95 • US$12.95

EVENTFUL DATES IN THE HISTORY OF THE WORLD, by Felix Berol. ISBN 1-59016-220-X • 176 pages • GB£11.95 • US$15.95

THE FIFTEEN DECISIVE BATTLES OF THE WORLD: From Marathon to Waterloo, by E. S. Creasy. ISBN 1-59016-238-2 • 364 pages • GB£18.95 • US$24.95

THE WORLD'S REVOLUTIONS, by Ernest Untermann. ISBN 1-59016-933-6 • 176 + ii pages • GB£10.95 • US$15.95

MEDIEVAL HISTORY

TALES OF THE CRUSADERS, by Anonymous. ISBN 1-59016-829-1 • 327 pages • illustrated • GB£17.95 • US$23.95

SCOTTISH CHIEFS: The Life Story of Sir William Wallace, by Jane Porter. ISBN 1-59016-758-9 • 350 + iv pages • GB£18.95 • US$24.95

THE HOLY GRAIL: SIX KINDRED ADDRESSES AND ESSAYS, by James A. B. Scherer. ISBN 1-59016-338-9 • 210 pages • GB£11.95 • US$16.95

KING ARTHUR AND HIS KNIGHTS, by Maude L. Radford. ISBN 1-59016-435-0 • 268 pages • illustrated • GB£14.95 • US$19.95

KING ARTHUR AND THE KNIGHTS OF THE ROUND TABLE, by Charles Morris. ISBN 1-59016-436-9 • 255 + vi + 5 illustrated pages • illustrated • GB£14.95 • US$19.95

A SYLLABUS OF MEDIEVAL HISTORY, by Dana Carleton Munro and George Clarke Sellery. ISBN 1-59016-824-0 • 148 + viii + (42 + iv) pages • GB£11.95 • US$16.95

ANTHROPOLOGY

PEASANTS & POTTERS, by Harold Peake and Herbert John Fleure. ISBN 1-59016-644-2 • 152 + vi pages • illustrated • GB£10.95 • US$14.95

THE CHAIN OF LIFE, by Lucretia Perry Osborn. ISBN 1-59016-112-2 • 189 + xiv + 14 illustrated pages • illustrated • GB£12.95 • US$17.95

THE FRUIT OF THE FAMILY TREE by Albert Edward Wiggam. ISBN 1-59016-262-5 • 389 + xiv pages • GB£20.95 • US$26.95

OUR PREHISTORIC ANCESTORS, by Herdman Fitzgerald Cleland. ISBN 1-59016-618-3 • 377 + xii pages • illustrated • GB£19.95 • US$26.95

PREHISTORIC MAN, by Joseph McCabe. ISBN 1-59016-670-1 • 428 + vi + 6 illustrated pages • illustrated • GB£9.95 • US$13.95

THE RISE OF MAN, by Paul Carus. ISBN 1-59016-728-7 • 103 + vi pages • illustrated • GB£9.95 • US$12.95

THE STORY OF AB, by Stanely Waterloo. ISBN 1-59016-786-4 • 292 + vi pages • GB£15.95 • US$21.95

THE STORY OF MANKIND, by Hendrik Van Loon. ISBN 1-59016-795-3 • 488 + xxxii + 16 illustrated pages • heavily illustrated • GB£24.95 • US$32.95

PALEONTOLOGY AND PREHISTORIC WORLD

ANIMALS OF THE PAST, by Frederic A. Lucas. ISBN 1-59016-034-7 • 207 + xii pages • illustrated • GB£12.95 • US$17.95

PREHISTORIC SUSSEX, by E. Cecil Curwen. ISBN 1-59016-71-X • 172 + x + 31 illustrated pages • illustrated • GB£12.95 • US$17.95

STORIES OF THE UNIVERSE: The Earth in Past Ages, by H. G. Seeley. ISBN 1-59016-783-X • 190 pages • illustrated • GB£11.95 • US$17.95

STORY OF LANGUAGE

THE STORY OF THE ALPHABET, by Edward Clodd. ISBN 1-59016-800-3 • 209 pages • illustrated • GB£12.95 • US$17.95

THE LIFE AND GROWTH OF LANGUAGE, by William Dwight Whitney. ISBN 1-59016-461-X • 327 + x pages • illustrated • GB£17.95 • US$23.95

THE SCIENCE OF ETYMOLOGY, by Walter W. Skeat. ISBN 1-59016-756-2 • 242 + xx pages • GB£14.95 • US$19.95

WRITING AND AUTHORSHIP

WRITING THE SHORT STORY, by Joseph Berg Esenwein. ISBN 1-59016-942-5 • 441 + xvi pages • illustrated • GB£22.95 • US$29.95

BRIEF BUSINESS ENGLISH AND BUSINESS LETTERS, by Benjamin J. Campbell and Bruce L. Vass. ISBN 1-59016-084-3 • 92 + viii pages • GB£11.95 • US$16.95

THE CENTURY HANDBOOK OF WRITING, by Garland Greever and Easley S. Jones. ISBN 1-59016-110-6 • 228 + xiv pages • GB£13.95 • US$18.95

ELEMENTARY COMPOSITION AND RHETORIC, by William Edward Mead. ISBN 1-59016-209-9 • 286 pages • GB£15.95 • US$20.95

THE HAND BOOK OF CONVERSATION: Its Faults and Graces, compiled by Andrew P. Peabody. ISBN 1-59016-302-8 • 152 pages • GB£9.95 • US$14.95

THE PREPARATION OF MANUSCRIPTS FOR THE PRINTER, by Frank H. Viztelly. ISBN 1-59016-673-6 • 148 + pages • illustrated • GB£9.95 • US$14.95

TECHNICAL WRITING, by T. A. Richard. ISBN 1-59016-831-3 • 78 + vi pages • GB£10.95 • US$15.95

ACTING AND CINEMATOGRAPHY

A CONDENSED COURSE IN MOTION PICTURE PHOTOGRAPHY, by the New York Institute of Photography. ISBN 1-59016-139-4 • 382 + 100 illustrated pages • illustrated • GB£22.95 • US$30.95

FILM FOLK, by Rob Wagner. ISBN 1-59016-241-2 • 356 + x pages • illustrated • GB£19.95 • US$26.95

SCREEN ACTING: Its Requirements and Rewards, by Inez and Helen Klumph. ISBN 1-59016-760-0 • 243 pages • illustrated • GB£13.95 • $18.95

THE ART OF MAKE-UP, by Helena Chalmers. ISBN 1-59016-039-8 • 159 + viii pages • illustrated • GB£10.95 • US$14.95

STAGE SCENERY AND LIGHTING, by Samuel Seldon and Hunton D. Sellman. ISBN 1-59016-772-4 • 433 + xiv pages • illustrated • GB£22.95 • US$29.95

THEATER AND DRAMA

THE ART OF PLAY PRODUCTION, by John Dolman, Jr. ISBN 1-59016-040-1 • 464 + xviii + 12 illustrated page • illustrated • GB£22.95 • US$30.95

BRITISH DRAMA, by Allardyce Nicoll. ISBN 1-59016086-X • 496+ viii + 16 illustrated pages • illustrated • GB£24.95 • US$32.95

THE COMIC SPIRIT IN RESTORATION DRAMA, by Anonymous. ISBN 1-59016-133-5 • 148 + viii pages • GB£9.95 • US$14.95

THE DEVELOPMENT OF THE DRAMA, by Branders Matthews. ISBN 1-59016-163-7 • 351 + vi pages • GB£18.95 • US$24.95

DRAMA AND MANKIND, by Halcott Glover. ISBN 1-59016-180-7 • 192 pages • GB£11.95 • US$16.95

THE DRAMA: Its Law and Its Technique, by Elisabeth Woodbridge. ISBN 1-59016-181-5 • 181 + xvi pages • GB£11.95 • US$16.95

HISTORIC COSTUME, by Katherine Morris Lester. ISBN 1-59016-313-3 • 244 pages • illustrated • GB£13.95 • US$18.95

HOW TO PRODUCE PLAYS AND PAGEANTS, by Mary M. Russell. ISBN 1-59016-346-X • 219 + 10 illustrated pages • illustrated • GB£12.95 • US$17.95

ON THE ART OF THE THEATRE, by Edward Gordon. ISBN 1-59016-610-8 • 296 + xxii + 14 illustrated pages • illustrated • GB£17.95 • US$23.95

THE POPULAR THEATRE, by George Jean Nathan. ISBN 1-59016-657-4 • 236 pages • GB£13.95 • US$18.95

RHYTHMIC ACTION PLAYS AND DANCES, by Irene E. Phillips Moses. ISBN 1-59016-722-8 • 164 + vi pages • illustrated • GB£10.95 • US$15.95

SCENES AND MACHINES OF THE ENGLISH STAGE DURING THE RENAISSANCE, by Lily B. Campbell. ISBN 1-59016-751-1 • 302 + x + 8 illustrated pages • illustrated • GB£169.95 • US$22.95

THE STORY OF THE THEATER, by Glenn Hughes. ISBN 1-59016-809-7 • 421 + x + 28 illustrated pages • illustrated • GB£22.95 • US$29.95

STUDIES IN STAGECRAFT, by Clayton Hamilton. ISBN 1-59016-815-1 • 298 + vi pages • GB£15.95 • US$21.95

THEATRON: An Illustrated Record of Twentieth Century Theater, by Clarence Stratton. ISBN 1-59016-838-0 • 260 + ii pages • illustrated • GB£15.95 • US$22.95

THE TWENTIETH CENTURY THEATRE, by William Lyon Phelps. ISBN 1-59016-873-9 • 147 + vi pages • GB£9.95 • US$14.95

SCIENCE AND TECHNOLOGY

THE ABCS OF WIRELESS RADIO, by Edward Trevert. ISBN 1-59016-004-5 • 116 pages • illustrated • GB£8.95 • US$12.95

THE EINSTEIN THEORY OF RELATIVITY, by Garrett P. Serviss. ISBN 1-59016-207-2 • 108 pages • illustrated • GB£7.95 • US$11.95

ABCS OF THE TELEPHONE, by James E Homans. ISBN 1-59016-002-9 • 347 + xxiv pages • illustrated • GB£19.95 • US$25.95

THE AGE OF INVENTION, by Holland Thompson. ISBN 1-59016-012-6 • 267 + x pages • GB£14.95 • US$20.95

DREAMS OF AN ASTRONOMER, by Camille Flammarion. ISBN 1-59016-187-4 • 223 pages • GB£12.95 • US$17.95

ELEMENTS OF GENERAL SCIENCE, by Otis William Caldwell and William Lewis Eikenberry. ISBN 1-59016-210-2 • 402 + xviii pages • illustrated • GB£20.95 • US$27.95

THE FAIRYLAND OF SCIENCE, by Arabella B. Buckley. ISBN 1-59016-228-5 • 266 pages • illustrated • GB£15.95 • US$19.95

A LABORATORY MANUAL IN PHYSICS, by N. Henry Black. ISBN 1-59016-451-2 • 115 + x pages • illustrated • GB£8.95 • US$12.95

MAKER'S OF PROGRESS, by William L. and Stella H. Nida. ISBN 1-59016-506-3 • 208 + vi pages • illustrated • GB£12.95 • US$17.95

MARVELS OF MODERN MECHANICS, by Harold T. Wilkins. ISBN 1-59016-508-X • 280 + xii + 15 illustrated pages • illustrated • GB£16.95 • US$22.95

TELSA, NIKOLA: Various Articles, Patents and Lectures - Coming Soon, Call 1 (800) 952-LOST for our current catalog.

NINETEENTH CENTURY PHOTOGRAPHY: Anthony's Annual International Photographic Bulletin, June 1891. ISBN 1-59016-569-1 • 468 + xxii + 14 illustrated pages • illustrated • GB£24.95 • US$32.95

PRINCIPLES OF BACTERIOLOGY, by Arthur A. Eisenberg. ISBN 1-59016-678-7 • 198 pages • illustrated • GB£11.95 • US$16.95

ROBINSON'S MANUAL OF RADIO TELEGRAPHY AND TELEPHONY, by Captain S. S. Robinson, U.S. Navy. ISBN 1-59016-732-5 • 307 + vi illustrated pages • illustrated • GB£16.95 • US$22.95

STEAM, STEEL AND ELECTRICITY, by James W. Steele. ISBN 1-59016-777-5 • 240 + viii pages • illustrated • GB£13.95 • US$18.95

THE STORY OF INVENTION, by Hendrik Van Loon. ISBN 1-59016-793-7 • 252 pages • heavily illustrated • GB£13.95 • US$19.95

THE STORY OF THE ART OF BUILDING, by P. Leslie Waterhouse. ISBN 1-59016-801-1 • 215 pages • illustrated • GB£12.95 • US$17.95

THE WONDERS OF SCIENCE IN MODERN LIFE, by Henry Smith Williams and Edward H. Williams. ISBN 1-59016-922-0 • 191 + viii + 8 illustrated pages • illustrated • GB£11.95 • US$16.95

GAMES, ENTERTAINMENT, HUMOR

THE AMERICAN CHECKER PLAYER'S HAND BOOK, by Erroll A. Smith. ISBN 1-59016-020-7 • 160 pages • illustrated • GB£9.95 • US$14.95

CHESS FOR BEGINNERS, by E. E. Cunnington. ISBN 1-59016-114-9 • 112 pages • illustrated • GB£8.95 • US$12.95

A COMIC HISTORY OF THE UNITED STATES, by Livingston Hopkins. ISBN 1-59016-132-7 • 223 pages • illustrated • GB£12.95 • US$17.95

COMMON SENSE IN CHESS, by Emanuel Lasker. ISBN 1-59016-136-X • 139 pages • illustrated • GB£9.95 • US$13.95

DANCES, DRILLS AND STORY PLAYS: For Every Day and Holidays, by Nina B. Lamkin. ISBN 1-59016-151-3 • 117 pages • GB£8.95 • US$12.95

DICK'S GAMES OF PATIENCE: SOLITAIRE WITH CARDS, edited by William B. Dick. ISBN 1-59016-166-1 • 154 + ii pages • GB£9.95 • US$14.95

FUN WITH CARDS, by Dean Bryden. ISBN 1-59016-266-8 • 165 + viii pages • GB£10.95 • US$15.95

FUN WITH PAPER FOLDING, by William D. Murray and Francis J. Rigney. ISBN 1-59016-267-6 • 95 + ii pages • illustrated • GB£7.95 • US$11.95

GAMES FOR THE PLAYGROUND, HOME, SCHOOL AND GYMNASIUM, by Jessie H. Bancroft. ISBN 1-59016-276-5 • 454 + viii + 22 illustrated pages • illustrated • GB£22.95 • US$30.95

THE GENTLEMEN'S HAND-BOOK ON POKER, by Florence. ISBN 1-59016-278-1 • 195 + viii pages • illustrated • GB£11.95 • US$16.95

HOW TO PLAY CHESS, by E. E. Cunnington. ISBN 1-59016-345-1 • 88 pages • GB£7.95 • US$11.95

MR. PUNCH'S AFTER DINNER STORIES, edited by J. A. Hammerton. ISBN 1-59016-683-3 • 192 + ii pages • illustrated • GB£11.95 • US$16.95

SONGS FOR LITTLE CHILDREN, composed and arranged by Eleanor Smith. ISBN 1-59016-769-4 • 213 + viii pages • illustrated with musical score • GB£12.95 • US$17.95

CRAFTWORK AND HOBBIES

THE GLAZER'S CLAY BOOK AND HOW TO USE IT, by E. L. Raes. ISBN 1-59016-285-4 • 137 + ii pages • tables • GB£9.95 • US$13.95

HOME TANNING AND LEATHER MAKING GUIDE, by Albert B. Farnham. ISBN 1-59016-340-0 • 176 pages • GB£10.95 • US$15.95

THE INDUSTRIAL ARTS IN SPAIN, by Juan F. Riaño. ISBN 1-59016-358-3 • 276 + vi pages • illustrated • GB£15.95 • US$20.95

INSTRUCTIONAL UNITS IN WOOD FINISHING, by R. A. McGee and Arthur G. Brown. ISBN 1-59016-363-X • 128 pages • illustrated • GB£8.95 • US$13.95

THE STAMP COLLECTOR, by Stanely C. Johnson. ISBN 1-59016-775-9 • 317 + 31 illustrated pages • illustrated • GB£17.95 • US$24.95

SWOOPE'S LESSONS IN PRACTICAL ELECTRICITY: Volume One, by Erich Hausmann. ISBN 1-59016-822-4 • 344 + xii pages • heavily illustrated • GB£18.95 • US$24.95

SWOOPE'S LESSONS IN PRACTICAL ELECTRICITY: Volume Two, by Erich Hausmann. ISBN 1-59016-823-2 • 348 + x pages • heavily illustrated • GB£18.95 • US$24.95

MUSIC STUDIES

CARUSO AND THE ART OF SINGING, by Salvatore Fucito and Barnet J. Beyer. ISBN 1-59016-104-1 • 219 + x + 12 illustrated pages • illustrated • GB£13.95 • US$18.95

THE THEORY AND PRACTICE OF MUSICAL FORM, by J. H. Cornell. ISBN 1-59016-836-4 • 214 + xviii pages • heavily illustrated • GB£14.95 • US$19.95

HOW TO LISTEN TO MUSIC, by Henry Edward Krehbiel. ISBN 1-59016-344-3 • 361 + xiv pages • illustrated • GB£18.95 • US$24.95

INTRODUCTORY TO MUSIC, by Thaddeus P. Giddings, Will Earhart, Ralph Baldwin and Elbridge Newton. ISBN 1-59016-372-9 • 176 + ii pages • GB£10.95 • US$15.95

LESSONS IN MUSICAL HISTORY, by John Comfort Fillmore. ISBN 1-59016-457-1 • 183 + xviii + 37 chronology pages • GB£13.95 • US$18.95

LISTENING LESSONS IN MUSIC, by Agnes Moore Fryberger. ISBN 1-59016-468-7 • 264 + xiv pages • GB£14.95 • US$20.95

MUSIC CLUB PROGRAMS FROM ALL NATIONS, by Arthur Elson. ISBN 1-59016-541-1 • 185 + x + 9 illustrated pages • illustrated • GB£11.95 • US$16.95

MUSICAL HARMONY SIMPLIFIED, by F. H. Shepard. ISBN 1-59016-545-4 • 242 + viii pages • heavily illustrated • GB£13.95 • US$19.95

THE NEW EDUCATIONAL MUSIC COURSE, by James M. McLaughlin. ISBN 1-59016-561-6 • 130 + viii pages • GB£9.95 • US$13.95

OUTLINES OF MUSIC HISTORY, by Clarence G. Hamilton. ISBN 1-59016-621-3 • 308 + xxxvi pages • illustrated • GB£17.95 • US$23.95

PRACTICAL GUIDE TO THE IDEAL HOME MUSIC LIBRARY, by Albert E. Wier. ISBN 1-59016-662-0 • 113 + viii pages • illustrated • GB£8.95 • US$12.95

STANDARD HISTORY OF MUSIC, by James Francis Cooke. ISBN 1-59016-776-7 • 260 + ii pages • heavily illustrated • GB£18.95 • US$19.95

SONG BOOKS

BEETON'S BOOK OF SONGS, edited by Ward, Lock & Co. ISBN 1-59016-059-2 • 162 + xiv pages • illustrated • GB£10.95 • US$15.95

FROM SONG TO SYMPHONY, by Daniel Gregory Mason. ISBN 1-59016-259-5 • 243 + vi pages • illustrated • GB£13.95 • US$19.95

GLEE AND CHORUS BOOK, by J. E. NeCollins. ISBN 1-59016-286-2 • 208 + ii pages • illustrated with musical score • GB£12.95 • US$17.95

THE IDEAL HOME MUSIC LIBRARY: Volume IX, Sentimental Music, compiled and edited by Albert E. Wier. ISBN 1-59016-355-9 • 256 + ii pages • illustrated with musical score • GB£14.95 • US$19.95

THE IDEAL HOME MUSIC LIBRARY: Volume X, Favorite Home Songs, compiled and edited by Albert E. Wier. ISBN 1-59016-356-7 • 336 + ii pages • illustrated with musical score • GB£17.95 • US$23.95

JUNIOR MUSIC, by Thaddeus P. Giddings, Will Earhart, Ralph L. Baldwin and Elbridge W. Newton. ISBN 1-59016-395-8 • 256 + ii pages • illustrated • GB£14.95 • US$19.95

LAUREL GLEE BOOK FOR MALE VOICES, by M. Teres Armitage. ISBN 1-59016-455-5 • 126 + iv pages • illustrated with musical score • GB£8.95 • US$13.95

OUR FAMILIAR SONGS AND THEIR AUTHORS: Volume One, by Helen Kendrick Johnson. ISBN 1-59016-612-4 • 290 + x pages • GB£15.95 • US$21.95

OUR FAMILIAR SONGS AND THEIR AUTHORS: Volume Two, by Helen Kendrick Johnson. ISBN 1-59016-613-2 • 368 + viii pages • GB£18.95 • US$25.95

SONG AND LEGEND FROM THE MIDDLE AGES, selected and arranged by William D. McClintock and Porter Lander McClintock. ISBN 1-59016-767-8 • 141 + ii pages • GB£9.95 • US$13.95

SONG TREASURY: 20th Century Americana, compiled and edited by Harriet Garton Cartwright. ISBN 1-59016-768-6 • 214 + xvi pages • illustrated with musical score • GB£12.95 • US$18.95

PAINTING AND DRAWING

AIMS AND IDEALS OF REPRESENTATIVE AMERICAN PAINTERS, written and arranged by John Rummell and E. M. Berlin. ISBN 1-59016-014-2 • 114 pages • GB£8.95 • US$12.95

ANATOMY AND DRAWING, by Victor Perard. ISBN 1-59016-024-X • 175 + xx pages • illustrated • GB£11.95 • US$16.95

APPLIED DRAWING, by Harold Haven Brown. ISBN 1-59016-036-3 • 266 + vi pages • illustrated • GB£14.95 • US$20.95

ART STUDIES FOR SCHOOLS, by Anna M. Von Rydingsvärd. ISBN 1-59016-043-6 • 185 + ii pages • heavily illustrated • GB£11.95 • US$15.95

DRAWING MADE EASY, by Joseph Cummings Chase. ISBN 1-59016-183-1 • 146 pages • GB£9.95 • US$13.95

ELECTRICAL DRAFTING and Design, by Calvin C. Bishop. ISBN 1-59016-208-0 • 165 + vi pages • illustrated • GB£10.95 • US$15.95

LETTERS AND LETTERING: A Treatise with Two Hundred Examples, by Frank Chouteau Brown. ISBN 1-59016-459-8 • 214 xviii pages • heavily illustrated • GB£12.95 • US$18.95

PAINTERS, PICTURES AND THE PEOPLE, by Eugen Neuhaus. ISBN 1-59016-631-0 • 224 + x + 31 illustrated pages • illustrated • GB£14.95 • US$19.95

PAINTING AND DECORATING WORKING METHODS, produced under the direction of Painting and Decorating Contractors of America. ISBN 1-59016-633-7 • 294 + xiv pages • illustrated • GB£16.95 • US$22.95

THE PRACTICE OF OIL PAINTING AND OF DRAWING, by Solomon J. Soloman. ISBN 1-59016-667-1 • 278 pages • illustrated • GB£14.95 • US$20.95

THE STORY OF DUTCH PAINTING, by Charles H. Caffin. ISBN 1-59016-789-9 • 210 + viii + 31 illustrated pages • illustrated • GB£13.95 • US$19.95

THE STORY OF FRENCH PAINTING, by Charles H. Caffin. ISBN 1-59016-792-9 • 232 + xii + 40 illustrated pages • illustrated • GB£15.95 • US$20.95

TOPOGRAPHICAL MAPS AND SKETCH MAPPING, by J. K. Finch. ISBN 1-59016-851-8 • 175 + xiv + 3 illustrated pages • heavily illustrated • GB£11.95 • US$16.95

FAMOUS PEOPLE

ABRAHAM LINCOLN: Volume One, by Carl Sandburg. ISBN 1-59016-007-X • 298 + x pages • GB£16.95 • US$22.95

ABRAHAM LINCOLN: Volume Two, by Carl Sandburg. ISBN 1-59016-008-8 • 304 + iv pages • GB£16.95 • US$22.95

BENJAMIN FRANKLIN: American Statesman, by John T. Morse, Jr. ISBN 1-59016-061-4 • 442 + xxii + 2 illustrated pages • illustrated • GB£22.95 • US$30.95

CELEBRATED FEMALE SOVEREIGNS, by Anna B. Jameson. ISBN 1-59016-109-2 • 245 pages • illustrated • GB£13.95 • US$18.95

FAMOUS WOMEN, by Joseph Adelman. ISBN 1-59016-231-5 • 328 + x pages • illustrated • GB£17.95 • US$23.95

THE LIFE OF BENJAMIN FRANKLIN, by M. L. Weems. ISBN 1-59016-466-0 • 239 + 5 illustrated pages • illustrated • GB£13.95 • US$18.95

MACAULAY'S LIFE OF SAMUEL JOHNSON, edited by Albert Perry Walker. ISBN 1-59016-501-2 • 92 + xxxii + 6 illustrated pages • illustrated • GB£8.95 • US$13.95

MEMORABLE ADDRESSES BY AMERICAN PATRIOTS, from a collection by John Clark Ridpath. ISBN 1-59016-513-6 • 112 + ii pages • GB£8.95 • US$12.95

MESSER MARCO POLO, by Donn Byrne. ISBN 1-59016-521-7 • 147 + iv pages • GB£9.95 • US$14.95

THE POCKET UNIVERSITY: Famous Explorers, edited by George Iles. ISBN 1-59016-648-5 • 171 + x pages • GB£10.95 • US$15.95

QUESTIONS AND ANSWERS

ANSWER THIS ONE: QUESTIONS FOR EVERYONE, compiled by Franklin P. Adams and Harry Hansen. ISBN 1-59016-035-5 • 192 pages • illustrated • GB£11.95 • US$16.95

ONE THOUSAND AND ONE RIDDLES, compiled by David McKay. ISBN 1-59016-609-4 • 203 + iv pages • GB£11.95 • US$16.95

THE QUESTION BOOK FOR YOUNG FOLKS, compiled by Sylvia Weil and Rosetta C. Goldsmith. ISBN 1-59016-688-4 • 95 pages • illustrated • GB£7.95 • US$11.95

WHAT'S THE ANSWER? edited by John A. Bassett. ISBN 1-59016-910-7 • 111 + iv pages • GB£8.95 • US$12.95

GEOLOGY AND MINERALS

DIAMONDS AND OTHER GEMS, by John Clyde Ferguson. ISBN 1-59016-164-5 • 160 pages • illustrated • GB£9.95 • US$14.95

THE TRAGEDY OF PELEE, by George Kennan. ISBN 1-59016-859-3 • 257 + 14 illustrated pages • illustrated • GB£14.95 • US$20.95

FIELD BOOK OF COMMON ROCKS AND MINERALS, by Frederic Brewster Loomis. ISBN 1-59016-236-6 • 278 + xvi + 73 illustrated pages • illustrated • GB£18.95 • US$24.95

A FIRST BOOK IN GEOLOGY, by N. S. Shaler. ISBN 1-59016-245-5 • 255 + xx pages • illustrated • GB£14.95 • US$20.95

GEOGRAPHIC INFLUENCES IN AMERICAN HISTORY, by Albert Perry Brigham. ISBN 1-59016-280-3 • 285 + x pages • illustrated • GB£15.95 • US$21.95

GEOGRAPHY OF CALIFORNIA, by Harold W. Fairbanks. ISBN 1-59016-281-1 • 239 + ii + 2 illustrated pages • illustrated • GB£13.95 • US$18.95

MINERAL TABLES FOR THE DETERMINATION OF MINERALS BY THEIR PHYSICAL PROPERTIES, by Arthur S. Eakle. ISBN 1-59016-522-5 • 73 + iv pages • tables • GB£7.95 • US$11.95

SAN FRANCISCO'S GREAT DISASTER, by Anonymous. ISBN 1-59016-746-5 • 422 pages • heavily illustrated • GB£20.95 • US$27.95

STORIES IN STONE, by Willis T. Lee. ISBN 1-59016-780-5 • 226 + x + 49 illustrated pages • illustrated • GB£15.95 • US$21.95

NATURAL HISTORY

MARVELS OF NATURAL HISTORY, by Henry Davenport Northrop. ISBN 1-59016-509-8 • 360 + 12 illustrated pages • heavily illustrated • GB£18.95 • US$24.95

NATURE'S PROGRAM, by Gaylord Johnson. ISBN 1-59016-454-3 • 181 + vi pages • GB£11.95 • US$15.95

THE POCKET UNIVERSITY: The Earth Around Us, edited by George Iles. ISBN 1-59016-649-3 • 191 + xxii pages • GB£12.95 • US$17.95

BIOLOGY

SEX SECRETS, by Robert B. Armitage, M.D. ISBN 1-59016-561-9 • 317 + ii pages • heavily illustrated • GB£16.95 • US$22.95

THE SEXUAL LIFE, by C. W. Malchow, M.D. ISBN 1-59016-562-7 • 317 pages • GB£16.95 • US$22.95

MISCELLANEOUS

THE ART OF THINKING, by Ernest Dimnet. ISBN 1-59016-342-8 • 221 + xii pages • GB£13.95 • US$18.95

CHARACTER READING THROUGH ANALYSIS OF THE FEATURES, by Gerald Elton Fosbroke. ISBN 1-59016-113-0 • 193 + xii + 56 illustrated pages • heavily illustrated • GB£14.95 • US$19.95

HEALTH AND NUTRITION

STRENGTH FROM EATING, by Bernarr MacFadden. ISBN 1-59016-812-7 • 194 pages • illustrated • GB£11.95 • US$16.95

A COMPEND OF MATERIA MEDICA AND THERAPEUTICS, by Samuel O. L. Potter. ISBN 1-59016-137-8 • 147 pages • GB£9.95 • US$13.95

DRUG ENCYCLOPEDIA, compiled by Brunswig Drug Company, circa 1908. ISBN 1-59016-190-4 • 241 pages • illustrated • GB£13.95 • US$18.95

EDUCATION AND SCHOOLING

COLLEGE: WHAT'S THE USE? by Herbert E. Hawkes. ISBN 1-59016-130-0 • 143 + vi pages • illustrated • GB£9.95 • US$14.95

A JUNIOR CLASS HISTORY OF THE UNITED STATES, by John J. Anderson. ISBN 1-59016-393-1 • 242 pages • illustrated • GB£13.95 • US$18.95

POISE: HOW TO ATTAIN IT, by D. Starke. ISBN 1-59016-650-7 • 159 pages • illustrated • GB£9.95 • US$14.95

COURSEWORK AND STUDY GUIDES

A COURSE IN PILOTING SEAMANSHIP AND SMALL BOAT HANDLING, by Charles F. Chapman. ISBN 1-59016-144-0 • 120 pages • illustrated • GB£9.95 • US$14.95

A COURSE IN WOOD TURNING, by Archie S. Milton and Otto K. Wohlers. ISBN 1-59016-145-9 • 200 pages • GB£11.95 • US$16.95

MONEY AND BUSINESS

THE THEORY AND HISTORY OF BANKING, by Charles F. Dunbar. ISBN 1-59016-835-6 • 199 + vi pages • illustrated • GB£11.95 • US$16.95

MONEY & INVESTMENTS, by Montgomery Rollins. ISBN 1-59016-525-X • 493 + xxii + 22 misc pages • graphs • GB£24.95 • US$33.95

PATENT OFFICE PRACTICE, by Archie R. McCrady. ISBN 1-59016-640-X • 385 + xx pages • illustrated • GB£20.95 • US$26.95

THE ROMANCE OF BUSINESS, by W. Cameron Forbes. ISBN 1-59016-734-1 • 258 + viii + 3 illustrated pages • illustrated • GB£14.95 • US$20.95

DICTIONARIES AND REFERENCE

A DESK-BOOK OF IDIOMS AND IDIOMATIC PHRASES, by Frank H. Vizetelly and Leander J. DeBekker. ISBN 1-59016-161-0 • 496 + x pages • GB£23.95 • US$31.95

THE ENGLISH DICTIONARIE OF 1623, by Henry Cockeram. ISBN 1-59016-212-9 • 197 + xxii pages • GB£12.95 • US$17.95

HANDY DICTIONARY OF ENGLISH SYNONYMS, by Thomas Fenby. ISBN 1-59016-305-2 • 268 + xii pages • GB£14.95 • US$20.95

A HANDY DICTIONARY OF SYNONYMS, by H. C. Faulkner. ISBN 1-59016-306-0 • 217 pages • GB£12.95 • US$17.95

THE NUTTALL DICTIONARY OF ANAGRAMS, A. R. Ball. ISBN 1-59016-584-5 • 120 pages • GB£8.95 • US$12.95

PRACTICAL SYNONYMS, by John H. Bechtel. ISBN 1-59016-664-7 • 226 + ii pages • GB£12.95 • US$17.95

PRONUNCIATION DICTIONARY, by John H. Bechtel. ISBN 1-59016-680-9 • 143 + ii pages • GB£9.95 • US$13.95

THE REPORTER'S WORD BOOK, by Anonymous. ISBN 1-59016-715-5 • 155 + iv pages • GB£9.95 • US$14.95

THE STORY KEY TO GEOGRAPHIC NAMES, by O. D. Von Engeln and Jane McKelway Urquhart. ISBN 1-59016-785-6 • 279 + xiv pages • GB£15.95 • US$21.95

WORDS: THEIR SPELLING, PRONUNCIATION, DEFINITION AND APPLICATION, compiled by Rupert P. SoRelle and Charles W. Kitt. ISBN 1-59016-925-5 • 127 + ii pages • tables • GB£8.95 • US$13.95

THE WRITER'S BLUEBOOK, by Leigh H. Irvine. ISBN 1-59016-938-7 • 82 pages • GB£7.95 • US$11.95

QUOTATIONS

THE BOOK OF FAMILIAR QUOTATIONS, compiled from Various Authors. ISBN 1-59016-070-3 • 503 + viii pages • GB£23.95 • US$32.95

THE WORLD'S BEST EPIGRAMS, by J. Gilchrist Lawson. ISBN 1-59016-931-X • 231 pages • GB£12.95 • US$17.95

BOOKS ON BOOKS

A BOOK FOR ALL READERS, by Ainsworth Rand Spofford. ISBN 1-59016-068-1 • 507 + vi pages • GB£24.95 • US$32.95

HOW TO FORM A LIBRARY, by H. B. Wheatley. ISBN 1-59016-343-5 • 248 + viii pages • GB£13.95 • US$18.95

THE STORY OF LIBRARIES AND BOOK COLLECTING, by Ernest A. Savage. ISBN 1-59016-794-5 • 230 + vi pages • GB£13.95 • US$18.95

WHAT I KNOW ABOUT BOOKS, by George C. Lorimer. ISBN 1-59016-908-5 • 110 pages • GB£8.95 • US$12.95

WHO WROTE IT? by William A. Wheller. ISBN 1-59016-915-8 • 174 + iv pages • illustrated • GB£10.95 • US$15.95

NOVELTY BOOKS

THE AMERICAN POETS BIRTHDAY BOOK, by Various Poets. ISBN 1-59016-022-3 • 183 pages • illustrated • GB£11.95 • US$15.95

BEASLEY'S CHRISTMAS PARTY, by Booth Tarkington. ISBN 1-59016-058-4 • 100 + iv pages • illustrated • GB£7.95 • US$11.95

A CAMPFIRE GIRL'S FIRST COUNCIL FIRE, by Jane L. Stewart. ISBN 1-59016-103-3 • 246 pages • illustrated • GB£13.95 • US$18.95

THE CHRISTMAS STORY FROM DAVID HARUM, by Edward Noyes Westcott. ISBN 1-59016-118-1 • 107 + x pages • GB£8.95 • US$12.95

CUPID'S CYCLOPEDIA, compiled by Oliver Herford and John Cecil Clay. ISBN 1-59016-148-3 • 100 pages • illustrated • GB£7.95 • US$11.95

FURNITURE AND DECORATING

DECORATIVE STYLES AND PERIODS IN THE HOME: Furnishings of the Nineteenth Century, by Helen Churchill Candee. ISBN 1-59016-159-9 • 297 + xx + 100 illustrated pages • illustrated • GB£20.95 • US$27.95

ENGLISH FURNITURE OF THE CABRIOLE PERIOD, by H. Avray Tipping. ISBN 1-59016-213-7 • 79 + vi + 32 illustrated pages • GB£8.95 • US$12.95

FURNITURE OF THE NINETEENTH CENTURY, compiled by the Century Furniture Company. ISBN 1-59016-270-6 • 156 pages • illustrated • GB£11.95 • US$14.95

INSIDE OF ONE HUNDRED HOMES, by William Martin Johnson. ISBN 1-59016-360-5 • 140 pages • illustrated • GB£9.95 • US$13.95

INSIDE THE HOUSE OF GOOD TASTE, edited by Richardson Wright. ISBN 1-59016-361-3 • 155 + x pages • illustrated • GB£9.95 • US$10.95

OLD GLASS: European and American, by N. Hudson Moore. ISBN 1-59016-594-2 • 389 + xx pages • illustrated • GB£20.95 • US$27.95

COOKING AND HOUSEHOLD

AUNT MARTHA'S CORNER CUPBOARD: Stories about Tea, Coffee, Sugar and Rice, by Mary and Elizabeth Kirby. ISBN 1-59016-046-0 • 144 pages • 32 illustrations • GB£9.95 • US$14.95

CHAFING DISH POSSIBILITIES, by Fannie Merritt Farmer. ISBN 1-59016-111-4 • 161 pages • GB£9.95 • US$14.95

ONE HUNDRED TESTED RECEIPTS, compiled by Jennie C. Benedict. ISBN 1-59016-606-X • 88 + ii pages • GB£7.95 • US$11.95

THE RUMFORD COMPLETE COOK BOOK, by Lily Haxworth Wallace. ISBN 1-59016-741-4 • 236 + xviii pages • GB£13.95 • US$19.95

THE SAGINAW COOK BOOK, compiled by the Women's Society of the First Congregational Church. ISBN 1-59016-744-9 • 247 + ii pages • GB£13.95 • US$19.95

THE SKANEATELES COOK BOOK, issued by the Women's Village Improvement Association. ISBN 1-59016-765-1 • 113 pages • GB£8.95 • US$12.95

THE TIDIOUTE COOK BOOK, compiled and arranged by Ladies from Tidioute, Pennsylvania. ISBN 1-59016-845-3 • 238 + ii pages • heavily illustrated • GB£13.95 • US$18.95

CHILDREN'S BOOKS

CHILDREN OF HISTORY, by Mary S. Hancock. ISBN 1-59016-116-5 • 192 + ii pages • illustrated • GB£11.95 • US$16.95

CHILDREN'S SAYINGS: Early Life at Home, by Caroline Hadley. ISBN 1-59016-117-3 • 160 pages • illustrated • GB£9.95 • US$14.95

MAGIC STORIES, by Frank N. Freeman, Grace E. Storm, Eleanor M. Johnson and W. C. French. ISBN 1-59016-505-5 • 288 + ii pages • illustrated • GB£15.95 • US$21.95

MOTHER HUBBARD'S MELODIES, with illustrations by Gordon Browne, R. Marriott Watson, L.L. Weedon and Others. ISBN 1-59016-527-6 • 146 + xiv pages • heavily illustrated • GB£9.95 • US$14.95

TOP OF THE WORLD STORIES FOR BOYS AND GIRLS, by Emilie Poulsson and Laura E. Poulsson. ISBN 1-59016-850-X • 206 + ii + 15 illustrated pages • illustrated • GB£12.95 • US$17.95

TRAVEL AND ADVENTURE

ADVENTURES BY LAND AND SEA, by Various Authors. ISBN 1-59016-010-X • 127 + x + 2 illustrated pages • illustrated • GB£9.95 • US$13.95

HOW THE WORLD TRAVELS, by A. A. Methley. ISBN 1-59016-342-7 • 127 + x + 2 illustrated pages • illustrated • GB£9.95 • US$13.95

LITTLE JOURNEYS TO THE HOMES OF GREAT REFORMERS, by Elbert Hubbard. ISBN 1-59016-472-5 • 170 + vi + 10 illustrated pages • illustrated • GB£11.95 • US$15.95

SCENES FROM EVERY LAND, by Gilbert H. Grosvenor. ISBN 1-59016-753-8 • 216 pages • heavily illustrated • GB£12.95 • US$17.95

SINBAD AND HIS FRIENDS, by Simeon Strunsky. ISBN 1-59016-764-3 • 261 + viii pages • GB£14.95 • US$20.95

WORLD CRUISE OF THE NORTHERN AND SOUTHERN HEMISPHERES, by Thomas Cook & Son. ISBN 1-59016-928-X • 103 pages • illustrated • GB£7.95 • US$11.95

SHORT STORIES

AMONG THE CAMPS: Young People's Stories of the Civil War, by Thomas Nelson Page ISBN 1-59016-023-1 • 163 pages • illustrated • GB£10.95 • US$15.95

A LITTLE BOOK OF PROFITABLE TALES, by Eugene Field. ISBN 1-59016-470-9 • 243 pages • illustrated • GB£13.95 • US$19.95

SPORTS AND ATHLETICS

SWIMMING SCIENTIFICALLY TAUGHT: A Practical Manual for Young and Old, by Frank Eugen Dalton. ISBN 1-59016-943-3 • 247 pages • illustrated • GB£13.95 • US$18.95

GREEK ATHLETICS, by F. A. Wright. ISBN 1-59016-295-1 • 123 + 8 illustrated pages • illustrated • GB£9.95 • US$13.95

PHYSICAL TRAINING MANUAL, by Sargent Arthur W. Wallander. ISBN 1-59016-646-9 • 159 pages • illustrated • GB£9.95 • US$14.95

TUMBLING, PYRAMID BUILDING AND STUNTS FOR MEN AND WOMEN, by Bonnie and Donnie Cotteral. ISBN 1-59016-868-2 • 143 + vi + 11 illustrated pages • illustrated • GB£9.95 • US$14.95

FBI FILES REVEALED

EINSTEIN, ALBERT: FBI Files Revealed - Coming Soon, Call 1 (800) 952-LOST for our current catalog.

TESLA, NIKOLA: FBI Files Revealed. ISBN 1-59016-833-X • 276 pages • GB£14.95 • US$19.95

AUDIO AND VIDEO TAPES (VHS NTSC)

REMOTE VIEWING TRAINING SESSIONS: Discovering Your Intuition, with Prudence Calabrese and TransDimensional Systems. RVT-00a • 13 Hours on 7 Audio Tapes • $60.00 postpaid / RVT-00 • 13 Hours on 7 VHS Video Tapes • $110.00 postpaid / Introductory tape only • RVT-01 • 2 hour Video • $19.95 • Other tapes available individually. Visit www.largeruniverse.com for more information.

ANCIENT MYSTERIES OF NORTH AMERICA with Tédd St. Rain. AMNA-01a • 110 min Audio • $12.00 / AMNA-01 • 110 min Video • $19.95

THE COSMIC ORIGINS OF MAN with Father Charles Moore. BACN-01a • 105 min Audio • $12.00 / BACN-01 • 105 min Video • $19.95

21ST CENTURY VISIONS OF NOSTRADAMUS with Dolores Cannon. BACN-02a • 105 min Audio • $12.00 / BACN-02 • 105 min Video • $19.95

HUMAN RELATIONSHIPS WITH ETS with Barbara Lamb. BACN-03a • 60 min Audio • $12.00 / BACN-03 • 60 min Video • $19.95

ET RELATIONSHIPS PANEL with Barbara Lamb, Pamela Stonebrooke, Eve Lorgen and Dolores Cannon. BACN-04a • 90 min Audio • $12.00 / BACN-04 • 90 min Video • $19.95

SCIENCE, POLITICS AND THE NEW MILLENNIUM with Dr. Nick Begich. BACN-05a • 2 hour Audio • $12.00 / BACN-05 • 2 hour Video • $19.95

MUSIC OF THE SPHERES with Randy Masters. BACN-06a • 90 min Audio • $12.00 / BACN-06 • 90 min Video • $19.95

TECHNOLOGY OF THE GODS with David Hatcher Childress. BACN-07a • 2 hour Audio • $12.00 / BACN-07 • 2 hour Video • $19.95

BIGFOOT / UFO CONNECTION with Jack "Kewaunee" Lapseritis. BACN-08a • 105 min Audio • $12.00 / BACN-08 • 105 min Video • $19.95

OUT-OF-BODY ADVENTURES with Albert Taylor. BACN-09a • 90 min Audio • $12.00 / BACN-09 • 90 min Video • $19.95

EGYPTIAN MYSTERIES with Karena Bryan. BACN-10a • 90 min Audio • $12.00 / BACN-10 • 90 min Video • $19.95

UFOS AND RELIGION PANEL with Stella Harder-Kucera. Moderator and Ted Peters, Jose Tirado and Matthew Fox, Panelists BACN-11a • 90 min Audio • $12.00 / BACN-11 • 90 min Video • $19.95

PARADIGM POLITICS with Daniel Sheehan. BACN-12a • 2 hour Audio • $12.00 / BACN-12 • 2 hour Video • $19.95

INTUITIVE ANIMAL COMMUNICATION with Raphaela Pope. BACN-13a • 90 min Audio • $12.00 / BACN-13 • 90 min Video • $19.95

FORBIDDEN ARCHEOLOGY with Michael Cremo. BACN-14a • 2 hour Audio • $12.00 / BACN-14 • 2 hour Video • $19.95

TALKING TO THE OTHER SIDE, with Mark Macy. BACN-15a • 105 min Audio • $12.00 / BACN-15 • 90 min Video • $19.95

NEW PARADIGMS FOR LOVE, with Deborah Taj Anapol. BACN-16a • 90 min Audio • $12.00 / BACN-16 • 60 min Video • $19.95

NEWS MEDIA DECEPTIONS, with Terry Hansen. BACN-17a • 90 min Audio • $12.00 / BACN-17 • 90 min Video • $19.95

MEDIA PANEL ON UFO'S – Lucia August, Moderator; Panelist Ralph Steiner, Leslie Kean, and Terry Hansen. BACN-18a • 75 min Audio • $12.00 / BACN-18 • 75 min Video • $19.95

THE TRUTH ABOUT 9-11, with Carol Brouillet. BACN-19a • 105 min Audio • $12.00 / BACN-19 • 105 min Video • $19.95

ANCIENT EGYPTIAN HI-TECH, with Christopher Dunn. BACN-20a • 105 min Audio • $12.00 / BACN-20 • 105 min Video • $19.95

NEW SCIENCE BREAKTHROUGHS, with Joe Firmage. BACN-21a • 90 min Audio • $12.00 / BACN-21 • 90 min Video • $19.95

THE INTERCEPTION: Roswell Crash Site Metal Recovery with Dennis Balthaser. Aztec-01a • 2 hour Audio • $12.00 / Aztec-01 • 2 hour Video • $19.95

MYSTERIOUS UFO INCIDENT IN PENNSYLVANIA AND BIG FOOT, with Stan Gordon. Aztec-02a • 2 hour Audio • $12.00 / Aztec-02 • 2 hour Video • $19.95

UFOS: THE TECHNOLOGY ISSUE, with John Schuessler. Aztec-03a • 2 hour Audio • $12.00 / Aztec-03 • 2 hour Video • $19.95

THE DAY AFTER ROSWELL: Revelations from Beyond the Grave, with Karl Pflock. Aztec-04a • 2 hour Audio • $12.00 / Aztec-04 • 2 hour Video • $19.95

CRITIQUE OF THE ROSWELL CRITICS, with Stanton Friedman. Aztec-05a • 2 hour Audio • $12.00 / Aztec-05 • 2 hour Video • $19.95

AZTEC 1949-1950: New Information on the Aztec UFO Crash, with Linda Moulton Howe. Aztec-06a • 2 hour Audio • $12.00 / Aztec-06 • 2 hour Video • $19.95

HOW THE WAR ON TERROR INTERRUPTED ET CONTACT, with Jim Marrs. Aztec-07a • 2 hour Audio • $12.00 / Aztec-07 • 2 hour Video • $19.95

AUDIO AND VIDEO TAPES (CONTINUED)

UFOS AND REALITY TRANSFORMATION, with Chris Styles. MUFON-01a • 76 min Audio • $12.00 / MUFON-01 • 76 min Video • $19.95

THE DAY AFTER PHIL CORSO, with William J. Birnes. MUFON-02a • 82 min Audio • $12.00 / MUFON-02 • 82 min Video • $19.95

SCIENTIFIC CONNECTIONS IN PHOTO/VIDEO UFOLOGY, with Jeff Sainio. MUFON-03a • 68 min Audio • $12.00 / MUFON-03 • 68 min Video • $19.95

THE LIMITS OF SCIENCE IN UFO RESEARCH, with Richard Dolan. MUFON-04a • 70 min Audio • $12.00 / MUFON-04 • 70 min Video • $19.95

IN SEARCH OF EBE'S, with William Hamilton. MUFON-05a • 75 min Audio • $12.00 / MUFON-05 • 75 min Video • $19.95

FIVE THEMES ON UFO ABDUCTION, with Dan Wright. MUFON-06a • 73 min Audio • $12.00 / MUFON-06 • 73 min Video • $19.95

BUILDING A PROFESSIONAL COMMUNITY, with David Jacobs. MUFON-07a • 73 min Audio • $12.00 / MUFON-07 • 73 min Video • $19.95

CONFLICTING INTEREST IN THE CONTROL OF EXTRATERRESTRIAL INTELLIGENCE, with Timothy Good. MUFON-08a • 77 min Audio • $12.00 / MUFON-08 • 77 min Video • $19.95

AIR TRAFFIC CONTROL ZONES, PILOTS, AIRCRAFT AND UFOS, with Don Ledger. MUFON-09a • 78 min Audio • $12.00 / MUFON-09 • 78 min Video • $19.95

THE ABDUCTION PHENOMENON - Where We Are Now? with Budd Hopkins. MUFON-10a • 72 min Audio • $12.00 / MUFON-10 • 72 min Video • $19.95

AN AMERICAN IN SUFFOLK: The Rendlesham Forest UFO Incident, with Peter Robbins. MUFON-11a • 90 min Audio • $12.00 / MUFON-11 • 90 min Video • $19.95

MIRACLES: UFO CONTACT, with Betty Hill. MUFON-12a • 68 Min Audio • $12.00 / MUFON-12 • 68 Min Video • $19.95

ARE THERE UFOS ON MARS? with Richard Thieme. MUFON-13a • 49 min Audio • $12.00 / MUFON-13 • 49 min Video • $19.95

TURKISH UFO INVESTIGATION, with Esen Sekerkarar. MUFON-14a • 79 min Audio • $12.00 / MUFON-14 • 79 min Video • $19.95

MUFON FIELD INVESTIGATOR TRAINING, with Dan Wright. MUFON-15a • 115 min Audio • $12.00 / MUFON-15 • 115 min Video • $19.95

EGYPT AND THE SCIENCE OF IMMORTALITY: Parts 1 and 2, with John Anthony West. SIGNS-01a & 02a • 2 92 min Audios • $19.95 / SIGNS-01 and 02 • 2 92 min Videos • $39.95

THE GREAT SPHINX AND THE QUEST TO REWRITE HISTORY, with John Anthony West. SIGNS-03a • 2 70 min Audios $19.95 / SIGNS-03 •139 min Video • $24.95

THE CROP CIRCLES PRIMARY MESSAGE, with Drunvalo Melchizedek. SIGNS-04a • 2 hour Audio • $12.00 / SIGNS-04 • 2 hour Video • $19.95

SACRED GEOMETRY WORKSHOP, with Drunvalo Melchizedek. SIGNS-05a • 2 hour Audio • $12.00 / SIGNS-05 • 2 hour Video • $19.95

THE IMPORTANCE OF WHERE AND HOW THE CROP CIRCLE PHENOMENON BEGAN, with Colin Andrews. SIGNS-06a • 2 min Audio • $12.00 / SIGNS-06 • 92 min Video • $19.95

THERMAL PLASMAS OF UNKNOWN ORIGIN: Hessdalen 002, with Linda Moulton Howe. SIGNS-07a • 60 min Audio • $12.00 / SIGNS-07 • 60 min Video • $19.95

THE CIRCLES, THE SCIENCE AND AN EYEWITNESS ACCOUNT, with Nancy Talbott. SIGNS-08a • 92 min Audio • $12.00 / SIGNS-08 • 92 min Video • $19.95

SCIENTIFIC ANALYSIS OF CROP CIRCLES: A Practical Guide, with Nancy Talbott. SIGNS-09a • 108 min Audio • $12.00 / SIGNS-09 • 108 min Video • $19.95

FIELD OF DREAMS: Crop Circles in Canada, with Paul Anderson. SIGNS-10a • 68 min Audio • $12.00 / SIGNS-10 • 68 min Video • $19.95

GROWING CROP CIRCLE SEEDS FOR FOOD, with Steve Burkable. SIGNS-11a • 26 min Audio • $12.00 / SIGNS-11 • 26 min Video • $19.95

ENGLAND'S CROP CIRCLES OF 2002, with Francine Blake. SIGNS-12a • 115 min Audio • $12.00 / SIGNS-12 • 115 min Video • $19.95

CROP CIRCLES IN GERMANY: Amazing Recent Developments, with Andreas Mueller. SIGNS-13a • 85 min Audio • $12.00 / SIGNS-13 • 85 min Video • $19.95

CROP CIRCLES REVEALED: A Spiritual Perspective, with Barbara Lamb. SIGNS-14a • 89 min Audio • $12.00 / SIGNS-14 • 2 min Video • $19.95

CROP CIRLCES 2001-2002: A Year of Surprises, with Dr. Chet Snow. SIGNS-15a • 53 min Audio • $12.00 / SIGNS-15 • 53 min Video • $19.95

For Audio/Video Tapes Only: To order individual tapes add $5.00 shipping and handling for the first item and $1.00 for each additional item. Send your check or money order to (CA residents add 8.25% sales tax): LOST ARTS MEDIA, POST OFFICE BOX 15026, LONG BEACH, CA 90815. Visit WWW.LOSTARTSMEDIA.COM or to order by credit card call 1 (800) 952-LOST or 1 (562) 596-ARTS.

NEWS AND INFORMATION

NEXUS MAGAZINE is an international bi-monthly alternative news magazine, covering the fields of Suppressed Science, Earth's Ancient Past, Alternative Health, UFOs, the Unexplained and much more. For subscription information visit www.nexusmagazine.com or call 1 (888) 909-7474.

ATLANTIS RISING MAGAZINE: One of the best magazines on Atlantis, ancient mysteries, lost continents, cryptozoology, and a whole host of other related subjects. For subscription information visit www.atlantisrising.com or call 1 (800) 228-8381.

STEAMSHOVEL PRESS is a zine that is dedicated to exposing the secrets behind the conspiracies that have shaped history. For subscription information visit www.steamshovelpress.com

PARANOIA – A CONSPIRACY READER focuses on the more paranoid aspects of society. For subscription information visit www.paranoiamagazine.com

THE EXCLUDED MIDDLE MAGAZINE publishes three times a year on all things paranormal. For information email exclmid@primenet.com. or write P.O. Box 481077, Los Angeles, CA 90048.

FLATLAND MAGAZINE publishes a once-per-year zine that reviews the suppressed and secret evidence around us. Contact www.flatlandbooks.com or call 1 (707) 964-8326.

THE BOOK TREE provides controversial and educational products to help awaken the public to new ideas and information that would otherwise not be available. For a free catalog visit www.thebooktree.com or call 1 (800) 700-TREE.

The INTERNATIONAL UFO CONGRESS holds a twice-yearly, week long conference and film festival on UFOs and a variety of other subjects. People attend from around the world and it is considered the best conference of its kind. For additional information visit www.ufocongress.com or call 1 (303) 543-9443.

The BAY AREA UFO EXPO and Conference holds an annual conference in the fall each year. For information and a free program guide visit www.thebayareaufoexpo.com or call 1 (209) 836-4281.

CONSPIRACY CON holds it's conference on Memorial Day weekend each year. For information and a free program guide visit www.conspiracycon.com or call 1 (209) 832-0999.

Cosmic Connections conducts the **EARTH MYSTERIES CONFERENCE** in the Fall and the **CRYSTAL HEALING CONFERENCE** in the Spring of each year. For more information visit www.chetsnow.com or call 1 (928) 204-1962.

The **BAY AREA CONSCIOUSNESS NETWORK** holds its annual conference in November each year. For information visit www.bacn.org

The **NORTHWEST UFO PARANORMAL CONFERENCE** is held in the late spring each year. For more information visit www.seattlechatclub.com

Adventures Unlimited holds its **WORLD EXPLORERS CLUB ANCIENT MYSTERIES CONFERENCE** several times a year. For more information or a program guide and a free book catalog visit www.wexclub.com or call 1 (815) 253-6390.

The **ANNUAL MUFON SYMPOSIUM** is held every year in various locations. For a program guide or information on local chapters of MUFON visit www.mufon.com or call 1 (303) 932-7709.

The **BUSINESS SPIRIT JOURNAL** produces several spiritual and consciousness-related conferences each year. For information visit www.bizspirit.com or call 1 (505) 474-7604.

The **AZTEC UFO SYMPOSIUM** is held once a year in the early spring in Aztec, NM, location of a famed UFO crash. For more information visit www.aztecufo.com or call 1 (505) 334-9890.

The **ALTERNATE REALITIES CONFERENCE** (ARC) hold its annual conference in the Summer each year. For more information visit www.dreaman.org or call 1 (423) 735-0848.

The **THINK ABOUT IT CONFERENCE** is held at various locations throughout the year. For more information visit www.think-aboutit.com or www.heartoftheheart.com or call 1 (319) 866-9560.

The **ROSWELL UFO ODYSSEY** commemorates a UFO crash in New Mexico for the first week in July each year. For information visit www.uforoswell.com

Problems-Solutions-Innovations sponsors the **CONTROLLED REMOTE VIEWING CONFERENCE** in the early summer each year. For more information visit www.crviewer.com

The International Remote Viewing Association holds its annual **REMOTE VIEWING CONFERENCE** in June each year. For more information visit www.rvconference.org

FREE REMOTE VIEWING TRAINING: Ongoing coursework live on the internet with Prudence Calabrese. For information visit www.aurorabomb.com or www.largeruniverse.com

LOST ARTS MEDIA produces a variety of **ANCIENT MYSTERIES CONFERENCES** and **TRAVEL PROGRAMS** throughout the year. Come travel with like-minded and kindred friends. For information visit www.lostartsmedia.com or call 1 (800) 952-LOST.

HAVE YOUR EVENT VIDEOTAPED AND/OR LISTED HERE
Call 1 (800) 952-LOST or Visit WWW.LOSTARTSMEDIA.COM

Printed in the United States
64960LVS00004B/57

9 781590 163160